Geography
for the IB Diploma

Patterns and Change

Paul Guinness

Cambridge University Press's mission is to advance learning, knowledge and research worldwide.

Our IB Diploma resources aim to:

- encourage learners to explore concepts, ideas and topics that have local and global significance
- help students develop a positive attitude to learning in preparation for higher education
- assist students in approaching complex questions, applying critical-thinking skills and forming reasoned answers.

CAMBRIDGE UNIVERSITY PRESS

CAMBRIDGE
UNIVERSITY PRESS

University Printing House, Cambridge CB2 8BS, United Kingdom

Cambridge University Press is part of the University of Cambridge.

It furthers the University's mission by disseminating knowledge in the pursuit of education, learning and research at the highest international levels of excellence.

www.cambridge.org
Information on this title: www.cambridge.org/9780521147330

© Cambridge University Press 2011

First published 2011
6th printing 2014

Printed in the United Kingdom by Cambrian Printers Ltd

A catalogue record for this publication is available from the British Library

ISBN 978-0-521-14733-0 Paperback

Cover image: Chepko Danil Vitalevich/Shutterstock

Header images: brianafrica/Alamy (refugee camp); thp73/iStock (polar bears); Shutterstock/Sculpies (oil rig)

Background images: iStock (compass); Shutterstock/Mark Breck (Joshua Tree, National Park); all other background images courtesy of Andrew Oliver

Illustrations by Kathy Baxendale
Reviewer: Ian Lycett, Head of IB Geography at Impington Village College, UK

Contents

Introduction

Patterns and Change covers the core theme of the IB Diploma Programme geography course for both Higher Level and Standard Level. The core theme accounts for 25% of the total assessment at Higher Level and 40% at Standard Level. The Diploma Programme geography course integrates both physical and human geography, with the objective of students acquiring elements of both scientific and socio-economic methodologies. This is clearly evident in the structure of the core theme. The core theme could form one continuous teaching block or be taught in two or more sections throughout the course where links with other modules may be exploited.

The overall objective of the core theme is to provide an overview of the geographical foundation for the key global issues of our times. This book follows the order of the syllabus, which is organised into four sections. Each sub-section in the Specification is the subject of a chapter, with the exception of 'Changing patterns of energy consumption' in Section 4. This sub-topic is covered in two chapters (15 and 16) because of the considerable content within it. The overall objective of this book is to provide comprehensive coverage of all topics included in the core theme. Key concepts are carefully explained and exemplified in case studies from a range of locations.

In the first section, 'Populations in transition', you will look at major demographic issues that have an impact on the environment of both individual countries and the planet as a whole. This section concludes with an analysis of gender and change. 'Change' may be a relatively new topic to you, depending on the specifications you have followed in previous years. The study of human population and its changes sets the scene for the global issues that follow in the rest of the book. It is the increase in human numbers and the activities undertaken by people that have caused stress to so many aspects of the global environment.

In Section 2, 'Disparities in wealth and development', you will study measurements of regional and global disparities, the origin of disparities, disparities and change, and strategies to reduce disparities. The scale of disparities is causing increasing tension both between and within countries. The United Nations and many other organisations have tried for years to narrow the gap between rich and poor, but with only limited success. Current efforts are very much focused around the Millennium Development Goals (MDGs); consideration of the MDGs is an important part of this section.

'Patterns in environmental quality and sustainability' is the title of Section 3. Here you will look at a range of environmental issues of global significance, covering the atmosphere, soil, water, biodiversity and sustainability. Global climate change remains the greatest concern because of the possibly huge scale of its impact as a whole and its linkage to so many 'individual' environmental issues. An understanding of this issue is fundamental to this section, and you will also examine the reasons for environmental change, along with human responses to such changes.

Section 4 examines 'Patterns in resource consumption'. Consideration of the ecological footprint is the important starting point. The opposing views of neo-Malthusians and anti-Malthusians are debated. You will look in detail at the global importance of oil as a resource , paying particular attention to geopolitical and environmental consequences, and analyse the changing importance of other energy resources. The final section is a discussion of conservation strategies.

The content of each chapter is posed at the start as a series of key questions that closely reflect the wording of the 'Development' section of the Specification. Each chapter includes a 'Theory of Knowledge' link highlighting issues of particular relevance to the study of the theory of knowledge. While these links are kept deliberately brief, they are designed to point you in the right direction to enable you to explore such issues in more detail.

Each main section of text within a chapter finishes with an 'Activities' section, allowing both students and teachers to check on the knowledge and understanding gained in terms of both concepts and content. A key 'Geographical skill' is highlighted in each chapter. Geographical skills reflect the subject's distinctive methodology and approach. While you are not expected to cover all the geographical skills in your study of the core theme, you should acquire or cement a significant number of the skills set out in the Specification. 'Discussion points' and 'Research ideas' are also a regular feature of the book. The first suggest ideas for group debate, while the research ideas can be used as extension exercises on both an individual and a group basis. Each chapter concludes with definitions of key terms (highlighted in bold in each chapter) and examination-style questions which follow the pattern of Section A in Paper 1.

Case studies are an important part of this book, with countries highlighted at different levels of economic development. Some countries are featured in several chapters, allowing you to develop a good overall understanding of such nations, but there are, too, more fleeting references to other nations across the world. Key countries featured in this book are also featured in the Higher Level extension book, *Global Interactions*, which will allow Higher Level students to further develop their knowledge of a range of countries. The aim throughout is to debate issues of national, regional and global importance, highlighting both the positive and negative aspects of change.

The Standard Level and Higher Level Diploma Programme geography course sets four Assessment Objectives. Having followed the course at either level you should be able to:

- demonstrate knowledge and understanding of specified content (45%)

- demonstrate application and analysis of knowledge and understanding (30%)

- demonstrate synthesis and evaluation (5%)

- select, use and apply a variety of appropriate skills and techniques (20%).

(The figures in brackets show the weighting of the Assessment Objectives for Paper 1.)

Full details of the Assessment Objectives for the Diploma Programme geography course can be found in the IBO Geography Guide. Higher Level students are required to study the core theme, the Higher Level extension and three option modules. Standard Level students study the core theme and two option modules. Internal assessment accounts for 20% of the total assessment at Higher Level and 20% at Standard Level.

Paul Guinness

01 Population change

KEY QUESTIONS

- How has the world's population changed over time?
- What is the global pattern of births, natural increase and mortality?
- What have been the major changes in these rates over time?
- How do fertility and life expectancy vary around the world?
- How do population pyramids show global variations in age and gender structure?
- What is population momentum and what impact does it have on population projections?

The grave of the poet W B Yeats, County Sligo, Ireland. The inscription reads: 'Cast a cold Eye/ On Life, on Death. / Horseman, pass by!'

Early humankind

The first hominids who were early ancestors of humans appeared in Africa around 5 million years ago, on a planet that is generally accepted to be 4600 million years old. They differed from their predecessors, the apes, in the fact that they walked on two legs and did not use their hands for weight-bearing. Other uses were soon found for these now liberated hands, with new skills acquired and charted in the evolutionary record as an increase in the size of the brain and the cranium (the hard bone case which gives the head its shape). After two million years cranial capacity (cc) had increased by 50% from the 600 cc of the earliest hominid, *Australopithecus*, to the 900 cc of the primitive man named *Homo erectus*. The final increase to *Homo sapiens'* current average of 1450 cc took place about 100 000 years ago.

The evolution of humankind was matched by its geographical **diffusion**. Whereas the locational evidence for *Australopithecus* is confined to Africa, remains of *Homo erectus* have been found stretching from Europe to South-east Asia. *Homo sapiens* roamed even further, making the first journeys into the cold environments of high latitudes.

During most of the period since *Homo sapiens* first appeared, global population was very small, reaching perhaps some 125 000 people a million years ago, although there is not enough evidence to be very precise about population in the distant past. It has been estimated that 10 000 years ago, when people first began to domesticate animals and grow crops, world population was no more than 5 million. Known as the Neolithic Revolution, this period of economic change significantly altered the

The pyramids at Giza, Egypt, build about 2000 BC when the world's population was only about 100 million.

relationship between people and their environments. But even then the average annual growth rate was less than 0.1% per year, extremely low compared with contemporary trends.

However, as a result of technological advance the **carrying capacity** of the land improved and population increased. By 3500 BC the global population had reached 30 million and by AD 1 this had risen to about 250 million.

A Roman amphitheatre in Tunisia, built around AD 50 when the world's population was about 250 million.

Demographers estimate that world population had reached 500 million by about 1500. From this time population grew at an increasing rate. By 1800 the global population had doubled to reach almost one billion (Figure 1). Table 1 shows the time taken for each subsequent billion to be reached, with the global total reaching six billion in 1999. It had taken only 12 years for the world population to increase from five billion to six billion – less than the time required for the previous billion to be added. It is estimated that 7 billion will be reached in 2013 – a 14-year gap. Table 2 shows population change in 2009, with a global population increase of almost 82 million in that year. The vast majority of this increase is in developing countries.

Each billion	Year	Number of years to add each billion
1st	1804	All of human history
2nd	1927	123
3rd	1960	33
4th	1974	14
5th	1987	13
6th	1999	12
7th	2013	14
8th	2028	15
9th	2054	26

Table 1 *World population growth by each billion..*

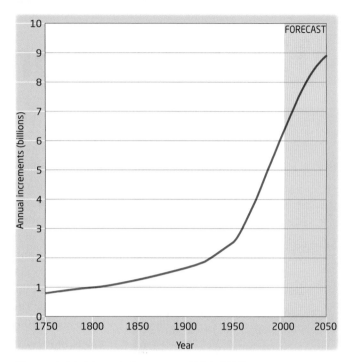

Figure 1 *World population growth, 1750–2050.*

Recent demographic change

Figure 2 shows that both total population and the rate of population growth are much higher in the developing world than in the more developed world. However, only since the Second World War has population growth in the developing countries overtaken that in the developed countries. The developed countries had their period of high population growth in the 19th and early 20th centuries, while for the developing countries high population growth has occurred since 1950.

The highest ever global population growth rate was reached in the early to mid-1960s when population growth in the developing world peaked at 2.4% a year. At this time the term 'population explosion' was widely used to describe this rapid population growth. By the late 1990s the rate of population growth was down to 1.8%. However, even though the rate of growth has been falling for three decades, **population momentum** meant that the numbers being added each year did not peak until the late 1980s (Figure 3).

The demographic transformation, which took a century to complete in the developed world, has occurred in a

		World	More developed countries	Less developed countries
Total population		6 809 972 000	1 232 100 000	5 577 872 000
Births per	Year	138 949 000	14 359 000	124 590 000
	Day	380 683	39 340	341 343
	Minute	264	27	237
Deaths per	Year	56 083 000	12 277 000	43 807 000
	Day	153 653	33 636	120 019
	Minute	107	23	83
Natural increase (births - deaths) per	Year	82 866 000	2 083 000	80 784 000
	Day	227 030	5 707	221 326
	Minute	158	4	154
Infant deaths per	Year	6 352 000	82 000	6 269 000
	Day	17 402	225	17 175
	Minute	12	0.2	12

Table 2 *World population clock, 2009.*

generation in some developing countries. Fertility has dropped further and faster than most demographers foresaw 20 or 30 years ago. The exceptions are in Africa and the Middle East, where in over 30 countries families of at least five children are the norm and population growth is still over 2.5%. Table 3 (page 4) shows the ten largest countries in the world in population size and their population projections for 2050.

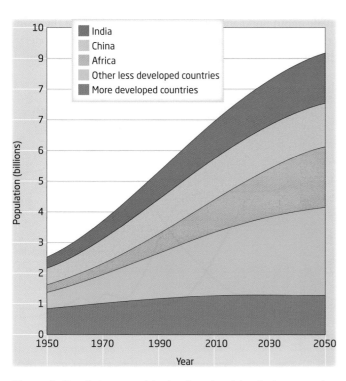

Figure 2 *Population growth in developed and developing countries, 1950–2050.*

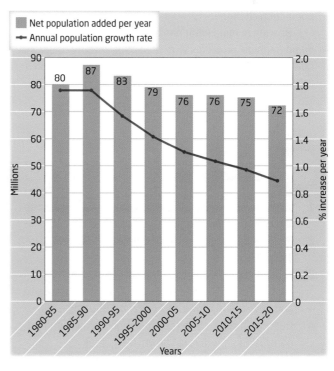

Figure 3 *Population increase and growth rate in five-year periods, 1980–2020.*

2009		2050	
Country	**Population (millions)**	**Country**	**Population (millions)**
China	1331	India	1748
India	1171	China	1437
USA	307	USA	439
Indonesia	243	Indonesia	343
Brazil	191	Pakistan	335
Pakistan	181	Nigeria	285
Bangladesh	162	Bangladesh	222
Nigeria	153	Brazil	215
Russia	142	Congo, Dem. Rep.	189
Japan	128	Philippines	150

Table 3 *The ten most populous countries in the world, 2009 and 2050.*

Theory of Knowledge

Patterns and processes can be examined at different time scales. The important thing is to choose the most appropriate time scale for your analysis.

    The concept of time lag is important in various types of geographical analysis. For example in this chapter the time lag between fertility falling to population replacement level in a country and the total population actually beginning to decline is a significant factor in population change.

    Bearing in mind what has been noted about demographers' problems with predicting fertility (page 3), how confident do you think we can be about population predictions 10, 20 or 50 years ahead?

Activities

1. With the help of Figure 1 and Table 1, briefly describe the growth of human population since 1750.
2. Produce a brief bullet point summary (8-10 points) of Table 2.
3. Look at Figure 2. Describe the differences in population growth and projected growth in developed and developing countries between 1950 and 2050.
4. Describe the trends in (a) population increase and (b) population growth rate shown in Figure 3.
5. Describe the changes in the world's most populous countries (Table 3) between 2009 and 2050.

Research idea

Find out in more detail about the advances in the Neolithic Revolution (page 1) which stimulated population growth.

Demographic transition

Although the populations of no two countries have changed in exactly the same way, some broad generalisations can be made about population growth since the middle of the 18th century. These generalisations are illustrated by the model of **demographic transition** (Figure 4) which is based on

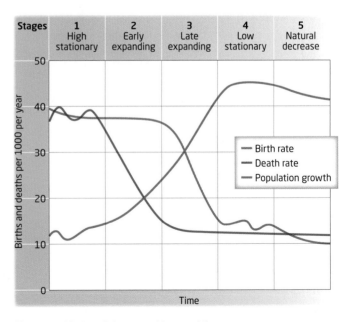

Figure 4 *Model of demographic transition.*

the experience of north-west Europe, the first part of the world to undergo such changes as a result of the significant industrial and agrarian advances that took place during the 18th and 19th centuries.

No country as a whole retains the characteristics of stage 1, which applies only to the most remote societies such as isolated tribes in New Guinea and the Amazon that have little or no contact at all with the outside world. All the developed countries of the world are now in stages 4 or 5, most having experienced all of the previous stages at different times. The poorest of the developing countries (e.g. Bangladesh, Niger, Bolivia) are in stage 2 but are joined in this stage by a number of oil-rich Middle East nations where increasing affluence has not been accompanied by a significant fall in fertility. Most developing countries that have registered significant social and economic advances are in stage 3 (e.g. Brazil, China, India), while some of the newly industrialised countries such as South Korea and Taiwan have entered stage 4. With the passage of time there can be little doubt that more countries will attain the demographic characteristics of the final stages of the model. The basic characteristics of each stage are as follows.

● High stationary Stage 1

The **crude birth rate** is high and stable while the **crude death rate** is high and fluctuating due to the sporadic incidence of famine, disease and war. The use of the word 'crude' means that the birth and death rates are based on the total population and as such they are very generalised, with clear limitations. In this stage population growth is very slow and there may be periods of considerable decline. Infant mortality is high and life expectancy low. A high proportion of the population is under the age of 15. Society is pre-industrial with most people living in rural areas, dependent on subsistence agriculture.

● Early expanding Stage 2

The death rate declines significantly. The birth rate remains at its previous level as the social norms governing fertility take time to change. As the gap between the two vital rates widens, the **rate of natural change** increases to a peak at the end of this stage. Infant mortality falls and life expectancy increases. The proportion of the population

Market in Morocco – a country in stage 3 of the demographic transition.

Graveyard in France dating from the 18th century. Inscriptions show that life expectancy at that time was very low.

under 15 increases. Although the reasons for the decline in mortality vary in intensity and sequence from one country to another, the essential causal factors are: better nutrition; improved public health, particularly in terms of clean water supply and efficient sewerage systems; and medical advance. Considerable rural-to-urban migration occurs during this stage. However, in recent decades for developing countries urbanisation has often not been accompanied by the industrialisation that was characteristic of the developed nations during the 19th century.

Case study

Demographic transition in England and Wales

In England and Wales in medieval times (stage 1) both the birth rate and the death rate hovered around 35/1000. The birth rate was generally a little higher, resulting in a slow rate of natural increase. While the birth rate tended to remain at a relatively stable level, the death rate varied considerably at times. For example, the 1348–49 epidemic of bubonic plague, known as the Black Death, killed something like a third of the population. These conditions of high fertility and high mortality persisted until about 1740 (Figure 5).

Stage 2, that lasted until about 1875, witnessed a period of rapid urbanisation which alerted both public officials and factory owners to the urgent need for improvements in public health. Factory owners soon realised that an unhealthy workforce had a huge impact on efficiency. The provision of clean piped water and the installation of sewerage systems, allied to better personal and domestic cleanliness, saw the incidence of the diarrhoeal diseases and typhus fall rapidly.

Although in many ways life in the expanding towns was little better than in the countryside, there was a greater opportunity for employment and a larger disposable income so that more food and a wider range of food products could be purchased. Contemporary studies in developing countries show a very strong relationship between infant nutrition and infant mortality. Infant mortality in England fell from 200/1000 in 1770 to just over 100/1000 in 1870.

The virulence of the common infectious diseases diminished markedly. For example, scarlet fever which caused many deaths in the 18th century had a much reduced impact in the 19th century. From about 1850 the mortality from tuberculosis also began to fall. A combination of better nutrition and the general improvements in health, brought about by legislation such as the Public Health Acts of 1848 and 1869, were the most likely causal factors.

The final factor to be considered in stage 2 is the role of medicine. Although some important milestones were reached, such as Jenner's discovery of a vaccination against smallpox, there was no widespread diffusion of medical benefits at this time. Of all the drugs available in 1850, fewer than ten had a specific action, so their impact on mortality was negligible. Surgery was no more advanced. Anaesthesia was unavailable until the last years of the century.

We can be much more sure about the accuracy of demographic data during this period. The first **census** of

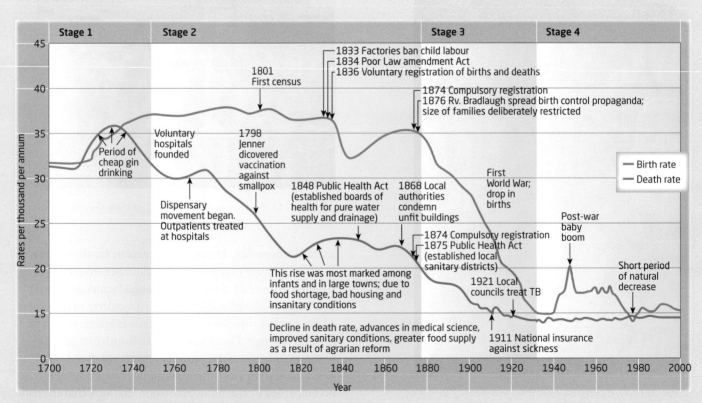

Figure 5 *Demographic transition in England and Wales.*

England and Wales was taken in 1801 and every ten years thereafter, and from 1836 the registration of births and deaths was introduced on a voluntary basis. The latter became compulsory in 1874.

After 1875 the continued decline of the death rate was accompanied by a marked downturn in the birth rate (stage 3). Medical science began to play an important role in controlling mortality and doctors were now able to offer potent, specifically effective drugs. From about 1906 increasing attention was paid to maternity and child welfare, and to school health. More measures to improve public health were introduced, while there were further gains in nutrition.

The beginning of the decline in fertility coincided with, and was partly the result of, much more widespread knowledge of contraception. However, perhaps the most important factor was the desire for smaller families now that people could be sure that the decline in mortality was permanent and because the monetary cost of children was higher in urban, compared with rural, areas.

Family size varied by social group, with the upper and professional middle classes leading the way in contraception. The birth rate, which had been 30.5/1000 in 1890, fell to 25/1000 in 1910 and was down to 17/1000 by 1930, at which time it is reasonable to assert that England and Wales was entering the final stage of demographic transition.

By 1940 the birth rate had fallen further to 14.5/1000 but this was undoubtedly influenced by the outbreak of war the previous year. The higher figures in the three decades following the end of the war are generally accounted for by the phenomenon known as the 'post-war baby boom'. However, by 1980 the birth rate was down again to 14/1000, remaining very close to that figure ever since. The introduction of the oral birth control pill in 1960 and improvements in other forms of contraceptive meant that the relationship between desired family size and achieved family size had never been stronger.

Geographical skill

Why can we be more certain about the accuracy of demographic data from the 19th century onwards than from the period before?

➲ Late expanding Stage 3

After a period of time social norms adjust to the lower level of mortality and the birth rate begins to decline. Urbanisation generally slows and average age increases. Life expectancy continues to increase and infant mortality to decrease. Countries in this stage usually experience lower death rates than nations in the final stage due to their relatively young population structures.

➲ Low stationary Stage 4

Both birth and death rates are low. The former is generally slightly higher, fluctuating somewhat due to changing economic conditions. Population growth is slow. Death rates rise slightly as the average age of the population increases. However, life expectancy still improves as age-specific mortality rates continue to fall.

➲ Natural decrease Stage 5

In an increasing number of countries the birth rate has fallen below the death rate, resulting in **natural decrease**. In the absence of net migration inflows, these populations are declining. Most countries in this stage are in eastern or southern Europe.

Critics of the demographic transition model see it as too Euro-centric. They argue that many developing countries may not follow the sequence set out in the model. It has also been criticised for its failure to take into account changes due to migration.

Theory of Knowledge

A model is a simplification of reality. Concentrating only on major characteristics and omitting the detail, it makes understanding easier at the start of the learning process. However, once clear about the framework of a situation or process, it is then not too difficult to unravel the detail. A good model will be helpful in this respect from the start. If, however, the model has clear limitations, then it needs to be improved (refined). In geography, models are useful in many areas of the subject. The model of demographic transition is the first to be examined in this book.

Discussion point

What do you think are the main factors responsible for the UK's current relatively low birth rate of approximately 13/1000?

Demographic transition in the developing world

There are a number of important differences in the way that developing countries have undergone population change compared with the experiences of most developed nations. In the developing world:

- Birth rates in stages 1 and 2 were generally higher. About a dozen African countries currently have birth rates of 45/1000 or over. Twenty years ago many more African countries were in this situation.

- The death rate fell much more steeply and for different reasons. For example, the rapid introduction of Western medicine, particularly in the form of inoculation against major diseases, has had a huge impact on lowering mortality. However, AIDS has caused the death rate to rise significantly in some countries, particularly in sub-Saharan Africa.

- Some countries had a much larger base population and thus the impact of high growth in stage 2 and the early part of stage 3 has been far greater. No countries that are now classed as developed countries had populations anywhere near the size of India and China when they entered stage 2 of demographic transition.

- For those countries in stage 3 the fall in fertility has also been steeper. This has been due mainly to the relatively widespread availability of modern contraception with high levels of reliability.

- The relationship between population change and economic development has been much more tenuous.

Different models of demographic transition

Although most countries followed the classical model of demographic transition illustrated in the last section, some countries did not. The Czech demographer Pavlik recognised two alternative types of population change (Figure 6). In France the birth rate fell at about the same time as the death rate and there was no intermediate period of high natural increase. In Japan and Mexico the birth rate actually

increased in stage 2 due mainly to the improved health of women in the reproductive age range.

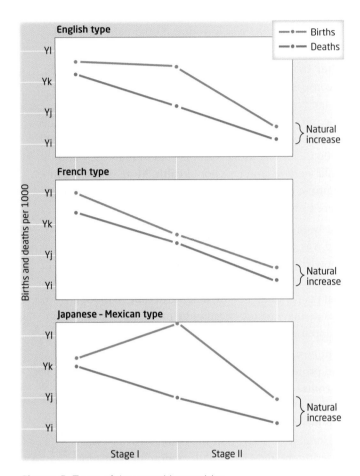

Figure 6 *Types of demographic transition.*

Activities

1 What is a geographical model (such as the model of demographic transition)?
2 Explain the reasons for declining mortality in stage 2 of demographic transition.
3 Why does it take some time before fertility follows the fall in mortality (stage 3)?
4 Suggest why the birth rate is lower than the death rate in some countries (stage 5).
5 Discuss the merits and limitations of the model of demographic transition.
6 Why has the death rate in developing countries fallen much more steeply over the last 50 years, compared with the fall in the death rate in earlier times in developed nations?

Look at the latest World Population Data Sheet on the Population Reference Bureau's website (www.prb.org). Select three countries which you feel reasonably fit each of stages 2, 3, 4 and 5 of the model of demographic transition.

The components of population change

The relationship between births and deaths (natural change) is not the only factor in population change. The balance between **immigration** and **emigration** – that is, **net migration** – must also be taken into account as the input-output model of population change shows (Figure 7). The corrugated divide in Figure 7 indicates that the relative contributions of natural change and net migration can vary over time within a particular country as well as between countries at any one point in time. The model is a simple graphical alternative to the population equation P = (B − D) +/− M, the letters standing for population, births, deaths and migration respectively.

Fertility varies widely around the world. According to the 2009 World Population Data Sheet the crude birth rate – the most basic measure of fertility – varied from a high of 53 / 1000 in Niger to a low of 7 / 1000 in Monaco. The word 'crude' means that the birth rate applies to the total population, taking no account of gender and age. The crude birth rate is heavily influenced by the age structure of a population. The crucial factor is the percentage of young women of reproductive age, as these women produce most children.

For more accurate measures of fertility, the **fertility rate** and the **total fertility rate** are used. The total fertility rate varies from a high of 7.4 in Niger to a low of 1.0 in China, Macao. Table 4 (page 10) shows the variations in birth rate and total fertility rate by world region alongside data for the percentage of women using contraception in each region. Contraception is a major factor influencing fertility. Figure 8 (page 11) shows in detail how the fertility rate varies by country around the world.

Factors affecting fertility

The factors affecting fertility can be grouped into four main categories:

➔ Demographic

Other population factors, particularly mortality rates, influence fertility. Where infant mortality is high, it is usual for many children to die before reaching adult life. In such societies, parents often have many children to compensate for these expected deaths.

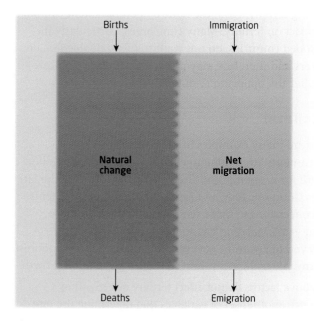

Figure 7 *Input-output model of population change.*

Nigerian woman and children.

Fertility and natural change

Region	Birth rate	Rate of natural change	Total fertility rate	Women aged 15–49 using contraception (%)
World	20	1.2	2.6	62
More developed world	12	0.2	1.7	68
Less developed world	22	1.4	2.7	61
Africa	36	2.4	4.8	28
Asia	19	1.2	2.3	67
Latin America/ Caribbean	20	1.4	2.3	71
North America	14	0.6	2.0	73
Oceania	18	1.1	2.5	59
Europe	11	0.0	1.5	68

Table 4 *Variations in birth rate, natural change, total fertility rate and percentage of women using contraception, by world region in 2009.*

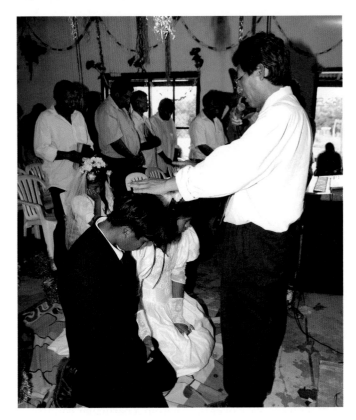

Traditional marriage ceremony, Paraguay.

➡ Social/Cultural

In some societies, particularly in Africa, tradition demands a high rate of reproduction. Here the opinion of women in the reproductive years may have little influence weighed against intense cultural expectations. Education, especially female literacy, is the key to lower fertility. With education comes a knowledge of birth control, greater social awareness, more opportunity for employment and a wider choice of action generally. In some countries religion is an important factor. For example, the Muslim and Roman Catholic religions oppose artificial birth control. Most countries that have population policies have been trying to reduce their fertility by investing in birth control programmes. Within developing countries it is usually the poorest neighbourhoods that have the highest fertility, due mainly to a combination of high infant mortality and low educational opportunities for women.

➡ Economic

In many of the least developed countries children are seen as an economic asset because of the work they do and also because of the support they are expected to give their parents in old age. In the more developed world the general perception is reversed, and the cost of the child dependency years is a major factor in the decision to begin or extend a family. Economic growth allows greater spending on health, housing, nutrition and education which is important in lowering mortality and in turn reducing fertility. Also, the nature of employment can have an impact on fertility. Many companies, particularly in developed countries, do not want to lose valuable female workers and therefore may provide workplace childcare and offer the opportunity of flexible working time.

➡ Political

There are many examples in the past century of governments attempting to change the rate of population growth for economic and strategic reasons. During the late 1930s Germany, Italy and Japan all offered inducements and concessions to those with large families. In more recent years Malaysia has adopted a similar policy. However, today, most governments that are interventionist in terms of fertility still want to reduce population growth.

The above factors do not affect fertility directly; they influence another set of variables that determine the rate and level of childbearing. Figure 9 shows these 'intermediate variables' that affect fertility. These factors operate in every country, but their relative importance can vary greatly.

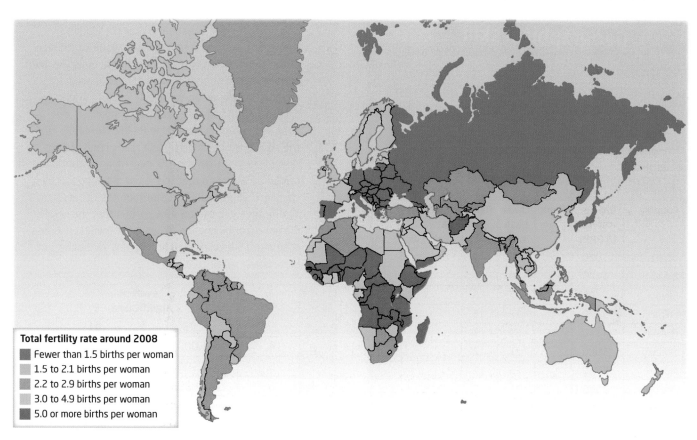

Figure 8 *Total fertility rate around 2008, by country.*

Total fertility rate around 2008
- ■ Fewer than 1.5 births per woman
- ■ 1.5 to 2.1 births per woman
- ■ 2.2 to 2.9 births per woman
- ■ 3.0 to 4.9 births per woman
- ■ 5.0 or more births per woman

Fecundity
- ability to have intercourse
- ability to conceive
- ability to carry a pregnancy to term.

Sexual unions (marriage and long-term relationships)
- the formation and dissolution of unions
- age at first intercourse
- proportion of women who are married or in a union
- time spent outside a union (e.g. separated, divorced, widowed)
- frequency of intercourse
- sexual abstinence (e.g. religious or cultural customs)
- temporary separations (e.g. military service).

Birth control
- use of contraceptives
- contraceptive sterilisation
- induced abortion.

Figure 9 *The intermediate variables that affect fertility.*

Theory of Knowledge

For the exercise on page 12 the author selected countries that he had used as case studies for teaching over a number of years. It is possible that this selection involved countries that would help 'prove' the expected result. Would systematic sampling, such as selecting every tenth country on the 2009 World Population Data Sheet give a more scientific, or more reliable outcome?

Spearman's rank correlation coefficient

Hypothesis: There is a negative correlation (inverse relationship) between GNI per capita and the crude birth rate.

Country	GNI per capita ($ PPP)	Rank	Crude birth rate	Rank	Difference between ranks (d)	d²
Venezuela	11 920		25	9		
Brazil	9 370		20	12		
Egypt	5 400		27	8		
China	5 370		12	16		
Bolivia	4 140		29	7		
Morocco	3 990		21	12		
India	2 740		23	11		
Pakistan	2 570		31	6		
Vietnam	2 550		16	15		
Mauritania	2 010		35	5		
Laos	1 940		34	4		
Tunisia	1 880		17	14		
Kenya	1 540		40	3		
Bangladesh	1 340		24	10		
Uganda	920		48	2		
Liberia	290		50	1		
					Σd²	

Table 5 *Spearman's rank correlation coefficient exercise.*

1 Rank the two data sets.
2 Calculate the difference in rank for each country (d).
3 Square the difference (d²).
4 Total the final column (Σd²).
5 Now use the formula to reach your result for SRCC.

$$r_s = 1 - \left[\frac{6\Sigma d^2}{n^3 - n}\right]$$

Σ = the sum of
d = difference in rank
n = the number of countries

6 Where does your result come on the scale below?

```
    -1.0                0               +1.0
     └───────────────────┴───────────────────┘
  perfect negative   no correlation   perfect positive
     correlation                         correlation
```

7 The final stage of Spearman's rank correlation coefficient exercise is to relate the result to the size of the sample. Clearly, the larger the sample, the more certain we can be that the result did not occur by chance. Chance, or 'unexpected', results frequently occur when the sample size is very small.

8 Look at the significance table (below) for SRCC. Find the size of your sample (n) and read across. If your result is higher than the .05 level of significance you can be 95% certain that the result did not occur by chance. If your result is higher than the 0.1 level of significance you can be 99% certain that the result did not occur by chance. However, if the result is less than the 0.5 level of significance it is said to be 'not statistically significant'.

n	Levels of significance	
	.05	**.01**
4	1.000	
5	.900	1.000
6	.829	.943
7	.714	.893
8	.643	.833
9	.600	.783
10	.564	.746
12	.506	.712
14	.456	.645
16	.425	.601
18	.399	.564
20	.377	.534
22	.359	.508
24	.343	.485
26	.329	.465
28	.317	.448
30	.306	.432

9 Now write a statement of significance for your result.
10 If a different set of 16 countries had been selected, would the result have been the same? Give reasons for your answer.

Fertility decline

A study by the United Nations published in 2007 predicted that global population would peak at 9.2 billion in 2050. This contrasts with a report published in 1996 which forecast that the world's population would peak at 10.6 billion in 2080. The global peak population has been continually revised downwards in recent decades. This is in sharp contrast to warnings in earlier decades of a population 'explosion'. The main reason for the slowdown in population growth is that fertility levels in most parts of the world have fallen faster than previously expected.

In the second half of the 1960s, after a quarter century of increasing growth, the rate of world population growth began to slow down. Since then some developing countries have seen the speediest falls in fertility ever known and thus earlier population projections did not materialise. The demographic transformation, which took a century to complete in the developed world, has occurred in a generation in some developing countries.

A fertility rate of 2.1 children per woman is **replacement level fertility**, below which populations eventually start falling. According to the 2009 World Population Data Sheet there are already 83 countries with total fertility rates at or below 2.1. This number is likely to increase. The movement to replacement level fertility is undoubtedly one of the most dramatic social changes in history, helping to enable many more women to work and children to be educated.

Theory of Knowledge

Religious belief can affect demography in a number of ways. It can influence attitudes to contraception, age of marriage and other relevant factors. However, adherence to religious values often falls with economic development. Why do you think this is? Does it make economic development more, or less, desirable?

Research idea

Find out how fertility has changed in the last 50 years in the country in which you live.

Carriages belonging to the Amish community, Indiana, USA. The Amish have a fertility rate much higher than the national average.

Activities

1 **a** Define the fertility rate.
   b Why is the fertility rate a better measure of fertility than the crude birth rate?
2 **a** Describe and explain the differences in fertility by world region shown in Table 4 (page 10).
   b Describe and attempt to explain the more detailed pattern of global fertility shown by Figure 8 (page 11).
3 How can (a) government policies and (b) religious philosophy influence fertility?
4 Why is replacement level fertility an important concept?
5 Discuss the importance of three of the intermediate variables shown in Figure 9 (page 11).

Like the crude birth rate, the crude death rate is a very generalised measure of mortality. It is heavily influenced by the age structure of a population. For example, the crude death rate for the US is 8/1000 compared with 6/1000 in Brazil. Yet life expectancy at birth in the US is 78 years compared with 73 years in Brazil. Brazil has a much younger population than the UK, but the average quality of life is significantly higher in the latter.

In 2009 the crude death rate varied around the world from a high of 23/1000 in Lesotho to a low of 1/1000 in Qatar. Table 6 shows variations by world region and also includes data for infant mortality and life expectancy at birth. The **infant mortality rate**, the **child mortality rate** and **life expectancy** are much more accurate measures of mortality. The infant and child mortality rates are age-specific rates – that is, they apply to one particular year of age or to a narrowly defined age range.

The causes of death vary significantly between developed countries and developing countries (Figure 10). In the developing world, infectious and parasitic diseases account for over 40% of all deaths. They are also a major cause of disability and social and economic upheaval. In contrast, in the developed world these diseases have a relatively low impact. In rich countries heart disease and cancer are the big killers. Epidemiology is the study of diseases. As countries develop, the ranking of major diseases tends to change from infectious to degenerative. This change is known as the epidemiological transition.

Drink and dangerous driving warning to motorists: a significant cause of death among young men.

Mortality and life expectancy

Region	Crude death rate	Infant mortality rate	Life expectancy at birth
World	8	46	69
More developed world	10	6	77
Less developed world	8	50	67
Africa	12	74	55
Asia	7	43	69
Latin America/ Caribbean	6	23	73
North America	8	6	78
Oceania	7	22	76
Europe	11	6	76

Table 6 *Death rate, infant mortality rate and life expectancy at birth, by world region 2009.*

Geographical skill

Using the data in Table 6:
1 Draw a scattergraph to show the relationship between the infant mortality rate and life expectancy at birth.
2 Insert a line of best fit.
3 Comment on the relationship between the two variables.
  Always consider the following points when analysing a scattergraph:
  ● the number of points plotted
  ● the general trend – positive correlation, negative correlation, no correlation
  ● the maximum and minimum values
  ● anomalies – how different are these from those points following the general trend?

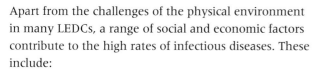

Apart from the challenges of the physical environment in many LEDCs, a range of social and economic factors contribute to the high rates of infectious diseases. These include:

- poverty
- poor access to health care
- antibiotic resistance
- evolving human migration patterns
- new infectious agents.

- social class
- ethnicity
- place of residence
- occupation
- age structure of the population.

Research idea

Find an example for each of the bullet points above to show how mortality can vary.

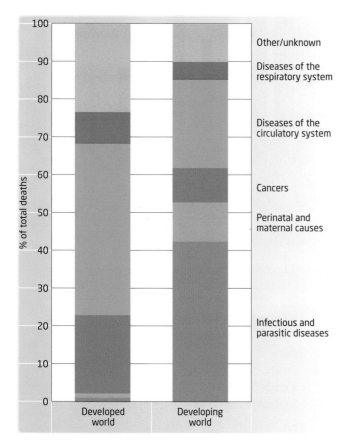

Figure 10 *Contrasts in the causes of death between developed and developing countries.*

When people live in overcrowded and insanitary conditions, communicable diseases such as tuberculosis and cholera can spread rapidly. Limited access to health care and medicines means that otherwise treatable conditions such as malaria and tuberculosis are often fatal to poor people. Poor nutrition and deficient immune systems are also key risk factors for several big killers such as lower respiratory infections, tuberculosis and measles.

Within most individual countries variations in mortality occur due to:

As Table 6 (page 14) shows, there is a huge contrast in infant mortality by world region. Africa has the highest rate (74/1000) and Europe and North America (6/1000) the lowest rate. The variation among individual countries is even greater. In 2009 the highest infant mortality rates were in Afghanistan (155/1000) and Angola (125/1000). In contrast the lowest rates were in Hong Kong and Luxembourg (1.8/1000). The infant mortality rate is frequently considered to be the most sensitive indicator of socio-economic progress, being heavily influenced by fundamental improvements in the quality of life, such as improvements in water supply, better nutrition, and improved health care. Once children survive the crucial first year, their life chances improve substantially.

Infant mortality in today's rich countries has changed considerably over time. In 1900, infant mortality in the USA was 120/1000. In 2009 it was down to 6.6/1000.

Child mortality

Figure 11 (page 16) shows how child mortality rates changed around the world between 1990 and 2006. Globally, the number of children under 5 years who died in 2006 dropped below 10 million for the first time. The United Nations International Children's Fund (UNICEF) estimated the total at 9.7 million, down from almost 13 million in 1990. The main reasons for the decline included measles vaccinations, mosquito nets and increased rates of breast-feeding. In some countries such as Morocco, Vietnam and the Dominican Republic, the number of children under 5 dying dropped by a third. The majority of child deaths occurred in sub-Saharan Africa (4.8 million) and south Asia (3.1 million). In Vietnam the steep fall has been attributed to the training of 30000 health workers to treat people in their own villages.

UNICEF argues that the majority of the remaining child deaths are preventable. In 2007 UNICEF called on the global community to invest another $5 billion to help the UN achieve its Millennium Development Goals (MDGs).

Falling mortality rates in less developed countries were responsible for most of the population growth in the 20th and early 21st centuries. Further reductions in mortality are likely to occur by focusing on particular causes and population groups. Maternal mortality is a case in point. Reducing material mortality is one of the United Nation's (UN) eight Millennium Development Goals. Globally, 1 in 92 women die from pregnancy-related causes. However, in more developed nations the risk is only 1 in 6000 compared with 1 in 22 in sub-Saharan Africa. Major influencing factors in maternal mortality are the type of pre-natal care and the type of attendance at birth.

The decline in levels of mortality and the increase in life expectancy has been the most important reward of economic and social development. On a global scale, 75% of the total improvement in longevity has been achieved in the 20th century and the early years of the 21st century. In 1900 the world average for life expectancy is estimated to have been about 30 years but by 1950–55 it had risen to 46 years. By 1980–85 it had reached a fraction under 60 years. The current global average is 68 years. Here there is a three-year gap between males and females (67 and 70 years). The gender gap is wider in the more developed world (74 and 81 years) than the less developed world (65 and 68 years).

Table 6 (page 14) shows that the lowest average life expectancy by world region is in Africa (55 years), with the highest average figure in North America (78 years). Rates of life expectancy at birth have converged significantly between rich and poor countries during the last 50 years or so, in spite of a widening wealth gap. These increases in life expectancy have to a certain extent offset the widening disparity between per capita incomes in developed and developing countries. However, it must not be forgotten that the ravages of AIDS in particular has caused recent decreases in life expectancy in some countries in sub-Saharan Africa. It is likely that the life expectancy gap between rich and poor countries will continue to narrow in the future.

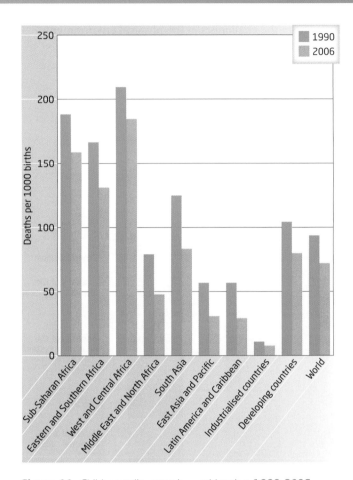

Figure 11 *Child mortality rates by world region, 1990–2006.*

Research idea

Find out how the infant mortality rate has changed in the last 20 years in one less developed country.

Activities

1 Define:
 a crude death rate
 b infant mortality rate
 c child mortality rate
 d life expectancy.
2 Why is the crude death rate a very limited measure of mortality?
3 Using Figure 10 (page 15), describe and explain the contrast in the causes of death between more developed and less developed countries.
4 To what extent does infant mortality vary around the world?
5 Discuss the main reasons for such large variations in infant mortality.
6 Describe the global variations in life expectancy.
7 Suggest reasons for the convergence of life expectancy rates between rich and poor countries over the last 50 years.

Analysing population pyramids

The structure, or composition, of a population is the product of the processes of fertility, mortality and migration. The most studied aspects of **population structure** are age and gender. Other aspects of population structure that can also be studied include ethnic origin, language, religion, and social/occupational groups.

Secondary school in Morocco: the country has a youthful population.

Age and gender structure is conventionally illustrated by the use of **population pyramids**. Pyramids can be used to portray either absolute or relative data. Absolute data shows the figures in thousands or millions while relative data shows the numbers involved in percentages. The latter is most frequently used as it allows for easier comparison of countries of different population sizes. Each bar represents a five-year age-group apart from the uppermost bar which usually illustrates the population 85 years old and over. The male population is represented to the left of the vertical axis with females to the right.

Population pyramids change significantly in shape as a country progresses through demographic transition (Figure 12, page 18):

- The wide base in the pyramid for Niger reflects extremely high fertility. The birth rate in Niger is 53/1000, the highest in the world. The marked decrease in width of each successive bar indicates relatively high mortality and limited life expectancy.

The death rate at 14/1000 is high, particularly considering how young the population is. The infant mortality rate is a very high, 88/1000. Life expectancy in Niger is 53 years, 49% of the population is under 15, with only 3% 65 or more. Niger is in stage 2 of demographic transition.

- The base of the second pyramid showing the population structure of Bangladesh is narrower, reflecting a considerable fall in fertility after decades of government-promoted birth control programmes. The almost equal width of the youngest three bars is evidence of recent falls in fertility. The birth rate is currently 23/1000. Falling mortality and lengthening life expectancy is reflected in the relatively wide bars in the teenage and young adult age groups. The death rate at 7/1000 is almost half that of Niger. The infant mortality rate is 48/1000. Life expectancy in Bangladesh is 65 years, 32% of the population are under 15, while 4% are 65 or over. Bangladesh is an example of a country in stage 3 of demographic transition.

- In the pyramid for the UK much lower fertility still is illustrated by narrowing of the base. The birth rate in the UK is only 13/1000. The reduced narrowing of each successive bar indicates a further decline in mortality and greater life expectancy compared with Bangladesh. The death rate in the UK is 9/1000, with an infant mortality rate of 4.6/1000. Life expectancy is 79 years, 18% of the population are under 15, while 16% are 65 or over. The UK is in stage 4 of demographic transition.

- The final pyramid, for Japan, has a distinctly inverted base, reflecting the lowest fertility of all four countries. The birth rate is 9/1000. The width of the rest of the pyramid is a consequence of the lowest mortality and highest life expectancy of all four countries. The death rate is 9/1000 with infant mortality at 2.6/1000. Life expectancy is 83 years. Japan has only 13% of its population under 15, with 23% at 65 or over. With the birth rate and the death rate in balance, Japan is on the boundary of stages 4 and 5 of demographic transition.

Figure 13 (page 19) provides some useful tips for understanding population pyramids. A good starting point is to divide the pyramid into three sections:

- the young dependent population
- the economically active population
- the elderly dependent population.

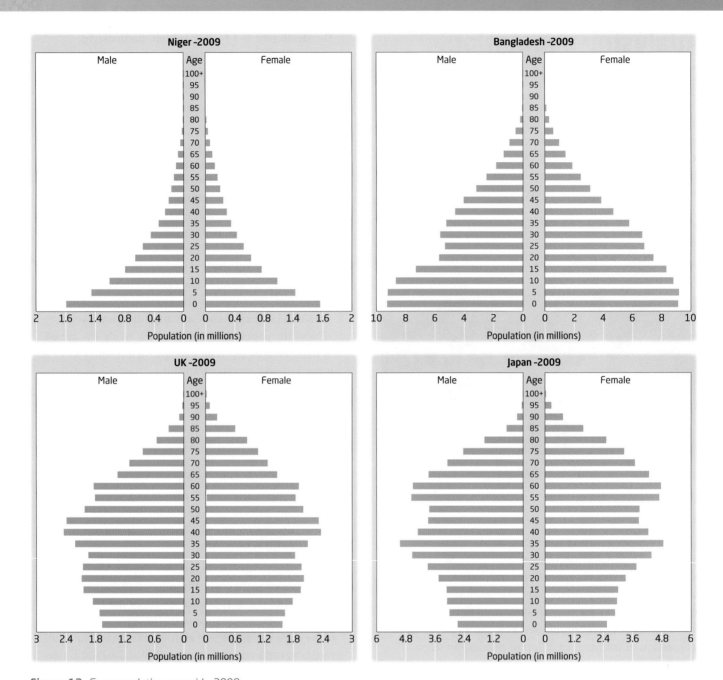

Figure 12 *Four population pyramids, 2009.*

Population structure: differences within countries

In countries where there is strong rural-to-urban migration, the population structures of the areas affected can be markedly different. These differences show up clearly on population pyramids. Out-migration from rural areas is age-selective with single young adults and young adults with children dominating this process.

Thus the bars for these age groups in rural areas affected by out-migration will indicate fewer people than expected in these age groups. In contrast, the population pyramids for urban areas attracting migrants will show age-selective in-migration, with substantially more people in these age groups than expected. Such migrations may also be gender-selective. If this is the case it should be apparent on the population pyramids.

Gender structure

The **sex ratio** is the number of males per 100 females in a population. Male births consistently exceed female births due to a combination of biological and social reasons. For

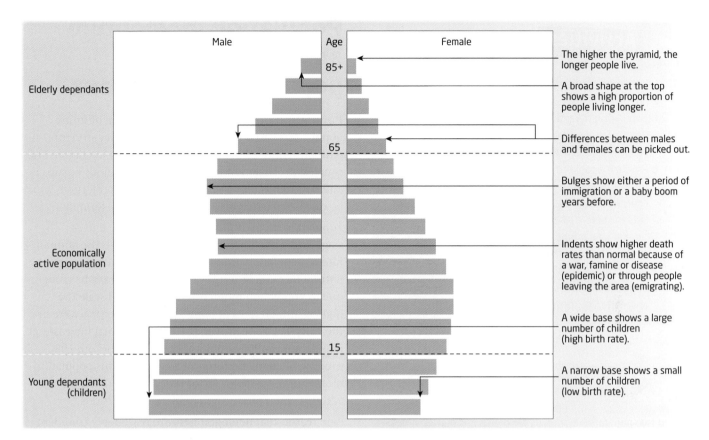

Figure 13 *Annotated population pyramid.*

The diagram annotations read:

- The higher the pyramid, the longer people live.
- A broad shape at the top shows a high proportion of people living longer.
- Differences between males and females can be picked out.
- Bulges show either a period of immigration or a baby boom years before.
- Indents show higher death rates than normal because of a war, famine or disease (epidemic) or through people leaving the area (emigrating).
- A wide base shows a large number of children (high birth rate).
- A narrow base shows a small number of children (low birth rate).

Left side labels:
- Elderly dependants
- Economically active population
- Young dependants (children)

example, more couples decide to complete their family on the birth of a boy than on the birth of a girl.

In the UK 105 boys are born for every 100 girls. However, after birth the gap generally begins to narrow until eventually females outnumber males, as at every age male mortality is higher than female mortality. This process happens most rapidly in the poorest countries where infant mortality is markedly higher among males than females. Here the gap may be closed in less than a year. In the UK it is not until the 45–59 age group that females outnumber males. In the age group 85 and over, females make up 74% of the population.

However, there are anomalies to the picture just presented. In countries where the position of women is often markedly subordinate and deprived, the overall sex ratio may show an excess of males. Such countries often exhibit high mortality rates in childbirth. For example, in India there are 107 males per 100 females for the population as a whole.

A report published in China in 2002 recorded 116 male births for every 100 female births due to the significant number of female foetuses aborted by parents intent on having a male child. Even within countries there can be significant differences in the sex ratio. In the USA, Alaska has the highest ratio at 103.2, while Mississippi has the lowest at 92.2.

Malaysian family in Penang.

Activities

1 What do you understand by the terms:
   a population structure
   b population pyramid?
2 **a** Describe and explain the differences between the four population pyramids shown in Figure 12 (page 18).
   b Produce a table to show all the statistical data given for the four countries. Keep the same order of countries as in the text. For how many of the data sets in there a clear trend?
3 How and why might the population structures of rural and urban areas in the same country differ?
4 **a** Define the sex ratio.
   b Suggest why the sex ratio can differ both between and within countries.

Research idea

Find two population pyramids for the same country which show clear changes in age/gender structure over time. Describe and explain these changes.

Population momentum and its impact on population projections

Population projections are the prediction of future populations based on the present age–gender structure, and with present rates of fertility, mortality and migration. The simplest projections are based on extrapolations of current and past trends, but a set of very different projections can be calculated based on a series of differing assumptions.

Population momentum occurs towards the end of stage 3 of demographic transition. Although the annual rate of population growth may be falling in a country, the natural increase in terms of total number may be rising due to population momentum. On a global scale the highest annual rates of population increase (%) were in the early 1960s. However, the highest annual increases in population (millions) did not occur until the late 1980s – a time lag of about a quarter of a century. Thus population momentum is a major factor that must be taken into account when producing population projections.

One reason that demographers are reasonably confident about short-term and medium-term population predictions is that through population momentum, much of the future is built into the current structure of populations. For example, in very high fertility countries, the current population structure guarantees very considerable future growth. This would occur even if the total fertility rate fell

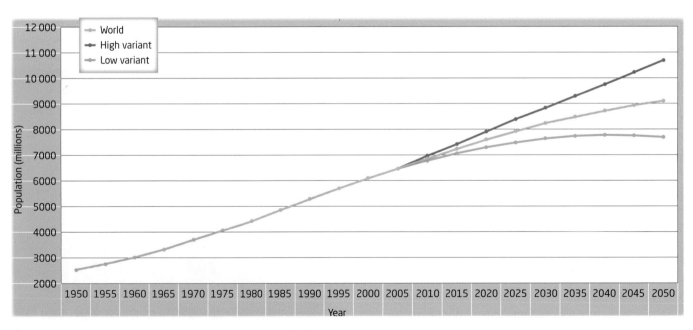

Figure 14 *World population 1950–2050: three variant projections.*

sharply almost overnight. Such populations would grow for another 50 years or so. In contrast, such low fertility countries as Germany, Italy and Spain do not have this 'positive momentum'. The positive momentum of these populations has been dissipated by decades of fertility below the replacement level.

Projections result from the assumptions made when they are prepared. Assumptions must be made about:

- declines in the future birth rate
- improvements in life expectancy at birth and infant mortality
- migration into and out of an area.

Any population projection is hypothetical in nature. It is always dangerous to assume that various demographic factors will stay the same in the future or change only marginally. The significant demographic changes that have occurred since 1950 in both developing and developed countries should make us very aware of this point. Many previous population projections have proved to be inaccurate to a considerable degree. Failure to foresee the 'baby boom' after the end of the Second World War, and the end of this boom, is an often quoted example.

Although total accuracy is almost impossible to achieve, population projections need to be accurate enough to serve as the basis for policies. As D.A. Coleman states in *The shape of things to come: world population to 2050* (Contribution to the Engelsberg Seminar 2005): 'Population matters because of its associated effects on power, environment and security arising from global and regional, and particularly differential, population growth and composition.' Coleman sees this differential population growth as radically transforming the international political and economic order.

Figure 14 shows three global projections to 2050:

- The central forecast expects world population to stabilise at about nine billion.
- The upper line is the UN's high variant, which assumes slow declines in fertility and faster increase in life expectancy.
- The low variant line shows that the UN now takes seriously the possibility that world population could actually decline before the end of the century.

Activities

1 Define (a) population momentum (b) population projection.
2 Why is population momentum applicable to many developing countries, but to few developed countries?
3 Why do individual countries and international organisations construct population projections?
4 Why are modern population projections likely to be more accurate than projections made 30 years ago?

Research idea

Find out about the population projections for the country in which you live. Try to obtain a graph showing variant projections and briefly describe what the graph shows.

Key terms

Diffusion the spread of a phenomenon over time and space.

Carrying capacity the largest population that the resources of a given environment can support.

Demography the scientific study of human populations.

Population momentum the tendency for population growth to continue beyond the time that replacement level fertility has been achieved, because of a relatively high concentration of people in the child-bearing years. This situation is due to past high fertility rates which results in a large number of young people.

Demographic transition the historical shift of birth and death rates from high to low levels in a population.

Crude birth rate (generally referred to as the 'birth rate') the number of births per 1000 population in a given year. It is only a very broad indicator as it does not take into account the age and gender distribution of the population.

Crude death rate (generally referred to as the 'death rate') the number of deaths per 1000 population in a given year. Again it is only a broad indicator as it is heavily influenced by the age structure of the population.

Rate of natural change the difference between the birth rate and the death rate.

Census an official periodic count of a population including such information as age, gender, occupation and ethnic origin.

Natural decrease when the number of births is lower than the number of deaths.

Immigration the migration of people into a country from one or a number of other countries.

Emigration the migration of people from a country to one or a number of other countries.

Net migration the difference between immigration and emigration for a particular country.

Fertility rate the number of live births per 1000 women aged 15–49 years in a given year.

Total fertility rate the average number of children that would be born alive to a woman (or group of women) during her lifetime, if she were to pass through her child-bearing years conforming to the age-specific fertility rates of a given year.

Replacement level fertility the level at which each generation has just enough children to replace themselves in the population. Although the level varies for different populations, a total fertility rate of 2.12 children is usually considered as replacement level.

Infant mortality rate the number of deaths of infants under 1 year of age per 1000 live births in a given year.

Child mortality rate the number of deaths of children under 5 years of age per 1000 live births in a given year.

Life expectancy (at birth) the average number of years a person may expect to live when born, assuming past trends continue.

Population structure the composition of a population, the most important elements of which are age and sex.

Population pyramid a bar chart, arranged vertically, that shows the distribution of a population by age and gender.

Sex ratio the number of males per 100 females in a population.

Population projection the prediction of future populations based on the present age-gender structure, and with present rates of fertility, mortality and migration.

Review

Examination-style questions

1 Refer to Figure 15.

a Define 'annual world population change'.

b Describe how annual population change varies for the time period shown.

c Examine the reasons for the variations in annual population change.

2 Refer to Figure 16.

a Suggest why the population pyramids are divided into three sections.

b Describe the differences between the three pyramids.

c Examine the reasons for the considerable changes between the three pyramids.

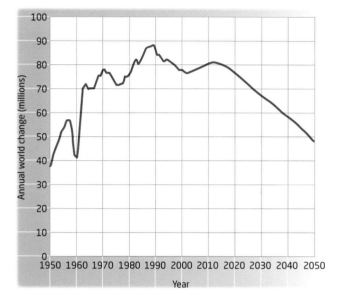

Figure 15 *Annual world population change, 1950–2050.*

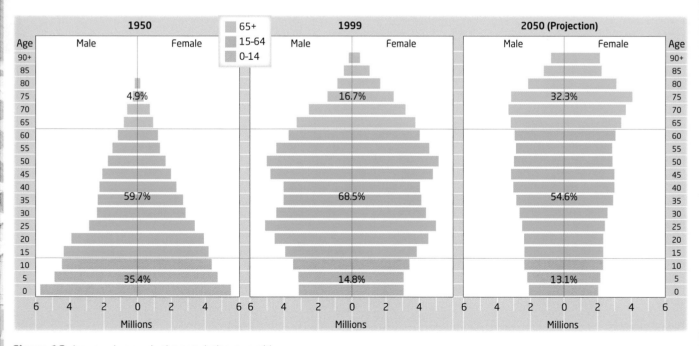

Figure 16 *Japan – changes in the population pyramid.*

Websites

www.prb.org
Population Reference Bureau

www.unfpa.org
UN Population Fund

www.un.org/popin/
UN Population Information Network

www.histpop.org/
Histpop – a collection of British historical population reports

www.census.gov/
US Census Bureau

www.statistics.gov.uk/
National Statistics Online (UK)

02 Responses to high and low fertility

KEY QUESTIONS

- What are the definitions and significance of the dependency and ageing ratios?
- What are the impacts of youthful and ageing populations?
- How successful have government policies to encourage births and to limit births been?

Gathering of young people, China.

The dependency and ageing ratios

Dependants are people who are too young or too old to work. The **dependency ratio** is the relationship between the working or economically active population and the non-working population. The formula for calculating the dependency ratio is as follows:

Dependency ratio

$$= \frac{\% \text{ population aged } 0\text{--}14 + \% \text{ population aged } 65 \text{ and over}}{\% \text{ population } 15\text{--}64} \times 100$$

A teacher talking to a group of 14-year-old students, London Docklands. These students are part of the UK's young dependent population.

A dependency ratio of 60 means that for every 100 people in the economically active population there are 60 people dependent on them. The dependency ratio in developed countries is usually between 50 and 75. In contrast, developing countries typically have higher ratios which may reach over 100. In developing countries, children form the great majority of the dependent population. In contrast, in developed countries there is much more of a balance between young and old dependents. Calculations of the **youth dependency ratio** and the **elderly dependency ratio** can show these contrasts more clearly.

$$\text{Youth dependency ratio} = \frac{\% \text{ population aged } 0\text{--}14}{\% \text{ population } 15\text{--}64} \times 100$$

$$\text{Elderly dependency ratio} = \frac{\% \text{ population } 65 \text{ and over}}{\% \text{ population } 15\text{--}64} \times 100$$

For any country or region the sum of the youth dependency ratio and the elderly dependency ratio is equal to the dependency ratio.

The dependency ratio is important because the economically active population will in general contribute more to the economy in terms of taxes on income, goods and business activity. In contrast, the dependent population tend to be bigger recipients of government funding, particularly for education, health care and public pensions. An increase in the dependency ratio can cause significant financial problems for a government if it does not have the financial reserves to cope with such a change.

The dependency ratio is an internationally agreed measure. Partly because of this it is a very crude indicator. For example:

- In developed countries, few people leave education before the age of 18 and a significant number go on to university and do not get a job before the age of 21. In addition, while some people will retire before the age of 65, others will go on working beyond this age.

- A significant number of people in the economically active age group, such as parents staying at home to look after children, do not work for various reasons. The number of people in this situation can vary considerably from one country to another.

- In developing countries a significant proportion of children are working full-time or part-time before the age of 15. In some developing countries there is very high unemployment and underemployment within the economically active age group.

A shop that stocks aids for elderly people: specialist companies also cater for the needs of the elderly.

However, despite its limitations the dependency ratio does allow reasonable comparisons between countries. It is also useful to see how individual countries change over time. Once an analysis using the dependency ratio has been made, more detailed research can look into any apparent anomalies.

Theory of Knowledge

Definitions of what is basically the same concept may differ to a certain extent between subjects and can change over time within one subject. For example, economists tend not just to look at the age profile of a population, but to delve deeper and assess whether or not people are economically active. The result of this more detailed analysis is termed the real (or effective) dependency ratio.

The Early Learning Centre shop caters for the needs of young dependants, creating economic demand and jobs.

Country	% population <15	% population 65 and over	Dependency ratio
USA	20	13	
Japan	13	23	
Germany	14	20	
UK	18	16	
Russia	15	14	
Brazil	28	6	
India	32	5	
China	19	8	
Nigeria	45	3	
Bangladesh	32	4	
Egypt	33	5	
Bolivia	38	4	

Table 1 *Dependency data, 2009*

Geographical skills

Calculate the dependency ratios for the 12 countries listed in Table 1.

The **ageing ratio** compares the percentage of people 65 years and over to the total population. As the ratio increases the **median age** of the population rises. The populations that are ageing most rapidly (**ageing population**) do so as a result of significant declines in fertility and increases in life expectancy. Table 2 shows how significantly the ageing ratio has increased for seven developed nations. Japan and Italy have particularly high ageing ratios. Figure 1 contrasts the overall age structures of the developed and developing worlds. The difference between the two populations is very substantial indeed.

Country	1950	1960	1970	1980	1990	2000	2008
Japan	5	6	7	9	12	17	23
USA	8	9	10	11	12	12	13
France	11	12	13	14	14	16	17
Germany	10	12	14	16	15	16	20
Italy	8	9	11	13	15	18	20
Sweden	10	12	14	16	18	17	18
UK	11	12	13	15	16	16	16

Table 2 *Increase in ageing ratios (percentage) for seven countries, 1950–2008.*

For all of these indicators, examining variations within countries can be as interesting as looking at international contrasts.

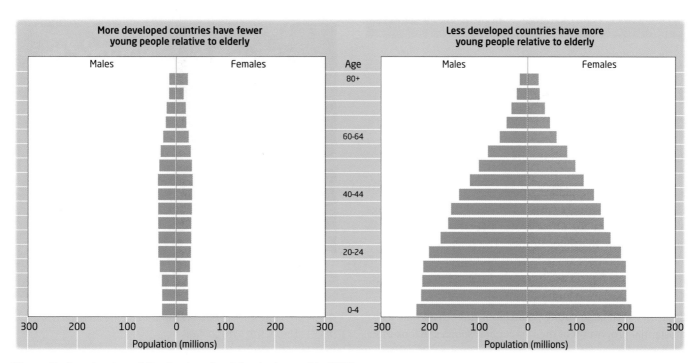

Figure 1 *Age structure of the developed and developing worlds, 2008.*

Activities

1 Define (a) the dependency ratio (b) the ageing ratio.
2 Identify two limitations of the dependency ratio.
3 Describe and explain the variations in the dependency ratio as a result of your calculations in using Table 1.
4 Identify and explain the differences between the two population pyramids shown in Figure 1.

Geographical skills

Construct a line graph to illustrate the data shown in Table 2. Produce a brief analysis of the trends shown on your graph.

Research idea

Find out how the dependency ratio varies within the country in which you live. Do some regions have a significantly higher dependency ratio than others?

The impacts of youthful populations

Rapid population growth results in a large young dependent population. The young dependent population is defined as the population under 15 years of age. Table 3 shows the huge variation around the world average of 27%. The 41% for Africa is over two and a half times higher than the figure for Europe. The highest figures for individual countries are in Uganda and Niger (49%). The world's lowest figures are in Japan, Bulgaria, China Hong Kong, China Macao, and Monaco (all 13%).

Countries with large young populations have to allocate a substantial proportion of their national resources to look after

Region	Total population under 15 years (%)
World	27
Africa	41
North America	20
Latin America/Caribbean	30
Asia	27
Europe	15
Oceania	24

Table 3 *The percentage of total population under 15 years of age, 2009.*

them. Young people require resources for health, education, food, water and housing. The money required to cover such needs may mean there is little left to invest in agriculture, industry and other aspects of the economy. The government of a developing country might see this as being too large a demand on the country's resources and as a result may introduce family planning policies to reduce the birth rate.

However, individual parents may have a different view, where they see a large family as valuable in terms of the work children can do on the land. Alongside this, people in poor countries often have to rely on their children in old age because of the lack of state welfare benefits.

A religious procession in Brazil, a Catholic country. Religion can affect attitudes to birth control.

Theory of Knowledge

Perceptions as to what is desirable can vary between different groups of people and organisations within a country. For example, a country's government may want to decrease fertility because of the high costs of providing for the needs of young people, but individual families may view more children as an economic benefit. Do governments have the right to control family size?

As a large young population moves up the age ladder over time, it will provide a substantial working population when it enters the economically active age group (15–64). This will be an advantage if a country can attract sufficient investment to create enough jobs for a large working population. Then, the large working population will contribute a lot of money in taxes to the country which can be invested in many different ways to improve the quality of life and to attract more foreign investment. Such a situation can create an upward spiral of economic growth.

On the other hand, if there are few employment opportunities for a large working population, the unemployment rate will be high. The government and most individuals will have little money to spend and the quality of life will be low. Many young adults may seek to emigrate because of the lack of opportunities in their own country.

Eventually, the large number of people in this age group will reach old age. If most of them enter old age in poverty, this creates even more problems for the government.

The impacts of ageing populations

According to the United Nations (UN), 'Population ageing is unprecedented, without parallel in human history, and the 21st century will witness even more rapid ageing than did the century just past.' In western Europe in 1800, less than 25% of men would live to the age of 60. Today, more than 90% do.

The world's population is ageing significantly. Ageing of population is a rise in the median age of a population. It occurs when fertility declines while life expectancy remains constant or increases.

The following factors have been highlighted by the UN:

- The global average for life expectancy increased from 46 years in 1950 to nearly 65 in 2000. It is projected to reach 74 years by 2050.
- In developing countries the population aged 60 years and over is expected to quadruple between 2000 and 2050.
- In developed countries the number of older people was greater than that of children for the first time in 1998. By 2050 older people in developed countries will outnumber children by more than two to one.
- The population aged 80 years and over (the oldest old) numbered 69 million in 2000. This was the fastest growing section of the global population and is projected to increase to 375 million by 2050.
- Europe is the 'oldest' region in the world. Those aged 60 years and over currently form 20% of the population. This should rise to 35% by 2050.
- Japan is the oldest nation with a median age of 41.3 years, followed by Italy, Switzerland, Germany and Sweden.
- Africa is the 'youngest' region in the world, with the proportion of children accounting for 43% of the population today. However, this is expected to decline to 28% by 2050. In contrast the proportion of older people is projected to increase from 5% to 10% over the same time period.

The impact of a young population in The Gambia is significant.

Case study

The impact of a young population in The Gambia

The Gambia, in West Africa, is a country with a young population which has placed big demands on the resources of the country. Muslims represent 95% of the country's population and until recently religious leaders were against the use of contraception. In addition, cultural tradition meant that women had little influence on family size. Children were viewed as an economic asset because of their help with crop production and tending animals. One in three children aged 10–14 are working. The country suffered from high infant and maternal mortality. With 45% of the population classed as young dependants and only 3% elderly dependants, the dependency ratio is 92.3%.

The World Health Organization (WHO) has stressed the link between high population growth and poverty for The Gambia and other countries. Many parents in The Gambia struggle to provide basic housing for their families. There is huge overcrowding and a lack of sanitation, with many children sharing the same bed. Rates of unemployment and underemployment are high, and wages are low, with parents struggling to provide even the basics for large families.

The government has insufficient financial resources for education and health. Because there are not enough schools, many schools operate a two-shift system with one group of pupils attending in the morning and a different group attending in the afternoon. The shortage of teachers means that some are working 12 hours a day. General facilities are poor and sanitation facilities are woefully inadequate. School books are in desperately short supply.

Another sign of population pressure is the large number of trees being chopped down for firewood. As a result desertification is increasing at a rapid rate. 'Forest educators' are working in rural areas in particular in an attempt to improve this situation.

In recent years the government has introduced a family planning campaign which has been accepted by religious leaders. It has been working with a non-governmental organisation (NGO) called Futures to deliver contraceptives and family planning advice to rural areas. The scheme has been subsidised by WHO. To some extent there has also been a change in male attitudes to family size and contraception. This has been very important to the success of the campaign.

Research idea

Use the latest World Population Data Sheet to produce a brief factfile on population in The Gambia.

Activities

1 Describe the variation in the percentage of population under 15 by world region shown in Table 3 (page 28).
2 Which resources in particular must a government provide for a large young population?
3 Produce a brief bullet-point summary of population pressure in The Gambia.
4 What impact will a large young population have as it gets older?

Discussion point

Why do individual families and governments often differ in their opinions about family size?

Table 4 shows that 8% of the world's population are aged 65 years and over. On a continental scale this varies from only 3% in Africa to 16% in Europe. Population projections show that the world population 65 years and over will rise to 10% in 2025, and to 16% by 2050.

The problem of demographic ageing has been a concern of developed countries for some time, but it is now also

Region	Population 65 years and over (%)
World	8
Africa	3
North America	13
Latin America/Caribbean	6
Asia	7
Europe	16
Oceania	10

Table 4 *The percentage of total population 65 years and over, 2009.*

Geographical skills

Draw a bar graph to illustrate the data in Table 4.
Describe the variations shown on your graph.

The demand for care homes in the UK is rising as the population ages.

beginning to alarm developing nations. Although ageing has begun later in developing countries it is progressing at a faster rate. This follows the pattern of previous demographic change, such as declining mortality and falling fertility where change in developing countries was much faster than that previously experienced by developed nations.

Demographic ageing will put health care systems, public pensions, and government budgets in general, under increasing pressure. In 1900, 4% of the USA's population was 65 years of age and older. By 1995 this had risen to 12.8% and by 2030 it is likely that one in five Americans will be senior citizens. The fastest-growing segment of the population is the so-called 'oldest-old': those who are 80 years or more. It is this age group that is most likely to need expensive residential care. The situation is similar in other developed countries.

A village in northern Spain now deserted due to out-migration and population ageing.

Some countries have made relatively good pension provision by investing wisely over a long period of time. However, others have more or less adopted a pay-as-you-go system, as the elderly dependent population rises. It is this latter group who will be faced with the biggest problems in the future.

For much of the post-1950 period the main demographic problem has been generally perceived as the 'population explosion', a result of very high fertility in the developing world. However, greater concern is now being expressed about demographic ageing in many countries where difficult decisions about the re-allocation of resources are having to be made. Very few countries are generous in looking after their elderly at present. Poverty amongst the

Case study

Population ageing in Japan

Japan has the most rapidly ageing population in the history of the world:

- one in five Japanese are over the age of 60
- nearly two million Japanese are now over 80 years of age
- the country's population peaked in 2005 at 128 million (Figure 2) – the most extreme population projection predicts a decline of 50 million by the end of this century
- fertility has declined substantially and the total fertility rate is an extremely low at 1.3
- no other country has a lower percentage of its population under 15.

A high age dependency ratio presents considerable economic and social challenges to the country, not least in terms of pensions, health care and long-term care. Japan's workforce peaked at 67.9 million in 1998 and has been in decline since then. This presents an increasing economic burden on the existing workforce. However, it must be noted that there is a high labour force participation rate among the elderly. Japanese men work an average of five years after mandatory retirement.

Japan has a long tradition of positive attitudes towards older people. Every year, National Respect the Aged Day is a public holiday. However, while there is a strong tradition of elderly people being looked after by their families, the number of old people living in care homes or other welfare facilities is steadily rising. The cost of care is shared between the elderly person, their family and the government. As the number of people in this situation increases, more pressure is placed on the country's economy. Social changes are also occurring, for example the emergence of ageing as a theme in films and books.

Younger workers are at a premium and there is considerable competition to recruit them. One solution is for manufacturers to set up affiliated companies in China or other countries, but past results have been mixed. The possibility of expanding immigration to help reduce the rising dependency ratio appears to be politically unacceptable in Japan. Foreigners make up only 1% of Japan's labour force. Legal immigration is practically impossible (except for highly skilled ethnic Japanese workers) and illegal immigration is strictly suppressed.

The UN predicts that by 2045, for every four Japanese aged 20–64, there will be three people aged 65 or over. The key question is what is a socially acceptable level of provision for the elderly in terms of the proportion of the country's total GDP? This is a question many other countries are going to have to ask themselves as well. Pension reforms have been implemented, with later retirement and higher contributions from employers. However, it is likely that further changes will be required as the cost of ageing rises.

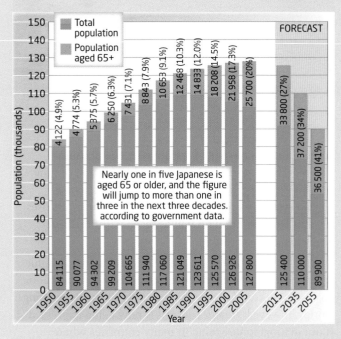

Figure 2 includes the note:
"Nearly one in five Japanese is aged 65 or older, and the figure will jump to more than one in three in the next three decades, according to government data."

Figure 2 *Population trends in Japan, 1950–2005.*

Activities

1. Why does Japan have a rapidly ageing population?
2. Suggest why this trend may contribute to changing attitudes towards the elderly.

elderly is a considerable problem but technological advances might provide a solution by improving living standards for everyone. If not, other less popular solutions, such as increased taxation, will have to be examined.

However, some demographers argue that there needs to be a certain rethinking of age and ageing, with older people adopting healthier and more adventurous lifestyles than people of the same age only one or two generations ago. Sayings such as '50 is the new 40' have become fairly commonplace. People argue that we should not just think of chronological age, but also of prospective age – the remaining years of life expectancy people have (Table 5).

It is of course easy to underestimate the positive aspects of ageing.

- Many older people make a big contribution to child care by looking after their grandchildren.
- Large numbers of older people work as volunteers, for example in charity shops.

Year	Age lived	Remaining life expectancy
1952	30 years	44.7 years
2005	30 years	54.4 years

Table 5 *Remaining life expectancy among French women, 1952 and 2005.*

Activities

1 Why is a large elderly dependent population generally viewed as a problem?
2 Discuss the possible benefits of a large elderly population.
3 Briefly explain Table 5.

Discussion point

In your opinion, at what age do people become 'elderly'? Do you think your attitude will change as you get older yourself? What do other people in your class think?

Population policies with regard to fertility

Population policy encompasses all of the measures explicitly or implicitly taken by a government aimed at influencing population size, growth, distribution, or composition.

Such policies may promote large families (**pro-natalist policies**) or immigration to increase its size, or encourage limitation of births (**anti-natalist policies**) to decrease it. A population policy may also aim to modify the distribution of the population over the country by encouraging migration or by displacing populations.

A significant number of governments have officially stated positions on the level of the national birth rate. However, forming an opinion on demographic issues is one thing, but establishing a policy to do something about it is much further along the line. Thus not all nations stating an opinion on population have gone as far as establishing a formal policy.

Most countries that have tried to control fertility have sought to curtail it.

In 1952 India became the first developing country to introduce a policy designed to reduce fertility and to aid development, with a government-backed family planning programme. Rural and urban birth control clinics rapidly increased in number. Financial and other incentives were offered in some states for those participating in programmes, especially sterilisation. In the mid-1970s the sterilisation campaign became increasingly coercive, reaching a peak of 8.3 million operations in 1977. Abortion was legalised in 1972 and in 1978 the minimum age of marriage was increased to 18 years for females and 21 years for males. The birth rate fell from 45/1000 in 1951–61 to 41/1000 in 1961–71. By 1987 it was down to 33/1000, falling further to 29/1000 in 1995. By 2008 it had dropped to 24/1000. It was not long before many other developing nations followed India's policy of government investment to reduce fertility. The most severe anti-natalist policy ever introduced has been in operation in China since 1979.

Vietnam is planning to return to a two-child policy to limit population growth. This policy was introduced in the 1960s, but stopped in 2003. However, with a current population of 86 million and two-thirds of the population under 35, the government is concerned that high population growth will hinder economic growth and put education and health services under too much strain.

Case study

Pro-natalist policy in France

France's relatively high fertility level (Figure 3) can be partly explained by its long-term active family policy, adapted in the 1980s to accommodate the entry of women into the labour force. The policy seems to have created especially positive attitudes towards two- and three-child families. France has taken steps to encourage fertility on a number of occasions over the last 70 years. In 1939 the government passed the 'Code de la Famille' which:

- offered financial incentives to mothers who stayed at home to look after children
- subsidised holidays
- banned the sale of contraceptives (this stopped in 1967).

More recent measures to encourage couples to have more children include:

- longer maternity and paternity leave; maternity leave, on near full pay, ranges from 20 weeks for the first child to 40 or more for the third child

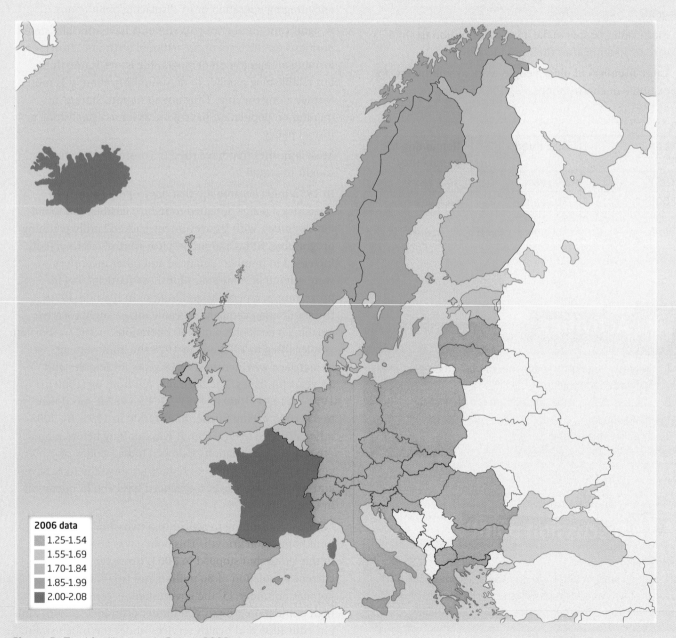

2006 data
- 1.25–1.54
- 1.55–1.69
- 1.70–1.84
- 1.85–1.99
- 2.00–2.08

Figure 3 *Total fertility rates in Europe, 2006.*

- higher child benefits
- improved tax allowances for larger families until the youngest child reaches 18
- pension scheme for mothers/housewives
- 30% reduction on all public transport for three-child families
- child-oriented policies, for example provision of crèches and day nurseries (state-supported day care centres and nursery schools are available for infants starting at the age of 3 months, with parents paying a sliding scale according to income)
- preferential treatment in the allocation of government housing.

Overall, France is trying to reduce the economic cost to parents of having children. In 2006, France overtook Ireland to become the highest-fertility nation in the European Union, with an average of two babies per woman. The 830 900 babies born in 2006 was the highest figure since 1981. France is close to the replacement level of 2.1 children per woman. A moderate positive net migration adds to fertility. This net migration is virtually equivalent to a surplus of 75 000 births.

The 2009 Population Data Sheet put France's total fertility rate at 2.0. This compares with 1.3 in Germany, 1.9 in the UK, 1.3 in Italy and 1.5 in Spain.

Although the average age of French mothers at childbirth is still rising, it is still less than in many other European countries. Almost half of the new arrivals in 2006 were born to unmarried mothers, although increasing numbers have legally recognised civil partnerships.

Within France, the highest level of fertility is among the immigrant population. But even for those born in France the average is 1.8 babies. French economists argue that although higher fertility means more expenditure on child-care facilities and education, in the longer term it gives the country a more sustainable age structure.

French politicians have talked about demography as a 'source of vitality' for the country. Some French commentators also argue that there is a better work–life balance in France than in many other European countries.

The central population forecast, based on the stability of fertility and migration at current levels, predicts stability in the population aged 60 or less, while the population aged 60 and over will increase as a consequence of the post-Second World War baby boom.

Activities

1 Define the terms:
   a population policy
   b pro-natalist policy.
2 Why has France, along with a number of other developed countries, taken measures to encourage fertility?
3 Produce a bullet-point summary of France's pro-natalist policy.
   a Describe the variations in the total fertility rate shown in Figure 3.
   b Suggest possible reasons for these differences.

A spokesperson for the Vietnam government's population and family planning office said that 'the demographic boom is damaging the country's sustainable development'. The UN Population Fund is puzzled by the reintroduction of the two-child policy as fertility levels have already fallen below replacement rates. However, population momentum means that the population will continue increasing for some time even with the recently reduced fertility levels.

What is perhaps surprising is the number of countries that now see their fertility as too low. Such countries are concerned about:

- the socio-economic implications of population ageing
- the decrease in the supply of labour
- the long-term prospect of population decline.

Russia has seen its population drop considerably since 1991. Alcoholism, AIDS, pollution and poverty are among the factors reducing life expectancy and discouraging births. In 2008 Russia began honouring families with four or more children with a Paternal Glory medal. The government has urged Russians to have more children, sometimes suggesting that it is a matter of public duty.

Case study

Anti-natalist policy in China

China, with a population in excess of 1.3 billion, operates the world's most severe family planning programme. Although it is the third largest country in the world in land area, 25% of China is infertile desert or mountain and only 10% of the total area can be used for arable farming. Most of the best land is in the east and south, reflected in the extremely high population densities found in these regions. Thus the balance between population and resources has been a major cause of concern for much of the latter part of the 20th century, although debate about this issue can be traced as far back in Chinese history as Confucius (a Chinese philosopher and teacher of ethics, 551–479 BC).

For people in the West it is often difficult to understand the all-pervading influence over society that a government can have in a centrally planned economy. In the aftermath of the communist revolution in 1949, population growth was encouraged for economic, military and strategic reasons. Sterilisation and abortion were banned and families received a benefit payment for every child. However, by 1954 China's population had reached 600 million and the government was now worried about the pressure on food supplies and other resources. Consequently, the country's first birth control programme was introduced in 1956. This was to prove short-lived, for in 1958 the 'Great Leap Forward' began. The objective was rapid industrialisation and modernisation. The government was now concerned that progress might be hindered by labour shortages and so births were again encouraged. But by 1962 the government had changed its mind, heavily influenced by a catastrophic famine due in large part to the relative neglect of agriculture during the pursuit of industrialisation. An estimated 20 million people died during the famine. Thus a new phase of birth control ensued in 1964. Just as the new programme was beginning to have some effect, a new social upheaval, the Cultural Revolution, got underway. This period, during which the birth rate peaked at 45/1,000, lasted from 1966 to 1971.

With order restored, a third family planning campaign was launched in the early 1970s with the slogan 'Late, Sparse, Few'. However, towards the end of the decade the government felt that its impact might falter and in 1979 the controversial 'One Child' policy was imposed. The Chinese demographer Liu Zeng calculated that China's optimum population was 700 million, and he looked for this figure to be achieved by 2080.

Table 6 shows key demographic changes in China's population between 1950 and 2005, while Figure 4 shows in graphic form the changes in the birth and death rates for the same period and beyond. The impact of the one child policy is very clear to see. Some organisations, including the UN Fund for Population Activities, have praised China's policy on birth control. Many others see it as a fundamental violation of civil liberties.

The policy has had a considerable impact on the sex ratio which at birth in China was 119 boys to 100 girls in 2009. This compares with the natural rate of 106:100. This is already causing social problems, which are likely to multiply in the future. Selective abortion after pre-natal screening is a major cause of the wide gap between the actual rate and the natural rate. But even if a female child is born, her lifespan may be sharply curtailed by infanticide or deliberate neglect.

China 's policy is based on a reward-and-penalty approach. Rural households that obey family planning rules get priority for loans, materials, technical assistance, and social welfare. The slogan in China is *shao sheng kuai fu* – 'fewer births, quickly richer'.

The one child policy has been most effective in urban areas where the traditional bias of couples wanting a son has been significantly eroded. However, the story is different in rural areas where the strong desire for a male heir remains the norm. In most provincial rural areas, government policy has been relaxed so that couples can now have two children without penalties.

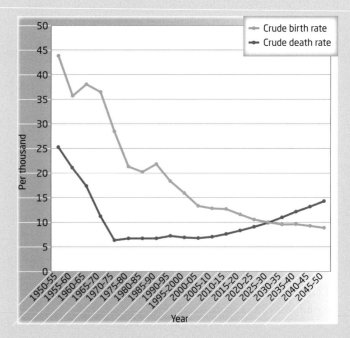

Figure 4 *Birth and death rates in China, 1950–2050.*

Indicators	1950–55	1955–60	1960–65	1965–70	1970–75	1975–80
Population (thousands)	554760	609005	657492	729191	830675	927808
Population growth rate (%)	1.87	1.53	2.07	2.61	2.21	1.48
Crude birth rate (per 1000 population)	43.80	36.10	38.00	36.60	28.60	21.50
Crude death rate (per 1000 population)	25.10	20.70	17.10	10.90	6.30	6.70
Total fertility rate (children per woman)	6.22	5.59	5.72	6.06	4.86	3.32
Infant mortality rate (per 1000 births)	195.00	178.70	120.70	80.80	61.10	52.00
Life expectancy at birth (male + female), years	40.80	44.60	49.50	59.60	63.20	65.30

Indicators	1980–85	1985–90	1990–95	1995–2000	2000–05
Population (thousands)	998877	1070175	1155305	1219331	1273979
Population growth rate (%)	1.38	1.53	1.08	0.88	0.65
Crude birth rate (per 1000 population)	20.40	22.10	18.30	16.0	13.60
Crude death rate (per 1000 population)	6.60	6.70	7.30	7.0	6.80
Total fertility rate (children per woman)	2.55	2.46	1.92	1.78	1.70
Infant mortality rate (per 1000 births)	52.00	50.00	47.10	41.50	34.70
Life expectancy at birth (male + female), years	66.60	67.10	68.10	69.70	71.50

Table 6 *Demographic changes in China's population data, 1950–2005.*

Beijing – crowds at the Forbidden City.

In July 2009, newspapers in the UK and elsewhere reported that dozens of babies had been taken from parents who had breached China's one child policy and sold for adoption abroad.

A paper published in 2008 estimated that China had 32 million more men aged under 20 than women. The imbalance is greatest in rural areas because women are 'marrying out' into cities. In recent years, reference has been made to the 'Four-Two-One' problem whereby one adult child is left with having to provide support for his or her two parents and four grandparents.

Figure 5 shows that there is a certain level of debate within China about the one child policy. The article from the newspaper *China Daily* highlights Shanghai's concerns about its ageing population.

Second child not right population recipe

Chen Weihua

Shanghai's announcement on encouraging couples who have no siblings to have a second child is sending a wrong signal.

By claiming the city is suffering from an increasingly ageing population and a possible shortage of workforce 40 years from now, these officials seem to talk as if Shanghai were an independent 'republic'.

This, of course, has no basis. If you count the 6.4 million people, mostly young, residing and working in Shanghai without a local *hukou*, or permanent residence permit, Shanghai's graying threat would not look that gloomy. These people actually make up a third of the city's 19 million.

Since Shanghai has long been a top destination in China for both young professionals and migrant rural workers, it would be near-sighted to examine the population problem from the viewpoint of the *hukou*-holding people, while ignoring those without a *hukou*.

With 1.3 billion people, China is the world's most populous country that would be surpassed by India in 2028, according to a recent study by the South Korea National Statistical Office.

The achievement of China moving towards becoming the second most populous country may be attributed to the last 30 years of family planning work, which translated into 300 to 400 million fewer births.

However, China still gives birth each year to some 8 million children.

Population pressure has long been an impediment to social and economic progress, despite the benefit China has reaped from its population dividend – the rise in the economic growth rate due to a rising share of working-age people.

On the employment side, China is still fighting a tough battle to create jobs for an estimated 10 million people entering the workforce each year. In addition, some 200 million surplus rural laborers are also in need of jobs.

It is true that the increasing graying population will and should be a matter of great concern. Yet that problem cannot be solved by ignoring the pressure from an even larger population – as a result of encouraging couples to have a second child.

There are other ways of dealing with this problem. Key among them is to build an effective social security system and better community service system offering good care to the elderly both in urban and rural areas. While having one more child might mean more attention for the elderly, it is by no means a guarantee.

The real problem we are facing now or in the future is not a shortage of people, but an excess of people who don't have access to proper education and medical resources, especially in the vast rural areas. We are challenged by a rural labor force that lacks proper training, and a rural population which still counts on more children for old age security and, that vicious cycle will continue if we choose to ignore the issues.

The right approach to the population problem is to divert more resources, such as in education and medical care, to the countryside.

Having fewer, yet healthy and well-educated children is a policy that should be encouraged.

It was only 60 years ago that China's population was around 450 million. If we had that number of people today, we would have faced fewer problems.

Figure 5 *Newspaper article from the China Daily.*

Activities

1 Write a brief bullet-point summary of the main changes in Chinese fertility policy since 1949.
2 Look at Table 6 (page 37) and Figure 4 (page 36).
  a Describe the changes in the birth rate from 1950 to 2005.
  b How did the total fertility rate change over the same period?
  c Comment on the changes in the death rate from 1950 to 2005.
  d How did these changes affect the population growth rate?
3 **a** Describe the changes in the infant mortality rate in China between 1950 and 2005.
  b How did this help in most people accepting the one child policy?

Websites

www.mortality.org
Human Mortality Database

www.demographic-research.org
Demographic Research

www.chinadaily.com.cn
China Daily

www.optimumpopulation.org
Optimum Population Trust

www.iussp.org
International Union for the Scientific Study of Population

Key terms

Dependency ratio the ratio of the number of people under 15 and over 64 years to those 15–64 years of age.

Youth dependency ratio the ratio of the number of people 0–14 to those 15–64 years of age.

Elderly dependency ratio the ratio of the number of people aged 65 and over to those aged 15–64 years.

Ageing ratio the proportion of people 65 years old and over to the total population.

Median age the age at which half the population is younger and half is older.

Ageing population a rise in the median age of a population which occurs when fertility declines while life expectancy remains constant or increases.

Population policy When a government has a stated aim on an aspect of its population and it undertakes measures to achieve that aim.

Pro-natalist policy a population policy that aims to encourage more births through the use of incentives.

Anti-natalist policy a population policy designed to limit fertility through the use both of incentives and deterrents.

Review

Examination-style questions

1 Refer to Figure 6.

a Define (i) the dependency ratio and (ii) the ageing ratio.

b Describe the relationship between the UK's population groups under 15, 15–64 and 65 and over for 2002.

c To what extent will the UK's age profile change by 2050?

2 Refer to Figure 7.

a Define the birth rate.

b Describe the general trend and the variations in the trend in the birth rate for European countries since 1960.

c With reference to a country you have studied, discuss what has been done to encourage an increase in fertility.

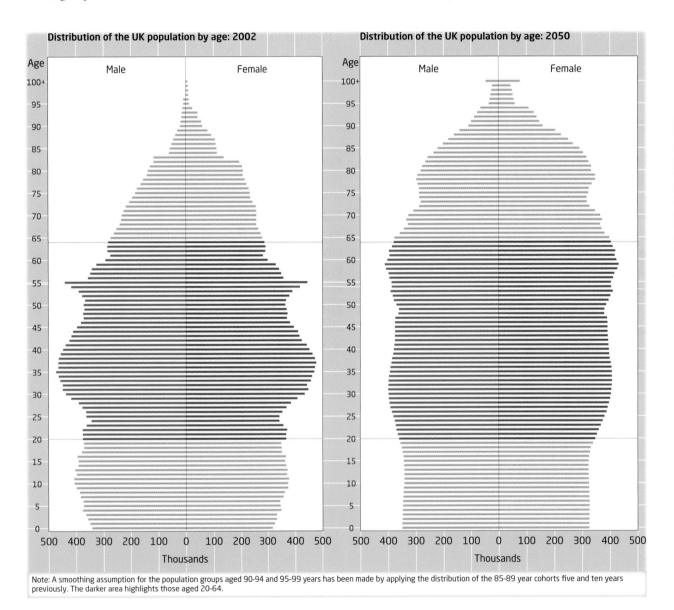

Note: A smoothing assumption for the population groups aged 90-94 and 95-99 years has been made by applying the distribution of the 85-89 year cohorts five and ten years previously. The darker area highlights those aged 20-64.

Figure 6 *Population pyramids for the UK, 2002 and 2050.*

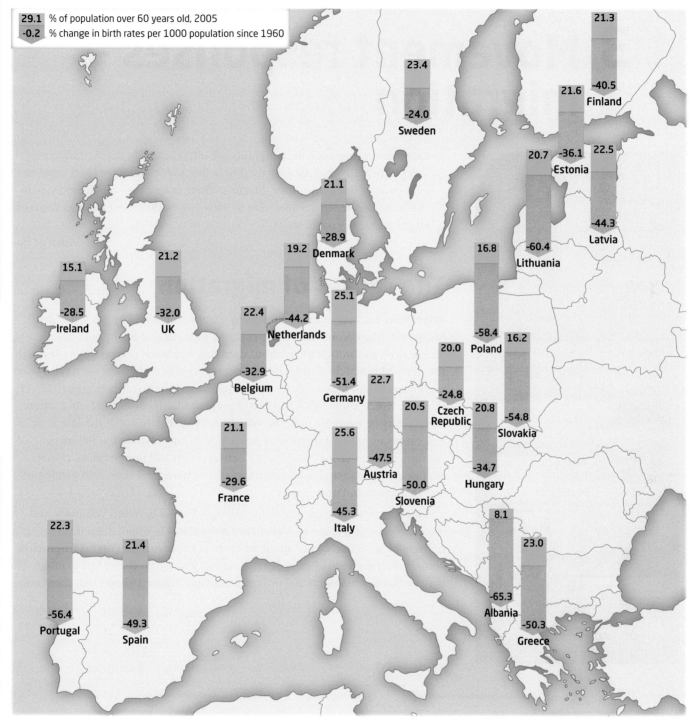

Figure 7 *Changes in birth rates since 1960 and in population over 60 for 2005 in Europe.*

03 Movement responses – migration

Views about migration and migrants are often based on the assumption of sedentarism, that populations used to be immobile and have been uprooted by economic or environmental factors. There is however much evidence to challenge this sedentary bias, and to view population movement as the norm rather than the exception.

Arjan de Haan

The causes of migration

Migration has been a major process in shaping the world as it is today. Its impact has been economic, social, cultural, political and environmental. Few people now go through life without changing residence several times. Through the detailed research of geographers, demographers and others we have a good understanding of the causes and consequences of the significant migrations of the past, which should make us better prepared for those of the future whose impact may be every bit as great. We can only speculate about the locations and causes of future migrations. Causal factors may include the following: continuing socio-economic disparity between rich and poor nations, climate change and all its implications, nuclear catastrophe, civil wars, and pandemics due to current and new diseases.

The most basic distinction drawn by demographers is between voluntary and forced migration (Figure 1). **Voluntary migration** is where the individual or household has a free choice about whether to move or not. **Forced migration** occurs when the individual or household has little or no choice but to move. This may be due to environmental or human factors. Figure 1 shows that there are

KEY QUESTIONS

- What are the causes of migrations, both forced and voluntary?
- What are the geographical impacts (socio-economic, political and environmental) of internal migrations at their origins and destinations?
- What are the geographical impacts of international migrations?

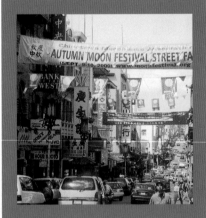

Chinatown, San Francisco. The city has had a significant Chinese community for over 150 years.

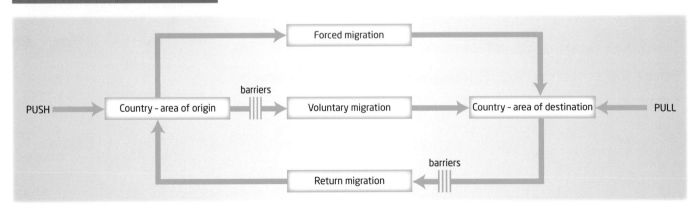

Figure 1 *Forced and voluntary migration.*

barriers to migration. In earlier times the physical dangers of the journey and the costs involved were major obstacles. However, the low real cost of modern transportation and the high level of safety have reduced these barriers considerably. In today's world it is the legal restrictions that countries place on migration that are the main barriers to migration. Most countries now have very strict rules on immigration, and some countries restrict emigration.

Voluntary migration

In terms of voluntary migration it is useful to differentiate between independent and dependent movements. In independent movements the decision to move to a new location is made by the individual, whereas in dependent movements the decision is taken collectively by the household. In the latter case the individual concerned may or may not have a significant say in the final decision, often depending on the age and gender of the prospective migrant. The reasons why people change their place of permanent residence on a voluntary basis can be viewed at three scales: macro-level, meso-level and micro-level.

Informal sector employment in Cairo (shoe shining), Egypt. Many migrants coming to Cairo can only find work in the informal sector.

The macro-level

This dimension highlights socio-economic differences at the national scale, focusing particularly on the core–periphery concept. The development of core regions in many developing countries had its origins in the colonial era. At this time migration was encouraged to supply labour for new colonial enterprises and infrastructural projects such as the development of ports and the construction of transport links between areas of raw material exploitation and the ports through which export would take place.

The introduction of capitalism, through colonialism, into previously non-capitalist societies had a huge influence on movement patterns. The demand for labour in mines, plantations and other activities was satisfied to a considerable extent by restricting access by local people to land, and by coercing people into migration to work either directly through forced labour systems or indirectly through taxation. The spread of a cash economy at the expense of barter into peripheral areas further increased the need for paid employment which, on the whole, could only be found in the economic core region.

In the post-colonial era most developing countries have looked to industrialisation as their path to a better world, resulting in disproportionate investment in the urban-industrial sector and the relative neglect of the rural economy. Even where investment in agriculture has been considerable, either the objective or the end result was to replace labour with machinery, adding further to rural out-migration.

The macro-level perspective, based on structural imbalances, provides a general explanation of migration patterns in developing countries. However, this approach has two weaknesses:

- it fails to explain why some people migrate and others stay put when faced with very similar circumstances in peripheral areas
- it offers no explanation as to why not all forms of migration occur in the direction of economic core regions.

Recent housing development on the outskirts of Manaus – a growth pole in the Amazon region.

The meso-level

The meso-level dimension includes more detailed consideration of the factors at the origin and destination, which influence people's migration decisions. E.S. Lee's origin-intervening obstacles–destination model (Figure 2) is a useful starting point in understanding this level of approach, which looks well beyond economic factors and recognises the vital role of the perception of the individual in the decision-making process.

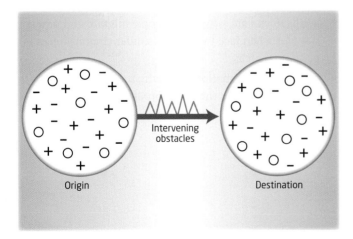

Figure 2 *E.S. Lee's migration model.*

Lee argues that migration occurs in response to the prevailing set of factors both in the migrant's place of origin and in one or a number of potential destinations. However, what is perceived as positive and what is viewed as negative at origin and destination may vary considerably between individuals, as may the intervening obstacles. Lee stressed the point that the factors in favour of migration would generally have to outweigh considerably those against, due to the natural reluctance of people to uproot themselves from established communities.

While recognising that individuals can react differently to similar circumstances, it is still important to consider the negative factors that act to 'push' people from rural areas of origin and the positive influences that 'pull' them towards towns and cities. **Push factors** and **pull factors** can vary from place to place. In Brazil the push factors responsible for rural-to-urban migration can be summarised as follows:

- the mechanisation of agriculture which has reduced the demand for farm labour in most parts of the country
- the amalgamation of farms and estates, particularly by agricultural production companies – in Brazil, as elsewhere in Latin America, the high incidence of landlessness has led to a much greater level of rural-to-urban migration than in most parts of Africa and Asia
- the generally poor conditions of rural employment – employers often ignore laws relating to minimum wages and other employee rights
- desertification in the north-east and deforestation in the north
- unemployment and underemployment
- poor social conditions, particularly in terms of housing, health and education.

High population growth is often cited as the major cause of rural-to-urban migration. However, in itself population growth is not the main cause of out-migration. Its effects have to be seen in conjunction with the failure of other processes to provide adequately for the needs of growing rural communities. Even when governments focus resources on rural development, the volume of out-migration may not be reduced. The irony in many developing nations is that people are being displaced from the countryside because in some areas change is too slow to accommodate the growing size and needs of the population, or because in other areas change is too rapid to enable redundant rural workers to find alternative employment in their home areas. In such circumstances out-migration provides an essential 'safety-valve'.

The evidence in Table 1 and in other similar studies is that the economic motive underpins the majority of rural-to-urban movements. During the 1960s most demographers cited the higher wages and more varied employment opportunities of the cities as the prime reason for **internal migration**. It was also widely held that the level of migration was strongly related to the rate of urban unemployment. However, while rural/urban income differentials are easy to quantify, they do not take into account the lower cost of living in the countryside and the fact that non-cash income often forms a significant proportion of rural incomes.

However, in the 1970s, as more and more cities in the developing world experienced large-scale in-migration in spite of high unemployment, demographers began to reappraise the situation. Michael Todaro was one of the first to recognise that the paradox of urban deprivation on the one hand, and migration in pursuit of higher wages on the other, could be explained by taking a long-term view of why people move to urban areas. Todaro argued that people are prepared to ensure urban hardship in the short term in the likelihood that their long-term prospects will be much better in the city compared with the countryside. Apart from employment prospects, the other perceived advantages of the cities are a higher standard of accommodation, a better education for migrants' children, improved medical facilities, the conditions of infrastructure often lacking in rural areas, and a wider range of consumer services. The most fortunate migrants find jobs in the **formal sector**. A regular wage then gives some access to the other advantages of urban life. However, as the demand for jobs greatly outstrips supply, many can do no better than the uncertainty of the **informal sector**.

Of all the factors that migrants take into account before arriving at a decision, the economic perspective invariably dominates the decision to leave the countryside. However, all the evidence shows that other factors, particularly the social environment, have a very strong influence on the direction that the movement takes. This largely explains why capital cities, with their wide range of social opportunities, attract so many rural migrants.

The micro-level

The main criticisms of the macro- and meso-scale explanations of migration are that:

- they view migration as a passive response to a variety of stimuli
- they tend to view rural source areas as an undifferentiated entity.

(a) Reasons for migration from village communities in rural Peru

Reason	Respondents citing reason (%)
To earn more money	39
To join kin already working	25
No work in the villages	12
Work opportunities presented themselves	11
Dislike of village life	11
To be near the village and family	11
To support nuclear and/or extended family	9
Poor	8
To pay for education	7

(b) Principal reasons for migration from village communities in north-east Thailand

Principal reason	Number of respondents citing reason	Respondents citing reason (%)
To earn more money for the household	138	52.9
To earn more money for self	57	21.8
To earn more money for parents	31	11.9
To further education	12	4.6
To earn money to build a house	10	3.8
To earn money to invest in farming	4	1.5
For fun	3	1.1
To earn money to purchase land/land title	2	0.8
To earn money to repay a debt	1	0.4
To earn money to pay for hired labour	1	0.4
To see Bangkok	1	0.4
To earn money to get married	1	0.4
Total	261	100.0

Table 1 *Reasons for migration from rural areas in (a) Peru and (b) Thailand.*

Geographical skills

Using full prose, briefly summarise tables (a) and (b) in Table 1 (page 45).

Expansion of the Ger (non-permanent housing) district onto a hillside on the outskirts of Ulaanbaatar due to high rural–urban migration.

The specific circumstances of individual families and communities in terms of urban contact are of crucial importance in the decision to move, particularly when long distances are involved. The alienation experienced by the unknown new migrant to an urban area should not be underestimated and is something that will be avoided if at all possible. The evidence comes from a significant number of sample surveys and of course from the high incidence of 'area of origin' communities found in cities. For example:

- A sample survey of rural migrants in Mumbai found that more than 75% already had one or more relatives living in the city, of whom 90% had received some form of assistance upon arrival.

- A survey of migration from the Peruvian Highlands to Lima found that 90% of migrants could rely on short-term accommodation on arrival in the city and for about 50%, their contacts had managed to arrange a job for them.

The importance of established links between urban and rural areas frequently results in the phenomenon of 'chain migration'. After one or a small number of pioneering migrants have led the way, subsequent waves of migration from the same rural community follow. The more established a migrant community becomes in the city the easier it appears to be for others in the rural community to take the decision to move and for them to assimilate into urban society.

Apart from contact with and knowledge of urban locations, differentiation between rural households takes the following forms:

- level of income
- size of land holding
- size of household
- stage in the life cycle
- level of education
- cohesiveness of the family unit.

All of these factors have an impact on the decision to migrate. Family ties and commitments may determine whether or not someone is able to migrate, and may also influence who from a family unit is most likely to take on the responsibility of seeking employment in the city. Here the stage in the life cycle is crucial and it is not surprising that the great majority of migrants in developing countries are aged between 15 and 25 years. In some communities the phenomenon of 'relay migration' has been identified whereby at different stages in a family's life cycle, different people take responsibility for migration.

Theory of Knowledge

It is only by examining all three dimensions – macro, meso and micro – that the complexity of the migration process can be fully understood. Migration is a highly charged political issue in many parts of the world. Would greater public understanding of the factors involved make it less of an emotive topic?

Activities

1 Define migration.
2 Briefly explain Figure 1 (page 42).
3 What do you understand by these terms as used in Figure 2 (page 44):
   a origin
   b intervening obstacles
   c destination?
4 Why is it important to consider voluntary migration at different scales (macro-, meso- and micro-)?

Forced migration

In the historical writings on developing world migration, there is an emphasis on the forced recruitment of labour. The abduction and transport of Africans to the Americas as slaves was the largest forced migration in history. In the 17th and 18th centuries, 15 million people were shipped across the Atlantic Ocean as slaves.

Even in recent times the scale of involuntary movement in the developing world is considerably higher than most people think. However, giving due consideration to such movements should not blind us to the increasing scale of free labour migration that has occurred in recent decades. Here the focal points have been the most dynamic of the developing world economies which have sucked in labour from more laggard neighbouring countries.

In the latter part of the 20th century and the beginning of the 21st century, some of the world's most violent and protracted conflicts have been in the developing world, particularly in Africa and Asia. These troubles have led to numerous population movements on a significant scale.

Not all have crossed international frontiers to merit the term **refugee** movements. Instead many are **internally displaced people**. This is a major global problem which is showing little sign of abatement.

A number of trends appear to have contributed to the growing scale and speed of forced displacement:

- the emergence of new forms of warfare involving the destruction of whole social, economic and political systems

- the spread of light weapons and land mines, available at prices that enable whole populations to be armed

- the use of mass evictions and expulsions as a weapon of war and as a means of establishing culturally and ethnically homogeneous societies – the term 'ethnic cleansing' is commonly used to describe this process.

In a number of locations around the world, whole neighbourhoods of states have been affected by interlocking and mutually reinforcing patterns of armed conflict and forced displacement, for example in the Caucasus and in Central Africa. The United Nations High

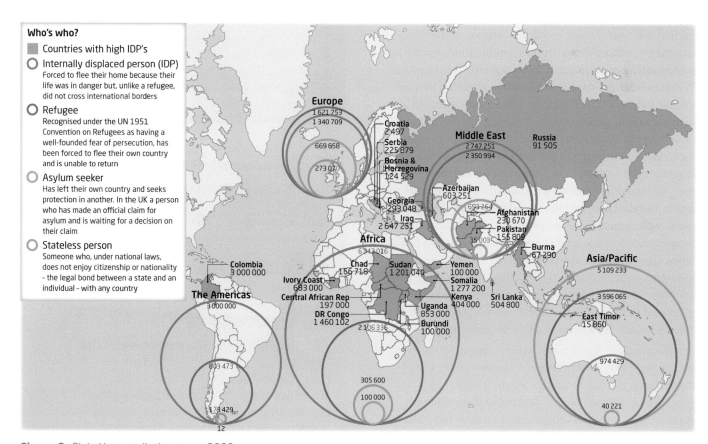

Figure 3 *Global human displacement, 2009.*

Commission for Refugees (UNHCR) is responsible for guaranteeing the security of refugees in the countries where they seek asylum and aiding the governments of these nations in this task. UNHCR has noted a growing number of situations in which people are repeatedly uprooted, expelled or relocated within and across state borders, forcing them to live a desperately insecure and nomadic existence. The UN High Commissioner for Refugees has observed that 'the forced displacement of minorities, including depopulation and repopulation tactics in support of territorial claims and self-determination, has become an abominable characteristic of the contemporary world'. Figure 3 (page 47) shows that a total of 42 million people were classed as displaced in 2009, with the largest numbers being in Africa and the Asia/Pacific region.

Many parts of the developing world are prone to natural disasters. Because poor nations do not possess the funds to minimise the consequences of natural disaster as developed nations can, forced migration is often the result. Some areas of the developing world have been devastated time and time again, often eliciting only a minimal response from the outside world. Ecological and environmental change are a common cause of human displacement. Much of Central Asia is affected by problems such as soil degradation and desertification, a situation created by decades of agricultural exploitation, industrial pollution and overgrazing. One of the worst situations is in and around the Aral Sea, a large lake located between Kazakhstan and Uzbekistan. In a large-scale effort to increase cotton production in the region, most of the river water flowing into the Aral Sea was siphoned off for irrigation. Since 1960 the surface area of the sea has been reduced by half. Dust from the dried-up bed of the sea, containing significant amounts of agricultural and industrial chemicals, is carried long distances by the wind, adding further to the pollution, salinisation and desertification of the land. Agricultural production has fallen sharply and food has increased in price. The fishing industry has been almost totally destroyed and local people are plagued by significant health problems. It has been estimated that more than 100 000 people have left the Aral Sea area since 1992 because of these problems.

Semipalatinsk in Kazakhstan, where almost 500 nuclear bombs were exploded between 1949 and 1989, 150 of them above ground, is another environmental disaster zone, which 160 000 people decided to leave due to concerns about the consequences of nuclear radiation. Around half of these people moved to other parts of Kazakhstan with the remainder moved to a number of other former Soviet states.

Tackling environmental degradation in this region will not be an easy task. The problem is so deep-rooted and was kept hidden for so long under Soviet rule that it may in some instances be too late for effective remedial action to be taken.

Increasingly large numbers of people have been displaced by major infrastructural projects and by the commercial sector's huge appetite for land. In the developing world the protests of communities in the way of 'progress' are invariably ignored for reasons of 'national interest' or pure greed. The World Bank and other international organisations have been heavily criticised in recent decades for financing numerous large-scale projects without giving sufficient consideration to those people who are directly affected.

It is predicted that climate change will force mass migrations in the future. In 2009 the International Organization for Migration estimated that worsening tropical storms, desert droughts and rising sea levels will displace 200 million people by 2050.

Activities

1 What is the difference between a refugee and an internally displaced person?
2 Describe the extent of global human displacement shown in Figure 3.
3 Suggest how climate change may cause forced migrations in the future.

Research idea

Study an example of a forced migration that has occurred in the last ten years. Write a 150-word summary of your findings.

Theory of Knowledge

Most religions encompass concepts such as sanctuary, refuge and asylum for people who are in distress. This provides an important historical background to modern attempts to protect and help such vulnerable people. How successfully have modern governments dealt with people affected by these issues?

The impacts of internal migration

Figure 4 provides a useful framework for understanding the costs and returns from migration. It highlights the main factors which determine how rural areas are affected by migration – namely the two-way transfers of labour, money, skills and attitudes. However, while all of the linkages seem fairly obvious none are easy to quantify. Therefore, apart from very clear-cut cases, it is often difficult to decide which is greater – the costs or benefits of migration.

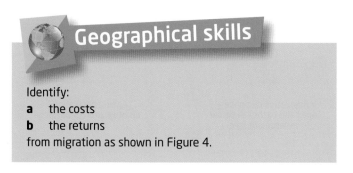

Geographical skills

Identify:
a the costs
b the returns
from migration as shown in Figure 4.

Socio-economic impact

Remittances from internal migration are even more difficult to estimate than those arising from international migration. It is not surprising, therefore, that research has produced a fairly wide range of conclusions, of which the following are but a sample:

- Williamson (1988) put urban–rural remittances at 10–13% of urban incomes in Africa.
- Reardon (1997) noted that in rural areas in Africa not close to major cities, migrant earnings accounted for only 20% of total non-farm earnings, whereas it

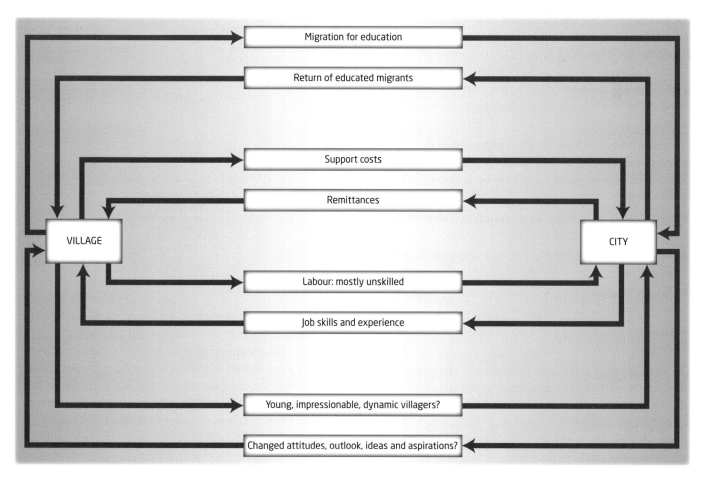

Figure 4 *The costs and returns from migration.*

reached as high as 75% of total non-farm earnings in areas close to major cities.

- Rempell and Lobdell (1978) concluded that remittances constituted up to 40% of the income of rural households.
- Adepoju and Mbugua (1997) note that migrants often remit up to 60% of their incomes.

De la Briere *et al.* (1997) note two types of economic model that attempt to explain remittance behaviour. The first model focuses on the notion of an insurance contract between the migrant and the household left behind, as a means of coping with household risk. A variation on this approach sees migration and remittances as a form of 'portfolio diversification'; potential remittances are weighed against the returns from local sources of income. The second model is based on the bequest motive, seeing remittances as investments in household assets that the migrant will later inherit.

Helweg (1983) studied the changing use of remittances over time, noting three stages: initially they are spent on family maintenance and improving land productivity; in the following stage spending tends to be on 'conspicuous' consumption; in the third and final stage remittances are also invested to start commercial, non-agricultural activities. Vijverberg and Zeager (1994) found that in Tanzania migrant workers in both public and private sectors initially received lower wages than native urban workers but the wage gap was eliminated in a decade or less.

The relationship between internal migration and development is complex and still the subject of much debate. The four questions that have been the subject of much research are:

- How does development in areas of destination affect migration?
- How does development in the area of origin affect migration?
- How does migration affect development in areas of destination?
- How does migration affect development in areas of origin?

The first question is the least problematic. The importance of pull factors in explaining migration is widely accepted. Clearly migrants do move in reaction to newly developed opportunities. However, a number of recent studies have shown that people in the poorest areas of developing countries do not exhibit the highest levels of out-

migration. In such regions levels of literacy and skill may be so low that access to even very menial urban jobs can be difficult.

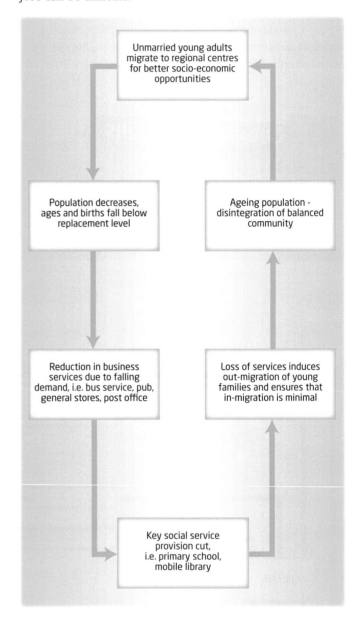

Figure 5 *The downward spiral of rural depopulation.*

It is in many ways ironic that development in rural areas of origin often acts as a stimulus to out-migration. In China the development of rural enterprises appears to increase rates of out-migration. In the Punjab, the Green Revolution witnessed both high rates of out-migration by the resident population and in-migration from a number of poorer Indian states. Development often acts as an important stimulus, widening the horizons of a significant number among the rural population.

There is some evidence that internal migration in developing countries is welfare-improving for receiving regions but quantification has generally proved to be difficult. The fact that rural migrants are often the most dynamic young adults from their communities should be of benefit to the receiving urban areas, providing enough opportunities are available for most to gain reasonable employment. It is of course a question of balance. On the one hand the influx of rural labour provides the foundation for industrialisation and other forms of economic development. On the other, newcomers can place a massive burden on over-stretched urban amenities and services, particularly if large numbers are unemployed.

The impact of out-migration on areas of origin is not at all clear. The traditional view has been that by reducing unemployment and underemployment, and providing inputs such as remittances and newly acquired skills, migration promotes development in rural areas of origin, narrows regional disparities and eventually makes migration unnecessary. However, recent research on this issue has in some respects been contradictory and the possibility of such mobility having an adverse effect on the economy of labour-exporting areas cannot be ruled out. Mukherji (1985) argues that circulation of Indian wage labourers 'occurs within, and in turn reinforces, the syndrome of poverty and mobility'.

Lipton, with reference to the Indian Village Studies Programme, emphasised the inequality-increasing effects of rural-to-urban migration in areas of origin. High emigration from a village was strongly related to the unequal distribution of resources, usually land. Migration frequently involved both the richest and poorest households in the village. Richer potential migrants were 'pulled' towards fairly firm job prospects in the formal sector whereas the poor were 'pushed' by rural poverty and labour-replacing methods. The much higher remittances from rich migrants compared with those from poorer migrants from the same community acted to increase inequalities in villages and between villages in the same region. Thus, although migration in many cases does alleviate poverty, it can also increase inequality.

An important issue is the impact of out-migration on local agriculture. In some cases out-migration undoubtedly causes a shortage of labour although in other instances it clearly alleviates unemployment and underemployment. In some areas large numbers of women now perform agricultural tasks which were once the preserve of men. This 'new' work is frequently in addition to an existing heavy household workload. Although remittances help,

they are often too low to hire-in labour. There is also a tendency for land to become concentrated in the hands of migrant families who gradually turn into non-farmers, resulting in a fall in agricultural production.

However, it is important to note that the flow of money and support in general is not always one-way. Some studies have highlighted village-to-town remittances to support education or the search for employment.

Within developed countries migration has been responsible for two major processes in the 20th and 21st centuries – rural depopulation and counter-urbanisation. Rural depopulation has affected both developed and developing nations alike, while counter-urbanisation has been largely restricted to the developed world. These processes have in fact become major political issues in some areas. Population decline in rural areas invariably results in service decline which can have a huge impact on the lives of the people remaining if key services such as schools and post offices are cut. Because the rural population in developed countries is now such a small proportion of the total population, rural dwellers often feel that their voice goes unheard by government. In areas within commuting distance of large urban areas in the developed world, counter-urbanisation became the dominant movement process in the latter part of the 20th century. While counter-urbanisation may benefit some of the established population in an area, it can have adverse social, economic and environmental consequences for others. A significant economic problem is for young people in the established population whose access to the housing market declines as demand for property in the area rises.

A deserted village on the island of Lemnos, Greece – the result of rural depopulation.

Political impact

Internal migration at a significant scale can have considerable political repercussions, which include the following:

- Lower political representation where migration results in depopulation: the reduced numbers of people in a region can reduce the 'political voice' of the community. A lower population can also result in decreased funding from central government. Such a downward spiral may result in a region becoming more and more peripheral to the country as a whole.

- In contrast, where population is growing rapidly, partly at least as a result of in-migration, the political voice of such regions becomes more important. In some developing countries in particular, capital cities have grown so rapidly as to attain an increasingly dominant political and economic role. Such economic and political primacy may be of considerable benefit to the residents of a capital city, but to the detriment of the rest of the country.

- Changing ethnic composition: internal migration can significantly change the ethnic composition of a region or urban area, which may result in tension. In the Niger delta many local people feel that most jobs go to members of the country's majority ethnic groups – the Igbo, Yoruba, Hausa and Fulani, who traditionally come from elsewhere in Nigeria. The local ethnic groups, whose numbers are small in national terms, feel that they have been largely overlooked by the government. This has resulted in a high level of resentment and is certainly one cause of the development of armed groups which have become a major threat to the large oil industry in the region.

Environmental impact

Large-scale rural-to-urban migration has led to the massive expansion of many urban areas in developing countries, which has swallowed up farmland, forests, floodplains and other areas of ecological importance. In turn, the increased impact of these enlarged urban areas is affecting environments even further afield in a variety of different ways. These include:

- deforestation due to the increasing demand for firewood
- greater and greater demands on regional water supplies and other resources
- the expansion of landfill sites
- air and water pollution from factories, households, power stations, transportation and other sources.

Internally displaced people and refugees can have a considerable impact on the environment. They often concentrate in marginal and vulnerable environments where the potential for environmental degradation is high. Apart from immediate problems concerning sanitation and the disposal of waste, long-term environmental damage may result from deforestation associated with the need for firewood and building materials. Increased pressure on the land can result in serious soil degradation.

Cairo has expanded rapidly due to both high in-migration and high natural increase.

A study of high in-migration into the coastal areas of Palawan in the Philippines found that the historical social processes which helped maintain reasonable patterns of environmental use had been overwhelmed by the rapid influx of migrants. The newcomers brought in new resource extraction techniques which were more efficient, but also more destructive than those previously employed by the established community. The study concluded that high in-migration had caused severe environmental damage to the coastal environment.

Activities

1 Discuss the importance of remittances to developing countries.
2 Examine the relationship between internal migration and development.
3 How can internal migration have a political impact?
4 Give two examples of the way internal migration can affect the environment.

Case study

Tibet's changing ethnic balance

In some countries governments have been accused of deliberately using internal migration to change the ethnic balance of a region. Tibet is an example where the in-migration of large numbers of Han Chinese has had a huge impact. Prior to the Chinese occupation of Tibet in 1950 very few Chinese lived in what is now the Tibetan Autonomous Region (TAR). This has changed completely with Chinese migrants now in the majority in some parts of Tibet. In the capital Lhasa there are 200 000 Chinese and 100,000 Tibetans. If the present influx continues Tibetans could become the minority population within a few decades. Most Tibetans see this as an immense threat to the survival of their culture and identity. The Dalai Lama, Tibet's exiled spiritual leader has stated that this policy of 'demographic aggression' has led to 'cultural genocide'.

Most in-migrants to Tibet are Han Chinese, by far the largest ethnic group in China. They fall into two general groups:

- Government officials and technical experts who can be thought of as involuntary migrants
- Economic migrants – miners, construction workers, retail and other service workers.

Incentives provided by the government for Han Chinese to go to Tibet include tax incentives, allowances, higher wages and better housing.

In 2006, the world's highest railway, the Qinghai–Tibet line, was opened. It runs from Golmud to Lhasa (Figure 6). China says the 1140 km line will bring economic opportunities to Tibet. However, many Tibetans fear it will encourage even more in-migration.

Figure 6 *The Qinghai–Tibet railway.*

The impacts of international migrations

Migration has played a major role in shaping the global cultural map. The phenomenon is essentially a series of exchanges between places. The impact of migration on population change has been greatest where mass migrations have overwhelmed relatively small indigenous populations, as exemplified by the demographic histories of the Americas and of Australia and New Zealand. In turn the old colonial powers have relatively cosmopolitan populations compared with most of their non-colonial counterparts, as significant numbers of people from former colonies have sought a higher standard of living in the 'mother' country. The African-Caribbean and Asian elements of the British population are a reflection of this process. In countries such as Britain, France, Germany, Italy and the USA there is a considerable difference in ethnic composition between the large metropolitan areas and rural regions, as most immigrants invariably head for large urban areas where the greatest concentration of employment opportunities can be found.

Discussion point

What is the evidence that international migration has occurred in the area in which you live?

International migration is a major global issue. In the past it has had a huge impact on both donor and receiving nations. In terms of the receiving countries the consequences have generally been beneficial. But today few countries favour a large influx of outsiders for a variety of reasons.

One in every 35 people around the world is living outside the country of their birth. This amounts to about 175 million people – more than ever before. Recent migration data reveals particular features:

- With the growth in the importance of labour-related migration and international student mobility, migration has become increasingly temporary and circular in nature. For example, in 2006/07 there were 583 000 foreign students in the USA. The international mobility of highly skilled workers increased substantially in the 1990s and 2000s.

- The spatial impact of migration has spread, with an increasing number of countries affected either as points of origin or destination. While many traditional migration streams remained strong, significant new streams have developed.

- The proportion of female migrants has steadily increased (now over 47% of all migrants). For some countries of origin, women now make up the majority of contract workers (e.g. the Philippines, Sri Lanka, Thailand and Indonesia).

- The great majority of international migrants from more developed countries go to other affluent nations. Migration from less developed countries is more or less equally split between more and less developed countries (Figure 7). However, there is an important qualification here in that the movement between less developed countries is usually from weaker to stronger economies.

- Developed countries have reinforced controls, in part in response to security issues, but also to combat illegal immigration and networks that deal in trafficking and exploitation of human beings.

Globalisation in all its aspects has led to an increased awareness of opportunities in other countries. With advances in transportation and communication and a reduction in the real cost of both, the world's population has never had a higher level of potential mobility. Also, in various ways, economic and social development has made people more mobile and created the conditions for emigration.

Each receiving country has its own sources, the results of historical, economic and geographical relationships. Earlier

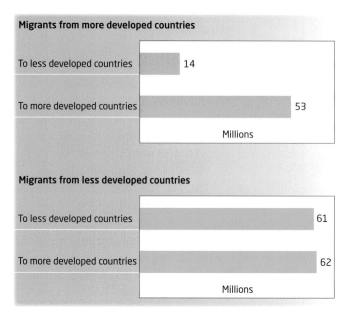

Figure 7 *Origin and destination of international migrants, 2005.*

generations of migrants form networks that help new ones to overcome legal and other obstacles. Today's tighter rules tend to confine immigration to family members of earlier 'primary' migrants.

Socio-economic impact

Recent international migration reports have stressed the sharp rise in the number of people migrating to the world's richest countries for work, although the 2008/09 global recession has had a considerable impact on this trend. Such movement is outpacing family-related and humanitarian movements in many countries. The rise in labour-related migration has been for both temporary and permanent workers and across all employment categories – skilled workers, seasonal employees, trainees, working holidaymakers, transfers of staff within Transnational Corporations (TNCs), and cross-border workers. Of the major industrial economies, only Japan has not had a significant influx of migrant workers.

While the inflow of skilled labour remains the priority for developed nations, some countries also welcome less skilled workers, particularly in agriculture (e.g. the USA, Australia, Spain and Greece), construction, care for the elderly and other business and household services (e.g. the UK, Italy, Portugal). The distribution of immigrants in receiving countries is far from uniform, with a significant concentration in economic core regions. Factors that influence the regional destination of immigrants into member countries of the Organisation for Economic Cooperation and Development (OECD) are:

- the extent of economic opportunities
- the presence of family members or others of the same ethnic origin
- the point of entry into the country.

The socio-economic status of OECD immigrants was frequently low. Immigrants were more likely to:

- be unemployed compared with nationals (in most European countries unemployment rates for foreigners are twice as high as for native workers)
- have jobs that were 'dirty, dangerous and dull/difficult' ('3D' jobs)
- be over-represented in construction, hospitality and catering, and in household services.

Although many migrants rely on family contacts and migrant networks, others may have little choice but to use a labour broker who will try to match a potential migrant to a job in a richer country. For example, in Bangladesh workers can pay up to $2000 to a broker for a job in Saudi Arabia.

Some international labour migration takes the form of commuting. Examples include:

- workers travelling daily from Malmo in Sweden to Copenhagen, the Danish capital city
- German, French and Belgium 'frontaliers' who commute daily into Luxembourg where they account for one-quarter of the labour force.

The World Bank estimates that international remittances totalled $397 billion in 2008, of which $305 billion went to developing countries, involving some 190 million

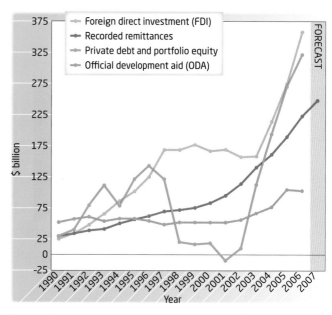

Figure 8 *Recorded remittances, 1990–2007.*

migrants or 3.0% of world population. Figure 8 shows how much remittances have increased since 1990. The graph also compares the value of remittances with official development assistance, foreign direct investment, and private debt and portfolio equity. Figure 9 shows (a) the top recipients of remittances by value in 2007 and (b) countries where remittances formed the highest percentage of GDP in 2006. Research in a number of countries has linked rising remittance payments to reduced levels of poverty. For example, Figure 10 (page 56) shows the relationship between remittances and poverty in Nepal.

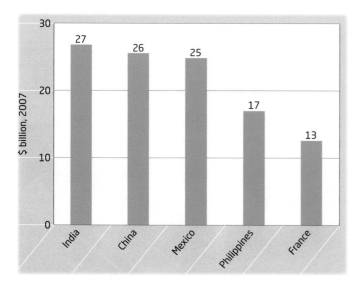

Figure 9 *(a) Top recipients of remittances, 2007.*

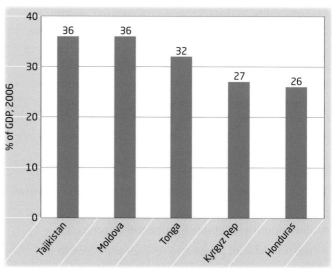

(b) Remittances forming the highest % of GDP, 2006.

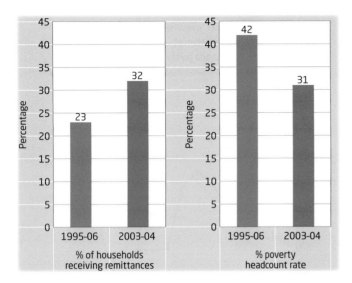

Figure 10 *Remittances and poverty in Nepal.*

Some economists argue that remittances are the developing world's most effective source of financing. Although foreign direct investment is larger, it varies with global economic fluctuations. Remittances exceed considerably the amount of official aid received by developing countries (Figure 8). Remittances have been described as 'globalisation bottom up'. Advocates of migration stress that these revenue flows:

- help alleviate poverty
- spur investment
- cushion the impact of global recession when private capital flows decrease.

The major sources of remittances are the USA, Western Europe and the Gulf. The number of foreigners working in these areas is rising significantly. About 1.3 million migrants settle in the USA annually, around one-third of them illegally. The top destinations of remittances are India, China, Mexico and the Philippines. The 20 million people who make up the Indian **diaspora** are scattered over 135 countries. In 2007 they sent back to India $27 billion – a source of foreign exchange that exceeds revenues generated by India's software industry. The Indian state of Kerala has nearly one million 'Gulf wives' living apart from their husbands.

Apart from the money that migrants send directly to their families, their home communities and countries also benefit from:

- donations by migrants to community projects
- the purchase of goods and services produced in the home country by migrants working abroad
- increased foreign exchange reserves.

All three forms of economic benefit mentioned above combine to form a positive **multiplier effect** in donor population countries.

In the past the perceived major disadvantage of emigration has been that it will lead to a 'brain drain' in which countries will lose their best workers. However, the direct and indirect effect of remittances may more than compensate for this. For some countries the proportion of graduates working overseas is high – 25% for Iran, 26% for Ghana, 10% for the Philippines, 6% for South Korea. It has been estimated that about $60 billion worth of investment by developing countries in tertiary education has been 'drained' to OEDC countries. However, it should be noted that some developing countries have more graduates in some areas than they need.

Social assimilation usually follows on the back of economic assimilation, although the speed and degree to which it is achieved tends to be strongly related to the socio-political maturity of the host society as well as to the degree of difference between an immigrant community and the host society. Racial differences create the greatest barrier to social assimilation but differences in language, religion and culture can also be important. As social barriers decline the benefits that different cultures can bring to society as a whole become more apparent. One of the great attractions of cities such as London and New York is their multiculturalism. The social impact on the donor country can also be considerable. This tends to occur in two stages. The first is the initial loss of many of its most dynamic individuals. The second stage occurs as new ideas from the adopted country filter back to the home country, often clashing with traditional values.

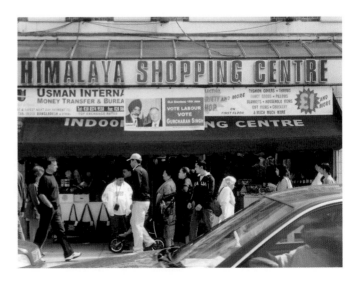

The Asian community in Southall, London.

The political impact

Significant levels of international migration can have a considerable political impact both within and between countries. In many countries there is a clear trend of immigrants being more likely to vote for parties of the centre and the left as opposed to political parties to the right of centre. In more developed countries immigrants tend to head for economic core regions and to inner city areas within these regions. Such concentrations can have a big impact on voting patterns.

Over time, immigrants gradually assimilate into host societies. In general, economic assimilation comes first, followed by social assimilation and then political assimilation. When immigrant groups reach a certain size and standing they begin to develop their own politicians as opposed to voting for politicians from the host society. This process is more likely to happen in mature democracies where there is a long history of immigration. The UK and the USA are examples of countries where this process has been evident.

High levels of international migration between one country and another can lead to political tension. The high level of Mexican migration into the USA, both legal and illegal, has created tensions between the US and Mexican governments. In recent years the USA has greatly increased the size of its Border Patrol. Critics refer to the 'militarisation of the Mexican border' which is costing $3 billion a year.

In a number of EU countries, immigration from Muslim countries over the last 50 years or so has resulted in sizeable Muslim communities. Some people and politicians have become worried about this trend, referring to the 'Islamisation of Europe'. One of the big concerns is the number of Muslims who favour introducing Sharia Law into European countries.

Many developing countries are looking to developed countries to adopt a more favourable attitude to international migration. The subject is brought up regularly at international conferences. This political pressure is known as 'the pro-migration agenda of developing nations'.

Living within a new political system can also affect the attitudes of immigrant communities to what goes on back in their home country. The harshest critics of authoritarian governments in the Middle East and Asia are invariably exiles living in other countries.

The environmental impact

In an article entitled *The Environmental Argument for Reducing Immigration to the United States*, Winthrop Staples and Philip Cafaro argue that 'a serious commitment to environmentalism entails ending America's population growth by implementing a more restrictive immigration policy. The need to limit immigration necessarily follows when we combine a clear statement of our main environmental goals – living sustainably and sharing the landscape generously with other species – with uncontroversial accounts of our current demographic trajectory and of the negative environmental effects of US population growth, nationally and globally.'

Staples and Cafaro explain how population growth contributes significantly to a host of environmental problems in the USA. They also argue that a growing population increases America's large environmental footprint beyond its borders and its disproportionate role in stressing global environmental systems.

There have been growing environmental concerns about immigration in other countries too, as the concept of sustainability has become understood in a more detailed way. However, some critics see such arguments as a disingenuous way of attempting to curtail immigration.

Activities

1 Briefly describe the information provided in Figure 7 (page 54).
2 Examine the trends shown in Figure 8 (page 55).
3 Describe the apparent relationship between remittances and poverty shown in Figure 10 (page 56).
4 Give two examples of the way international migration can have a political impact.
5 How can international migration have an impact on the environment?

Key terms

Migration the movement of people across a specified boundary, national or international, to establish a new permanent place of residence. The UN defines 'permanent' as a change of residence lasting more than one year.

Voluntary migration when the individual or household has a free choice about whether to move or not.

Forced migration forced migration occurs when the individual or household has little or no choice but to move.

Push factors negative conditions at the point of origin which encourage or force people to move.

Pull factors positive conditions at the point of destination which encourage people to move.

Internal migration migration within the same country.

Formal sector jobs in the formal sector are known to the government department that is responsible for taxation, and to other government offices. Such jobs generally provide better pay and much greater security than jobs in the informal sector.

Informal sector the part of the economy operating outside of official recognition. Employment is generally low-paid and often temporary and/or part-time in nature.

Refugee a person who has been forced to leave home and country because of 'a well-founded fear of persecution' on account of race, religion, social group or political opinion.

Internally displaced people as for a refugee, people who are forced to leave their home, but in this case they remains in the same country.

Remittances money sent back by migrants to their family in the home community.

Diaspora the dispersal of a people from their original homeland.

Multiplier effect where an increase in the money supply in a region sets off an upward spiral of development as this money circulates in the economy.

Websites

www.forcedmigration.org
Forced Migration Online

jrs.oxfordjournals.org
Journal of Refugee Studies

www.iom.int/
International Organization for Migration

http://pstalker.com/migration
Stalker's Guide to International Migration

www.migrationinformation.org
Migration Policy Institute

Review

Examination-style questions

1 Refer to Figure 11.

a What is the difference between intra-national and international migration?

b Discuss the possible impact of high levels of rural–urban migration on rural areas in developing countries.

c What are the advantages and disadvantages of large in-migration into urban areas in the developing world?

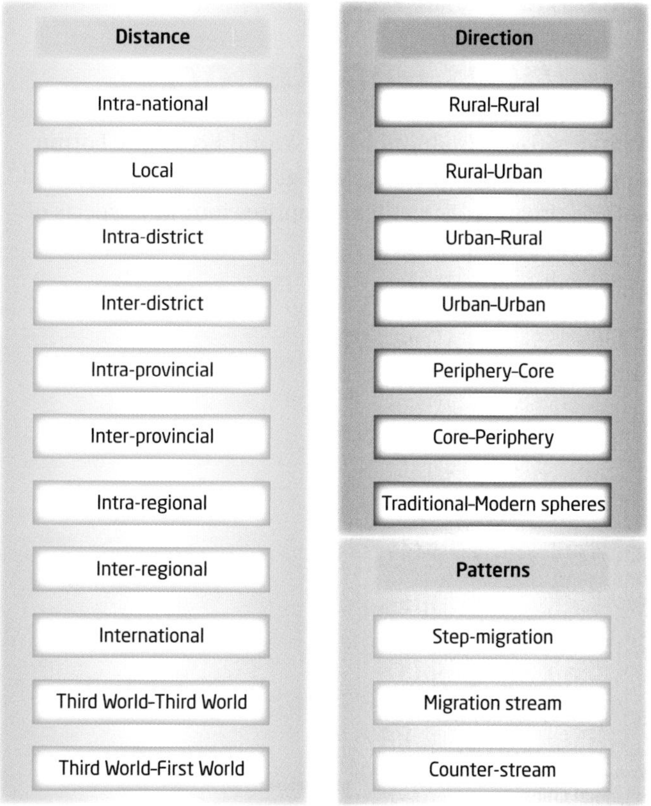

b Identify and explain the relationship or lack of relationship between the two data sets.

c Explain the importance of remittances to many developing countries.

	Country	Amount (US$ thousands)	Share of GDP (%)
1	India	25 700	2.9
2	Mexico	24 732	3.0
3	China	22 492	0.9
4	Philippines	14 923	14.6
5	Bangladesh	5 485	9.1
6	Pakistan	5 400	4.3
7	Morocco	5 048	9.1
8	Egypt	5 017	4.3
9	Lebanon	4 924	20.7
10	Vietnam	4 800	7.5

Table 2 *Top ten countries with the greatest value of remittances, 2006.*

	Country	Amount (US$ thousands)	Share of GDP (%)
1	Moldova	1 182	38.2
2	Tonga	66	30.9
3	Guyana	201	21.6
4	Haiti	985	21.2
5	Lebanon	4 924	20.7
6	Tajikistan	1 019	20.2
7	Honduras	1 796	19.6
8	Jordan	2 500	19.6
9	Bosnia-Herzegovina	1 943	19.4
10	Armenia	1 175	19.1

Table 3 *Top ten countries with remittances representing the highest share of gross domestic product (GDP), 2006.*

Distance
Intra-national
Local
Intra-district
Inter-district
Intra-provincial
Inter-provincial
Intra-regional
Inter-regional
International
Third World–Third World
Third World–First World

Direction
Rural-Rural
Rural-Urban
Urban-Rural
Urban-Urban
Periphery-Core
Core-Periphery
Traditional-Modern spheres

Patterns
Step-migration
Migration stream
Counter-stream

Figure 11 *Spatial dimensions of population movement in developing countries.*

2 Refer to Tables 2 and 3.

a Briefly describe the data presented in the tables.

04 Gender and change

Gender, like socio-economic status, shapes the life opportunities and experiences of individuals. **Social norms** and values result in significant gender differences and inequalities. There are many ways in which gender inequalities are present around the world (Figure 1). They exist in all societies, the difference is in degree. Such differences empower one group (males) to the detriment of the other (females).

Women in developed countries generally have more opportunities than those in developing nations. They are more likely to be highly educated, have greater employment opportunities and face less discrimination generally. However, gender norms and values are not fixed and they tend to evolve over time. It is not so long ago that the gender situation in the developed world was similar to that in the developing world today.

The Global Gender Gap Report

The Global Gender Gap Index was introduced by the World Economic Forum in 2006. It is a framework for illustrating the scale of gender disparities around the world and tracking their progress. The index comprises four key aspects of the quality of life:

- economic participation and opportunity
- educational attainment
- political empowerment
- health and survival.

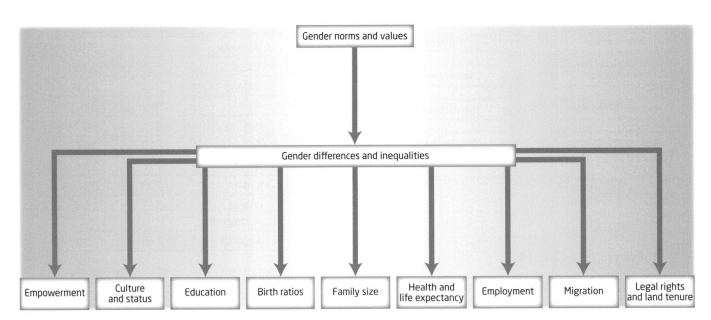

Figure 1 *Gender inequalities.*

Subindex	Variables	Sources
Economic participation and opportunity	Ratio: Female labour force participation over male value	International Labour Organisation, *Key Indicators of the Labour Market*, 2006
	Wage equality between women and men for similar work (converted to female-over-male ratio)	World Economic forum. Executive Opinion Survey 2008
	Ratio: Estimated female earned income over male value	United Nations Development Programme, *Human Development Report 2007/2008*, 2005 or latest data available
	Ratio: Female legislators, senior officials and managers over male value	International Labour Organisation, *LABORSTA Internet*, online database, 2007 or latest data available; United Nations Development Programme, *Human Development Report 2007/2008*
Educational attainment	Ratio: Female literacy rate over male value	United Nations Development Programme, *Human Development Report 2007/2008*, 2005 or latest data available; UNESCO Institute for Statistics, *Education Indicators*, 2007 or latest data available; World Bank's *World Development Indicators*, online database, 2005 or latest data available
	Ratio: Female net primary level enrolment over male value	UNESCO Institute for Statistics, *Education Indicators*, 2007 or latest data available; World Bank's *World Development Indicators*, online database, 2007 or latest data available
	Ratio: Female net secondary level enrolment over male value	UNESCO Institute for Statistics, *Education Indicators*, 2007 or latest data available; World Bank's *World Development Indicators*, online database, 2007 or latest data available
	Ratio: Female gross tertiary level enrolment over male value	UNESCO Institute for Statistics, *Education Indicators*, 2007 or latest data available; World Bank's *World Development Indicators*, online database, 2007 or latest data available
Political empowerment	Ratio: Women with seats in parliament over male value	Inter-Parliamentary Union – *National Women in Parliaments*, 2008
	Ratio: Women at ministerial level over male value	Inter-Parliamentary Union – *E-Parliament Report*, 2008
	Ratio: Number of years of a female head of state or government (last 50 years) over male value	Own calculations, as of June 2008
Health and survival	Ratio: Female healthy life expectancy over male value	World Health Organization, Online Database (WHOSIS), data from 2003
	Sex ratio at birth (converted to female-over-male ratio)	Central Intelligence Agency, *The CIA World Factbook*, 2008 edition

Table 1 *Structure of the Global Gender Gap Index.*

Table 1 shows the detail for each of these criteria, along with the sources of information available for each variable examined. Table 3 (page 62) lists the 30 top-ranking countries according to the 2008 Index. No country in the world has completely eliminated the gender gap. It would have to reach a figure of 1.0 on the Index to do so.

The Nordic countries of Norway, Finland, Sweden, Iceland and Denmark continue to occupy prominent positions on the list. There are clearly significant cultural reasons for this strong geographical grouping. It is interesting to note that a number of counties in the top 30, for example the Philippines, Sri Lanka and Lesotho, are from the developing world.

Camel driver preparing food for camels, India.

Additionally, a number of more affluent countries, such as Japan, do not appear in this top band. Table 2 also lists the 30 countries at the bottom of the 2008 rankings. Most of these countries are in Africa, the Middle East and Asia. Even in the short period of time that the index has been published there have been positive changes, as Table 2 illustrates.

Figure 2 shows the gender gap situation by world region. Oceania leads the way, followed by Western Europe and North America. All three regions have closed 70% of the gender gap. The Middle East and North Africa has the lowest score, having closed only 58% of its gender gap.

Country	2008 rank	2008 score
Norway	1	0.8239
Finland	2	0.8195
Sweden	3	0.8139
Iceland	4	0.7999
New Zealand	5	0.7859
Philippines	6	0.7568
Denmark	7	0.7538
Ireland	8	0.7518
Netherlands	9	0.7399
Latvia	10	0.7397
Germany	11	0.7394
Sri Lanka	12	0.7371
UK	13	0.7366
Switzerland	14	0.7360
France	15	0.7341
Lesotho	16	0.7320
Spain	17	0.7281
Mozambique	18	0.7266
Trinidad and Tobago	19	0.7245
Moldova	20	0.7244
Australia	21	0.7241
South Africa	22	0.7232
Lithuania	23	0.7222
Argentina	24	0.7209
Cuba	25	0.7195
Barbados	26	0.7188
USA	27	0.7179
Belgium	28	0.7163
Austria	29	0.7153
Namibia	30	0.7141

Table 3 *(a) The Global Gap Index 2008 rankings – top 30.*

Number of countries	2007 to 2008	2006 to 2007	2006 to 2008
With widening gaps	41	24	22
With narrowing gaps	87	91	93
Improving (%)	68	79	81
Deteriorating (%)	32	21	19
Total	128	115	115

Table 2 *Gender gap changes, 2006–08.*

Geographical skills

Describe the geographical locations of the top 30 and bottom 30 countries on the Global Gender Gap Index.

Country	2008 rank	2008 score
Kuwait	101	0.6358
Nigeria	102	0.6339
Tunisia	103	0.6295
Jordan	104	0.6275
United Arab Emirates	105	0.6220
Zambia	106	0.6205
Syria	107	0.6181
North Korea	108	0.6154
Mali	109	0.6117
Mauritania	110	0.6117
Algeria	111	0.6111
Guatemala	112	0.6072
India	113	0.6060
Angola	114	0.6032
Burkina Faso	115	0.6029
Iran	116	0.6021
Cameroon	117	0.6017
Oman	118	0.5960
Qatar	119	0.5948
Nepal	120	0.5942
Bahrain	121	0.5927
Ethiopia	122	0.5867
Turkey	123	0.5853
Egypt	124	0.5832
Morocco	125	0.5757
Benin	126	0.5582
Pakistan	127	0.5549
Saudi Arabia	128	0.5537
Chad	129	0.5290
Yemen	130	0.4664

Table 3 *(b) The Global Gap Index 2008 rankings – bottom 30.*

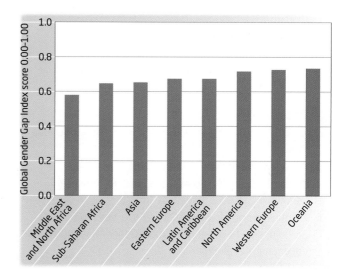

Figure 2 *Regional performance on the Global Gender Gap Index, 2008.*

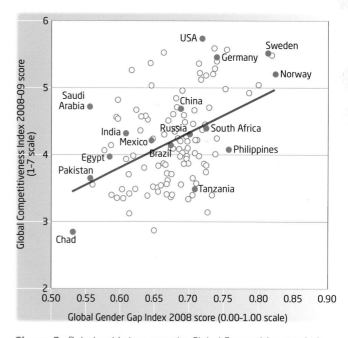

Figure 3 *Relationship between the Global Competitiveness Index and the Global Gender Gap Index.*

Figures 3 and 4 show that there is a significant link between gender equality and economic performance. Numerous studies in recent years have illustrated that reducing gender inequality improves productivity and economic growth.

The 130 countries included in the Global Gender Gap Index comprise over 90% of the world's population.

For these countries the gender gap has been closed by:

- 97% on health outcomes
- 95% on educational attainment
- 62% on economic participation
- 16% on political empowerment.

Activities

1 Define the terms:
   a gender
   b social norms.
2 Briefly discuss the structure of the Global Gender Gap Index.
3 Analyse the data provided in Table 2.
4 Describe the differences in regional performance shown in Figure 2 (page 63).
5 With reference to Figures 3 and 4, assess the relationship between the Global Gender Gap Index and economic development.

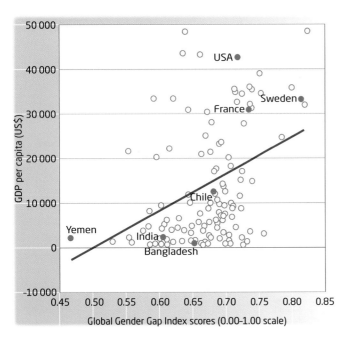

Figure 4 *Relationship between GDP per capita and the Global Gender Gap Index.*

What is the evidence that there is a gender gap in the community and country in which you live?

Culture and status

Culture can be defined as the total of the inherited ideas, beliefs, values and knowledge which constitutes the shared bases of social action. Culture shapes the way things are done in a society. With regard to gender, **status** may be defined as 'the relative position or standing of men and women in a society'.

To some degree, every society assigns different traits, tasks and expectations to males and females. In many societies there are clear patterns of supposed 'men's work' and 'women's work', both in the wider community and in the household, and cultural explanations of why this has come to be so (Figure 5). Such patterns and explanations vary from country to country and are subject to change over time.

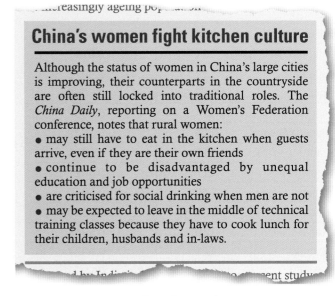

Figure 5 *China's women fight kitchen culture.*

A common characteristic of gender differences is that women have:

- less personal autonomy
- fewer resources at their disposal
- less influence over the decision-making processes that shape the societies in which they live and the factors affecting their own lives.

Such differences based on gender are both a human rights issue and a development issue.

In almost all countries it is women rather than men who take primary responsibility for keeping the home and family going. Women assume the greater share of care-giving which can be extremely time-consuming. This is frequently unpaid and occurs on the basis that women 'naturally' fill this role.

Societies and cultures are dynamic rather than static. Cultural change occurs in response to economic and social movement due to globalisation, technological advance, environmental pressures, development projects,

Women working in a clothing factory, India.

international and civil wars and other factors. An example of such change has been in Bangladesh, with the growth of the clothing industry drawing large numbers of women into the urban labour force. This has challenged the traditional social norm of purdah (female seclusion) for the households and communities concerned. The much greater visibility of women in large urban areas such as Dhaka has also influenced public perceptions in general.

Change also occurs through changes in the law and government policy. Attempts to redefine values with regard to women and gender relations have focused on female education, women's access to paid employment and public attitudes to domestic violence. However, in some countries and communities there are concerns that promotion of gender equality will 'interfere with local culture' and thus some may argue that gender equality should not be promoted for ethical reasons. Religion can play a huge part in cultural characteristics in some parts of the world. There is currently much debate about the status of women in communities and countries where Islamic fundamentalism is strong.

Education

There are large differences in educational attainment with regard to gender around the world. Research has shown that investment in girls' education reduces fertility rates, lowers infant and child mortality, cuts maternal mortality, increases women's labour force participation rates and fosters educational investment in children. It is thus an important part of the development process. Figure 6 shows UNESCO data comparing male and female literacy in 135 countries. For adult literacy the global male rate was 84.9% with the female rate at 72.1%.

Figure 6 compares the male and female literacy rates in 135 countries. The male literacy rate is plotted along

the horizontal axis and the female literacy rate along the vertical axis. For each country, up to two points are drawn, one for adult literacy and one for youth literacy. The location of a country relative to the 45 degree line indicates whether more men or women are literate. If the literacy rate of men and women is the same, the country's marker is located on the 45 degree line. If the male literacy rate is higher than the female literacy rate, the marker is below the 45 degree line. In countries above the 45 degrees line, a higher share of women is literate.

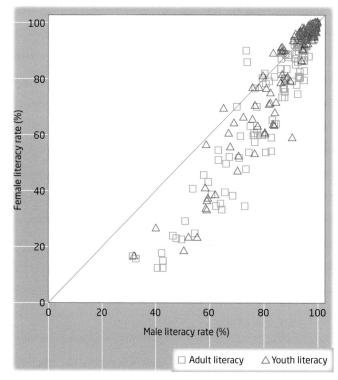

Figure 6 *Comparison of male and female literacy.*

India accounts for 30% of the world's total illiterate population and around 70% of these illiterates are women. According to the 2001 Census, women constitute 48% of the total population in India, but around 46% of women are still classed as illiterate. A major research paper published in April 2008 entitled *Gender Equity in Education: A Review of Trends and Factors* noted the following:

- Although female enrolment has risen rapidly since the 1990s, there is still a substantial gap in upper primary and secondary schooling.

- Girls have persistently high rates of drop-out and poor attendance relative to boys.

- Gender inequalities interlock with other forms of social inequality, notably caste, ethnicity and religion.

- There are considerable inter-state variations in gender parity. While the largest increases in female enrolment have been achieved in the most educationally disadvantaged states such as Bihar and Rajasthan, these states still have a long way to go to catch up with the best-performing states of Kerala, Tamil Nadu and Himachal Pradesh.

In an article entitled *Challenging gender inequalities in the information society*, Anita Gurumurthy of the Indian Institute of Management describes how women, particularly poor women, often lack the necessary infrastructure, skills, literacy and knowledge of English to make the most of opportunities opened up by ICT. This analysis stresses how women are further marginalised from the information sector through:

- domestic responsibilities
- cultural restrictions on mobility
- less economic power
- the lack of relevant material on the internet.

Figure 7 illustrates one scheme that is working to increase access to ICT for women.

In contrast to the situation in many developing countries, in some developed countries girls perform better than boys in school examination results and recently qualified female graduates outnumber their male counterparts.

I used to wonder about the working of a mobile phone. Then I began to use it to call up the wholesale market for prices. This helped me to get direct orders. Now I am recognised as a businesswoman, growing and selling sesame seeds, and not anybody's wife or sister. Ever since I have begun to use [an] electronic weighing machine, people rely more on me. I have also learnt how to use computers.
Jasuben Malik *(Surendranagar)*

The Self Employed Women's Association (SEWA) is a union of about 53 000 poor women working in the informal sector in India. SEWA's aim is to achieve full employment and self-reliance for women workers and does so by focusing both on work and on support in other related areas like income, food and social security (health, childcare, and shelter). Having understood the effect of poor access to information on poverty, SEWA embarked on a journey to include ICTs within its work. The vision was to make ICTs a tool for empowering its ever-increasing numbers of grassroots members. It now runs programmes which develop women's abilities in the use of computers, radio, television, video, the telephone, fax machines, mobile phones and satellite communication.

Appropriate technology for supporting micro enterprise

SEWA's provision, training and capacity-building with ICTs at the grassroots level has helped in bridging the existing digital divide through the use of technologies appropriate to the needs of its members. It has shown that such technologies can support women working in the informal sector, bringing greater livelihood security to economically vulnerable households living in increasingly fragile environments. SEWA's capacity building measures include computer awareness programmes and training on basic computer skills for its members. The organisation received a donation of 400 computers from the World Computer Exchanges in the United States, to strengthen its capacity-building resources at the grassroots. Members are now able to manage their own micro enterprises, which has led to a surge in confidence and better decision-making abilities.

Earlier I used my savings to buy gold ornaments. Then I decided to get a telephone. I have direct and faster communication with everyone. I use the telephone to confirm meetings and bus schedules and decide my work plans. I just dial whenever we are ready for more work!
Jomiben, Bakutara *(Patan)*

Figure 7 *Empowering women at the grassroots: SEWA and ICTs.*

Pupils studying in a classroom, Beijing, China.

Activities

1 Define:
   a culture
   b status.
2 With reference to Figure 5 (page 64), briefly explain how culture can affect the status of women in a society.
3 How did the growth of the clothing industry challenge traditional cultural attitudes in Bangladesh?
4 Briefly describe the extent of gender inequality in education in India.
5 With reference to Figure 7, explain how SEWA is trying to improve ICT skills among poor women in India.

Research idea

Find out the extent of the gender gap in education for the country in which you live.

Theory of Knowledge

The development of true knowledge is impeded if important aspects of reality are ignored or distorted. Many geography textbooks produced before the 1980s were very male biased. Do you think it is ever possible to produce geography textbooks that are unbiased? Would it help if they were written by a woman, or people from the parts of the world being discussed? How important is personal history and experience?

Birth ratios

The birth ratio (or sex ratio at birth) is a fundamentally important gender issue. The 'natural' global rate is about 105 male births for every 100 female births. This excess of male births compensates for higher male mortality throughout the life cycle. However, in some countries the excess of male births is significantly higher than the average because of a preference for male children resulting in the abortion of female foetuses and female infanticide. The CIA estimates that the current birth ratio is 107 boys to 100 girls.

Nowhere is this issue more current than in China where men will outnumber women by 30 million in 2020 if current trends continue. In 2005 China's birth ratio was 119 males to 100 females. In some provinces it is estimated the figure may be as high as 140. Feminist writers in China see 'son preference' as a blatant form of gender discrimination and gender-based violence. However, this is an issue that affects other countries besides China (Figure 8, page 68).

Family size

Because of the preference for male children in many societies, family size is often concluded on the birth of a male child and parents may continue to have children until this is so. Studies have shown that women are more likely to use modern contraceptive methods when they have boys or both boys and girls than when they have only girls.

In some regions of the developing world women have been found to prefer male offspring, possibly because they are afraid of being disinherited if they do not produce a male heir for their husbands.

A research study in Egypt hypothesised that smaller family size may lead to more equitable childrearing practices: when parents have fewer children, they may be

★ Vietnam could experience a major social crisis as a result of a skewed birth rate. Traditionally and for historical reasons Vietnamese women have been more numerous than men but in the last few years this trend has been reversed causing dangerous changes whose consequences can can now be seen in countries like China and India.

The General Statistics Office of Vietnam sounded the alarm bell in a recently released study that indicated that 'in 2007 the male-to-female ratio at birth was 112 to 100,' up from 110 to 100 a year before and much higher than the average world sex ratio which stands at about 103–105 to 100. The study also showed that the skewed sex ratio is higher in some areas of the country, most notably in the north-west mountain regions.

One basic reason for this trend is the traditional preference for boys which has been aggravated by the possibility now available for sex selection.

Contraception and targeted pregnancies allow parents to have baby boys and abort the foetus if it is that of a baby girl.

If left unchecked this trend will create a dreadful future that is not far off with a sex ratio of 123 males per 100 females, like in India, or China (where the one child policy is in place), with selective foeticide or infanticide at birth practiced at the expense of females.

In about 15 years men are likely to find themselves without enough women for marriage and will be forced to look for wives abroad or remain unmarried. For women the danger is even greater because they might become victims of prostitution rings or human traffickers.

Figure 8 *Skewed birth ratios raise fears of social crisis in Vietnam.*

more attentive to the survival and well-being of all their children. Therefore girls may be more highly valued and less subject to discrimination.

Research in the USA examining the relationship between the gender of children already born, and the likelihood of having subsequent children, found that couples with previous children of the same gender are consistently more likely to bear an additional child. This relationship is more pronounced among Anglo-Americans than Mexican Americans.

Health and life expectancy

In the UK the *Independent Inquiry into Inequalities in Health Report* noted that mortality is higher for males compared with females at all ages. The overall result is that life expectancy is five years longer for women. The report's findings included the following:

- up to the age of 14 higher male mortality occurs because boys are more likely to die from poisoning and injury
- by the age of 15 boys have 65% higher mortality than girls
- for the 20–24 age group, male mortality is 2.8 times higher; in youth and early adult life the higher rates of male death are due to car accidents, other accidents and suicide
- across the whole of adult life, mortality rates are higher for men for all the major causes of death
- the least well-off women still have lower mortality than the most well-off men
- gender differences are least in affluent areas and greatest in the most deprived areas.

On a global scale the World Health Organization (WHO) has highlighted the following facts about women's health:

- Women have a significantly higher risk of becoming visually impaired than men. However, they do not have

An Anglo-American family with three children.

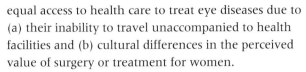

equal access to health care to treat eye diseases due to (a) their inability to travel unaccompanied to health facilities and (b) cultural differences in the perceived value of surgery or treatment for women.

- Around 1600 women and more than 10 000 newborn children die every day from preventable complications during pregnancy and childbirth. Almost 99% of maternal mortalities occur in the developing world.
- About 14 million adolescent girls become a mother every year, with more than 90% living in developing countries.
- Up to 1 in 5 women have been sexually abused before the age of 15.
- Between 15% and 71% of women around the world have suffered physical or sexual violence committed by an intimate male partner at some point in their lives.
- Of all adults living with HIV in sub-Saharan Africa, 61% are women. The proportion of women living with HIV has been increasing for over a decade
- Indoor smoke from cooking is responsible for half a million of the 1.3 million annual deaths due to chronic obstructive pulmonary disease (COPD) among women worldwide. In contrast, only about 12% of COPD deaths among men each year are related to indoor smoke.

HIV/AIDS

Gender inequality is a key factor driving the HIV/AIDS epidemic. Due to their lower social and economic power, women and girls are at greater risk of infection and have more difficulty in trying to protect themselves from it. The World Health Organization states that gender norms related to masculinity can encourage men to have more sexual partners and older men to have sexual relations with much younger women. The WHO notes:

- in some areas this contributes to higher infection rates for young women than for young men
- homosexual men are very vulnerable to HIV infection but social stigma often leads to this problem being ignored
- women who fear or experience violence lack the power to ask their partners to use condoms or refuse unprotected sex
- social norms relating to women can prevent women, particularly in the younger age group, from accessing HIV information and services
- their lower status and limited livelihood opportunities often force women and girls to turn to transactional sex to survive.

Activities

1 Explain why (a) birth ratios and (b) family size are gender issues.
2 With reference to examples, explain how health and life expectancy can vary by gender.

Employment

A report by the UN Economic and Social Commission for Asia and the Pacific countries stated that restricting job opportunities for women costs the region between $42 billion and $46 billion a year. Similarly, a study by the World Bank found that restricting employment opportunities for women in the Middle East resulted in huge additional costs. In the latter region there has been substantial investment in reducing the gender gap in health and education, but much less progress in terms of economic opportunities, with only a third of women participating in the labour force.

Two female police officers in Vienna, Austria – police forces in most countries employ more women now than they did 20 years ago.

It has been estimated that closing the gender employment gap would boost GDP in:

- the USA by as much as 9%
- the EU by up to 13%
- Japan by as much as 13%.

The argument throughout all of these reports is that women account for half the world's talent – and undervaluing and under-using this talent results in big economic costs.

Research in the UK has shown that their different occupational and domestic positions make women more vulnerable to poverty than men, both during their working lives and in retirement. This is in part due to the fact that women are more likely to have had breaks in employment and to work part-time in low wage jobs.

Reference has also frequently been made to the following:

- The 'double shift syndrome' – this refers to the fact that many working women with families have heavy household responsibilities which may mean they are unable to compete with male colleagues in terms of involvement in (a) overtime, (b) business trips and (c) informal interactions with colleagues after business hours that may help to strengthen promotion prospects within a company. Looking after children at home when they are ill also falls disproportionately on women.

- The 'glass ceiling syndrome' – although equal opportunities legislation in many countries should result in a much higher level of employment equality, there are reasons why legal equality (*de jure*) is not always translated into actual equality (*de facto*). A major reason seems to be a so-called invisible 'glass ceiling' that is deemed to prevent most women progressing above a certain level within many companies.

However, changes have been occurring quite quickly in some countries. A recent Cambridge University study (Figure 9) reports a 'quiet revolution in the workplace' with women increasingly occupying positions in the

Women now dominate the 'status' professions

By Martin Beckford
Social Affairs Correspondent

WOMEN outnumber men in the most high status professions after a 'quiet revolution in the workplace', according to a Cambridge University study.

The report claims that the majority of lawyers, doctors and architects are now female thanks to improvements in education and the changing nature of 'women's work'.

However, although more women now have high status occupations, they are still paid less than men and are less likely to be found in senior positions.

Dr Robert Blackburn, emeritus reader in sociology and Fellow of Clare College, Cambridge, said: 'The findings are very important, but not widely recognised until now.

A quiet revolution in the workplace means that the widespread idea that women do the low status jobs is now wrong – in fact they are more likely to be found working in the sorts of occupations that both men and women think are higher up the social scale.

'There was not always this advantage to women; it is part of a significant change in industrialised societies in the last 50 years.'

For his paper, called Gender Inequality at Work in Industrial Countries, Dr Blackburn and colleagues looked at official census and labour force surveys in 10 European countries including Britain.

He focused on 200 occupations whose social status has been rated using a scale called the Cambridge Social Interaction and Stratification Scale.

This ranks jobs according to how interesting and desirable they appear to others, and how much autonomy the worker is believed to have. It places professions in fields such as law, medicine and architecture at the top of the scale along with managers and scientists.

Overall, there were more women in 'prestigious' occupations. The difference in Britain was found to be 'statistically significant' but smaller than in other countries headed by Russia and Sweden.

Dr Blackburn said that part of the change was because women were more likely to go on to university than in previous generations.

But the main reason was the changing face of the job market, he claimed, with a decline in the number of low-skilled jobs for women, such as domestic service roles, while the number of office jobs and professional roles has risen.

'Formerly, women were more likely than men to be in manual occupations, but as manual work has declined, it is predominantly women who have moved into non-manual jobs, so that now it is men who are more likely than women to be manual workers,' he said. 'Initially, in the change from manual to non-manual work, women tended to be employed in low-level non-manual occupations, especially clerical work. More recently, they have contributed to the expansion of professional employment.'

The figures show, however, that the British workplace remains segregated in terms of pay, with men earning more. The Women and Work Commission claimed last month that the gender pay gap widened to 22.6 per cent last year.

This is partly because men tend to be employed in more senior positions such as company directors, but also because they do more dangerous or physically demanding work.

Figure 9 *From* The Daily Telegraph, *11 August 2009.*

'status' professions. Nevertheless the study also notes that women are still paid less than men, and they are still less likely to be found in senior positions.

The **unemployment gender ratio** varies significantly between countries. Table 5 (see page 75) shows a sample of 30 countries. The reasons for a high unemployment gender ratio can vary from country to country. Heavy gender bias may be the major reason in one country, while general affluence and a favourable benefits system for mothers may be a significant reason in another. Likewise the reasons for a low unemployment gender ratio can vary.

The European Public Health Alliance has noted that:

- women are more likely to be employed part time, increasing the risk of underemployment and reducing opportunities for promotion
- a vicious circle of gender discrimination is perpetuated because senior positions are often linked to the ability to work long or unsocial hours, which segregates women into lower-paid jobs.

A nurse checking a patient's blood pressure, Peru, South America.

Women make up more than 40% of the world's agricultural workforce. The Food and Agriculture Organization of the UN (FAO) states: 'women's roles in food production frequently go beyond providing labour and encompass major responsibilities for organising the production process – recruiting additional labour and hiring mechanised services, as well as storing, selling or controlling the use of the crop'.

The International Poverty Centre studied the relationship between poverty and gender inequalities in eight countries in Latin America. This research found that:

- women have a markedly lower rate of economic activity than men
- rates of female informality (working in the informal sector) and unemployment are usually higher than those for men
- women receive lower hourly wages.

The study concluded that while it is important to eliminate other aspects of gender inequality, promoting women's participation in the labour market is the aspect with the greatest potential to enhance **pro-poor growth**.

Empowerment

There are different ways of viewing empowerment. In terms of political empowerment, Figure 10 shows the changes in parliamentary seats by world region occupied by women for 1995, 1999 and 2004. All regions apart from Oceania showed a continuous increase in the percentage of seats occupied by women. In Oceania there was a slight dip between 1999 and 2004. The highest representation of women in parliament is in Europe (20.56%) and the lowest in Oceania (7.5%).

At a lower level, which can affect many more women, Figure 11 (page 72) illustrates the objectives of providing micro-credit facilities for women. The diagram attempts to show how providing relatively small loans can improve women's economic, social and political empowerment.

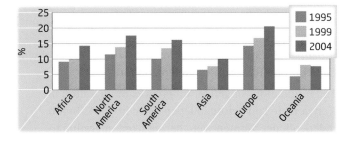

Figure 10 *Trends in the representation of women in national parliaments, 1995–2004.*

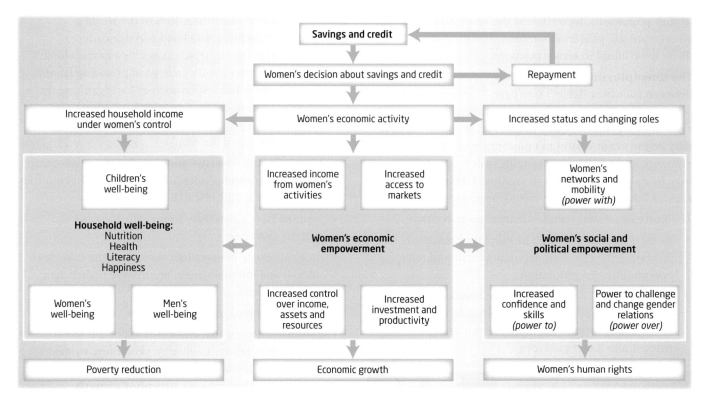

Figure 11 *Objectives of micro-credit for women.*

Migration

In recent decades gender has come to occupy a significant place in migration literature. This has made a crucial contribution to understanding the institutions that structure migration processes. The gendered nature for motives of remitting, as determined by gender-differentiating inheritance rules, is an important aspect of this approach.

Recent research has extended the Todaro hypothesis by suggesting that males receive larger monetary returns than females as a result of migration and consequently have a greater incentive to move to urban areas. In a study of rural-to-urban migration in Kenya, J. Agesa and R. Agesa found that rural men are significantly more educated than rural women and hence will migrate to urban areas in greater numbers as urban jobs generally demand higher educational requirements than those in rural areas. In addition the urban/rural wage gap is larger for males than females, giving higher economic returns to migration for men.

The foundations of gender differences in migration in Kenya were laid before independence in 1963. Before independence women were barred from migrating to urban areas and these restrictions helped to create a pattern of migration that is pervasive in Kenya today. The high rate of fertility in Kenya – one of the highest in the world – also reduces the likelihood of female migration. Child-rearing over a long period of time and the responsibility of looking after a large family inevitably reduce the propensity to migrate. On the other hand, for many families it makes male migration all the more necessary. Although women account for 56% of the country's population, approximately 87% of women live in rural areas compared with 54% of men.

In contrast, recent studies show that women in Latin America equal or outnumber men in urban-destined migration streams and that the majority of women are economically active in their urban destinations. However, a higher percentage of women than men work in the informal sector where incomes are low and labour protection is poor. An important stimulus to female rural-to-urban migration has been an increase in the type of industrial jobs that employers see as being particularly suitable for women. The establishment of free trade zones and export-led growth strategies have added to this effect. Radcliffe's study of peasant households in the Peruvian province of Calca in the southern Andes found that one-third of eldest daughters had out-migrated compared with only 14% of sons. This is largely because in this region women are considered as marginal to agricultural work and therefore are regarded as 'surplus' labour. Similarly

research by Gilbert *et al.* (1994) in the Campoo and Misque provinces of Bolivia noted that young unmarried women in rural peasant households are frequently migratory. Two influences are dominant here: the importance for women to bring a dowry to their marriage, and inheritance patterns that have favoured passing scarce land to male offspring.

Legal rights and land tenure

Women face widespread discrimination around the world with regard to land and property. The agrarian reforms implemented in many countries from the 1950s through the 1970s were 'gender blind'. They were often based on the assumption that all household members would benefit equally, when this was simply not the case. For example, many women in developing countries lose their homes, inheritance and possessions, and sometimes even their children, when their partner dies. This may force women to adopt employment practices that increase their chances of contracting HIV.

In most societies women have very unequal access to, and control over, rural land and associated resources. The UN's Food and Agriculture Organization has stated that 'denying large segments of rural society equitable access to land and to the benefits of land tenure regularisation creates unanticipated costs and is a major contributing factor to extreme poverty, dependence, rural migration leading

Addressing HIV/AIDS and gender equality in food security and rural livelihoods programming

In Namibia, legislation exists to prevent property/asset grabbing, yet it is still common practice in many areas in the north for a husband's family to grab resources, including livestock, from a widow and/or remaining children upon the husband's death. Losing livestock immediately impacts the woman and/or her children as she loses her 'food security' bank, potential draught power, fertilizer, and source of income.

Figure 12 *Gender equality and inheritance/property rights in Namibia.*

to land abandonment, social instability and many other negative conditions because of the unforeseen externalities that arise'. It is now generally accepted that societies with well-recognised property rights are also the ones that thrive best economically and socially.

The impact of globalisation

Some writers have argued that globalisation has increased gender inequalities in some parts of the world. This stance stresses the fact that women are very differently positioned in relation to markets in different parts of the world. In some places women are socially excluded from leaving their homes and are being largely by-passed by economic change. In other places the need is to create markets that are more friendly to women's participation. The UN's Women Watch Online Working Group on Women's Economic Inequality found that in China and Vietnam globalisation had brought new opportunities to young women with English language skills in new service sector jobs. In contrast many women over 35 were redundant because they were either working in declining industries or had outdated skills.

Microcredit is one solution to female participation in the economy that has gained much praise in recent years. However, research in Bangladesh revealed that:

- many female borrowers reported an increase in verbal and physical aggression from male relatives after taking out loans
- women run the risk of losing control of their loans to male relatives due to their restricted economic mobility set by social norms.

Activities

1 Provide evidence to show that constraints on employment opportunities for women can hinder the economic development of a country.
2 Give a brief summary of Figure 9 (page 70).
3 Describe the variations in the political empowerment of women shown in Figure 10 (page 71).
4 How has the creation of micro-credit facilities in some countries helped to empower women?
5 Suggest reasons why migration is often gender selective.
6 Briefly review how legal rights and land tenure can vary in some countries.

Key terms

Gender according to the World Health Organization, gender refers to the socially constructed roles, behaviours, activities and attributes that a given society considers appropriate for men and women.

Social norms the rules for how people should act in a given group or society. These rules are often different for men and women. Any behaviour that is outside these norms is considered abnormal.

Culture the total of the inherited ideas, beliefs, values and knowledge that constitutes the shared bases of social action.

Status (with regard to gender) the relative position or standing of men and women in a society.

Unemployment gender ratio the female unemployment rate as a percentage of the male unemployment rate.

Pro-poor growth to increase incomes of the poorest people at rates above the national average.

Websites

www.epha.org/a/2865
European Public Health Alliance

www.who.int/en/
World Health Organization (WHO)

www.isiswomen.org
Isis International

www.bridge.ids.ac.uk
BRIDGE, Institute of Development Studies

www.femnet.or.ke/
The African Women's Development and
Communication Network

www.twnside.org.sg
Third World Network

www.unhabitat.org
UN Habitat

www.fao.org
UN Food and Agriculture Organization (FAO)

Review

Examination-style questions

1 Refer to Table 4.

a Define (i) the adult literacy rate (ii) the youth literacy rate.

b Complete the final column of Table 4 and then describe the differences between male and female literacy.

c Examine the reasons for the differences in male and female literacy.

Adult or youth literacy	Countries with data	Male literacy rate (%)	Female literacy rate (%)	Difference male-female literacy rate (%)
Adult literacy (15 years and older)	135	84.9	72.1	
Youth literacy (15–24 years)	132	89.4	82.2	

Table 4 *Male and female literacy rates.*

2 Refer to Table 5.

a Define the unemployment gender ratio.

b Describe the variations in the data and any geographical patterns you notice.

c Suggest reasons for the variations shown in Table 5.

Rank	Country	Amount (%)
1	Greece	228
2	Spain	212
3	Italy	180
4	Luxembourg	173
5	Netherlands	161
6	Portugal	159
7	Iceland	158
8	Belgium	156
9	Czech Rep.	144
10	France	140
11	Switzerland	136
12	Poland	126
13	Denmark	123
14	Mexico	117
15	Finland	116
16	Germany	113
17	USA	105
18	Slovakia	100
19	Turkey	99
20	Austria	97
21	Ireland	97
22	Canada	96
23	New Zealand	95
24	Japan	91
25	Australia	89
26	Norway	88
27	Sweden	87
28	Hungary	81
29	UK	79
30	South Korea	71
	Weighted average	123.9

Table 5 *Unemployment gender ratio.*

05 Measurements of regional and global disparities

KEY QUESTIONS

- How can regional and global disparities be measured?
- What are the definitions of the indices of infant mortality, education, nutrition, income, marginalisation and the Human Development Index?
- What is the value of the different indices used to measure global and regional disparities?

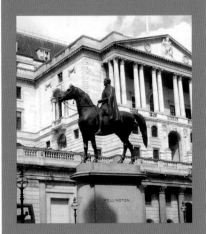

The Bank of England, with a statue of the Duke of Wellington. The UK is one of the wealthiest countries in the world.

Development and its traditional income measures

Development, or improvement in the quality of life, is a wide-ranging concept. It includes wealth, but it also includes other important aspects of our lives. For example, many people would consider good health to be more important than wealth. People who live in countries that are not democracies, where freedom of speech cannot be taken for granted, often envy those who do live in democratic countries. Development occurs when there are improvements to individual factors making up the quality of life. Figure 1 shows one view of the factors that comprise the quality of life. For example, development occurs in a low-income country when:

- local food supply improves due to investment in machinery and fertilisers
- the electricity grid extends outwards from the main urban areas to rural areas
- a new road or railway improves the accessibility of a remote province
- levels of literacy improve throughout the country.

Figure 1 *Factors comprising the quality of life.*

The traditional indicator of a country's wealth has been the **Gross Domestic Product (GDP)**. The GDP is the total value of goods and services produced by a country in a year. A more recent measure, the **Gross National Income (GNI)**, has to some extent taken over from GNP as a preferred measure of national wealth. Gross National Income comprises the total value of goods and services produced within a country (that is, its gross domestic product), together with its income received from other countries (notably interest and dividends), less similar payments made to other countries.

To take account of the different populations of countries the **Gross National Income per capita** is often used. Here, the total GNI of a country is divided by the total population. Per capita figures allow for more valid comparisons between countries when their total populations are very different. However, 'raw' or 'nominal' GNI data does not take into account the way in which the cost of living can vary between countries. For example, a dollar buys much more in China than it does in the USA. To account for this the GNI at 'purchasing power parity' (PPP) is calculated. Figure 2 shows how **GNI at purchasing power parity per capita** varied globally in 2007. The lowest GNI figures are concentrated in Africa and parts of Asia. The highest figures are in North America, the EU, Japan, Australia and New Zealand.

Table 1 (page 78) shows the top and bottom 20 countries in GNI per capita (PPP) for 2006–07. The **development gap** between the world's wealthiest and poorest countries is huge. However, a major limitation of GNI and other national data is that these are 'average' figures for a country which tell us nothing about:

- the way in which wealth is distributed within a country – in some countries the gap between rich and poor is much greater than in others

- how government invests the money at its disposal – for example, Cuba has a low GNI per capita but high standards of health and education because these have been government priorities for a long time.

Development not only varies between countries, it can also vary significantly within countries. Most of the measures that can be used to examine the contrasts between countries can also be used to look at regional variations within countries.

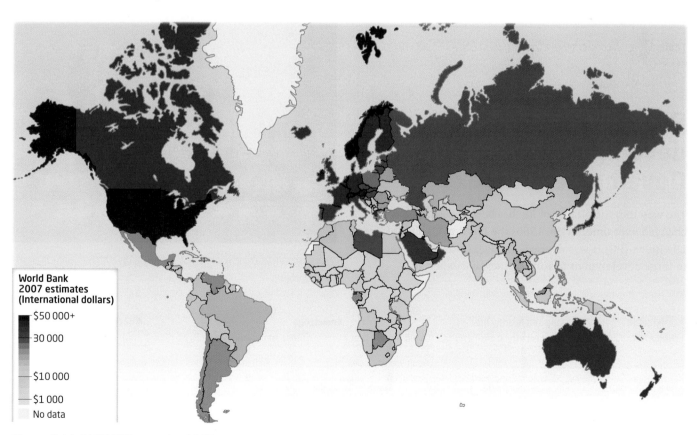

World Bank 2007 estimates (International dollars)

- $50 000+
- 30 000
- $10 000
- $1 000
- No data

Figure 2 *World GNI PPP per capita, 2007.*

Top 20 countries		Bottom 20 countries	
Luxembourg	64 320	Comoros	1 170
Norway	58 500	Burkina Faso	1 160
Kuwait	52 610	Chad	1 160
Macau	52 260	Uganda	1 140
Brunei	50 200	Nepal	1 120
Singapore	47 940	Mali	1 090
USA	46 970	Madagascar	1 040
Switzerland	46 640	Rwanda	1 010
Hong Kong	43 960	Ethiopia	870
Netherlands	41 670	Malawi	830
Sweden	38 180	Togo	820
Austria	37 680	Mozambique	770
Ireland	37 350	Sierra Leone	750
Denmark	37 280	Central African Rep.	730
Canada	36 220	Niger	680
UK	36 130	Eritrea	630
Germany	35 940	Guinea-Bissau	530
Finland	35 660	Burundi	380
Japan	35 220	Liberia	300
Belgium	34 760	Congo, Dem. Rep.	290

Table 1 *Top 20 and bottom 20 countries in GNI (PPP) per capita, 2006–07.*

Broader measures of development: the Human Development Index

The way that the quality of life has been measured has changed over time. In the 1980s the Physical Quality of Life Index (PQLI) was devised. The PQLI was the average of three development factors: literacy, life expectancy and infant mortality. However, in 1990 the **Human Development Index (HDI)** was devised by the United Nations as a better measure of the disparities between countries. The HDI contains three variables:

- life expectancy
- educational attainment (adult literacy and combined primary, secondary and tertiary enrolment)
- GDP per capita (PPP$).

The actual figures for each of these three measures are converted into an index (Figure 3) which has a maximum value of 1.0 in each case. The three index values are then combined and averaged to give an overall HDI value. This also has a maximum value of 1.0. Every year the United Nations (UN) publishes the Human Development Report (HDR) which uses the HDI to rank all the countries of the world in their level of development. Table 2 shows the top 25 countries listed in the HDR for 2009.

Every measure of development has merits and limitations. No single measure can provide a complete picture of the differences in development between countries. This is why the United Nations combines three measures of different aspects of the quality of life to arrive at a figure of human

The Waterfront, Vancouver – Canada has a very high level of human development.

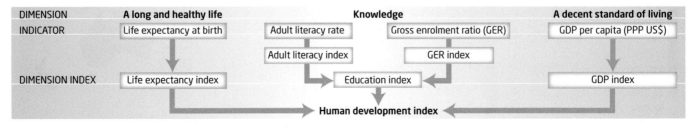

DIMENSION	A long and healthy life	Knowledge		A decent standard of living
INDICATOR	Life expectancy at birth	Adult literacy rate	Gross enrolment ratio (GER)	GDP per capita (PPP US$)
		Adult literacy index	GER index	
DIMENSION INDEX	Life expectancy index	Education index		GDP index

Human development index

Figure 3 *Constructing the Human Development Index.*

Human development index rank	Human development index value	Life expectancy at birth (years)	Adult literacy rate (% aged 15 and above)	Combined gross enrolment ratio in education (%)	GDP per capita (PPP US$)	Life expectancy index	Education index	GDP index	GDP per capita rank minus HDI rank
	2007	2007	1999–2007	2007	2007	2007	2007	2007	
1 Norway	0.971	80.5	–	98.6	53433	0.925	0.989	1.000	4
2 Australia	0.970	81.4	–	114.2	34923	0.940	0.993	0.977	20
3 Iceland	0.969	81.7	–	96.0	35742	0.946	0.980	0.981	16
4 Canada	0.966	80.6	–	99.3	35812	0.927	0.991	0.982	14
5 Ireland	0.965	79.7	–	97.6	44613	0.911	0.985	1.000	5
6 Netherlands	0.964	79.8	–	97.5	38694	0.914	0.985	0.994	8
7 Sweden	0.963	80.8	–	94.3	36712	0.930	0.974	0.986	9
8 France	0.961	81.0	–	95.4	33674	0.933	0.978	0.971	17
9 Switzerland	0.960	81.7	–	82.7	40658	0.945	0.936	1.000	4
10 Japan	0.960	82.7	–	86.6	33632	0.961	0.949	0.971	16
11 Luxembourg	0.960	79.4	–	94.4	79485	0.906	0.975	1.000	–9
12 Finland	0.959	79.5	–	101.4	34526	0.908	0.993	0.975	11
13 USA	0.956	79.1	–	92.4	45592	0.902	0.968	1.000	–4
14 Austria	0.955	79.9	–	90.5	37370	0.915	0.962	0.989	1
15 Spain	0.955	80.7	97.9	96.5	31560	0.929	0.975	0.960	12
16 Denmark	0.955	78.2	–	101.3	36130	0.887	0.993	0.983	1
17 Belgium	0.953	79.5	–	94.3	34935	0.908	0.974	0.977	4
18 Italy	0.951	81.1	98.9	91.8	30353	0.935	0.965	0.954	11
19 Liechtenstein	0.951	–	–	86.8	85382	0.903	0.949	1.000	–18
20 New Zealand	0.950	80.1	–	107.5	27336	0.919	0.993	0.936	12
21 UK	0.947	79.3	–	89.2	35130	0.906	0.957	0.978	–1
22 Germany	0.947	79.8	–	88.1	34401	0.913	0.954	0.975	2
23 Singapore	0.944	80.2	94.4	–	49704	0.920	0.913	1.000	–16
24 Hong Kong	0.944	82.2	–	74.4	42306	0.953	0.879	1.000	–13
25 Greece	0.942	79.1	97.1	101.6	28517	0.902	0.981	0.944	6

Table 2 *Top 25 countries, Human Development Report 2009.*

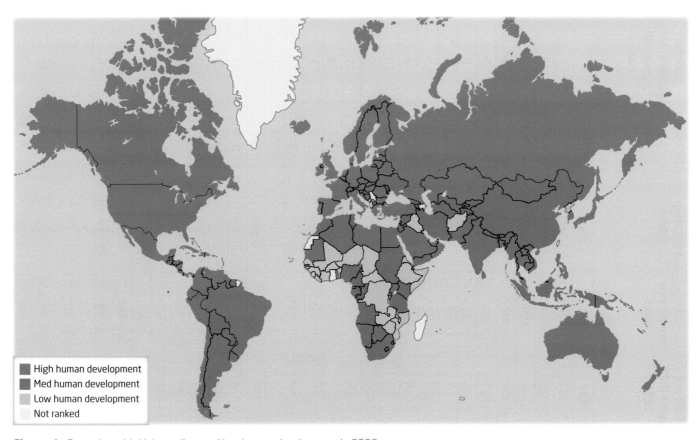

Figure 4 *Countries with high, medium and low human development in 2009.*

development for each country. Although the development gap can be measured in a variety of ways it is generally taken to be increasing.

Figure 4 shows the variation in human development in 2007. Countries are divided into three categories: high, medium and low human development. The 'high' category also includes those countries with 'very high' human development shown in Table 3. Table 3 shows the HDI values for each of these categories.

Level of human development	HDI value	Number of countries 2007
Very high	0.900 and over	38
High	0.800–0.899	45
Medium	0.500–0.799	75
Low	Below 0.500	24

Table 3 *HDI values.*

The Human Development Report

The Human Development Index is published annually. It is a key part of the Human Development Report (HDR). According to a recent edition of the HDR, 'Human development is about putting people at the centre of development. It is about people realizing their potential, increasing their choices and enjoying the freedom to lead lives they value. Since 1990, annual HDRs have explored challenges including poverty, gender, democracy, human rights, cultural liberty, globalization, water scarcity and climate change.'

In assessing the progress made in reducing global poverty, the HDR has noted that:

- in the past 60 years poverty has fallen more than in the previous 500 years
- poverty has been reduced in some respects in almost all countries
- child death rates in developing countries have been cut by more than half since 1960
- malnutrition rates have declined by almost a third since 1960

- the proportion of children not in primary education has fallen from more than half to less than a quarter since 1960
- the share of rural families without access to safe water has been cut from nine-tenths to about a quarter since 1960.

These are just some of the achievements made during what the HDR calls the 'second Great Ascent from poverty', which started in the 1950s in the developing world, eastern Europe and the former Soviet Union. The first Great Ascent from poverty began in Europe and North America in the late 19th century in the wake of the industrial revolution.

However, although the global poverty situation is improving, approximately one in six people worldwide struggle on a daily basis in terms of:

- adequate nutrition
- uncontaminated drinking water
- safe shelter
- adequate sanitation
- access to basic health care.

These people have to survive on $1 a day or less and are largely denied access to public services for health, education and infrastructure. The United Nations estimates that 20 000 people die every day of dire poverty, for want of food, safe drinking water, medicine and other vital needs.

Different stages of development

Although the global development picture is complex, a general distinction can be made between the developed 'North' and the developing 'South'. These terms were first used in *North–South: A Programme for Survival* published in 1980. This publication is generally known as the *Brandt Report* after its chairperson Willy Brandt.

Other terms used to distinguish between the richer and poorer nations are:

- developed and developing
- more economically developed countries (MEDCs) and less economically developed countries (LEDCs).

Over the years there have been a number of descriptions and explanations of how countries moved from one level of development to another. A reasonable division of the world in terms of stages of economic development is shown in Figure 5.

Farmers working an irrigation water pump, sub-Saharan region.

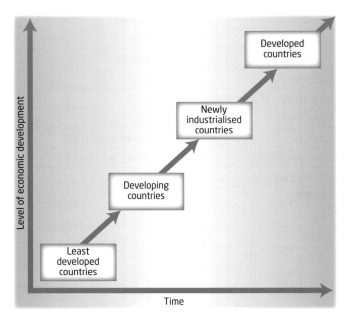

Figure 5 *Stages of development.*

The concept of **least developed countries (LDCs)** was first identified in 1968 by the United Nations Conference on Trade and Development (UNCTAD). These are the poorest of the developing countries. They have major economic, institutional and human resource problems. These are often made worse by geographical handicaps and natural and human-made disasters. *The Least Developed Countries Report 2009* identified 49 countries as LDCs. With 10.5% of the world's population, these countries generate only one-tenth of 1% of its income. The list of LDCs is reviewed every three years by the UN. When countries develop beyond a certain point they are no longer considered to be LDCs.

Many of the LDCs are in Sub-Saharan Africa. Others are concentrated in the poverty belt of Asia (including Nepal and Afghanistan) or are small island nations in the South Pacific. As the gap between the richest and poorest countries in the world widens, LDCs are being increasingly marginalised in the world economy. Their share of world trade is declining and in many LDCs national debt now equals or exceeds GDP. Such a situation puts a stranglehold on all attempts to halt socio-economic decline.

Least developed countries are usually dependent on one or a small number of exports for their survival. Table 4 shows a classification of LDCs according to their export specialisation.

Research idea

Go to www.unctad.org to find out the latest information on least developed countries.

The first countries to become **newly industrialised countries (NICs)** were South Korea, Singapore, Taiwan and Hong Kong. The media referred to them as the 'four Asian tigers'. A 'tiger economy' is one that grows very rapidly. This group is now often referred to as the first generation of NICs. The reasons for the success of these countries were:

- a good initial level of infrastructure
- a skilled but relatively low-cost workforce
- cultural traditions that revere education and achievement
- governments welcoming foreign direct investment (FDI) from transnational corporations
- all four countries having distinct advantages in terms of geographical location
- ready availability of bank loans, often extended at the government's behest and at attractive interest rates.

The success of these four countries provided a model for others to follow, such as Malaysia, Brazil, China and India. In the last 15 years the growth of China has been particularly impressive. South Korea and Singapore have developed so much that many people now consider them to be developed countries.

The relative wealth of countries has a big impact on their use of resources. Table 5 shows the huge gap in energy consumption per capita in different countries.

Oil exporters	Sierra Leone
Angola	Zambia
Chad	**Manufactures exporters**
Equatorial Guinea	Bangladesh
Sudan	Bhutan
Timor-Leste	Cambodia
Yemen	Haiti
Agricultural exporters	Lesotho
Afghanistan	Nepal
Benin	**Services exporters**
Burkina Faso	Cape Verde
Guinea Bissau	Comoros
Kiribati	Djibouti
Liberia	Eritrea
Malawi	Ethiopia
Solomon Islands	Gambia
Somalia	Maldives
Tuvalu	Rwanda
Uganda	Samoa
Mineral exporters	São Tomé/Principe
Burundi	Tanzania
Central African Rep.	Vanuatu
Congo, Dem. Rep.	**Mixed exporters**
Guinea	Laos
Mali	Madagascar
Mauritania	Myanmar
Mozambique	Senegal
Niger	Togo

Table 4 *Classification of LDCs according to their export specialisation, 2003–05.*

	Total energy consumption per capita
High-income countries	5435
Middle-income countries	1390
Low-income countries	494

Table 5 *Energy consumption per capita for high, middle and low-income countries, 2003 (kg of oil equivalent per person).*

Explaining the development gap

There has been much debate about the causes of development. Detailed studies have shown that variations between countries are due to a number of factors.

⊙ Physical geography

- Landlocked countries have generally developed more slowly than those that have a coast.

- Small island countries face considerable disadvantages in development.

- Tropical countries have grown more slowly than those in temperate latitudes, reflecting the cost of poor health and unproductive farming in the former. However, richer non-agricultural tropical countries such as Singapore do not suffer a geographical deficit of this kind.

- A generous allocation of natural resources has spurred economic growth in a number of countries.

Low-income housing on the banks of the river Nile, Egypt.

⊙ Economic policies

- Open economies that welcomed and encouraged foreign investment have developed faster than closed economies.

- Fast-growing countries tend to have high rates of saving and low spending relative to GDP.

- Institutional quality in terms of good government, law and order and lack of corruption generally result in a high rate of growth.

⊙ Demography

- Progress through demographic transition is a significant factor, with the highest rates of growth experienced by those nations where the birth rate has fallen the most.

Figure 6 shows how such factors have combined in developing countries to produce higher and lower levels of development. In diagram (a) the area where the three factors coincide gives the highest level of development. In contrast, in diagram (b) the area where the three factors combine gives the lowest level of development.

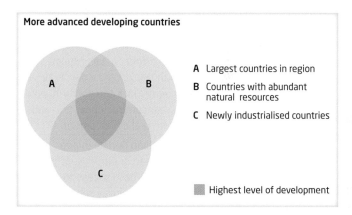

A Largest countries in region

B Countries with abundant natural resources

C Newly industrialised countries

■ Highest level of development

Figure 6(a) *Highest level of development.*

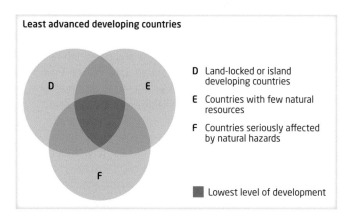

D Land-locked or island developing countries

E Countries with few natural resources

F Countries seriously affected by natural hazards

■ Lowest level of development

Figure 6(b) *Lowest level of development.*

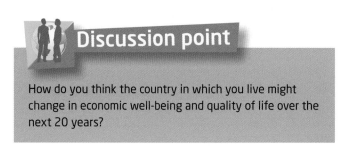

Discussion point

How do you think the country in which you live might change in economic well-being and quality of life over the next 20 years?

Consequences of the development gap

The development gap has significant consequences for people in the most disadvantaged countries. The consequences of poverty can be economic, social, environmental and political (Table 6). Development may not bring improvements in all four areas at first, but over time all four categories should witness advances.

Economic	Global integration is spatially selective: some countries benefit, others it seems do not. One in five of the world's population live on less than a dollar a day, almost half on less than two dollars a day. Poor countries frequently lack the ability to pay for (a) food (b) agricultural innovation and (c) investment in rural development.
Social	More than 850 million people in poor countries cannot read or write. Nearly a billion people do not have access to clean water and 2.4 billion to basic sanitation. Eleven million children under five die from preventable diseases each year. Many poor countries do not have the ability to combat the effects of HIV/AIDS.
Environmental	Poor countries have increased vulnerability to natural disasters. They lack the capacity to adapt to droughts and other natural events induced by climate change. Poor farming practices lead to environmental degradation. Often, raw materials are exploited with very limited economic benefit to poor countries and little concern for the environment. Landscapes can be devastated by mining, vast areas of rainforest felled for logging and clearance for agriculture, and rivers and land polluted by oil exploitation.
Political	Poor countries that are low on the development scale often have non-democratic governments or they are democracies that function poorly. There is usually a reasonably strong link between development and improvement in the quality of government. In general, the poorer the country the worse the plight of minority groups.

Table 6 *The consequences of poverty.*

Activities

1 Look at Figure 1 (page 76). Select what you think are the four most important aspects of the quality of life. Justify your selections.
2 Define:
   a GNI per capita
   b GNI at purchasing power parity
   c the development gap.
3 Describe the global distribution of GNI per capita (PPP) shown in Figure 2 (page 77).
4 Why are organisations such as the United Nations (UN) increasingly using GNI data at purchasing power parity?
5 Discuss the extent of the development gap shown in Table 1 (page 78).
6 Look at Figure 4 (page 80). Use an atlas to identify at least three countries in each colour category of the key.
7 Suggest three countries for each stage of development shown in Figure 5 (page 81).
8 Draw a graph to illustrate the data presented in Table 5 (page 82).
9 With reference to Figure 6 (page 83), suggest why some poorer countries have been able to develop into NICs while many have not.

Discussion point

Imagine that the UN has decided to add one more measure of development to the HDI. What do you think it should be, and why?

Infant mortality

The **infant mortality rate** is regarded as one of the most sensitive indicators of socio-economic progress. It is defined as the number of deaths of children under one year of age per 1000 live births. The infant mortality rate is an important measure of health equity both between and within countries.

There are huge differences in the infant mortality rate around the world, despite the wide availability of public health knowledge. Differences in material resources certainly provide a large part of the explanation for how international populations can share the same knowledge but achieve disparate mortality rates.

In addition, differences in the efficiency of social institutions and health systems can enable countries with similar resource levels to register disparate mortality levels. Figure 7 shows the extent of global variations in infant mortality. The highest rates are clearly concentrated in Africa and southern Asia.

However, many countries have significant intra-national disparities in infant mortality where populations share similar resource levels and health technology but achieve different health outcomes in various regions of the same country.

In countries where civil registration and vital statistics are lacking, the most reliable sources of information on infant mortality are demographic surveys of households.

Where these are not available, other sources and general estimates are made which have limitations in terms of reliability. Where countries lack comprehensive and accurate systems of civil registration, infant mortality statistics by gender are particularly difficult to collect or to estimate with any degree of reliability because of reporting biases.

Geographical skills

Describe the global variations in the infant mortality rate shown in Figure 7. Ensure that you refer to all seven elements of the key, identifying world regions and individual countries where particularly significant.

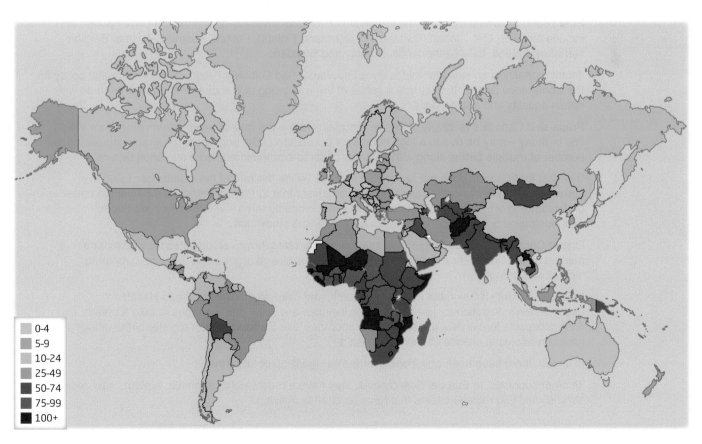

Figure 7 *Global variations in the infant mortality rate.*

However, even in affluent nations with comprehensive systems of recording data, there is some debate about the accuracy of infant mortality data when international comparisons are made (Figure 8). It seems that Canada's relatively high rate of infant mortality may be due to countries adopting slightly different definitions of 'live births'.

Infant mortality generally compares well with other indicators of development. Figure 12 (page 91) is a scatter graph comparing the infant mortality rate with electricity consumption per capita. While the relationship is far from a perfect correlation, it is clearly significant.

Canwest News Service

Canada's infant mortality rate high among developed nations

By Jorge Barrera, Canwest News Service, 29 September 2009

STORY PHOTOS

Canada continues to have one of the highest infant mortality rates in the developed world, a trend that has held since the 1990s, according to a new study.

Canada recorded five deaths for every 1000 live births in 2006, placing it 15th out of 17 peer countries, according to a report card of health indicators released by the Conference Board of Canada.

While Canada has improved its infant morality rate since the 1960s, it has been unable to match the success of the majority of its peers which have managed to improve at a much more rapid pace.

Peer countries are members of the Organization for Economic Co-operation and Development and include the U.S., U.K., Japan, Switzerland, Denmark, Finland, France, Australia, Austria, Belgium, Germany, Ireland, Italy, Netherlands, Norway and Sweden.

'Infant mortality is an indicator that is quite important,' said Gabriele Prada, director of health policy for the Conference Board. 'It gives you a sense of the well-being of a society and it has a lot to do with health equality and quality of life.'

Prada said Canada's relatively high infant mortality rate – the rate at which infants die before their first birthday – may be due to a high number of premature births and fertility programs increasing the number of multiple births, along with a variety of socio-economic and environmental factors.

'The fact that Canada does not seem able to break below the rate of five deaths per 1,000 live births, while 14 peer countries already have, suggests that further attention must be paid to better understanding of international differences in infant mortality rates – whether they are due to methodological or socio-economic factors, or both,' the study said.

One of Canada's foremost experts on infant mortality rates, however, disputes the dire picture painted by the Conference Board's international rankings and argues that they are comparing 'apples and oranges'.

University of British Columbia Prof. K.S. Joseph said Canada follows the World Health Organization's definition for live births which includes any baby that manages to take a breath, even if the prospects for survival are slim. Some countries, like Sweden, do not register births unless they have a reasonable chance of survival, he said.

In Japan, there have been questions over the categorizing of stillbirths.

'In other countries, in Europe, Scandinavia, they have a much more pragmatic system,' said Joseph. 'Why should you register babies that have no chance of living?'

Figure 8 *On Canada's infant mortality.*

Education

Education is undoubtedly the key to socio-economic development. It can be defined as the process of acquiring knowledge, understanding and skills. Education has always been regarded as a very important individual indicator of development and it has figured prominently in aggregate measures. It is one of the three components of the HDI. Here 'educational attainment' comprises:

- adult literacy
- combined primary, secondary and tertiary enrolment in schools and colleges.

Quality education generally, and female literacy in particular, are central to development. The World Bank has concluded that improving female literacy is one of the most fundamental achievements for a developing nation to attain, because so many aspects of development depend on it. For example, there is a very strong relationship between the extent of female literacy and infant and child mortality rates. People who are literate are able to access medical and other information that will help them to a higher quality of life compared with those who are illiterate. Figure 9 shows the extent to which the **adult literacy rate** varies around the world.

A secondary school in Tunisia.

The UN sees education for **sustainable development** as being absolutely vital for the future of the planet. Sustainable development is seeking to meet the needs of the present without compromising those of future generations. The year 2005 was the beginning of the United Nations Decade for Sustainable Development which will run until 2014. The UN Educational, Scientific and Cultural Organisation (UNESCO) is the lead agency in this

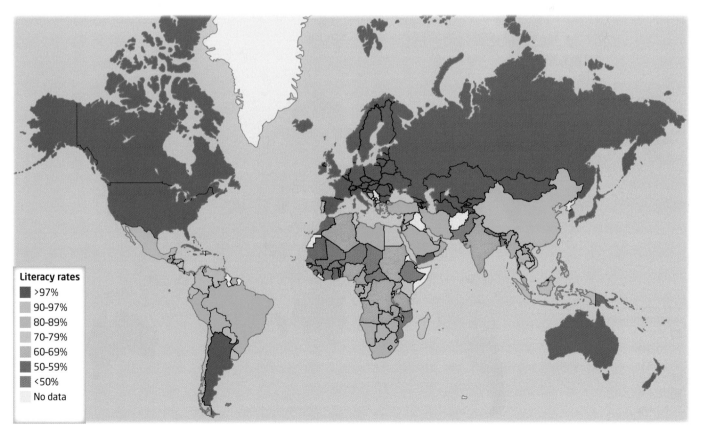

Literacy rates
- >97%
- 90–97%
- 80–89%
- 70–79%
- 60–69%
- 50–59%
- <50%
- No data

Figure 9 *Adult literacy rates.*

important campaign. It argues that we have to learn our way out of current social and environmental problems and learn to live sustainably, stating that 'sustainable development is a vision of development that encompasses populations, animal and plant species, ecosystems, natural resources and that integrates concerns such as the fight against poverty, gender equality, human rights, education for all, health, human security, intercultural dialogue, etc.'

Nutrition

Figure 10 shows the percentage of population undernourished around the world. Undernourishment is concentrated in the least developed countries, particularly in Sub-Saharan Africa and South Asia. The remaining problem areas are found in former Soviet Union countries. However, transitory areas of undernourishment can be caused by natural or human-made disasters.

Hunger may be defined as a condition resulting from chronic under-consumption of food and/or nutritious food products. It can be a short-term or long-term condition. If long-term it is usually described as chronic hunger.

Malnutrition is the condition that develops when the body does not get the right amount of the vitamins,

minerals and other nutrients it needs to maintain healthy tissues and organ function. Malnutrition occurs in people who are undernourished. Undernutrition is a consequence of consuming too few essential nutrients or using or excreting them more rapidly than they can be replaced. The leading cause of death in children in developing countries is protein-energy malnutrition. This type of malnutrition is the result of inadequate intake of calories from proteins, vitamins and minerals. Malnutrition is not confined to developing countries. It can also have an impact on the very poor in more affluent nations.

The global recession of 2008/09 has increased malnutrition for many of the most vulnerable people in developing countries. A paper published by the UN Standing Committee on Nutrition found that:

- in many countries the hours of work needed to feed a household of five increased by 10–20% during 2008
- the nutritional consequences of food price increases are likely to be considerable
- currently some 50 million, or 40%, of pregnant women in developing countries are anaemic; this number is likely to rise because of the current economic situation; nutritional problems very early in pregnancy will influence later foetal and infant growth.

% of population undernourished
- 35%
- 20-34%
- 5-19%
- 2.5-4%
- <2.4
- No data

Figure 10 *Undernourished people around the world.*

Increased and diversified agricultural production is one of the most reliable, sustainable interventions to improve nutrition and reduce infant and child malnutrition and mortality.

Marginalisation

Marginalisation is the process of being pushed to the edge of economic activity, of being largely left out of positive economic trends. The term can be applied to countries, regions within countries and to groups within a population. In terms of the last group its applicability is to the poorest, the unemployed and the most vulnerable. In some countries, such as the UK, the government has adopted a range of policies under the general umbrella term of 'social inclusion' in an attempt to bring marginalised (excluded) people into mainstream society. The term 'underclass' is also sometimes used to identify those who are socially and economically marginalised.

There are great concerns that marginalisation has increased under the processes of globalisation and deregulation. On a global scale the least developed countries are the most marginalised and are subject to UN assistance to try to change this situation. Figure 11 shows the components of the Marginalisation Index used in Mexico and how this condition varies across the country. There is a fairly clear regional pattern.

Socio-economic dimension	Indicator for measuring exclusion intensity	National (%)
Education	% of population of 15 years or more:	
	• illiterate	9.5
	• without complete primary education	28.5
Housing	% of private household occupants:	
	• without running water	11.2
	• without sewerage or private toilet facilities	9.9
	• with dirty floors	14.8
	• without electricity	4.8
	• with some degree of overcrowding	45.9
Income	% of employed population with income of up to two minimum wages	51.0
Population distribution	% of population in localities with fewer than 5000 inhabitants	31.0

Table 7 *Components of the Marginalisation Index in Mexico.*

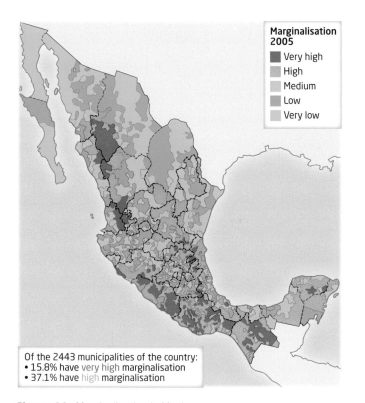

Marginalisation 2005
- ■ Very high
- ▨ High
- ▨ Medium
- ▨ Low
- ▨ Very low

Of the 2443 municipalities of the country:
• 15.8% have very high marginalisation
• 37.1% have high marginalisation

Figure 11 *Marginalisation in Mexico.*

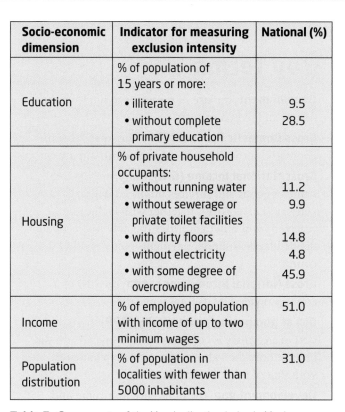

Activities

1 Briefly summarise the issues over international comparisons in infant mortality discussed in Figure 8 (page 86).
2 Look at Figure 9 (page 87).
   a Identify two countries for each colour used in the key.
   b Describe the general pattern shown on the map.
3 Look at Figure 10 (page 88).
   a Identify two countries for each type of shading used in the key.
   b Describe the general pattern shown on the map.
4 What is the extent of the correlation between Figures 9 (page 87) and 10 (page 88) ?
5 With the aid of an atlas map of Mexico, describe the pattern of marginalisation shown in Figure 11.

Key terms

Development the use of resources to improve the quality of life in a country.

Gross Domestic Product (GDP) the total value of goods and services produced in a country in a year.

Gross National Income (GNI) comprises the total value of goods and services produced within a country (i.e. its GDP), together with its income received from other countries (notably interest and dividends), less similar payments made to other countries.

Gross National Income per capita the GNI of a country divided by its total population.

GNI at purchasing power parity (PPP) here the GNI of a country is converted into US dollars on the basis of how the value of the currency compares with that of other countries.

Development gap the difference in income and the quality of life in general between the richest and poorest countries in the world.

Human Development Index (HDI) a measure of development which combines three important aspects of human well-being: life expectancy, education and income.

Least developed countries (LDCs) the poorest and weakest economies in the developing world as identified by UNCTAD.

Newly industrialised countries (NICs) countries that have undergone rapid and successful industrialisation since the 1960s.

Infant mortality rate the number of deaths of children under one year of age per 1000 live births.

Education the gradual process of acquiring knowledge, understanding and skills.

Adult literacy rate the percentage of the adult population with basic reading and writing skills.

Sustainable development development that seeks to meet the needs of the present without compromising the needs of future generations.

Malnutrition the condition that develops when the body does not get the right amount of the vitamins, minerals and other nutrients it needs to maintain healthy tissues and organ function.

Marginalisation the process of being pushed to the edge of economic activity, of being largely left out of positive economic trends.

Websites

hungerreport.org/2009/mdgs/child-mortality
Bread for the World Institute Development Goal

www.edc.org
Education Development Center

www.unesco.org/en/esd
UN Educational, Scientific and Cultural Organisation (UNESCO)

www.who.int/nutrition
World Health Organization (WHO)

www.unicef.org
UN Children's Fund (UNICEF)

www.unctad.org
UN Conference on Trade and Development (UNCTAD)

Review

Examination-style questions

1 Refer to Figure 12.

a Define the infant mortality rate.

b Describe the relationship between the infant mortality rate and electricity consumption per capita shown in Figure 12.

c Examine the factors responsible for the wide variations in infant mortality around the world.

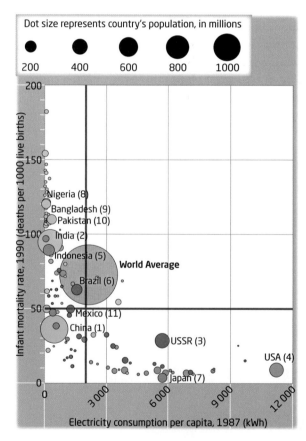

Figure 12 *The relationship between infant mortality and electricity consumption.*

2 Refer to Table 8.

a Define the adult literacy rate.

b Describe the changes in the adult literacy rate in the Asian countries identified in Table 7 (page 89).

c Why is the adult literacy rate generally regarded as a good indicator of the socio-economic development of a country?

East and north-east Asia		1990	2000-04
China	Male	87.2	95.1
	Female	68.9	86.5
Hong Kong	Male	95.6	–
	Female	83.4	–
Macao	Male	94.6	95.3
	Female	86.8	87.8
Mongolia	Male	98.4	98.0
	Female	97.1	97.5
South Korea	Male	98.4	–
	Female	93.4	–
South-east Asia		**1990**	**2000-04**
Brunei	Male	91.0	95.2
	Female	79.4	90.2
Cambodia	Male	77.7	84.7
	Female	48.8	64.1
Indonesia	Male	86.7	–
	Female	72.5	–
Laos	Male	70.3	77.0
	Female	42.8	60.9
Malaysia	Male	86.9	92.0
	Female	74.4	85.4
Myanmar	Male	87.4	93.7
	Female	74.2	86.2
Philippines	Male	92.2	92.5
	Female	91.2	92.7
Singapore	Male	94.4	96.6
	Female	83.2	88.6
Thailand	Male	95.3	94.9
	Female	89.4	90.5
Vietnam	Male	94.0	93.9

Table 8 *Adult literacy rate for selected Asian countries.*

06 Origin of disparities

The extent of income disparities within countries

The scale of disparities within countries is often as much an issue as the considerable variations between countries. The **Gini coefficient** is a technique frequently used to show the extent of income inequality. It allows:

- analysis of changes in income inequality over time in individual countries and comparison between countries.

Figure 1 shows global variations in the Gini coefficient for 2007–08. It is defined as a ratio with values between 0 and 1.0. A low value indicates a more equal income distribution while a high value shows more unequal income distribution. A Gini coefficient of zero would mean that everyone in a country had exactly the same income (perfect equality). At the other extreme a Gini coefficient of 1 would mean that one person had all the income in a country (perfect inequality). Figure 1 shows that in general more affluent countries have a lower income gap than lower-income countries. In 2007–08 the global gap ranged from 0.232 in Denmark to 0.707 in Namibia.

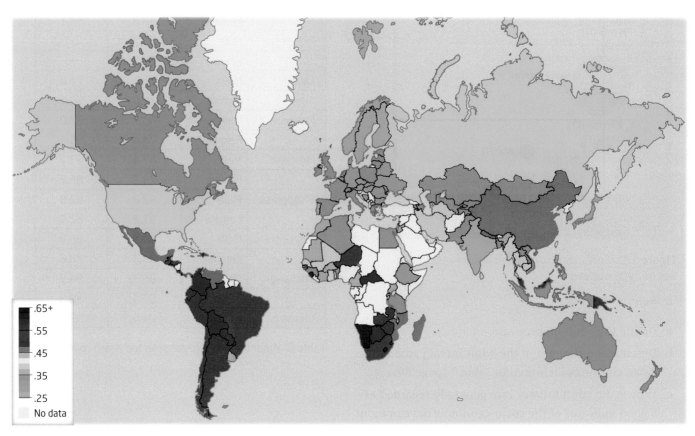

Figure 1 *Variations in Gini coefficient, 2007–08.*

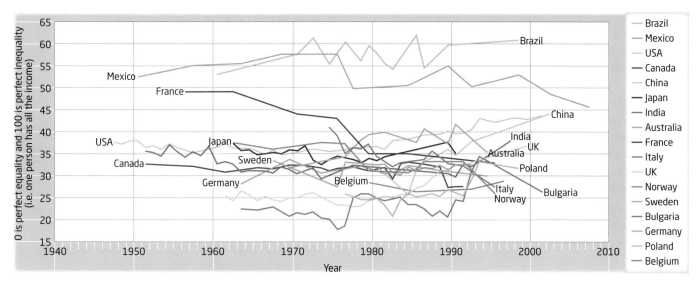

Figure 2 *Gini index – income disparity since the Second World War for selected countries.*

Figure 2 shows income disparity within a number of countries over a period of more than four decades. In countries like France and Mexico there has been a clear decline in income inequality, whereas China and Brazil show a significant increase. The abrupt changes that have occurred from time to time for some countries are often related to economic recessions which generally have the greatest impact on people on low incomes.

The Lorenz curve is a graphical technique that shows the degree of inequality that exists between two variables. It is often used to show the extent of income inequality in a population (Figure 3). The diagonal line represents perfect equality in income distribution. The further the curve is away from the diagonal line the greater the degree of income inequality. Thus, in Figure 3 income inequality in the UK was greater in 2002–03 than it was in 1961.

Discussion point

Suggest reasons for the increase in income inequality in the UK between 1961 and 2002/03.

A report published in October 2008 entitled *Growing Unequal? Income Distribution and Poverty in OECD (Organisation for Economic Cooperation and Development) Countries* found that:

- the gap between rich and poor has grown in more than three-quarters of OECD countries over the past two decades

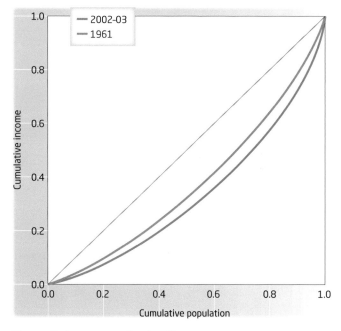

Figure 3 *Lorenz curve for the UK.*

- the economic growth of recent decades has benefited the rich more than the poor – in some countries, such as Canada, Finland, Germany, Italy, Norway and the USA, the gap also increased between the rich and the middle-class

- countries with a wide distribution of income tend to have more widespread income poverty

- social mobility is lower in countries with high inequality, such as Italy, the UK and the USA, and higher in the Nordic countries where income is distributed more evenly.

In China, the income gap between urban residents and the huge farm population reached its widest level ever in 2008 as rural unemployment in particular rose steeply. The ratio between more affluent urban dwellers and their rural counterparts reached 3.36 to 1, up from 3.33 to 1 in 2007. This substantial income gap is a very sensitive issue in China, as more and more rural people feel they have been left behind in China's economic boom. The size of the income gap is not just a political problem, but is also causing considerable national economic concern. Falling purchasing power in rural areas is hindering efforts to boost domestic consumer spending. The government wants to do this to help compensate for declining exports caused by the global recession.

Geographical skills

1 What is the Gini coefficient?
2 Describe the global variation in the Gini coefficient shown in Figure 1 (page 92).
3 How has the Gini coefficient varied over time for the countries shown in Figure 2 (page 93)?

Research idea

What are the regional disparities in income in the country in which you live? How have these differences changed over time?

Theory of Knowledge

Statistical techniques such as the Gini coefficient, and graphical techniques such as the Lorenz curve, help to improve our understanding of patterns and processes through clear visual representation. Is anything lost in this process of increasing abstraction?

Theory of regional disparities

The Swedish economist Gunnar Myrdal produced his **cumulative causation** theory in 1957. Figure 4 is a simplified version of the model Myrdal produced. Cumulative causation theory was set in the context of developing countries but the theory can also reasonably be applied to more advanced nations. According to Myrdal a three-stage sequence can be recognised:

- the pre-industrial stage when regional differences are minimal
- a period of rapid economic growth characterised by increasing regional economic divergence
- a stage of regional economic convergence when the significant wealth generated in the most affluent region/s spreads to other parts of the country.

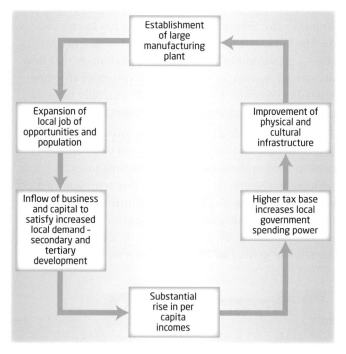

Figure 4 *Simplified model of cumulative causation.*

Figure 5 shows how the regional economic divergence of the earlier stages of economic development can eventually change to regional economic convergence.

In Myrdal's model, economic growth begins with the location of new manufacturing industry in a region with a combination of advantages greater than elsewhere in the country. Once growth has been initiated in a dominant region, spatial flows of labour, capital and raw materials develop to support it and the growth region undergoes

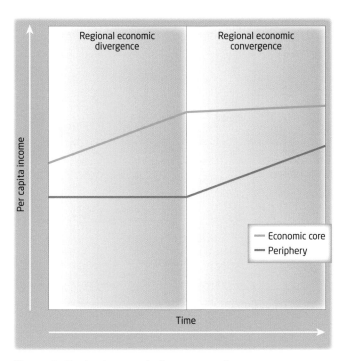

Figure 5 *Regional economic divergence and convergence.*

A village in eastern Siberia. The standard of living in most parts of Asiatic Russia (the periphery) is lower than in European Russia.

further expansion by the cumulative causation process. A detrimental 'backwash effect' is transmitted to the less developed regions as skilled labour and locally generated capital are attracted away. Manufactured goods and services produced and operating under the scale economies of the economic 'heartland' flood the market of the relatively underdeveloped 'hinterland', undercutting smaller-scale enterprises in such areas.

However, increasing demand for raw materials from resource-rich parts of the hinterland may stimulate growth in other sectors of the economies of such regions. If the impact is strong enough to overcome local backwash effects, a process of cumulative causation may begin leading to the development of new centres of self-sustained economic growth. Such 'spread effects' are spatially selective and will only benefit those parts of the hinterland with valuable raw materials or other significant advantages.

The American economist Hirschman (1958) produced similar conclusions to Myrdal although he adopted a different terminology. Hirschman labelled the growth of the **economic core region** (heartland) as 'polarisation', which benefited from 'virtuous circles' or upward spirals of development, whereas the **periphery** (hinterland) were impeded by 'vicious circles' or downward spirals. The term 'trickle-down' was used to describe the spread of growth from core to periphery. The major difference between Myrdal and Hirschman is that the latter stressed to a far greater extent the effect of counterbalancing forces overcoming polarisation (backwash), eventually leading to

economic equilibrium being established. The subsequent literature has favoured the terms 'core' and 'periphery' rather than Myrdal's alternatives.

Activities

1 Suggest reasons why income disparities are narrowing in some countries but getting wider in others.
2 Define the terms:
   a economic core region
   b periphery.
3 Explain in your own words the process shown in Figure 4 (page 94).
4 Describe and explain the trends shown in Figure 5 (above).
5 What is the evidence in the photo above that this region is part of the economic periphery of Russia?

Factors affecting internal disparities

Residence

Where people are born and where they live can have a significant impact on their quality of life. The focus of such study has been mainly on:

- regional differences within countries
- urban/rural disparities
- intra-urban contrasts.

Case study

Regional contrasts in Brazil

The South-east region (Figure 6) is the economic core region of Brazil. Over time the South-east has benefited from spatial flows of labour, raw materials and capital (Figure 7a). The last two have come from abroad as well as from internal sources. The region grew rapidly through the process of cumulative causation. This process not only resulted in significant economic growth in the core, but also had a considerable negative impact on the periphery. The overall result was widening regional disparity.

However, more recently some parts of the periphery, with a combination of advantages above the level of the periphery as a whole, have benefited from spread effects (trickle-down) emanating from the core (Figure 7b). Such spread effects are spatially selective and may be the result of either market forces or regional economic policy or, as is often the case, a combination of the two. The South has been the most important recipient of spread effects from the South-east, but the other regions have also benefited

Figure 6 *South-east Brazil.*

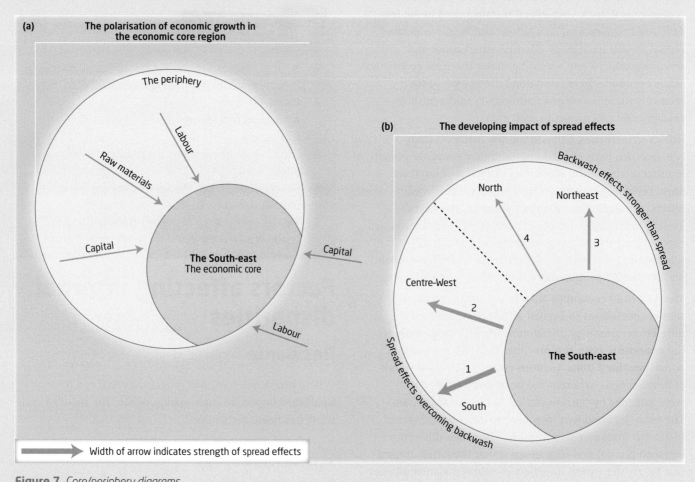

Figure 7 *Core/periphery diagrams.*

to an extent. This process has caused the regional gap to narrow at times, but often not for very long. However, in Brazil income inequality still remains very wide.

Region	Population (millions)
South-east	72.4
North-east	47.7
South	25.1
North	12.9
Centre-west	11.6

Table 1 *The population of Brazil's five regions (from Census 2000).*

The South-east's primary, secondary, tertiary and quaternary industries generate large amounts of money for Brazil. The natural environment of the South-east provided the region with a number of advantages for the development of primary industries.

- The warm temperature, adequate rainfall and rich terra roxa soils (weathered from lava) have provided many opportunities for farming. The region is important for coffee, beef, rice, cacao, sugarcane and fruit.

- Large deposits of iron ore, manganese and bauxite have made mining a significant industry. Gold is still mined.

- The region is energy rich, with large deposits of oil and gas offshore. Hydro-electric power is generated from large rivers flowing over steep slopes.

- The temperate rainforest provides the raw material for forestry.

- Fishing is important for many of the coastal settlements.

The South-east is the centre of both foreign and domestic investment in manufacturing industry. In the 1950s and 1960s the government wanted Brazil to become a newly industrialised country. Because the South-east had the best potential of all Brazil's five regions, investment was concentrated here. The region is the focus of the country's road and rail networks.

The South-east region contains the main airports and seaports. It also has a significant pipeline network for oil and gas. More transnational corporations (TNCs) are located in the South-east than in the rest of Brazil. With the highest population density in Brazil, the labour supply is plentiful. The region also has the highest educational and skill levels in the country.

The car industry is a major activity in the region. Most of the world's large car makers are here, including Ford, GM, Toyota, WV and Fiat. Other manufacturing industries include food processing, textiles, furniture, clothing, printing, brewing and shoemaking.

The raw materials located in the region and the large market have provided favourable conditions for many of these industries. However, cheaper imports of shoes, clothes and textiles from Asia have led to a number of companies in the region closing.

São Paulo is by far the largest financial centre in Latin America. The headquarters of most Brazilian banks are in São Paulo. Most major foreign banks are also located there. This is not surprising, as Brazil dominates the economy of Latin America and São Paulo is the largest city in South America.

The South-east is the centre of research and development in both the public and private sectors. Just 80 km from São Paulo is São Jose dos Campos, where the Aerospace Technical Centre is located. It conducts teaching, research and development in aviation and outer space studies. Many people would be surprised to know that aircraft and aircraft parts make up Brazil's largest export category by value.

The success of the first large wave of investment by foreign TNCs in the South-east encouraged other TNCs to follow suit. For the last 50 years the South-east has experienced an upward cycle of growth (cumulative causation).

Intra-urban variations: the growth of slums and urban poverty

Residence as a factor in inequality within countries can also be examined at a more detailed scale. The focus of such analysis has been on intra-urban variations and the large number of people living in slum housing. Thirty-two per cent of the world's urban population – almost 1 billion people – are housed in slums, with the great majority being in developing countries. A **slum** is a heavily populated urban area characterised by substandard housing and squalor. However, virtually all large cities in developed countries also contain slum districts. The UN recognises that the focus of global poverty is moving from rural to urban areas, a process known as the **urbanisation of poverty**. Without significant global action the number of slum dwellers will double over the next 30 years. The urban poor live in inner-city slums, peripheral shanty towns and in almost every other conceivable space, such as on pavements and traffic roundabouts, under bridges, and in sewers.

The number of people living in urban poverty is increased by a combination of economic problems, growing inequality and population growth – particularly growth due to in-migration (Figure 8). As *The Challenge of Slums* (2003) states, 'Slums result from a combination of poverty or low incomes with inadequacies in the housing provision system, so that poorer people are forced to seek affordable accommodation and land that has become

The middle-income Jardins district of São Paulo.

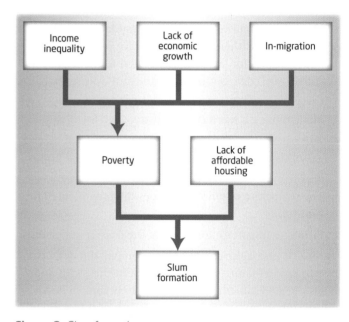

Figure 8 *Slum formation.*

increasingly inadequate.' The report identifies women, children, widows and female-headed households as the most vulnerable among the poor. In urban African slums, women head over 30% of all households.

The Challenge of Slums groups the dimensions of urban poverty as follows:

- Low income: consisting of those who are unable to participate in labour markets and lack other means of support, and those whose wage income is so low that they are below a nominal poverty line.

Favela in São Paulo.

- Low human capital: low education and poor health. Health 'shock' in particular can lead to chronic poverty.
- Low social capital: this involves a shortage of networks to protect households from shocks; weak patronage on the labour market; labelling and exclusion. This particularly applies to minority groups.
- Low financial capital: lack of productive assets that might be used to generate income or avoid paying major costs.

Table 2 sums up the constituents of urban poverty. The complexities of urban poverty indicate how difficult it is for individuals to improve their socio-economic situation. In many countries in recent times, social mobility has become more difficult rather than easier.

• Inadequate income, and thus inadequate consumption of necessities including food and, often, safe and sufficient water; often problems of indebtedness, with debt repayments significantly reducing income available for necessities.
• Inadequate, unstable or risky asset base (non-material and material including educational attainment and housing) for individuals, households or communities.
• Inadequate shelter – typically poor quality, overcrowded and insecure.
• Inadequate provision of 'public' infrastructure, e.g. piped water, sanitation, drainage, roads, footpaths, which increases the health burden and often the work burden.
• Inadequate provision of basic services such as day care/ schools/vocational training, health care, emergency services, public transport, communications, law enforcement.
• Limited or no safety net to ensure basic consumption can be maintained when income falls; also to ensure access to shelter and health care when these can no longer be paid for.
• Inadequate protection of poorer groups' rights through the operation of the law, including laws and regulations regarding civil and political rights, occupational health and safety, pollution control, environmental health, protection from violence and other crimes, protection from discrimination and exploitation.
• Voicelessness and powerlessness within political systems and bureaucratic structures leading to little or no possibility of receiving entitlements.

Table 2 *The constituents of urban poverty.*

Ethnicity and employment

The development gap often has an ethnic and/or religious dimension whereby some ethnic groups in a population have income levels significantly below the dominant group/s in the same population. This is invariably the result of discrimination which limits the economic, social and political opportunities available to the disadvantaged groups. Examples include South Africa (Table 3), Indonesia and Bolivia. Because of such obvious differences in status, tensions can arise between majority and minority groups resulting in:

- social unrest
- migration
- new political movements.

In South Africa the wide gap in income originated in the apartheid era, but since then it has proved extremely difficult to close for a variety of reasons. Political change often occurs well in advance of significant economic and social change. Table 3 shows the 2005 mean per capita income for the white population at 7646 Rand. In contrast the mean for the African population was only 775 Rand. The Asian population occupies an intermediate position with a 2005 figure of 2785 Rand.

Activities

1. Explain the processes illustrated in Figure 7 (page 96).
2. Produce a graph to illustrate the regional breakdown of Brazil's population (Table 1, page 97).
3. Examine the factors that lead to the formation of slums in developing countries.
4. Compare the photos on page 98 showing different residential districts in São Paulo.
5. Discuss the constituents of urban poverty shown in Table 2.

Inequality of wealth distribution is higher in Latin America than in any other part of the world. Indian and black people make up a third of the population, but have very limited parliamentary representation. Figure 9 (page 100) shows the situation in five Latin American countries in 2005, prior to political transformation in Bolivia. The changes that have occurred in Bolivia have given hope to indigenous peoples elsewhere in Latin America.

	1995	2000	2005
African: mean	615.36	575.64	775.46
African: median	333.23	278.46	406.95
*Coloured: mean	935.65	1141.80	1384.95
Coloured: median	583.72	655.11	651.47
Asian: mean	2299.15	2021.84	2785.50
Asian: median	1596.02	1306.92	1583.09
White: mean	4436.18	5129.21	7645.56
White: median	3442.72	3544.50	5331.61
Total: mean	1101.48	1074.29	1514.81
Total: median	428.74	356.27	483.87

Table 3 *South Africa: income differences by ethnic group, 2007. *The term 'coloured' is used in South Africa as a recognised ethnic grouping.*

Indians and blacks – poorly represented in parliament

In Ecuador, Guatemala and Peru, indigenous people make up 34–60% of the population but have had few seats in parliament. Even in Bolivia the majority Indian population only has 26% of seats – though its power to change government policy through mass protest has been growing, an alarming development for governments fearful of 'mob rule'. Part of the popular enthusiasm for Hugo Chavez – and the fear and loathing he inspires in traditional elites – arises from the fact that he is part Indian and part black, thus representing two of the most disadvantaged groups in Latin American history.

Country (ethnic group)	% of population	% representation in lower house
Bolivia (indigenous)	61	26
Ecuador (indigenous)	34	3
Guatemala (indigenous)	60	12
Peru (indigenous)	43	1
Brazil (African descent)	44	3

Figure 9 *Parlimentary representation in Latin America.*

Bolivia: ethnicity, employment and income

The **indigenous population** of Bolivia has always had to endure a much lower quality of life than people of Spanish descent. Two-thirds of Bolivia's population are indigenous, the largest number of any country within the region. However, the advent of 'participative democracy' in the last decade or so has resulted in a startling transformation of political power in the country. The key to this change was the indigenous population organising itself in an increasingly sophisticated manner. An important staging post was the success of Bolivia's poor in major protests over water and gas **privatisation**.

The privatisation of water has been a major issue. The resulting large increases in water bills provoked huge demonstrations, such as that in Cochabamba, Bolivia's third largest city. The Bolivian government withdrew its water contract with the TNC Bechtel and its operating partner Abengoa. As a result the companies sued the Bolivian government for $50 million. However, in 2006 the companies agreed to abandon their legal action in return for a token payment.

The indigenous population has been particularly susceptible for various reasons:

- a lack of economic opportunities in rural areas, where there are particularly high concentrations of indigenous peoples, resulting in large-scale migration to urban areas
- low employment rates in the formal sector, so there is a heavy reliance on the informal sector
- lack of access to land
- lack of access to basic social services (education, health care, energy)
- continued discrimination and stereotyping
- higher adjustment costs to the economic reforms of the 1990s (privatisation etc.).

Table 4 shows the indigenous/non-indigenous schooling gap for Bolivia and four other Latin American countries. The smallest gap for these five countries is 2.3 years in Peru, rising to a very significant high of 3.7 years in Bolivia. Figure 10 shows the considerable gap between incomes achieved in the formal and informal sectors in Bolivia. The indigenous population are heavily over-represented in the latter.

The main driving force of political change was the Movement Towards Socialism (MAS) party led by Evo Morales. He became the first fully indigenous head of state when he was elected president in December 2005. He was elected on a pledge to challenge the free market reforms that most people felt the country had been pressurised into adopting. There was widespread concern that these policies benefited large TNCs and the rich in Bolivia to the detriment

Country	Non-indigenous	Indigenous	Schooling gap (years)
Bolivia	9.6	5.9	3.7
Ecuador	6.9	4.3	2.6
Guatemala	5.7	2.5	3.2
Mexico	7.9	4.6	3.3
Peru	8.7	6.4	2.3

Table 4 *The indigenous/non-indigenous schooling gap.*

2 Disparities in wealth and development

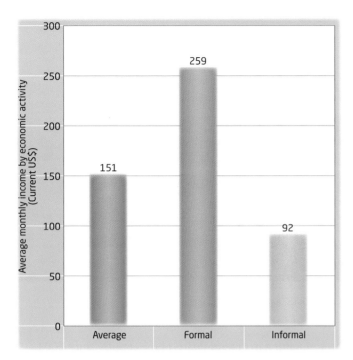

Figure 10 *The income gap between the formal and informal economy.*

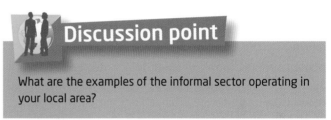

The informal sector – a beach artist in Agadir, Morocco.

Discussion point

What are the examples of the informal sector operating in your local area?

of the poor and the environment. The party's stated aims were to give more power to indigenous and poor people by means of land reforms and redistribution of gas wealth.

The formal and informal sectors of employment

Jobs in the formal sector will be known to the government department responsible for taxation and to other government offices. Such jobs generally provide better pay and much greater security than jobs in the informal sector. Fringe benefits such as holiday and sick pay may also be available. Formal sector employment includes health and education service workers, government workers, and people working in established manufacturing and retail companies.

In contrast, the informal sector is that part of the economy operating outside official recognition. Employment is generally low paid and often temporary and/or part-time in nature. While such employment is outside the tax system, job security will be poor with an absence of fringe benefits. About three-quarters of those working in the informal sector are employed in services. Typical jobs are shoe-shiners, street food stalls, messengers, repair shops and market traders. Informal manufacturing tends to include both the workshop sector, making for example cheap furniture, and the traditional craft sector. Many of these goods are sold in bazaars and street markets.

Education

Education is a key factor in explaining disparities within countries. Those with higher levels of education invariably gain better-paid employment. In developing countries there is a clear link between education levels and family size, with those with the least education having the largest families. Maintaining a large family usually means that saving is impossible and varying levels of debt are likely. In contrast, people with higher educational attainment have smaller families and are thus able to save and invest more for the future. Such differences serve to widen rather than narrow disparities.

Brazil has a greater disparity in income levels than most other countries. An important research study in the late 1990s concluded that the main cause was the huge variation in access to education. One of the authors of the study, Ricardo Paes de Barros, stated: 'There are not two Brazils. The poor and the rich live together in the same cities. They often work in the same multinational companies. The problem is that their educational background is absurdly unequal, and this results from the very poor quality of the public basic education system.' The report concluded that educational attainment explains 35–50% of income inequality.

Land ownership (tenure)

The distribution of land ownership has had a major impact on disparities in many countries. The greatest disparities tend to occur alongside the largest inequities in land ownership. The ownership of even a very small plot of land provides a certain level of security that those in the countryside without land cannot possibly aspire to.

Case study

Brazil: Marching for Real Land Reform

By Fabiana Frayssinet

RESENDE, Brazil, August 12 2009 (IPS) – After 10 years of waiting for secure title to the land they occupy and farm, 35 families in Resende, in the southeastern Brazilian state of Rio de Janeiro, have joined a huge march organised by the Landless Workers Movement (MST) in Brasilia to demand effective agrarian reform.

Mario Laurindo knows all about protest demonstrations. Some 14 years ago, he and others in the MST set up a roadside camp and were evicted. For the past 10 years he and his family have lived in the 'Terra Libre' (Free Land) settlement, 176 kilometres from the city of Rio de Janeiro, the state capital.

'We may grow old in the attempt, but we will continue the struggle,' Laurindo told IPS. A long time ago, he left the 'favela' (shantytown) where he lived, because he had no job, food or health care, and wanted to escape the high levels of urban violence.

Now, at least, he has plenty of food. With his wife and two children – they had two more, but they died – the family produces enough to subsist on, from honey to bananas. They also keep chickens and a few dairy cows.

Like other families in the settlement, Laurindo sells his surplus produce at a nearby town where he goes every day, crossing a river on boats built by another neighbour. Barter with other settlers complements the family diet.

'I'll never work for someone else again. Now I'm my own boss,' says Laurindo, who has taken up the way of life a small farmer and ekes out the family income with odd jobs such as bricklaying, but always on a self-employed basis, he stresses.

Like Osvaldo Cutis, a teacher and the spokesman for Terra Libre, Laurindo shares the goals of the settlement and of the MST, which is mobilising 3000 of its activists in Brasilia from Augest 10–19.

The demonstration in the capital, which includes marches, debates, cultural events and other activities, is an effort by the MST to put pressure on the government of leftwing President Luiz Inàcio Lula da Silva to distribute land within the next six months to at least 90 000 families who have

Crop production in Brazil.

been squatting in different parts of the country since 2003, many of them camping by the roadside.

The landless movement has carried out land occupations for the past 25 years 'calling for fulfilment of the law,' Cutis told IPS. It also seeks better living conditions for another 45 000 families 'who have been resettled on paper only,' and are 'suffering hardship' because they are still waiting for resources for housing, infrastructure and production, he said.

People in the Terra Libre settlement are all too familiar with this situation. The state Institute for Agrarian Reform (INCRA) has not legalised their ownership of the land where they have lived 'on a temporary basis' for over a decade because of red tape and endless battles over inheritance and compensation for expropriation in the courts.

Terra Libre occupies 460 hectares of an old estate, which was deemed unproductive according to official criteria set out in the law on agrarian reform, and which owed its workers the equivalent of one million dollars before it was taken over by the MST.

The problem is that until they have legal title to the land, the settlers do not have access to credits and tools from INCRA. But according to the MST, many families to whom the government has already granted title deeds have not yet received this assistance.

'It's hard to convince some farmers to put effort and work into a plot of land that they might be forced to leave tomorrow,' Cutis said.'

Land reform in Brazil

The distribution of land in terms of ownership has been a divisive issue since the colonial era. Then the monarchy rewarded those in special favour with huge tracts of land, leaving a legacy of highly concentrated ownership. For example, 44% of all arable land in Brazil is owned by just 1% of the nation's farmers, while 15 million peasants own little or no land. Many of these landless people are impoverished, roving migrants who have lost their jobs as agricultural labourers due to the spread of mechanisation in virtually all types of agriculture.

At least a partial solution to the problem is land reform. This involves breaking up large estates and redistributing land to the rural landless. Although successive governments have vowed to tackle the problem, progress has been limited due to the economic and political power of the big *fazenda* or farm-owners. The latter have not been slow to use aggressive tactics, legal or otherwise, to evict squatters and delay expropriation.

In the mid-1990s land reform clearly emerged as Brazil's leading social problem, highlighted by a number of widely publicised squatter invasions. Such land occupations have occurred in both remote regions and established, prosperous farmlands in the South and South-east. Each year, in April the Landless Rural Workers' Movement (known as the MST) organises a series of land invasions, takeovers of buildings and other protests. The purpose is twofold: (a) to keep the issue high on the national political agenda, and (b) to commemorate the killing eleven years ago of 19 landless protestors by police in the state of Para.

Activities

1 Produce a graph to show selected data from Table 3 (page 100).
2 Describe the data presented in Figure 9 (page 100).
3 Comment on the education gap between non-indigenous and indigenous peoples shown in Table 4 (page 100).
4 Describe and attempt to explain the differences in average monthly income shown in Figure 10 (page 101).
5 Write a 100-word summary on land reform in Brazil referring to the case study and text.

Key terms

Gini coefficient a statistical technique used to show the extent of income inequality in a country. With values between 0 and 1, a low value indicates a more equal income distribution while a high value means more unequal income distribution.

Cumulative causation the process whereby a significant increase in economic growth can lead to even more growth as more money circulates in the economy.

Economic core region the most highly developed region in a country with advanced systems of infrastructure and high levels of investment resulting in high average income.

Periphery the parts of a country outside the economic core region. The level of economic development in the periphery is significantly below that of the core.

Slum a heavily populated urban area characterised by substandard housing and squalor.

Urbanisation of poverty the gradual shift of global poverty from rural to urban areas with increasing urbanisation.

Indigenous population people descending from the original ethnic groups(s) to populate a country. Other ethnic groups migrating to that country at a later period of time may come to dominate the indigenous population in various ways.

Privatisation the sale of state-owned assets to the private sector.

Websites

www.wider.unu.edu
World Institute for Development
Economics Research of the UN University
(UNU-WIDER)

http://epp.eurostat.ec.europa.eu
European Commission Eurostat

www.globalpolicy.org
Global Policy Forum

www.carnegieendowment.org
Carnegie Endowment for International Peace

Review

Examination-style questions

1 Refer to Table 5.

a Define GDP.

b Describe the changes that have occurred in the relationship between GDP and population for the four regions of China.

c Discuss the possible reasons for such changes.

	1980		1990		2000		2005	
	GDP	**Population**	**GDP**	**Population**	**GDP**	**Population**	**GDP**	**Population**
Eastern	43.8	33.9	45.9	34.1	53.5	35.1	55.6	35.8
Central	22.3	28.3	21.8	28.5	19.2	28.1	18.8	27.5
Western	20.2	28.7	20.3	28.5	17.3	28.3	16.9	28.2
North-eastern	13.7	9.1	11.9	8.8	9.9	8.6	8.7	8.4

Table 5 *GDP by region in China (% share).*

2 Refer to Figure 11.

a What is the Lorenz curve designed to show?

b How did income inequality in Brazil change between 1996 and 2005?

c Suggest possible reasons for the change in income inequality you have identified.

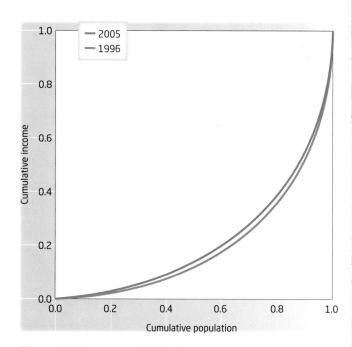

Figure 11 *Lorenz curve for Brazil.*

07 Disparities and change

Statue of Chinggis Khan, north of Ulaanbaatar, Mongolia. Chinggis Khan ruled the Mongol Empire which once occupied a huge part of Asia and Europe. Today Mongolia is a relatively poor country with a population of only 2.8 million.

The theories used to explain the global development gap

Modernisation theory: the stages of development

In 1960, the American economist W.W. Rostow recognised five stages of economic development (Figure 1). The richest countries were in the final stage, having passed through all or most of the previous stages. Countries at all five stages could be recognised in the modern world. Rostow concluded that the development gap was explained by the fact that countries were at different stages of the model. The model was based on the economic history of over a dozen European countries. Like all models it is a simplification of reality.

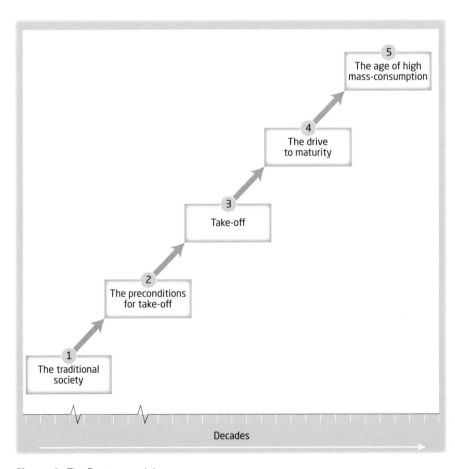

Figure 1 *The Rostow model.*

The crucial part of Rostow's model is the 'take-off' stage, the decade or two when economy and society are transformed in such a way that thereafter a steady rate of growth can be sustained. Take-off is launched by an initial stimulus and is characterised by:

- a rise in the rate of productive investment to over 10% of national income
- the development of one or more substantial manufacturing sectors with a high rate of growth
- the emergence of administrative systems that encourage development.

In reality, take-off has proved very difficult to achieve in many countries.

Rostow argued that capitalism was fundamental to economic development. In his view a communist system of government stifled enterprise. **Modernisation theory** held sway in the 1950s and early 1960s when there was general optimism about narrowing the development gap. But as the painfully slow progress became more and more obvious, criticism of modernisation theory grew.

Dependency theory

The apparent failure of the capitalist Rostow model resulted for a while in the ascendancy of Marxist and neo-Marxist ideas on the development gap. Andre Gunder Frank, a Chicago-trained economist, popularised many of these ideas in 1966 with his 'development of underdevelopment theory' which is generally referred to as **dependency theory**. Frank used a historical approach to argue that:

- poverty in the developing world arose through the spread of capitalism and that many countries had been prosperous before the arrival of European colonists
- the process of absorption into the capitalist system sowed the seeds of underdevelopment
- the development of the rich world was achieved by exploiting the raw materials of the developing world
- developing countries became even more dependent on the rich countries by farming export crops where once local food crops prevailed
- the stronger the links to the developed world the worse the level of development.

Frank used a simple model (Figure 2) to explain how the 'metropolis' (the developed world) exploited the 'periphery' (the developing world). The model shows a chain of exploitation which begins with small towns in the periphery expropriating surplus from the surrounding

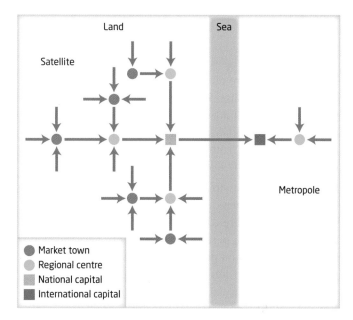

Figure 2 *The Frank model.*

rural areas. This process of exploitation works its way up the urban hierarchy in the periphery until, finally, the largest settlements are exploited by cities in the 'metropolis'. The intensity of poverty increases with the number of stages down the chain of exploitation.

Frank and others saw socialist systems of government as providing a better basis than capitalism for a fairer society, both between countries and within countries.

The Houses of Parliament, London. The UK is part of the world's economic core.

World system (core/periphery) theory

New approaches are often stimulated by the shortcomings of previous theorising. **World system theory** was popularised in the mid-1970s by Immanuel Wallerstein. It asserts that a capitalist world economy has been in existence since the 16th century. Before this, global interdependence did not exist.

From then on a growing number of previously more or less isolated societies were brought into the capitalist system. A small number of core countries transformed a much larger external area into a periphery. A semi-periphery developed between the core and periphery (Figure 3). Within the world system a division of labour operated. The core countries were manufacturers and the peripheral countries were agricultural and other raw material producers. The terms of trade were heavily skewed in favour of the core. The process of underdevelopment started with the incorporation of an external area into the world system.

The semi-periphery forms the most dynamic part of the system. The rising semi-peripheries of the present, the NICs, are competing to varying degrees for core status. Thus the world system approach has a degree of optimism lacking in dependency theory, recognising that some countries can escape from the state of underdevelopment.

Activities

1   Describe the stages of development shown in Figure 1 (page 106).
2   With reference to Figure 2 (page 107), briefly explain dependency theory.
3   With the help of Figure 3, write a bullet-point summary of world system theory.

Life expectancy: patterns and trends

The decline in levels of mortality and the increase in life expectancy have been the most important rewards of economic and social development. On a global scale, 75% of the total improvement in longevity has been achieved in the 20th century and the early years of the 21st century. In 1900 the world average life expectancy is estimated to have been about 30 years but by 1950–55 it had risen to 46 years. By 1980–85 it had reached a fraction under 60 years.

Table 1 shows current global variations in life expectancy. The world average of 69 years shows a four-year gap between males and females in favour of the latter. The difference between the more developed world and the less developed world is ten years. In the more developed world the male–female gap is seven years compared with three years in the less developed world.

World region	Total	Male	Female
World	69	67	71
Developed countries	77	74	81
Developing countries	67	65	68
Africa	55	53	56
North America	78	75	80
Latin America/Caribbean	73	70	76
Asia	69	68	71
Europe	76	72	80
Oceania	76	74	78

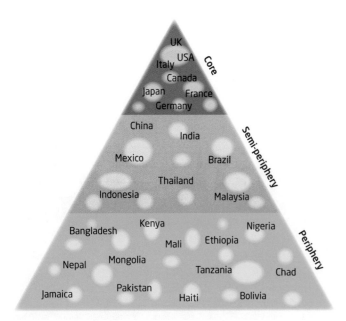

Figure 3 *Examples of countries in the global core, semi-periphery and periphery.*

Table 1 *Global variations in life expectancy, 2009.*

Highest life expectancy		Lowest life expectancy	
Japan	83	Sierra Leone	48
Italy	82	Rwanda	48
Switzerland	82	Mali	48
Hong Kong	82	Nigeria	47
Macao	82	Chad	47
San Marino	82	Guinea-Bissau	46
Canada	81	Malawi	46
Israel	81	Swaziland	46
Singapore	81	Angola	46
Iceland	81	Central African Rep.	45
Sweden	81	Afghanistan	44
Australia	81	Zambia	43
Norway	81	Mozambique	43
Spain	81	Zimbabwe	41
France	81	Lesotho	40

Table 2 *Countries with the highest and lowest life expectancies, 2009.*

In terms of continental areas, North America (the USA and Canada) records the highest figure of 78 years while Africa has by far the lowest life expectancy at 55 years. Africa, along with Asia, also has the smallest male–female life expectancy difference at only three years.

Table 2 shows the individual countries that have an average life expectancy of 81 years or more. Japan leads the way followed by Italy, Switzerland, Hong Kong, Macao and San Marino. The table also shows the countries with the lowest life expectancies. Lesotho and Zimbabwe are at the bottom of the list with a life expectancy of only 40 and 41 years respectively. Apart from Afghanistan, all the lowest life expectancy countries in Table 2 are in Sub-Saharan Africa, the poorest region in the world.

Global convergence

Rates of **life expectancy at birth** have converged significantly between rich and poor countries during the last 50 years or so, in spite of a widening wealth gap. These increases in life expectancy have to a certain extent offset the widening disparity between per capita incomes in developed and developing countries. However,

it must not be forgotten that the ravages of AIDS in particular have caused recent decreases in life expectancy in some countries in Sub-Saharan Africa. United Nations projections show that the life expectancy gap between rich and poor countries will continue to narrow in the future.

According to the World Health Organization (WHO), life expectancy increased by an average of 23 years between 1960 and 2000 in the poorest 50% of countries, but only by 9 years in the richest 50%. East Asia and the Pacific recorded the greatest increase during this period, up from 42 to 71 years. In contrast the lowest increase was in North America where life expectancy rose from 70 to 77 years.

Influences on life expectancy

- The incidence of disease – certain diseases are common in some areas but not others. For example, diseases that are big killers in many developing countries (cholera, typhoid, tuberculosis, malaria, measles) are rare in developed countries. In some developing countries a large number of diseases can take a huge toll on human life.
- Physical environmental conditions – natural hazards such as tsunamis, floods, earthquakes and volcanic eruptions affect some parts of the world but not others.
- Human environmental conditions – factors such as the quality of housing, the extent of atmospheric pollution, the dangers of road traffic and health and safety conditions at work all have an impact on people's lives.
- Personal lifestyle – smoking, alcohol consumption, obesity, lack of exercise and other factors that people have control over can have a big impact on the number of years that people live.

Who uses life expectancy figures?

It is important for international and national government agencies to know about variations in life expectancy as this is a key measure of inequality. It helps development programmes to target those in most need. Insurance companies use life expectancy data to set their premiums (the cost of insurance to an individual), and they use life expectancy data to produce an actuarial chart which determines how many years a potential client could be expected to live. Banks take life expectancy into account when considering loan applications. Pension plans may also be based on life expectancy data.

Case study

Life expectancy in Russia

Russia is one of the few developed countries where life expectancy has fallen in recent years. Russia's average of 68 years is fifteen years behind that of Japan. Mortality from non-communicable diseases is the main cause of death, being three to five times higher than average rates in the EU.

In Russia heart diseases account for 52% of all deaths each year. Death rates from road traffic injuries, cancer, homicide and suicide are all high and well above the EU average. Mortality for Russian men (life expectancy 61 years) is much higher than in other countries with similar per capita income levels. The situation is different for women (life expectancy 74 years), who live about thirteen years longer than men in Russia.

Russian orthodox church in Moscow.

Research idea

Find out how life expectancy has changed in the country in which you live. What do you think are the main reasons for these changes?

Income: patterns and trends

The first detailed calculations of global income inequality were done in the 1980s. Since then there has been much debate among academics about the ways in which income inequality should be calculated. This is because there are a number of things to consider. The difference in the cost of living between countries is one such factor. As a result there has been some discrepancy in the conclusions of various studies on income inequality. It is important for you to be aware of this because if you delve into this topic in more detail you may come across tables and graphs where the data is a little different from that presented in this section.

Live poultry for sale in a food market in Morocco. A reasonable income is required for a healthy diet.

Figure 4, from the World Development Report 2009, uses the coefficient of variation of GDP per capita to show that the global GDP per capita gap:

- widened (diverged) between 1950 and 1970 and
- narrowed (converged) from 1970 to 2005.

The coefficient of variation is the ratio of the standard deviation to the mean. However, it is important to understand that the convergence in the post-1970 period shown in Figure 4 was driven in particular by the increasingly strong performance of Asian economies – the 'Asian tigers' of South Korea, Taiwan, Singapore and Hong Kong initially, and more recently by the booming economies of China and India. It is the large number of people in China and India in particular that influences the global picture. GDP per capita in China grew at 8.4% a year between 1990 and 2005.

Other parts of the developing world have been left out of this process and thus the development gap for these countries has widened rather than narrowed. Figure 5 shows the wide variation in growth rates of GDP per capita between 1960 and 2006 for regions in the developing world. The four subdivisions of Africa had the slowest growth rates by far. Total GDP in the Central African region increased threefold between 1960 and 2006 compared with north-east Asia's thirty-fold increase. However, with population growth outpacing economic growth, per capita incomes in Central Africa fell by 8%.

Incomes in the poorest countries of the world declined by 5% during the 1990s. These countries are populated by the 'bottom billion' of the world's population – nations that are mostly landlocked, with many in Africa.

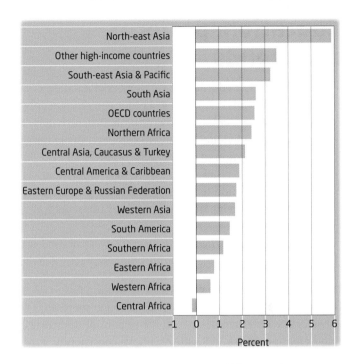

Figure 5 *Average annual growth rates of GDP per capita, 1960–2006.*

Hoh Indian Reservation, Washington, USA. Incomes on Indian reservations are well below the US national average.

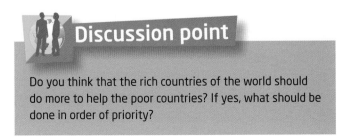

Discussion point

Do you think that the rich countries of the world should do more to help the poor countries? If yes, what should be done in order of priority?

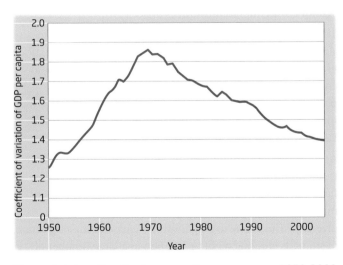

Figure 4 *Internationally: divergence, then convergence, 1950–2000.*

Education: patterns and trends

Providing higher education to all sectors of a nation's population means confronting social inequalities deeply rooted in history, culture and economic structure that influence an individual's ability to compete. Geography, unequal distribution of wealth and resources all contribute to the disadvantage of certain population groups. Participation tends to be below national average for populations living in remote or rural areas and for indigenous groups.

Trends in Global Higher Education: Tracking an Academic Revolution, Executive Summary, page v, 2009.

Figure 6 shows that on a global scale education has become more equal since the 1980s, although there are considerable differences between the regions of the world. Sub-Saharan Africa and South Asia have consistently been in the bottom three regions since 1960 although moderate improvements have been made in the timeframe illustrated by the graph. In contrast, the Middle East and North Africa, which recorded the lowest figure in 1960, has recorded a much faster improvement. However,

Study in Russia poster. Increasing the education and skills of a population is an important part of the development process.

a substantial gap still exists between the high-income countries and the other regional groups shown in Figure 6.

On average, low-income countries devote almost half their total education spending on primary education. This falls to about a quarter in high-income countries where higher proportions of total education spending go towards the secondary and tertiary sectors. As development progresses it is likely that the pattern of educational spending of low-income countries will gradually move towards that of more affluent nations.

Much has been done to improve the education of girls in developing countries. However, although the gender gap in education has narrowed in most countries, girls in the developing world are often seen as the last priority in a family to go to school and the first to be taken out of school if difficult circumstances arise.

The number of years of schooling generally has a very significant impact on the quality of life of the individual and the economic development of the communities and countries in which they live. For example, in the USA people without a college certificate or degree are twice as likely to live in poverty as those with such qualifications. Data for other countries show a similar pattern.

According to The United Nations Educational, Scientific and Cultural Organisation (UNESCO), 'An academic revolution has taken place in higher education in the past half century marked by transformations unprecedented in scope and diversity.' This is due to a significant increase in the proportion of students entering higher education in a large number of countries in every world region. However, the gap between the richest and poorest countries remains extremely wide.

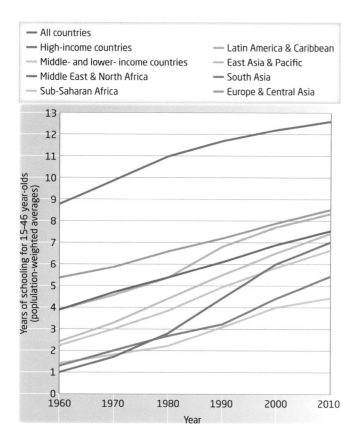

Figure 6 *Education has become more equal since the 1980s.*

Figure 7 shows tertiary enrolment by geographical region for 2000 and 2007. Globally, the percentage of young people in the relevant age cohort enrolled in tertiary education rose from 19% in 2000 to 26% in 2007. While every world region showed an increase during this period, the rate of change varied widely.

The terms 'core' and 'periphery' can be applied to the academic world in much the same way as they can to the economic world. The strongest universities which have a long-standing reputation for research prowess and excellent teaching are at the core or centre of global higher education. In contrast, African universities are very much at the periphery. They barely register on global institutional rankings and produce a minute percentage of the world's research output.

Activities

1 To what extent has life expectancy converged between the developed and developing worlds?
2 Describe the life expectancy data presented in Table 1 (page 108).
3 Comment on the gap between the highest and lowest life expectancy countries shown in Table 2 (page 109).
4 Look at Figures 4 and 5 (page 111). How is it that global income convergence has occurred since 1970 when the development gap for some world regions has widened?
5 Summarise the trends relating to education shown in Figure 6.
6 Describe the global variations in tertiary education illustrated in Figure 7.

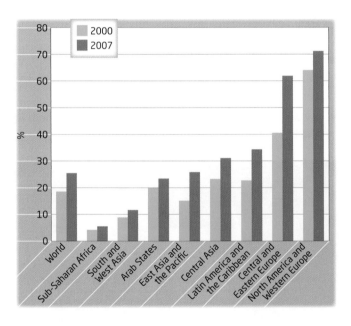

Figure 7 *Tertiary gross enrolment ratio by geographical region, 2000 and 2007.*

The last few decades have witnessed many more students travelling abroad to study. This is a very visible aspect of globalisation. The result of this increasing student mobility means that more than 2.5 million students are now studying outside their home countries. This figure is predicted to rise to 7 million by 2020.

Theory of Knowledge

Over time the importance of education to all other aspects of development has been increasingly recognised. The high value of education in the development process operates at individual, community, regional and national scales. Do those receiving high value education such as IBDP students, have an obligation to give something in return to those less previleged?

The Millennium Development Goals

Looking ahead to 2015 and beyond, there is no question that we can achieve the overarching goal: we can put an end to poverty. We know what to do. But it requires an unswerving, collective, long-term effort.

United Nations Secretary-General Ban Ki-moon, 2008

For the first time in history, global economic prosperity, brought on by continuing scientific and technological progress and the self-reinforcing accumulation of wealth, has placed the world within reach of eliminating extreme poverty altogether.

J.D. Sachs, United Nations Millennium Project

The Millennium Development Goals (MDGs), established in 2000 by international agreement, comprise probably the most significant major attempt to defeat poverty ever undertaken. The UN set out MDGs to reduce global poverty substantially by 2015. They are viewed as basic human rights – the rights of every person on Earth to health, education, shelter and security. Measurement of progress is based on 1990 figures. All 191 UN member states have pledged to meet these goals by 2015. The eight MDGs are as follows:

1 Eradicate extreme poverty and hunger

Targets:

- Halve, between 1990 and 2015, the proportion of people whose income is less than $1 a day.
- Achieve full and productive employment and decent work for all, including women and young people.
- Halve, between 1990 and 2015, the proportion of people who suffer from hunger.

2 Achieve universal primary education

Target:

- Ensure that, by 2015, children everywhere, boys and girls alike, will be able to complete a full course of primary schooling.

3 Promote gender equality and empower women

Target:

- Eliminate gender disparity in primary and secondary education, preferably by 2005, and in all levels of education no later than 2015.

4 Reduce child mortality

Target:

- Reduce by two-thirds, between 1990 and 2015, the under-five mortality rate.

5 Improve maternal health

Targets:

- Reduce by three-quarters, between 1990 and 2015, the maternal mortality ratio.
- Achieve, by 2015, universal access to reproductive health.

6 Combat HIV/AIDS, malaria and other diseases

Targets:

- Have halted by 2015 and begun to reverse the spread of HIV/AIDS.
- Achieve, by 2010, universal access to treatment for HIV/AIDS for all those who need it.
- Have halted by 2015 and begun to reverse the incidence of malaria and other major diseases.

7 Ensure environmental sustainability

Targets:

- Integrate the principles of sustainable development into country policies and programmes and reverse the loss of environmental resources.
- Reduce biodiversity loss, achieving by 2010 a significant reduction in the rate of loss.
- Halve, by 2015, the proportion of the population without sustainable access to safe drinking water and basic sanitation.
- By 2020, to have achieved a significant improvement in the lives of at least 100 million slum dwellers.

Women collecting water from a well in Gambia.

8 Develop a global partnership for development

Targets:

- Address the special needs of the least developed countries, landlocked countries and small island developing states.
- Develop further an open, rule-based, predictable, non-discriminatory trading and financial system.
- Deal comprehensively with developing countries' debt.
- In cooperation with the private sector, make available the benefits of new technologies, especially information and communication.

Geographical skills

Study the eight MDGs. Which, in your opinion, are the four most important MDGs? Justify your decisions.

The Millennium Development Goals Report 2009

This major report, more than halfway to the 2015 deadline to achieve the MDGs, noted that considerable advances in the battle against poverty and hunger had begun to slow or even reverse. This was largely as a result of the global economic and food crises. The UN Secretary-General advised that overall progress has been too slow to meet most targets by 2015.

Progress towards the MDGs has been threatened by:

- slow or even negative economic growth
- diminished resources
- fewer trade opportunities for developing countries
- possible reductions in aid from donor nations
- the increasingly apparent effects of climate change.

Poverty reduction

Figure 8 shows the proportion of people living on less than $1.25 a day in 1990, 1999 and 2005. This is the level for **extreme poverty** set by the UN. Worldwide, the

number of people in this income category fell from 1.8 billion in 1990 to 1.4 billion in 2005. As a result the total number of people considered extremely poor fell from almost a half of the world's population in 1990 to slightly more than a quarter in 2005. The most significant fall, in Eastern Asia, was largely due to rapid economic growth in China. However, the number of people in extreme poverty in 2009 is expected to be 55–90 million higher than anticipated before the global economic crisis.

Projections suggest that overall poverty rates will still fall but at a much slower rate than before the global economic crisis. For some countries this could be the difference between reaching or not reaching their poverty reduction target. In Sub-Saharan Africa and Southern Asia, both the number of poor and the poverty rate are expected to increase further in some of the most vulnerable and low-growth economies.

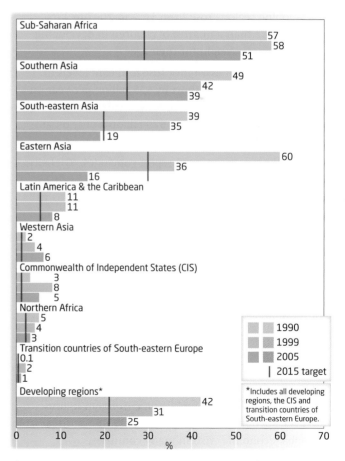

Figure 8 *The number of people living on less than $1.25 a day, 1990, 1999 and 2005.*

Cave dwellings in North Africa.

Higher food prices meant that progress in the eradication of hunger was reversed in 2008. The prevalence of hunger in developing regions rose from 16% in 2007 to 17% in 2008. More than a quarter of children in developing regions are underweight for their age.

While development assistance rose to record levels in 2008, donors are falling short by $35 billion per year on the 2005 pledge on annual aid flows made by the Group of Eight in Gleneagles, and by $20 billion a year on aid to Africa.

In terms of poverty the 2009 report concludes: 'Globally, the target of reducing the poverty rate by half by 2015 seems likely to be achieved. However, some regions will fall short, and as many as 1 billion people are likely to remain in extreme poverty by the target date.'

Education

Globally, enrolment in primary education increased from 83% in 2000 to 88% in 2007. Most of this progress was in the worst-performing regions. In Sub-Saharan Africa and Southern Asia, enrolment rose by 15% and 11% respectively during this time period (Figure 9). In many countries, increases in national spending on education have had a considerable impact on enrolment figures. However, such increases in spending are under threat from the global economic crisis in many countries.

Globally, 77 million children were denied the right to education in 2007. Almost half of these children live in Sub-Saharan Africa. Nearly half of the children currently out of school have never had any contact with formal education. There are concerns that the large number of

out-of-school children will have a clear negative impact on other MDGs.

While the 2009 report welcomes the improvements made, it concludes: 'Globally, numbers of out-of-school children are dropping too slowly and too unevenly for the target to be reached by 2015.'

The **gender gap in education** is also an important MDG. Two out of three countries have achieved gender parity at the primary level. However, of the 113 countries that failed to achieve gender parity in primary and secondary enrolment combined by the target date of 2005, only 18 are likely to achieve the goal by 2015. Globally, girls account for 55% of the out-of-school population. Sub-Saharan Africa, Oceania and Western Asia have the largest gender gaps in primary enrolment.

Figure 10 shows the gender gap for secondary school enrolment. The gap is wider at secondary level than at primary level, with many more countries falling behind. The gap is especially wide in countries where overall enrolment is low. In Sub-Saharan Africa the ratio of girls' to boys' enrolment in secondary education fell from 82 in 1999 to 79 in 2007. There were also decreases in Oceania and the Commonwealth of Independent States (CIS).

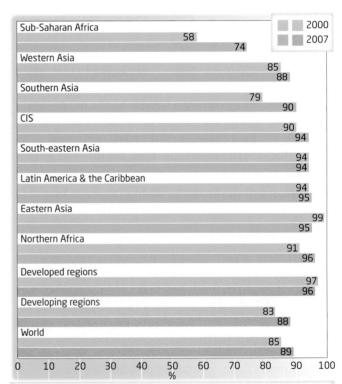

The number of pupils of the theoretical school age for primary education enrolled either in primary or secondary school, expressed as a percentage of the total population in that age group.
Note: Data for Oceania are not available.

Figure 9 *Enrolment in primary education by world region, 2000 and 2007.*

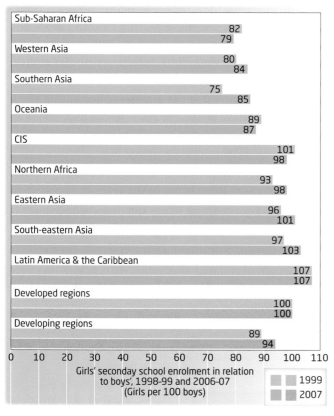

Figure 10 *The gender gap in secondary school enrolment, 1999 and 2007.*

At higher levels of education a very different situation exists. The ratio of enrolment of girls to boys globally at the tertiary level rose from 96 in 1999 to 108 in 2007. However, there are substantial differences around the world. There is a large gap in favour of girls in the developed regions, the CIS, Latin America and the Caribbean, and South-eastern Asia. The gap in favour of girls is smaller in Northern Africa where the ratio changed from 68 in 1999 to 104 in 2007. In all other regions the ratio favours boys. In Sub-Saharan Africa there was actually a decline in the ratio from 69 in 1999 to 67 in 2007.

Health

Infant and maternal mortality

Significant improvements have been made in child mortality, with the number of worldwide deaths of children under 5 falling steadily from 12.6 million in 1990 to 9 million in 2007. For developing regions as a whole the child mortality rate fell from 103 in 1990 to 74 in 2007 (Figure 11). However, in many countries, particularly in Sub-Saharan Africa and Southern Asia, little progress has

been made. In Sub-Saharan Africa the actual number of under-5 deaths rose from 4.2 million in 1990 to 4.6 million in 2007. Sub-Saharan Africa now accounts for half of all under-5 deaths around the world.

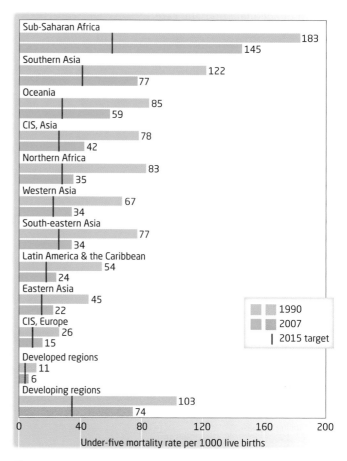

Figure 11 *Under-5 mortality, 1990 and 2007.*

In some developing regions there have been major improvements in several key child-survival interventions that should lead to further significant falls in child mortality. These include:

- vitamin A supplementation
- the use of insecticide-treated bed nets
- exclusive breastfeeding and immunisation.

Maternal mortality is among the health indicators that show the greatest gap between developed and developing countries (Figure 12). In 2005 the **maternal mortality rate** in developed regions was 9 per 100,000 live births compared with 450 in developing regions. Half of all maternal deaths are in Sub-Saharan Africa and another third in Southern Asia. These two regions combined account for 85% of all maternal deaths. Figure 12 (page 118) shows how far these and other regions need to progress to meet their 2015 targets.

Obstetric complications, including post-partum haemorrhage, infections, eclampsia, prolonged or obstructed labour, and complications of unsafe abortion, account for the majority of maternal deaths. Fewer than half of pregnant women in developing countries have the benefit of adequate prenatal care.

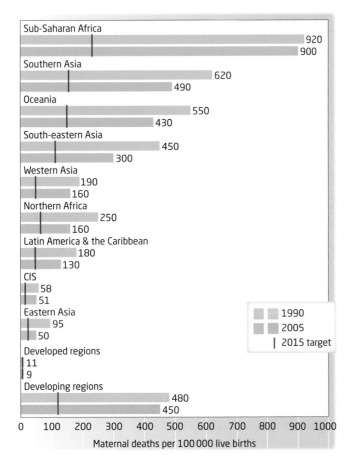

Figure 12 *Maternal deaths, 1990 and 2005.*

HIV/AIDS

Figure 13 shows that the number of people newly infected with **HIV** peaked in 1996 and has since fallen to 2.7 million in 2007. This trend is due to a fall in the number of new infections in some countries in Asia, Latin America

and Sub-Saharan Africa. However, infection rates continue to increase in other regions, especially Eastern Europe and Central Asia. In these last two regions, HIV prevalence has almost doubled since 2001. Infection with HIV is the underlying cause of **AIDS**.

Figure 13 also shows that the number of deaths due to AIDS seems to have peaked in 2005, falling to 2 million in 2007. In 2007 an estimated 33 million people were living with HIV. The 2009 report also noted that:

- two-thirds of those living with HIV are in Sub-Saharan Africa, most of them being women
- accurate knowledge of HIV is still unacceptably low
- wider access to treatment has contributed to the first decline in AIDS deaths since the epidemic began
- the plight of children affected by AIDS is inspiring new approaches directed to children, their families and their communities.

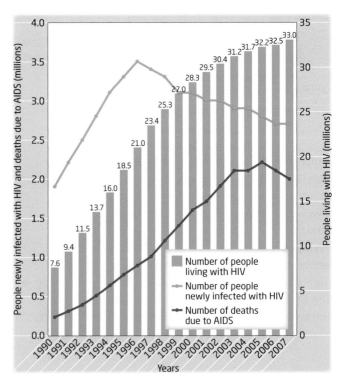

Figure 13 *HIV and AIDS, 1990–2007.*

World AIDS Day is recognised all over the world.

Malaria

Nearly a million people died of malaria in 2006. Around 95% of these deaths occurred in Sub-Saharan Africa and the great majority were children under 5. However, significant progress has been made in recent years with new objectives set out in the 2008 Roll Back Malaria Global Action Plan. International funding for malaria control has risen from $250 million in 2004 to over $1 billion in 2008. Among other things this has allowed a major increase in the procurement of artemisinin-based combination therapies since 2004. However, many children, particularly in Africa, are still using less effective medicines.

Activities

1 Refer to Figure 8 (page 115).
   a What progress has been made since 1990 in the fight against poverty?
   b What remains to be done to achieve this MDG?
2 With reference to Figure 9 (page 116), assess the progress made in achieving universal primary education.
3 Comment on the gender gap in secondary school enrolment shown in Figure 10 (page 117).
4 What progress has been made in reducing under-5 mortality since 1990 and what remains to be done to achieve the MDG in this respect?
5 Describe the data on maternal deaths shown in Figure 12 (page 118). How likely is it that the world will achieve the 2015 target?
6 Produce a summary of the data illustrated in Figure 13 (page 118).

Research idea

Look at the Millennium Goals Report 2009 (www.un.org/millenniumgoals) to assess progress on the other millennium goals not covered in this section.

Key terms

Modernisation theory a deterministic approach based on the economic history of a number of developed countries. Distinct economic and social changes are required for a country to move from one stage to another.

Dependency theory blames the relative underdevelopment of the developing world on exploitation by the developed world, first through colonialism and then by the various elements of neo-colonialism.

World system theory based on the history of the capitalist world economy. Countries fall into three economic levels, and can move from one level to another if their contribution to the world economy changes.

Life expectancy at birth the average number of years that a newborn baby is expected to live if the age-specific mortality rates effective at the year of birth apply throughout their lifetime.

Extreme poverty the most severe state of poverty with an inability to meet basic needs. It is now defined as living on less than $1.25 per day.

Gender gap in education girls' school enrolment in relation to boys (girls per 100 boys).

Maternal mortality rate the annual number of deaths of women from pregnancy-related causes per 100 000 live births.

HIV human immunodeficiency virus. The underlying cause of AIDS is infection with HIV-1 or HIV-2.

AIDS acquired immune deficiency syndrome.

Websites

www.worlded.org
World Education

www.uis.unesco.org
UNESCO Institute for Statistics

www.un.org/millenniumgoals/pdf/MDG_Report_2009_ENG.pdf
UN Millennium Goals Report 2009

www.unaids.org
Joint UN Programme on HIV/AIDS

Review

Examination-style questions

1 Refer to Figure 14.

a What trend is the graph attempting to show?

b Describe the variations by world region from 1950 to 2001.

c Discuss the main reasons for the variations you have described.

2 Refer to Figure 15.

a Define HIV.

b Describe the patterns and trends shown in Figure 15.

c Suggest reasons for the variations between the different world regions.

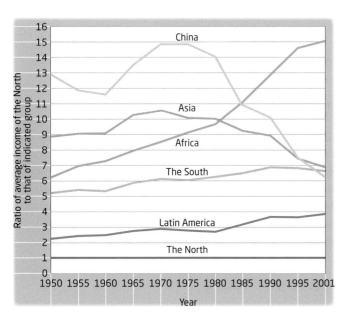

Figure 14 *Ratio of average income of the North to different groupings of countries.*

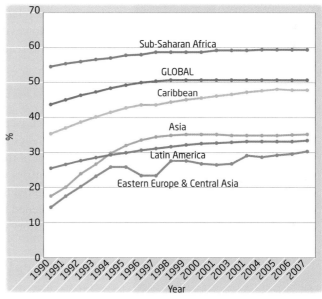

Figure 15 *Female adults (15+ years) living with HIV, 1990–2007.*

08 Reducing disparities

A giant banner for Expo 2010, Shanghai, China. The export of large volumes of goods has been a major factor in China's economic development.

The theories and approaches that underpin attempts to reduce the development gap

Public, private and voluntary organisations often have different philosophies about narrowing the development gap. It is thus not surprising that the initiatives they develop reflect these philosophies. In the early decades after the Second World War there was general optimism that the development gap could be narrowed relatively quickly. Theory at the time reflected this fairly simplistic approach. However, it did not take too long for governments and international institutions to realise that the path to development was a more complex issue.

Modernisation theory

This approach (see also page 106), which was very influential in the late 1950s and 1960s, relies heavily on the philosophy of the free market and the historical development of the developed countries. It postulated that lack of development in poor countries was mainly down to pre-modern socio-economic structures. These prohibited the adoption of efficient modes of production. Thus developing countries needed to make significant internal changes in order to follow the economic history of the industrialised nations.

Neo-liberal economic theory

This approach developed in the 1980s and 1990s as the process of globalisation intensified. It advocated abolishing tariff barriers which should encourage international trade. Unrestricted markets would lead to development through trade. Privatisation, deregulation and cutting public expenditure are important elements of neo-liberalism. In the UK Margaret Thatcher, and in the USA Ronald Reagan, were seen as the architects of this approach. At the time the terms 'Thatcherism' and 'Reaganomics' were commonplace. This approach has been at the heart of the actions of the World Bank, the International Monetary Fund (IMF) and the World Trade Organization (WTO).

Supporters of neo-liberalism point to the emergence of successive generations of newly industrialised countries as proof of the success of the free market in generating development. They argue that countries which can attract significant **foreign direct investment** (FDI) are able to widen their range of economic activities and increase their volumes of trade. FDI sets off a chain of cumulative causation (see also page 94) whereby a phase of economic growth generates even more growth in the future. This process begins in the economic core region of a country. Eventually economic growth should 'spread' to spatially selected areas in the periphery.

Marxist and populist approaches

Critics of free market approaches argue that only a relatively small number of developing countries have evolved into NICs. For most developing countries the development gap has widened rather than narrowed. They argue that the operation of the free market can often have devastating consequences for the fragile economies of poor countries. Internal policies require a certain level of government intervention to ensure a fairer distribution of wealth within countries, while external policies lobby international bodies to change the world's financial and trading systems to try to distribute the benefits of globalisation in a more equitable way.

The Marxist approach has historically been based on a very high degree of central planning (a top-down approach). In contrast, the populist approach is based on participatory bottom-up planning. So-called 'grassroots action' is an important element of 'bottom-up' planning. Such ideas began on the fringes of **non-governmental organisations** (NGOs). Both the Marxist and populist approaches are left-wing, but they view development from a different perspective.

Generally NGOs adopt a pragmatic approach in an effort to maximise the development impact of the funding available to them. They emphasise the local and the small-scale, putting significant emphasis on sustainability. Figure 1 shows WaterAid's approach to development.

Working in the informal sector.

Geographical skills

Draw up a table to compare the main aspects of (a) modernisation theory (b) neoliberal theory (c) Marxist approaches and (d) populist approaches to development.

Activities

1   Briefly explain in your own words WaterAid's approach to development shown in Figure 1.
2   Define (a) foreign direct investment and (b) resource nationalisation (page 124).

Research idea

Look at the *Bolivia Times* website (www.boliviatimes.com) for information on some of the latest economic issues concerning Bolivia.

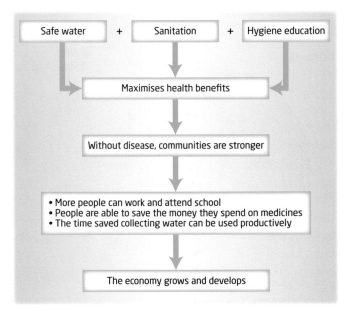

Figure 1 *WaterAid's approach to development.*

Case study

Bolivia is an example of a country challenging the free market philosophy. Bolivia has recently introduced a **resource nationalisation** policy. Along with Cuba and Venezuela it forms the so-called 'radical block' of nations in Latin America which are concerned about US economic power in the region and the exploitative action of TNCs in general.

In May 2006 President Morales of Bolivia nationalised the country's gas and oil industry. Bolivia has the second largest natural gas reserves in Latin America, but produces only a small amount of oil for domestic use. The foreign energy companies were told they had six months to sign new operating contracts or leave the country. All signed new contracts, which should result in higher revenues for the government. Now, all foreign energy companies have to deliver all their production to the state-run YPFB for distribution and processing. Overall, Bolivia has taken control of 82% of the oil and gas in the country, leaving the remainder to foreign companies.

Bolivia is adopting a socialist model of regional commerce and cooperation as opposed to what it sees as 'US-backed free trade'. Bolivia views the concept of the free trade area of the Americas as an attempt by the USA to 'annex' Latin America. The government is trying to attract foreign investment while at the same time giving the state a larger role in managing the economy.

The role of trade and investment in development

Trade and investment play a key role in the development gap and global wealth distribution. Investment in a country is the key to it increasing its trade. Some developing countries have increased their trade substantially. These countries have attracted the bulk of foreign direct investment. Such low-income countries as China, Brazil, India and Mexico, which have been able to embrace globalisation, have increased their trade-to-GDP ratios significantly. Figure 2 shows the regional share of world merchandise trade for 2005.

The emergence of newly industrialised countries has been a key element in the process of globalisation. In Asia four generations of NICs can be recognised in terms of the timing of industrial development and the current economic characteristics of these countries. They have all benefited from a high level of foreign direct investment, which has been a key element in their growth as trading nations. Within this region, only Japan is at a higher economic level than the NICs (Table 1).

Nowhere else in the world is the filter-down concept of industrial location better illustrated. When Japanese companies first decided to locate abroad in the quest for cheap labour, they looked to the most developed of their neighbouring countries, particularly South Korea and Taiwan. Most other countries in the region lacked the physical infrastructure and skill levels required by Japanese companies. Companies from elsewhere in the

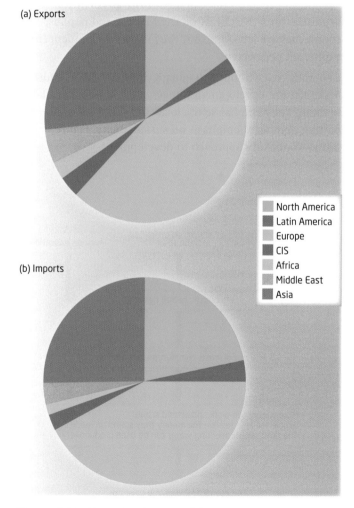

Figure 2 World merchandise trade, 2005.

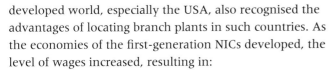

developed world, especially the USA, also recognised the advantages of locating branch plants in such countries. As the economies of the first-generation NICs developed, the level of wages increased, resulting in:

- Japanese and Western TNCs seeking locations in second generation NICs where improvements in physical and human infrastructures now satisfied their demands but where wages were still low
- indigenous companies from the first-generation NICs also moving routine tasks to their cheaper labour neighbours such as Malaysia and Thailand.

With time, the process also included the third-generation NICs, a significant factor in the recent very high growth rates in China and India. The least developed countries in the region, nearly all hindered by conflict of one sort or another at some time in recent decades, are now beginning to be drawn into the system. It should not be too long before the economic journals recognise a fourth generation of NICs in Asia. Vietnam would seem to be a prime candidate for such recognition.

Figure 3 (page 126) shows the inflow of foreign direct investment for a number of world regions from 1970. The substantial increase in the early 1990s was an important stimulus to growth in a number of countries, particularly those classed as NICs.

However, on the other side of the coin are the two billion people who live in countries that have become less rather than more globalised (in an economic sense) as trade has fallen in relation to national income. This group includes most African countries. In these 'non-globalising' countries income per person fell by an average of 1% a year during the 1990s. An Oxfam report published in April 2002 stated that if Africa increased its share of world trade by just 1% it would earn an additional £49 billion a year – five times the amount it receives in aid.

Organisations such as Christian Aid and Oxfam argue strongly that trade is the key to real development, being worth 20 times as much as aid. However, the trading situation of Africa will only improve if the trading relationship between developed and developing countries is made fairer to bring more benefits to the latter. In fact, Africa's share of world trade has fallen in recent decades. According to Oxfam, if Sub-Saharan Africa had maintained its exports at the same level as 1980, its economy would be worth an extra $280 billion a year.

Container ships and port, Seattle, USA. Much of the world's trade is carried in containers.

Level	Countries	GNP per capita 2005 (US$)
1	Japan: an MEDC	38 984
2	First-generation NICs, e.g. Taiwan	16 764
3	Second-generation NICs, e.g. Malaysia	4 963
4	Third-generation NICs, e.g. China	1 735
5	Fourth-generation NICs, e.g. Vietnam	623
6	Least developed countries, e.g. Mongolia	380

Table 1 *Level of development in some Asian countries.*

A timber train on the Trans-Siberian railway. The export of raw materials has become an important source of income in eastern Russia.

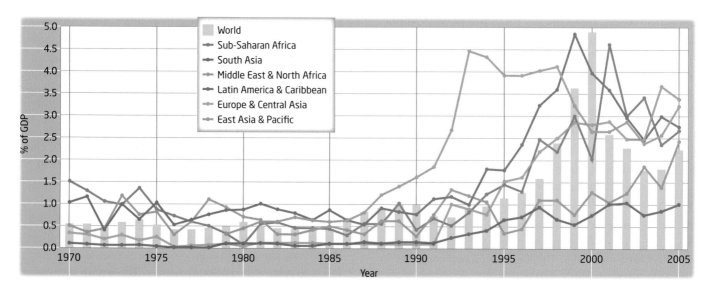

Figure 3 *Foreign direct investment by world region, 1970–2005.*

The terms of trade

The most vital element in the trade of any country is the terms on which it takes place (the **terms of trade**). If countries rely on the export of commodities that are low in price and need to import items that are relatively high in price they need to export in large quantities to be able to afford a relatively low volume of imports. Many poor nations are **primary product dependent** – that is, they rely on one or a small number of primary products to obtain foreign currency through export. The world market price of primary products is in general very low compared with that of manufactured goods and services. Also, the price of primary products is subject to considerable variation from year to year, making economic and social planning extremely difficult. The terms of trade for many developing countries are worse now than they were a decade ago. It is not surprising, therefore, that so many nations are struggling to get out of poverty.

Trade deficits

Because the terms of trade are generally disadvantageous to the poor countries of the South, many developing countries have a very high **trade deficit** (Figure 4). Among lower-income countries the average trade balance is a deficit of 12.3% of GDP. Such a level is a rarity amongst developed nations.

Conventional neo-liberal economists generally welcome the large transfers of capital linked to high trade deficits. They say that trade deficits are strongly related to stages

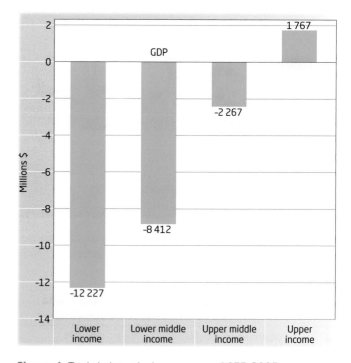

Figure 4 *Trade balance by income group, 1975–2005.*

of economic development. The argument is that capital inflows swell the available pool of investment funds and thus generate future growth in the developing world. However, Marxist and populist writers argue that:

* If the expansion of trade volumes brings benefits to developing countries, the accompanying expansion of trade deficits may bring considerable problems.

- Trade deficits have to be financed. One way is to borrow more money from abroad, but this will increase a country's debt. Another is to divert investment away from important areas of the economy such as agriculture, industry, education and health.

- Thus high trade deficits in the developing world constrain growth and produce a high level of dependency.

Trans-Siberian railway train at a station in eastern Siberia. Mongolian traders display their goods to Russian shoppers during a 20-minute stop at the station. The railway is an important trade route.

Research idea

The World Investment Report (UNCTAD) is published annually. Look at the latest report to see how much foreign direct investment is flowing into each world region.

Fair trade

At one end of the ideological spectrum are those who see trade as a force for good that will lift people out of poverty, while at the other end are those who argue that trade is responsible for widening the gulf between rich and poor. Oxfam has pointed out what it thinks needs to be done to make trade fairer to poorer countries (Table 2, page 128).

Many supermarkets and other large stores in Britain and other developed countries now stock some **fair trade**

products. Most are agricultural products such as bananas, orange juice, nuts, coffee and tea, but the market in non-food goods such as textiles and handicrafts is also increasing. The fair trade system operates as follows:

- Small-scale producers group together to form a cooperative or other democratically run association with high social and environmental standards.

- These cooperatives deal directly with companies (cutting out 'middlemen') such as Tesco and Sainsbury in developed countries.

- Developed country companies (through their customers) pay significantly over the world market price for the products traded. The price difference can be as large as 100%. This might mean, for example, supermarket customers paying a few pence more for a kilo of bananas.

- The higher price achieved by the developing country cooperatives provides both a better standard of living (often saving producers from bankruptcy and absolute poverty) and some money to reinvest in their farms.

Advocates of the fair trade system argue that it is a model of how world trade can and should be organised to tackle global poverty. This system of trade began in the 1960s with Dutch consumers supporting Nicaraguan farmers. It is now a global market worth £315 million a year, involving over 400 companies in developed countries and an estimated 500,000 small farmers and their families in the world's poorest countries. Food sales are growing by more than 25% a year, with Switzerland and Britain being the largest markets.

Regional trade agreements

Regional trade agreements have proliferated in the last two decades as they became increasingly viewed as an important factor in the generation of trade and development. In 1990 there were fewer than 25; by 1998 there were more than 90. The most notable of these are the European Union, NAFTA in North America, ASEAN in Asia, and Mercosur in Latin America. The United Nations (1990) refer to such organisations as 'geographically discriminatory trading arrangements'. Nearly all of the WTO's members belong to at least one regional pact. All such arrangements have one unifying characteristic: the preferential terms that trade participants enjoy over non-participating countries. Although no regional group has as yet adopted rules contrary to those of the WTO, there are some concerns:

1. End the use of conditions attached to International Monetary Fund (IMF)-World Bank programmes which force poor countries to open their markets regardless of the impact on poor people. Often, poor countries have been forced to open their markets far too quickly and to a much greater extent than rich countries.

2. Improve market access for poor countries and end the cycle of subsidised agricultural over-production and export dumping by rich countries. Rich nations spend $1 billion every day on agricultural subsidies which encourage surplus production, much of which is dumped on world markets, undermining small farmers in poor countries. When developing countries export to developed countries they face tariff barriers that are four times higher than those encountered by developed countries. These barriers cost developing countries $100 billion a year – twice the amount they receive in aid. WTO rules need to be changed so that developing countries can protect domestic food production.

3. Create a new international commodities institution to promote diversification and end over-supply in order to raise prices for producers and give them a reasonable standard of living. Low and unstable commodity prices are a major cause of poverty. Between 1997 and 2002 coffee prices fell by 70%, costing exporters in developing countries $8 billion in lost foreign-exchange earnings. Change corporate practices so that companies pay fair prices to producers. For example, coffee farmers in developing countries receive an average of $1 a kilogram while consumers in developed countries pay $15 a kilogram – a mark-up of 1500%.

4. Establish new intellectual property rules to ensure that poor countries are able to afford new technologies and basic medicines. Many of the current WTO rules protect the interests of developed countries and powerful TNCs, but impose huge costs on developing countries.

5. Prohibit rules that force governments to liberalise or privatise basic services that are vital for poverty reduction.

6. Enhance the quality of private-sector investment and employment standards. For example, Oxfam argue that in many countries export-led success is built on the exploitation of women and girls. The foreign sales of the largest TNCs are equivalent in value to one-quarter of world trade. TNCs are continually linking producers in developing countries more closely with consumers in developed countries. Many governments, in order to attract foreign investment, deny workers rights that are commonplace in developed countries.

7. Democratise the WTO to give poor countries a stronger voice. In principle, every nation has an equal vote in the WTO. In practice, the rich world shuts out the poor world from key negotiations. In recent years agreements have become more and more difficult to reach, with some economists forecasting the stagnation or even the break-up of the WTO.

8. Change national policies on health, education and governance so that poor people can develop their capabilities, realise their potential, and participate in markets on more equitable terms.

Table 2 *Some of Oxfam's aims in its 'Make Trade Fair' campaign.*

- regional agreements can divert trade, inducing a country to import from a member of its trading bloc rather than from a cheaper supplier elsewhere
- regional groups might raise barriers against each other, creating protectionist blocks
- regional trade rules may complicate the establishment of new global regulations.

There is a growing consensus that international regionalism is on the ascendency. The EU, NAFTA and ASEAN+ (associated agreements with other countries) triad of regional trading arrangements dominate the world economy, accounting for 67% of all world trade. Whether the regional trade agreement trend causes the process of world trade liberalisation to falter in the future remains to be seen.

Apart from trade blocs there are a number of looser trade groupings aiming to foster the mutual interests of member countries. These include:

- Asia-Pacific Economic Co-operation forum (APEC). Its 21 members border the Pacific Ocean and include Canada, the USA, Peru, Chile, Japan, China and Australia. The member countries have pledged to facilitate free trade.

- The Cairns Group of agricultural exporting nations was formed in 1986 to lobby for freer trade in agricultural products. Its members include Argentina, Brazil, Canada, New Zealand, Australia, the Philippines and South Africa.

Case study

The emergence of China as a major trading nation

Soon after the death of Mao Zedong (Mao Tse-Tung) in 1976, China's economic policy changed significantly. Mao's successor, Deng Xiaoping, sought to end the relative isolation of China from the world economy and to imitate East Asia's export-led success. Economic growth increased by an average of over 10% a year and exports (by value) by 15% a year in the 1980s and 1990s. During this 20-year period the Chinese economy grew eight times bigger and between 1990 and 1998 the number of Chinese living on less than a dollar a day fell by 150 million. Growth has continued strongly in the first decade of the new millennium. The value of China's international trade rose to $2562 billion in 2008, compared with only $1.13 billion in 1950. Foreign exchange reserves totalled more than $2000 billion in 2008. China is now the world's third largest economy. Per capita incomes have risen significantly as a result of strong economic growth and trade (Table 3).

Chinese entry into the WTO was an important milestone in its economic development. On 15 November 1999 the USA and China agreed in principle to a deal that would allow China to join the WTO. Although there were other hurdles to get over, this was the most important obstacle to clear. The success of the USA-China negotiations was hailed as a triumph for the moderate, reformist policies of Chinese President Jiang Zemin. For the developed world in particular the main benefits of Chinese entry were its huge market potential, and that China would be bound by WTO rules on a range of issues concerning production and trade. The main concerns for China were the problems caused by the new rules that China had signed up to, as the country struggled to identify and specialise in fields of comparative advantage.

China attracted a record $92 billion in foreign direct investment in 2008. The Chinese government has made it easier for foreign companies to expand in China since the country joined the WTO. The major attraction to manufacturers is the cheap labour market where wages are less than 5% of those in the USA.

China now makes 60% of the world's bicycles and over half of the world's shoes. It accounts for 20% of the world's garment exports, with the prediction that this will rise to 50% in 2010 as quotas on imports are eliminated around the world. However, worries about Chinese goods swamping global markets seem to be exaggerated. China's share of world trade is still only 4% with a trade surplus of about $30 billion (similar to Canada's). Although China is steadily producing more capital-intensive goods, these are mainly destined for the domestic market where demand is rising rapidly.

China has considerably more control over its economy than most other countries. Its currency is not freely convertible. The country was therefore not vulnerable to the speculation and resulting panic that affected so many of its neighbours in the late 1990s.

Year	Per capita income (yuan)
1980	463
1990	1644
2000	7858
2008	22698

Table 3 *China: increase in per capita income, 1980–2008.*

Beijing street market.

Case study

The trade in tea

Tea, like coffee, bananas and other raw materials, exemplifies the relatively small proportion of the final price of the product that goes to producers. The great majority of the money generated by the tea industry goes to the post-raw material stages (processing, distributing and retailing), usually benefiting companies in developed countries rather than the poorer producing nations.

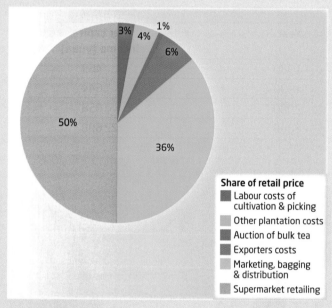

Share of retail price
- Labour costs of cultivation & picking
- Other plantation costs
- Auction of bulk tea
- Exporters costs
- Marketing, bagging & distribution
- Supermarket retailing

Figure 5 *The tea value chain.*

A report by the Dutch Tea Institute in 2006 drew particular attention to:

- the problems of falling prices and rising input costs
- the consequent pressure to limit labour costs of tea production workers
- the urgent need for improvement of labour, social, ecological and economic conditions throughout the tea sector in the developing countries.

The global tea market is dominated by a small number of companies including Unilever and Sara Lee. About half of all the tea produced is traded internationally. Annual export sales of tea in its raw material state are worth almost $3 billion. The retail value of the global tea business is of course much higher. The large tea companies wield immense power over the industry. As many countries now produce tea they have to compete with each other in an increasingly competitive market. Global supply is rising at a faster rate than consumption, keeping prices low. Tea producers complain that the global trading system prevents them from moving up the value chain by processing and packing the tea they grow. This is mainly because they would have to compete with very powerful brands and they would find it very difficult to achieve the economies of scale of the global tea companies.

Activities

1 Describe the share of world merchandise trade for exports and imports shown in Figure 2 (page 124).
2 Analyse the trends shown in Figure 3 (page 126).
3 Briefly summarise the conflicting views about the impact of trade deficits on development.
4 Discuss the figures shown in the tea value chain (Figure 5).
5 **a** What is fair trade?
   b Examine two of the issues raised by Oxfam's 'Make Trade Fair' campaign, Table 2.
6 What is the advantage for a country's being part of a regional trade agreement?

How effective are different aid strategies in development?

Investment involves expenditure on a project in the expectation of financial (or social) returns. Transnational corporations are the main source of foreign investment. TNCs invest to make profits. Aid is assistance in the form or grants or loans at below market rates.

Most developing countries have been keen to accept foreign aid because of the:

- 'foreign exchange gap' whereby many developing countries lack the hard currency to pay for imports such as oil and machinery which are vital to development

- 'savings gap' where population pressures and other drains on expenditure prevent the accumulation of enough capital to invest in industry and infrastructure

- 'technical gap' caused by a shortage of skills needed for development.

Figure 6 shows how these factors combine to form the 'vicious circle of poverty'.

Figure 7 shows the different types of **international aid**. The basic division is between official government aid and voluntary aid:

- Official government aid is where the amount of aid given and who it is given to are decided by the government of an individual country.

- Voluntary aid is run by NGOs or charities such as Oxfam, ActionAid and CAFOD. NGOs collect money from individuals and organisations. However, an increasing amount of government money goes to NGOs because of their expertise in running aid efficiently.

Official government aid can be divided into (a) bilateral aid which is given directly from one country to another and (b) multilateral aid which is provided by many countries and organised by an international body such as the United Nations.

Aid supplied to poorer countries is of two types:

- short-term emergency aid which is provided to help cope with unexpected disasters such as earthquakes, volcanic eruptions and tropical cyclones

- long-term development aid which is directed towards the continuous improvement in the quality of life in a poorer country.

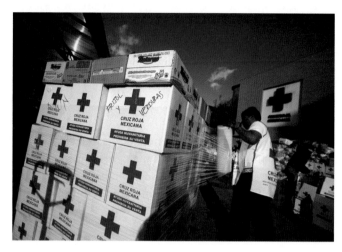

Red Cross worker packing aid for Haiti, 2010.

Critics of international aid argue that:

- too often aid fails to reach the very poorest people and when it does the benefits are frequently short-lived

- a significant proportion of foreign aid is 'tied' to the purchase of goods and services from the donor country and often given for use only on jointly agreed projects

- the use of aid on large capital-intensive projects may actually worsen the conditions of the poorest people

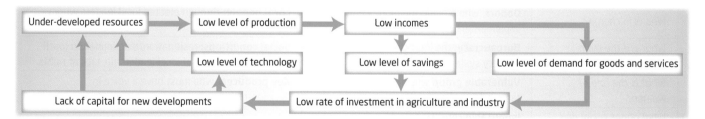

Figure 6 *The vicious circle of poverty.*

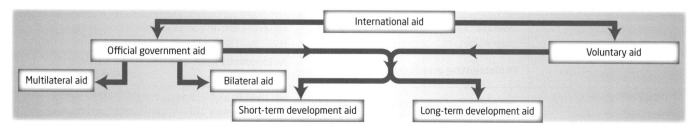

Figure 7 *The different types of international aid.*

- aid may delay the introduction of reforms, for example the substitution of food aid for land reform
- international aid can create a culture of dependency.

Many development economists argue there are two issues more important to development than aid:

- changing the terms of trade so that developing nations get a fairer share of the benefits of world trade
- writing off the debts of the poorest countries.

Table 4 shows official development assistance (ODA) received by world region.

NGOs have often been much better at directing aid towards sustainable development than government agencies. The selective nature of such aid has targeted the poorest communities using **appropriate technology** and involving local people in decision-making.

	Total (US$ millions)	Per capita (US$)	As % of GDP	
	2005	2005	1990	2005
Developing countries	86 043.0	16.5	1.4	0.9
Least developed countries	25 979.5	33.9	11.8	9.3
Arab States	29 612.0	94.3	2.9	3.0
East Asia and the Pacific	9 541.6	4.9	0.8	0.2
Latin America and the Caribbean	6 249.5	11.3	0.5	0.3
South Asia	9 937.5	6.3	1.2	0.8
Sub-Saharan Africa	30 167.7	41.7	5.7	5.1
Central and Eastern Europe and Russia	5 299.4	13.1	–	0.3

Table 4 *ODA by world region.*

Service delivery versus empowerment

A new way of thinking about hunger and abject poverty

	The conventional top-down service delivery model	**The Hunger Project's bottom-up empowerment model**
Who are the hungry people?	**Beneficiaries** whose basic needs must be met.	**Principal authors and actors in development:** hardworking, creative individuals who lack opportunities.
What must be done?	**Provide services** through government or charities.	**Mobilise and empower** people's self-reliant action, and stand in solidarity with them for their success.
What's the primary resource for development?	**Money** and the **expertise** of consultants and programme managers.	**People:** their vision, mobilisation, entrepreneurial spirit and confidence.
Who is in charge?	**Donors**, who provide the money and hold implementers to account.	**Local people:** through elected local leaders whom they hold to account.
What are the main constraints?	**Bureaucracy:** the inefficiency of the delivery system.	**Social conditions:** resignation, discrimination (particularly gender), lack of local leadership, lack of rights.
What is the role of women?	**Vulnerable group** who must be especially targeted beneficiaries.	**Key producers** who must have a voice in decision-making.
What about social and cultural issues?	**Immutable conditions** that must be compensated for.	**Conditions** that people can transform.
How should we focus our work?	Carefully **target beneficiaries** on an objective-needs basis.	**Mobilise everyone** as broadly as possible – build spirit and momentum of accomplishment.
What is the role of central government?	**Operate** centrally managed service-delivery programmes.	**Decentralise** resources and decision-making to local level; build local capacity; set standards; protect rights.
What is the role of local government?	**Implementing arm** of central programmes.	**Autonomous** leadership directly accountable to people.
What is the role of civil society?	**Implementing arm** of central programmes.	**Catalyst** to mobilise people; fight for their rights; empower people to keep government accountable.

Figure 8 *Contrasting top-down and bottom-up aid models.*

Case study

Local democracy in Kerala

In 1996 the government of the Indian state of Kerala launched a campaign (The People's Campaign for Decentralised Planning) to make village democracy a major development mechanism. The 'Kerala Model', hailed for its very high rate of political participation, has resulted in high levels of literacy and life expectancy and low levels of infant mortality and caste discrimination.

Initial concentration was on:

- building development infrastructure

- improving public services
- creating jobs
- involving local people in planning and decision-making
- channelling resources to women and to the poorest castes and classes.

In 2002, the People's Campaign was extended to a follow-up project known as the Mararikulam Experiment.

The effectiveness of aid: top-down and bottom-up approaches

Over the years most debate about aid has focused on the amount of aid made available. However, in recent years the focus has shifted somewhat to the effectiveness of aid. This has involved increasing criticism of the traditional top-down approach to aid.

The financing of the Pergau Dam in Malaysia with UK government aid is an example of a capital-intensive government-led aid programme, set up without consulting the local population. Work began in 1991 and around the same time Malaysia bought £1 billion worth of arms from the UK, leading many people to believe that the £234 million in aid was 'tied' to the arms deal.

The Hunger Project is one of a number of organisations that have adopted a radically different approach (Figure 8). The Hunger Project has worked in partnership with grassroots organisations in Africa, Asia and Latin America to develop effective bottom-up strategies. The key strands in this approach have been:

- mobilising grassroots people for self-reliant action
- intervening for gender equality
- strengthening local democracy.

Research idea

Look at UN-Habitat's best practices database: www.unhabitat.org/bestpractices/2006 to find out more about the Kerala model (see case study above).

The level of official development assistance

At the UN General Assembly in 1970 the rich donor governments promised to spend 0.7% of GNP on international aid. The deadline for reaching the target was the mid-1970s. However, the reality has been that almost all donor countries have consistently failed to reach this target. International aid is more of a priority in some countries than others.

The importance of remittances

In recent decades remittances have become a very important source of income for many developing countries. The value of remittances has already been covered in Chapter 3.

Debt relief

Experts from a variety of disciplines blame the rules of the global economic system for excluding many countries from its potential benefits. Many single out debt as the major problem for the world's poorer nations. An ever-increasing proportion of new debt is used to service interest payments on old debts. While supporters of globalisation argue that economic growth through trade is the only answer, critics say that developed countries should do more to help the poor countries through debt relief and by opening their markets to exports from developing countries.

The Heavily Indebted Poor Countries (HIPC) Initiative was first established in 1996 by the IMF and the World Bank. Its aim is to provide a comprehensive approach to debt reduction for heavily indebted poor countries. To qualify for assistance, countries have to pursue IMF and World Bank supported adjustment and reform programmes. By early 2008, debt reduction packages had been approved for 33 countries, 27 of them in Africa. Eight additional countries are eligible for HIPC Initiative assistance (Figure 9).

Microcredit and social business

The development of the Grameen Bank in Bangladesh has illustrated the power of **microcredit** in the battle against poverty. Muhammad Yunus highlights **social business** as the next phase in the battle against poverty in his book *Creating a World Without Poverty*. He presents a vision of a new business model that combines the operation of the free market with the quest for a more humane world.

Activities

1. Write a brief explanation of the flow diagram in Figure 6 (page 131).
2. Describe the different types of aid shown in Figure 7 (page 131).
3. Draw a graph to illustrate the data presented in Table 3 (page 129).
4. Examine the differences between the top-down and bottom-up approaches to aid (page 133).
5. a Explain the HIPC initiative.
   b On an outline map of the world, label the countries in receipt of assistance under the HIPC initiative (Figure 9).
6. Explain the terms (a) microcredit and (b) social business.

Post-Completion-Point countries (23)		
Benin	Honduras	Rwanda
Bolivia	Madagascar	São Tomé & Principe
Burkina Faso	Malawi	Senegal
Cameroon	Mali	Sierra Leone
Ethiopia	Mauritania	Tanzania
The Gambia	Mozambique	Uganda
Ghana	Nicaragua	Zambia
Guyana	Niger	
Interim countries (between Decision and Completion Point) (10)		
Afghanistan	Congo, Republic	Haiti
Burundi	Congo, Dem. Rep.	Liberia
Central African Republic	Guinea	
Chad	Guinea Bissau	
Pre-Decision-Point countries (8)		
Comoros	Kyrgyz Republic	Sudan
Eritrea	Nepal	Togo
Ivory Coast	Somalia	

Figure 9 *Countries concerned with the HIPC Initiative.*

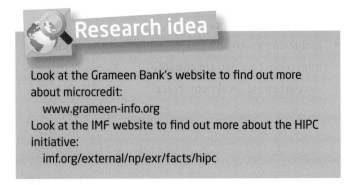

Research idea

Look at the Grameen Bank's website to find out more about microcredit:
www.grameen-info.org
Look at the IMF website to find out more about the HIPC initiative:
imf.org/external/np/exr/facts/hipc

Case study

Mauritania – struggling to develop

The West African nation of Mauritania, at over four times the size of the UK, covers more than one million km² (Figure 10). It borders Western Sahara, Algeria, Mali, Senegal and the Atlantic Ocean. Water is a prime concern not just in the desert and semi-desert areas but also in those zones where rain-fed agriculture is possible. Agricultural production varies hugely from year to year because of the unpredictability of the rains.

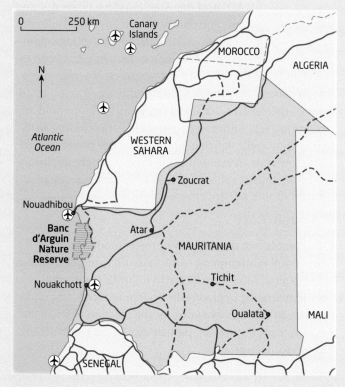

Figure 10 *Map of Mauritania.*

With a relatively small population of 2.365 million, Mauritania is classed as a least developed country. In 2007 its GDP per capita at PPP was estimated at $2000. For the same year its HDI ranking was 137 out of 177 countries. Net ODA in 2006 was US$ 93.7 million. Major development partners include the International Development Association (IDA), the African Development Fund and France.

A food crisis hit Mauritania in 2008, when food prices rose sharply, leading to a big increase in food insecurity levels. The level of malnutrition is high at 12.6% and exceeding 15% in some regions. The February 2009 food survey showed that 138 000 people in the country are severely food insecure and 246 000 are moderately food insecure.

When the country gained independence from France in 1960, slavery still formally existed and under 5% of the population lived in urban areas. Today the urban population numbers over 60%. In an effort to shed its poverty the country has embraced privatisation and other aspects of structural adjustment favoured by the World Bank and the IMF. Mauritania is one of the first countries to benefit from the HIPC debt reduction scheme.

Although starting from a low base there are significant signs of economic and social progress. For example:

- between 1990 and 2004, the proportion of Mauritanians living below the poverty line fell from 56% to 40%
- the gross primary enrolment ratio reached almost 99% in 2006 – since 1995 the gap between enrolment ratios of boys and girls has almost closed.

Exports have depended almost totally on two commodities: iron ore and fish. Iron ore accounts for almost 50% of total exports by value. The relatively low price of iron ore on the world market and the depletion of some of the best reserves have made Mauritania's dependency on iron ore very risky. Fortunately the fishing sector has developed strongly in recent decades but the problem of overfishing by foreign boats is now causing considerable concern.

Nouadhibou is the main port of export for the mining and fishing industries. Its turnover makes it one of the most important ports in West Africa. It does though have one great disadvantage – there is no road link with the capital Nouakchott. However, this situation will change when the West Coast pan-African highway is completed. An important development in the south was the construction, with Chinese aid, of a half-million tonne capacity deepwater port near Nouakchott. There has been talk of turning Nouakchott port into a major gateway for landlocked Mali which would be of considerable benefit to both countries.

Discoveries of other minerals, including gold and diamonds, offer possibilities for the future but further exploration will be required to ascertain the economics of development. Mauritania, like all oil-poor developing countries, can do nothing but pay the fluctuating market price for its essential oil imports. However, the discovery of oil off the coast in mid-2001 may solve this problem if the reserves prove economic to exploit.

Import substitution has long been an objective but earlier attempts at establishing an oil refinery and other industrial plants ended in failure. The very small size of the domestic market has proved to be a major limitation in this respect.

The periodic need to import food is a major obstacle to achieving a trade balance. Traditionally, the nomadic desert Moors were largely self-sufficient, while in the south, the predominantly black African farmers also grew their own food. However, a high rate of rural–urban migration in recent decades has increased the number of people dependent on others to produce their food. Acute periods of drought, notably in the 1970s and 1980s, have exacerbated the situation. Rice production, the staple food of many Mauritanians, has been of particular concern. Yields can vary significantly from year to year, depending on rainfall and other factors. Thus Mauritania is not always self-sufficient in rice. In addition, imported rice is often favoured as it tends to be less expensive. Livestock rearing accounts for 15% of GDP. There are more goats than people in Mauritania and more than a million camels.

Since independence, France has remained Mauritania's main trading partner. Migrant workers based in France remit significant sums home. In total the EU accounts for just over 60% of both imports and exports. Mauritania is a signatory to the Cotonou Agreement, which links more than 70 African, Caribbean and Pacific countries to the EU, giving them various trade and aid concessions. China and Japan have also been important trade and aid partners.

A number of development programmes are in operation:

➔ Sustainable Rural Development

The promotion of sustainable rural development is vital if the drift to the towns is to slow. Among the government agencies and projects involved in this process is the Programme for Managing Natural Resources in Rain-fed Zones (PGRNP). The main objective of this programme is to stem the degradation of vegetation cover and to improve the environment by enabling local populations to rationalise the use of natural resources. There has been a push to replace firewood with butane as the main domestic fuel.

➔ The Senegal River Valley

In this region, where irrigation enables far more intensive farming than elsewhere, a project jointly funded by the World Bank and the government is under way. The objectives of the Programme for Integrated Development of Irrigated Agriculture in Mauritania (PDIAIM), which has been organised in three phases from 2000 to 2010, are higher agricultural output, wider crop diversification, a reduction in rural poverty, improved food security, and a better ecological balance.

➔ The Oasis Development Project

This project, which was established in the mid-1980s, is assisted by the UN's International Fund for Agricultural Development (IFAD) and the Arab Fund for Economic and Social Development. The objective is to improve the living standards of poor people in the oasis zones. An important part of this participatory development scheme has been the establishment of microcredit cooperatives, of which there are now about 70. Members can borrow small amounts of money, interest-free, for up to ten years for household and community self-sufficiency projects (e.g. purchasing seed, digging new wells, fencing land). When the project ended in 2002 private investment came to play a more important role as the tourist value of oasis settlements is developed.

➔ Nouakchott

A ten-year urban development project funded by the World Bank is attempting to alleviate the worst deprivation in the capital. Its objectives are to improve water and electricity supply, upgrade educational facilities, and make microcredit facilities available for the creation of small and medium-sized businesses, particularly in the construction and service sectors.

➔ Tourism

Until the late 1990s tourism was not a priority in Mauritania because:

- there was concern that an influx of tourists would damage the nation's cultural and religious heritage
- the huge strain on government finances could not justify investing in the infrastructure required for a significant tourist industry.

However, in recent years the government has looked more favourably on tourism in order to (a) generate revenue and (b) as a contributing factor in ecological and cultural preservation. The aim is to avoid mass tourism and its pitfalls and to target special interest groups and adventure tourists.

The development gap: what are the possibilities for the future?

Table 5 shows that there is a range of factors which could either enhance or hinder the processes of development in the near future and beyond.

Factors encouraging future development in developing countries	Factors hindering future development in developing countries
Developed countries as a whole increasing international aid to the 0.7% of GDP agreed in 1970	Declining international aid in real terms
Reform of the WTO to allow developing countries greater access to the benefits of world trade	High food and energy prices drawing money away from other investment priorities
Reform of World Bank/IMF policies to better fit the individual circumstances of developing countries	Adverse climate change reducing agricultural production and increasing the impact of climatic hazards
The wider spread of good governance in the developing world	Deterioration in the terms of trade for developing countries
Significant technological advances in agriculture to bring food security to more people	The existence of a significant number of anti-democratic and corrupt governments
Increased levels of investment in developing countries from TNCs	Developed countries increasing barriers to trade to protect their own industries
A reduction in the barriers to migration from developing countries to developed countries	Developed countries increasing the barriers to migration from developing countries

Table 5 *Factors affecting development.*

The global economic situation

The future of the development gap is uncertain, particularly in the light of the recent global credit crisis. It remains to be seen what impact this will have on much needed investment in developing countries. The significant increases in the prices of energy and food were already creating considerable problems in many poorer countries before the full extent of the global credit crisis unravelled.

Many countries are struggling more than ever before to pay for vital imports. While significant reductions in poverty have already taken place, the global problems that have emerged in the latter part of the first decade of the 21st century must cast doubt on further progress in a number of countries, at least in the short term. For example, a newspaper article in the *Daily Telegraph* in October 2008 was entitled 'Rising oil prices push Pakistan to verge of bankruptcy'. The article noted that Pakistan's foreign exchange reserves were so low that the country could only afford one more month of imports.

Sustainable development

If the development gap is to narrow in the future, sustainable strategies will be of vital importance. Figure 11 summarises the sustainable livelihoods approach to raise people from rural poverty towards food security. Reducing poverty in rural areas will take the pressure of poverty off urban areas by dampening down rural to urban migration.

Figure 11 *Sustainable livelihoods approach to sustainable development.*

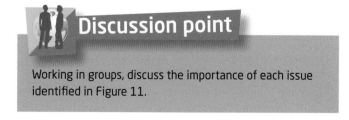

Discussion point

Working in groups, discuss the importance of each issue identified in Figure 11.

New development thinking

Many experts and ordinary people are frustrated that the considerable effort that has gone into the fight against poverty in developing countries in the post-1945 period has not produced better results. There can be little doubt that much of the international aid provided and the other efforts made have often not been very effective. According to J.D. Sachs, an expert in the field of development economics, 'A new kind of development economics needs to emerge, one that is better grounded in science – a "clinical economics" akin to modern medicine. Development economists need better diagnostic skills to recognise that economic pathologies (problems) have a wide variety of causes.'

Perceptions about the reasons for underdevelopment have changed over time. Race was once thought to be the most significant factor. Later explanations focused on culture, examining such characteristics as caste systems, religious divisions and taboos, gender inequalities and a lack of entrepreneurship. More recently 'poor governance', meaning inefficient and corrupt government action, has been highlighted. However, Sachs argues that geography, including natural resources, climate, heavy disease burdens, topography, and proximity to trade routes and major markets, is at least as important as good governance. It is not surprising that most landlocked countries have developed more slowly than coastal nations. Lack of direct access to ports increases transport costs and makes trade more difficult. Research has shown that tropical countries with a high incidence of malaria have experienced significantly slower economic growth than other tropical countries free from the disease. A high incidence of disease can hinder development potential in a range of ways.

Of course technology can do much to offset adverse geographical factors. For example, irrigation has had a huge impact on dry areas in both developed and developing countries.

A most important factor is to encourage overall economic growth in a country where the benefits are widespread rather than a situation where increasing wealth is concentrated in the hands of a small elite. For some countries an increasing GNP can mask the fact that conditions for the poorest people have not changed at all. If increasing wealth is widely spread, the process of cumulative causation is much more likely to take off.

J.D. Sachs argues that carefully targeted spending on basic government services is essential for economic growth, stating that 'Many of the recommendations of the past two decades emanating from Washington, that governments in low-income countries should cut back on their spending to make room for the private sector, miss the point. Government spending, directed at investment in critical areas, is itself a vital spur to growth, especially if its effects are to reach the poorest of the poor.'

Theory of Knowledge

Values and attitudes can change over time. Such change is most likely to occur when there is general agreement that a certain way of thinking is failing to provide solutions to problems. It then becomes clear that a new approach (or approaches) is required. What can be done to speed up effective action to reduce world poverty?

Activities

1 With reference to Table 5 (page 137), discuss the factors that will encourage and hinder the progress of development in poor countries.
2 Describe the sustainable livelihoods approach to development illustrated in Figure 10 (page 137).
3 After reviewing the case study (pages 135–136) draw up a fact file on Mauritania to show:
   a its present state of development
   b what is being done to promote development.

Conclusion

Extreme poverty remains concentrated in Sub-Saharan Africa, the Andean and Central American Highlands and the landlocked nations of Central Asia. Only a very concerted and well-targeted effort by the affluent nations can significantly change this situation. It remains to be seen if this will be done. The past tells us that the good intentions agreed at international conferences are frequently not carried through when it comes to finding the money. The UN Secretary-General has stressed that it is in the rich nations' own interests to supply the investment required to eliminate poverty and create development, stating: 'There will be no development without security, and no security without development.'

Key terms

Foreign direct investment overseas investments in physical capital by transnational corporations.

Non-governmental organisations national or international private organisations, which are distinct from governmental or intergovernmental agencies.

Resource nationalisation when a country decides to take part, or all, of one or a number of natural resources under state ownership.

Terms of trade the price of a country's exports relative to the price of its imports, and the changes that take place over time.

Primary product dependent countries that rely on one or a small range of primary products for most of their exports.

Trade deficit when the value of a country's exports is less than the value of its imports.

Fair trade when producers of food, and some non-food products, in developing countries receive a fair deal when they are selling their products.

International aid the giving of resources (money, food, goods, technology etc.) by one country or organisation to another poorer country. The objective is to improve the economy and quality of life in the poorer country.

Appropriate technology aid supplied by a donor country whereby the level of technology and the skills required to service it are properly suited to the conditions in the receiving country.

Microcredit tiny loans and financial services to help the poor, mostly women, start businesses and escape poverty.

Social business forms of business that seek to profit from investments that generate social improvements and serve a broader human development purpose.

Websites

www.cia.gov
US Central Intelligence Agency (CIA)

www.worldbank.org
The World Bank

www.grameen-info.org
Grameen Bank

www.undp.org
UN Development Programme (UNDP)

www.hipc.cbp.org
California Budget Project

Review

Examination-style questions

1 Refer to Figure 12.

a Describe the trends shown in Figure 12a.

b Comment on the trends shown in Figure 12b.

c Describe and explain the relationship between the two graphs.

2 Refer to Figure 13, produced by a Mexican development agency. The objective is to reverse the vicious circle of poverty and transform it into a human development cycle.

a Which of the four sections of the diagram is the logical starting point for the development cycle? Justify your choice.

b Describe the progression of the development cycle as a whole.

c Examine the importance of one of the four sections in detail. This should be a different section to the one you chose for (a).

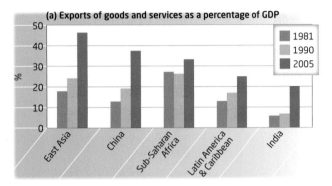

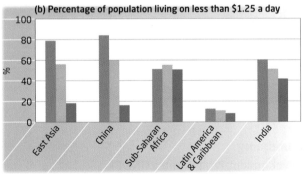

Figure 12 *(a) Exports as a percentage of GDP and (b) percentage of population living on less than $1.25 a day.*

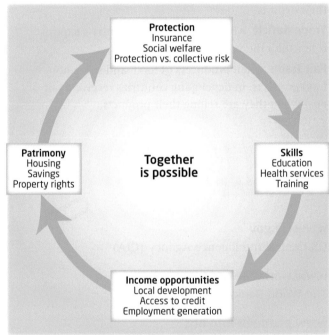

Figure 13 *Human development cycle.*

09 Atmosphere and change

KEY QUESTIONS

- How does the atmospheric system function in terms of the energy balance between solar and longwave radiation?
- How has this balance changed due to external forcings (changes in solar radiation, changes in the albedo of the atmosphere, and changes in the longwave radiation returned to space)?
- What are the causes and environmental consequences of global climatic change?

Red sky at sunset, Australia – a country that has suffered much in recent years from drought and bush fires.

The Stern Review, published in the UK in 2006 (Figure 1, page 142), stated that **climate change** is the greatest challenge facing humankind. The Stern Review was a major study into the economics of climate change commissioned by the UK government in 2005. It was designed to point the way ahead for government policy making. This major report concluded:

- climate change is the result of the externality associated with greenhouse gas emissions – it entails costs that are not paid for by those who create the emissions
- there is still time to avoid the worst impacts of climate change, if we take strong action now
- the benefits of strong and early action far outweigh the economic cost of not acting.

Although there is not unanimous agreement among scientists, most believe that the **natural greenhouse effect** has been significantly altered by human activity. Now an **enhanced greenhouse effect** is causing temperatures to increase beyond the limits of the natural greenhouse effect. For such scientists the issue is how far **global warming** has progressed and whether the **tipping point** has been reached. This is the level at which the effects of climate change will become irreversible to varying degrees.

The energy balance between solar and terrestrial radiation

The atmosphere is an open energy system receiving energy from both the sun and the Earth. The energy received from the Earth is extremely small compared with that from the sun, but it does have an important local effect as in the case of urban climates.

The sun has a surface temperature of nearly 6000°C. It constantly emits radiant energy or **insolation**. Solar energy comes from nuclear reactions within the sun's hot core while visible radiation (light) originates from the sun's surface. However, only a very small proportion of solar output – about 0.0005% – actually reaches the Earth as the sun's energy is emitted in all directions. Solar radiation is transmitted in the form of short waves because the sun is so hot. About 45% of solar radiation can be perceived as light. The rest is made up of ultraviolet and infrared waves which cannot be seen. The sun's insolation is vital in maintaining the Earth's climate and life support systems. In contrast to solar

An overwhelming body of scientific evidence now clearly indicates that **climate change is a serious and urgent issue**. The Earth's climate is rapidly changing, mainly as a result of increases in greenhouse gases caused by human activities.

Most climate models show that **a doubling of pre-industrial levels of greenhouse gases is very likely to commit the Earth to a rise of between 2 and 5°C in global mean temperatures**. This level of greenhouse gases will probably be reached between 2030 and 2060. A warming of 5°C on a global scale would be far outside the experience of human civilisation and comparable to the difference between temperatures during the last ice age and today. Several new studies suggest up to a 20% chance that warming could be greater than 5°C.

If annual greenhouse gas emissions remained at the current level, concentrations would be more than treble pre-industrial levels by 2100, committing the world to 3–10°C warming, based on the latest climate projections.

Some impacts of climate change itself may amplify warming further by triggering the release of additional greenhouse gases. This creates a real risk of even higher temperature changes.

- Higher temperatures cause plants and soils to soak up less carbon from the atmosphere and cause permafrost to thaw, potentially releasing large quantities of methane.
- Analysis of warming events in the distant past indicates that such feedbacks could amplify warming by an additional 1–2°C by the end of the century.

Warming is very likely to intensify the water cycle, reinforcing existing patterns of water scarcity and abundance and increasing the risk of droughts and floods.

Rainfall is likely to increase at high latitudes, while regions with Mediterranean-like climates in both hemispheres will experience significant reductions in rainfall. Preliminary estimates suggest that the fraction of land area in extreme drought at any one time will increase from 1% to 30% by the end of this century. In other regions, warmer air and warmer oceans are likely to drive more intense storms, particularly hurricanes and typhoons.

As the world warms, the risk of abrupt and large-scale changes in the climate system will rise.

- Changes in the distribution of heat around the world are likely to disrupt ocean and atmospheric circulations, leading to large and possibly abrupt shifts in regional weather patterns.

- If the Greenland or West Antarctic Ice Sheets began to melt irreversibly, the rate of sea level rise could more than double, committing the world to an eventual sea level rise of 5–12 m over several centuries.

The body of evidence and the growing quantitative assessment of risks are now sufficient to give clear and strong guidance to economists and policy-makers in shaping a response.

Figure 1 *Key messages from the Stern Review.*

radiation, the much cooler Earth emits longwave infrared or 'thermal' radiation. Figure 2 shows the contrasting wavelengths of solar and terrestrial radiation.

The natural greenhouse effect

Until recent human-induced global warming became evident, the atmosphere was not getting any hotter. There was an **energy balance** (budget) between inputs (insolation) and outputs (re-radiation from the Earth). This relationship is shown in Figure 3 (page 145).

The amount of insolation received at the outer edge of the atmosphere is known as the **solar constant**. The Earth receives approximately 342 watts of solar energy for each square metre of its spherical surface. Of this, 32% is immediately reflected by (a) clouds (b) dust particles in

the atmosphere and (c) the Earth's surface. This leaves a balance of 235 watts per square metre to be absorbed by the surface. For a stable climate on Earth the planet must radiate the same amount back into space. However, this would mean an average global surface temperate of −19°C rather than the 14°C it actually is. The difference of 33°C is due to the natural greenhouse effect.

The natural greenhouse effect is due to several gases in the atmosphere that absorb and emit infrared radiation. The main mechanism by which these gases absorb infrared radiation is through the vibrations of their molecules. The main greenhouse gases are water vapour, carbon dioxide, methane, nitrous oxides and ozone. These gases allow incoming solar radiation to pass through unaffected, but they trap infrared radiation emitted from the surface of the Earth. As a result there is reduced radiation back to

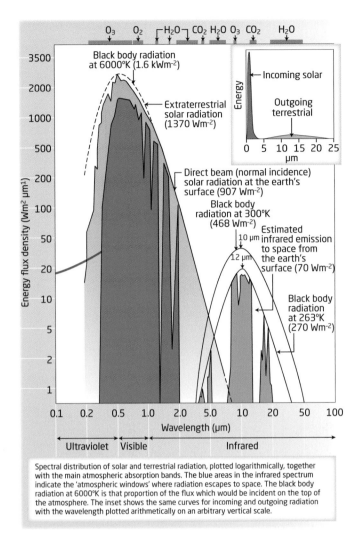

Spectral distribution of solar and terrestrial radiation, plotted logarithmically, together with the main atmospheric absorption bands. The blue areas in the infrared spectrum indicate the 'atmospheric windows' where radiation escapes to space. The black body radiation at 6000°K is that proportion of the flux which would be incident on the top of the atmosphere. The inset shows the same curves for incoming and outgoing radiation with the wavelength plotted arithmetically on an arbitrary vertical scale.

Figure 2 *Wavelengths of solar and terrestrial radiation.*

space and the Earth is warmed until a new balance is achieved. The overall effect is that the atmosphere acts like a blanket which is the natural greenhouse effect. The contribution that each of the greenhouse gases makes to the total effect depends on two main factors: how efficient it is at absorbing outgoing longwave radiation, and its atmospheric concentration.

Other important energy transfer processes operate in addition to radiation. These are:

- **Sensible heat** transfer – sensible heat is heat energy transferred between the surface and air when there is a difference in temperature between them. The transfer of sensible heat is felt by people as a rise or fall in the temperature of the air. Heat is initially transferred into the air by **conduction** as air molecules collide with those at the surface. As the air warms it rises in the atmosphere through **convection**. Thus the transfer of sensible heat is accomplished in a two-step process. Because air is such a poor conductor of heat, it is convection that is the most efficient way of transferring sensible heat into the air.

- **Latent heat** transfer – this occurs with a change in state or phase in the atmosphere. For example, heat is required for the change in state from water to water vapour. The heat added during **evaporation** breaks the bonds between the clusters of water molecules creating individual molecules that escape from the surface as a gas. The heat used in the phase change from a liquid to a gas is called the *latent heat of vaporisation*. It is 'latent' because it is being stored in the water molecules to later be released during the condensation process.

- **Condensation** is the phase change from a gas to a liquid when the latent heat that was taken up during evaporation is released from the water molecule and passed into the surrounding air. During this process latent heat is converted to sensible heat, causing an increase in the temperature of the air.

- **Ground heat** transfer – this is the warming of the subsurface of the Earth. Heat is transferred from the surface downwards through conduction. As in sensible heat transfer, a temperature gradient must exist between the surface and the subsurface for heat transfer to occur. Heat is transferred downwards when the surface is warmer than the subsurface. If the subsurface is warmer than the surface then heat is transferred upwards.

Table 1 (page 144) and Figure 3 show the net effect of energy transfers in the Earth-atmosphere system. Of all the radiation received at the edge of the atmosphere, 32 out of every 100 units of solar radiation are reflected back to space. This figure is a combination of reflection both from clouds (23 units) and from the Earth's surface (9 units). This process is known as the **albedo** or reflectivity of the Earth.

Forty-nine units of solar radiation are absorbed at the Earth's surface. In addition, 95 units of 'back' radiation are absorbed by the surface because of the greenhouse effect. So the total surface gain is 144 units. These units are lost as outgoing radiation (114 units), latent heat transfer (23 units), and sensible heat transfer (7 units). This results in a surface energy balance.

Within the atmosphere, Table 1 and Figure 3 show that there are gains of 20 units from solar radiation, 103 units from surface radiation, 23 units from latent heat and 7 units from sensible heat. This comes to a total gain (after rounding) of 152 units. Losses in the atmosphere are

	Shortwave		Longwave and thermal			
	Gain	Loss	Gain	Loss	Total gain	Total loss
Outer edge of atmosphere						
Incoming solar radiation	100				100	
Solar radiation reflected from clouds		23				
Solar radiation reflected from surface		9				
Thermal radiation from atmosphere				48		
Thermal radiation from clouds				9		
Thermal direct radiation from surface				12		100
Atmosphere						
Solar radiation absorbed by atmosphere	20					
Thermal radiation from surface to atmosphere			103			
Sensible heat transfer			7			
Latent heat transfer (evaporation)			23			
Thermal radiation from atmosphere to space				48		
Thermal radiation from clouds to space				9		
Back radiation from atmosphere to surface				95	152	152
Earth's surface						
Incoming solar radiation absorbed by surface	49					
Back radiation from atmosphere			95			
Sensible heat transfer				7		
Evaporation (latent heat transfer)				23		
Surface radiation to atmosphere				103		
Surface radiation straight to space				12	144	144

Note: Solar (shortwave) radiation in red. Thermal (longwave) radiation and other heat energy transfers in blue. Total inputs and outputs in green.
Total gain and total loss figures differ slightly due to rounding errors.

Table 1 *Transfers of energy in the Earth-atmosphere system.*

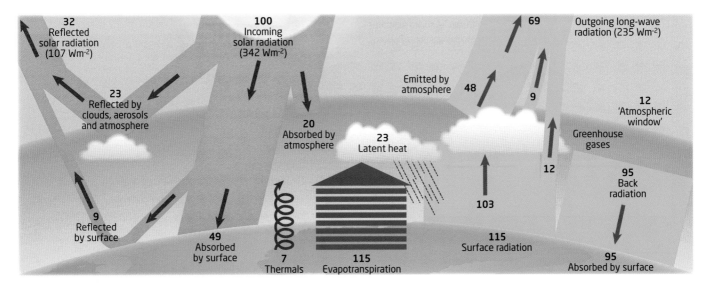

Figure 3 *Transfers of energy in the Earth-atmosphere system.*

thermal radiation back to the surface (95 units), thermal radiation from clouds (9 units) and from the atmosphere itself to space (48 units). Again, after rounding there is a balance.

At the edge of the atmosphere the gain of every 100 units of incoming solar radiation is balanced by (after rounding) the loss of 69 units of outgoing longwave radiation and 32 units which are reflected from clouds and the Earth's surface.

The energy balance varies across the Earth's surface. Latitude is the main factor here, with low latitudes receiving a net surplus of energy and high latitudes (greater than 40° North and South) a net deficit. Figure 4 shows why low latitude areas close to the equator and tropics receive more heat than high latitude areas close to the poles. Near the equator the sun's rays reach the surface from a position that is directly overhead (90°) or not far from this angle. At higher latitudes the angle of the sun's rays reaching the Earth is much lower so that the same amount of heat is spread out over a much larger surface area. In addition, there is more likelihood of a loss of solar radiation by absorption and scattering as the radiation is passing through a greater mass of atmosphere.

For example, London, UK is at a latitude of 51½°N. For London the sun is highest in the sky on 21 June, the summer solstice, when the sun is directly over the Tropic of Cancer (23½°N). This is a latitudinal difference of 28 degrees. The sun is lowest in the sky for London on 21 December, the

winter solstice, when the sun is directly over the Tropic of Capricorn (23½°S). Now the latitudinal difference between London and the overhead sun is 75 degrees.

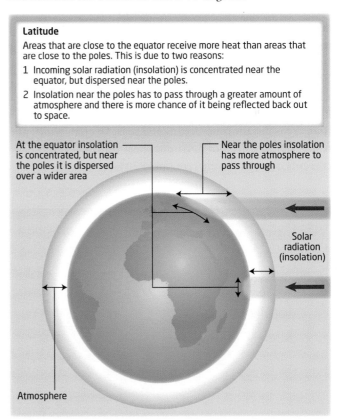

Latitude

Areas that are close to the equator receive more heat than areas that are close to the poles. This is due to two reasons:

1 Incoming solar radiation (insolation) is concentrated near the equator, but dispersed near the poles.
2 Insolation near the poles has to pass through a greater amount of atmosphere and there is more chance of it being reflected back out to space.

At the equator insolation is concentrated, but near the poles it is dispersed over a wider area

Near the poles insolation has more atmosphere to pass through

Solar radiation (insolation)

Atmosphere

Figure 4 *The relationship between temperature and latitude.*

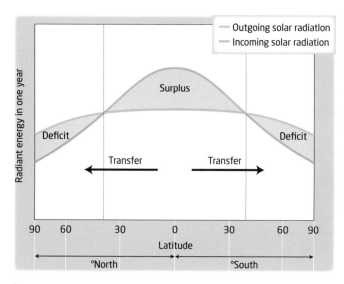

Figure 5 *Heat transfer from low to high latitudes.*

As the areas of heat surplus are not getting warmer and the areas of heat deficit are not becoming colder, heat must be being transferred between areas of surplus and deficit. The two agents of heat transfer are winds and ocean currents (Figure 5). In low latitudes the ocean moves more heat poleward than does the atmosphere, but at higher latitudes the atmosphere becomes the big carrier. The thermal capacity of the oceans imparts a moderating effect on global temperatures. Areas close to large water bodies generally have a lower annual temperature range than areas distant from oceans and seas. Overall, winds are responsible for 80% of horizontal heat transfers and ocean currents account for the remaining 20%.

Sunbeams through cloud on water, Australia. Cloud absorbs and scatters solar radiation.

Activities

1. Why is the atmosphere said to be an open energy system?
2. Define (a) insolation (b) energy balance (c) solar constant.
3. Write a brief description and explanation of Figure 2 (page 143).
4. Describe and explain the energy transfers shown in Table 1 (page 144) and Figure 3 (page 145).
5. Briefly explain sensible heat transfer, latent heat transfer and ground heat transfer.
6. With reference to Figure 4 (page 145), explain the relationship between temperature and latitude.
7. Look at Figure 5 (opposite). Explain how heat is transferred from areas with a net surplus of energy to areas with a net deficit of energy.

Discussion point

Suggest why governments such as that in the UK are interested in the economics of climate change.

Changes in the energy balance due to external forcings

There are processes both outside and within the atmosphere that can force changes in climate. Outside the atmosphere, climate forcing can occur due to variations in the amount of solar energy that reaches the Earth's atmosphere and because of variations in the Earth's orbit around the sun. Within the atmosphere, changes in atmospheric composition, changes in ocean circulation and the impact of singular events such as volcanic eruptions can influence climate. Such **external forcings** have been the subject of considerable recent research.

Changes in solar radiation

The total amount of solar radiation reaching the Earth can vary due to changes in the sun's output, such as those associated with sunspots, or in Earth's orbit. Orbital oscillations can also lead to different parts of the Earth getting more or less sunlight even when the total amount of solar energy reaching the Earth remains constant – similar to the way the tilt in the Earth's axis produces the hemispheric seasons. There may also be more subtle effects but these remain to be proved.

Research into the amount of radiation emitted by the sun has found that a solar cycle occurs approximately every eleven years. This is when the sun undergoes a period of increased magnetic and sunspot activity called the 'solar maximum' which is followed by a quiet period called the 'solar minimum'. Sunspots are seen as small darker spots on the surface of the sun. They are intense 'bubbles' of magnetic energy which somehow cool down the hot gases within so that they appear dark in relation to the surrounding solar atmosphere. Figure 6 shows changes in sunspot activity since 1900.

Decreases of solar energy of 0.2% occur during the weeklong passage of large sunspot groups across our side of the sun. Since the late 1970s, the amount of solar radiation the sun emits during times of quiet sunspot activity has increased by nearly .05% per decade, according to a NASA

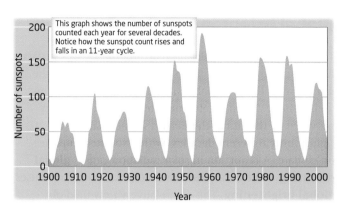

Figure 6 *Changes in sunspot activity.*

funded study. There is debate about how much this trend could influence climate change on Earth. Figure 7 is part of a recent article in the *New Scientist* which concludes that there has been no corresponding rise in any kind of solar activity to account for the strong warming in the last 40 years. In fact, the 2007 report by the Intergovernmental Panel on Climate Change halved the maximum likely influence of **solar forcing** on warming over the past 250 years from 40% to 20%.

Sunspot activity

What role have solar fluctuations had in temperature changes on Earth?

This is a difficult question to answer, as there is no first-hand record of the variations in solar output associated with sunspot activity prior to the 20th century.

Information on sunspot activity can be traced back to the 17th century, but it is lacking in one very important aspect: sunspots block the sun's radiation. It is the smaller bright spots (faculae) that actually increase the Sun's output, but these were not recorded until quite recently. The relationship between sunspots and bright faculae is not perfect and as such estimates of solar activity based on sunspot records may be missing the mark by as much as 30%.

An alternative method of assessing past solar activity is to measure levels of carbon-14 and beryllium-10 in tree rings and ice cores. These isotopes were formed when cosmic rays penetrated the atmosphere. Higher sunspot activity is related to increases in the solar wind that deflects more galactic cosmic rays away from Earth. Again, the relationship is not perfect. Recent evidence also suggests that the deposition of beryllium-10 can be affected by climate changes, making it even less reliable as an indicator of past solar activity.

Recent changes

In spite of these issues, most analyses suggest that before the Industrial Revolution, there was a good relationship between natural forcings (solar fluctuations and other factors such as volcanic dust) and average global temperatures. Solar forcings may have largely caused the warming in the late 19th and early 20th centuries and its levelling off in the mid-century cooling.

A 2007 report by the Intergovernmental Panel on Climate Change (IPCC) reduced the likely maximum effect of solar forcing on global warming over the past 250 years from 40% to 20%. This was based on a new analysis of the likely changes in solar forcing since the 17th century. Even if solar forcing in the past was more important than this estimate suggests, as some scientists believe, there is no significant relationship between solar activity and the strong warming during the past 40 years. Arguments that this is the case have not stood up to close examination.

Since 1978, direct measurements of solar output have shown a steady increase and decrease over the 11-year sunspot cycle, but with no upward or downward trend. Also, there is no noticeable trend in direct measurements of the Sun's ultraviolet output in cosmic rays. Thus, for the period for which there are direct reliable records, the Earth has warmed significantly although there has been no corresponding increase in any kind of solar activity.

Figure 7 *Solar fluctuations and temperatures.*

Global brightening/dimming

The amount of solar radiation reaching the Earth's surface has been recorded since 1923. However, it is only in the last 50 years that a global monitoring network has been taking shape. The data obtained shows that the energy provided by the sun at the Earth's surface has varied significantly in recent decades, with associated impacts on climate. A reduction in solar radiation causes **global dimming** while an intensification of solar radiation causes **global brightening**. This is a relatively new field of research.

The amount of solar radiation reaching the Earth's surface fell considerably between the 1950s and the 1980s, but has been gradually increasing again since 1985. At present it is not clear whether it is clouds or aerosols that trigger global brightening or dimming, or even interactions between the two. Research continues into these issues and others including how greatly the effects differ between urban and rural areas, where fewer aerosols are released into the atmosphere. Another challenge to researchers is to incorporate the effects of global dimming/brightening more effectively in climate models in order to understand their impact on climate change better.

Sea mist off Vancouver Island, Canada.

Changes in the albedo of the atmosphere

The Earth's albedo is the proportion of solar energy reflected from the Earth back into space. The lower the albedo of the Earth, the greater amount of solar radiation it will absorb, and the greater the albedo, the more solar radiation is reflected. This has an impact on surface temperatures. Dark objects tend to absorb most of the light that falls on them and thus they have a low albedo. Typical albedos are as follows:

- snow 80–90%
- sand 30–35%
- tropical rainforest 7–15%
- deciduous forest 15–18%
- clouds 35–90%.

Snow and ice have an extremely high albedo, so the loss of large **ice sheets** and glaciers would mean much more solar radiation being absorbed by the Earth's surface. Changes in surface albedo occur naturally but climate forcing is also caused by anthropogenic (caused by humans) changes. Significant changes in albedo occur:

- in regions undergoing desertification, as sand has a higher albedo than soil or vegetation – model studies of the Sahel in Africa reveal that albedo increased from 14% to 35% due to desertification during the 20th century
- in areas of deforestation – depending on the albedo of the underlying soil, reductions in vegetative land cover may give rise to albedo increases of as much as 20%, as soil has a higher albedo than vegetation
- in the Arctic where the loss of sea ice, which has a high albedo, is replaced by ocean water with a relatively low albedo
- when there are substantial changes in cloud cover – clouds have the greatest potential for changing albedo on a short timescale.

The Earthshine project conducted at the Big Bear Solar Observatory in California has found that there have been considerable changes in the albedo of the atmosphere. The Earth's albedo has risen in the past few years. By doing reconstructions of the past albedo, it appears that there was a significant reduction in the Earth's albedo leading up to a lull in 1997. Then the albedo increased, making the Earth more reflective.

Changes in the longwave radiation returned to space

The changing composition of the atmosphere, including its greenhouse gas and aerosol content, is a major internal forcing mechanism of climate change. Such changes have a significant impact on the longwave radiation returned to space. Changes in the greenhouse gas content of the atmosphere can occur as a result of both natural and anthropogenic factors. The latter has been the focus of much research in recent decades and will be looked at in detail in the following section.

The causes and environmental consequences of global climate change

There is no doubt that the Earth is getting warmer. Many parts of the world are experiencing changes in their weather that are unexpected. Some of these changes could have disastrous consequences for the populations in the areas affected if they continue to get more severe.

There is much evidence to tell us that the global climate changed naturally before humankind was able to influence it with large-scale economic activity. The ice ages that have occurred throughout geological time are clear evidence of such climate change. Natural changes to the global climate are caused by changes in the output of energy from the sun, slow variations in the Earth's orbit and slow changes in the angle of the Earth's axis.

However…

- The present rate of change is greater than anything that has happened in the past. In the 20th century, average global temperatures rose by 0.6°C. Most of this increase took place in the second half of the century (Figure 8). The 1990s was the warmest decade on record. The greatest increases have occurred over the middle and high latitudes of the northern hemisphere continents.

- Most climate experts believe that this high rate of temperature change is due to human activity. The visual evidence of atmospheric pollution is clear to see in more and more parts of the world.

- The predictions are for a further global average temperature increase of between 1.6°C and 4.2°C by 2100.

The argument is that human activity has significantly increased the amount of greenhouse gases in the

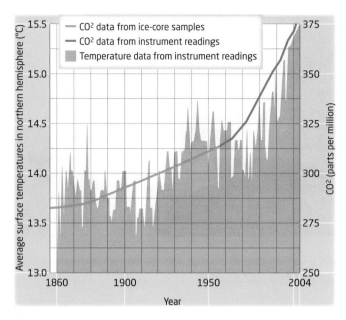

Figure 8 *Evidence of global warming.*

atmosphere and this has caused temperatures to rise more rapidly than ever before. As the economies of China, India and other NICs expand even further, greenhouse gas emissions will continue to increase.

Factory pollution in Tunisia, North Africa.

Wood-burning stove in an urban Asian settlement where this is a significant cause of pollution.

The following are the greenhouse gases:

➔ Carbon dioxide

It accounts for the largest share of greenhouse gases. It is produced by burning fossil fuels in power stations, factories and homes. Vehicle emissions are also a major source. Carbon dioxide is also released into the atmosphere by deforestation and the burning of rainforests. Global carbon dioxide emissions from the burning of fossil fuels grew at 3.1% a year between 2000 and 2006, more than twice the rate of growth during the 1990s.

➔ Methane

This gas is released from decaying plant and animal remains and from farms (particularly from cattle and rice padi fields). Other sources include swamps, peat bogs and landfill sites. Methane is the second-ranked contributor to global warming with a current annual increase of 1%. Cattle convert up to 10% of the food they eat into methane, emitting 100 million tonnes of methane into the atmosphere annually. It has been estimated that padi fields emit up to 150 million tonnes of methane each year. Of great concern is the fact that bogs trapped in permafrost will melt as temperatures rise, releasing large quantities of methane.

➔ Nitrous oxides

The main forms of reactive nitrogen in the air are nitrogen monoxide (NO) and nitrogen dioxide (NO2). Together they are called nitrous oxides (NOx). The main sources are from power stations, vehicle emissions, fertilisers and burning biomass. Catalytic converters fitted to cars can decrease production of these harmful compounds.

➔ Chlorofluorocarbons

These are synthetic chemicals that destroy ozone as well as absorbing longwave radiation. The main sources are aerosols, refrigerators, foam packaging and air conditioning. Chlorofluorocarbons (CFCs) have a lifetime of about 20 to 100 years, and consequently one free chlorine atom from a CFC molecule can do a lot of damage, destroying ozone molecules for a long time. Although emissions of CFCs from the developed world have largely ceased due to international control agreements, the damage to the stratospheric ozone layer will continue for a number of years to come.

➔ Ozone

Naturally occurring ozone found in the stratosphere has been called 'good' ozone because it protects the Earth's surface from dangerous ultraviolet light. Ozone can also be found in the **troposphere**, the lowest layer of the atmosphere. **Tropospheric ozone** (often termed 'bad' ozone) is human-made, a result of air pollution from vehicle and power plant emissions. In Europe, ozone is thought to be increasing by 1–2% a year.

Together these gases form only 0.1% of the atmosphere, but they play a major role in the way the atmospheric system works. Before the Industrial Revolution, which began in the middle of the 18th century, the carbon dioxide concentration in the atmosphere was 280 parts per million (ppm). By 2000 it had risen to 367 ppm. Most scientists argue that about three-quarters of this increase is due to the burning of fossil fuels. Some forecasts indicate that by the end of the current century carbon dioxide concentrations in the atmosphere could be double those before the Industrial Revolution. Much of this will be due to the phenomenal growth rates of the newly industrialised countries. As carbon dioxide increases, the other greenhouse gases are likely to increase as well. Analysis of ice cores from Greenland and Antarctica shows a very strong correlation between carbon dioxide levels in the atmosphere and temperatures.

There is debate about the level of future warming for a number of reasons. In itself a doubling of greenhouse gases should result in the Earth warming by about 1°C. Warmer air can hold more water vapour which is an important greenhouse gas in its own right. The combined impact of both a warmer and a moister atmosphere should result in an increase in global temperature of 2°C. Because an increase of one phenomenon results in an increase in another, the effect is one of **positive feedback**.

Such warming will lead to the melting of snow and ice, reducing the albedo of the Earth. This will result in more solar radiation being absorbed by the Earth's surface. This additional positive feedback effect should increase the total warming to over 4°C.

On the other hand the increase in water vapour will result in more cloud. The effect here can vary depending on the type of cloud:

- If the additional cloud is mainly high and thin, more outgoing longwave radiation will be trapped. This would be another positive feedback effect which would increase global warming further.

- The more likely scenario is that there would be an increase in low, thick clouds. Here, more solar radiation would be reflected resulting in less warming than expected. This is an example of negative feedback. However, overall global warming might still be more than 1°C.

There are also other uncertainties. There is debate about how much more carbon dioxide can be absorbed by the oceans and how vegetation will respond to increasing levels of carbon dioxide. Table 2 charts some of the major events in the global warming debate. Are there any more to add by the time you read this chapter?

Research idea

Some scientists disagree that human activity is having a big impact on the atmosphere. Use the internet to find out the views of these scientists.

Geographical sources of greenhouse gases

Figure 9 shows the top polluting countries in both absolute and relative terms. In absolute terms China and the USA are by far the largest polluters. The emissions of both countries are over four times those of Russia in third place. In relative terms the USA and Canada are the largest polluters, with Russia again in third place. Per capita pollution in China is just over a quarter of that in the USA. Looking at the time period between 1840 and 2004, the USA has been responsible for over 28% of all carbon dioxide emissions. This is way beyond the contribution of any other nation.

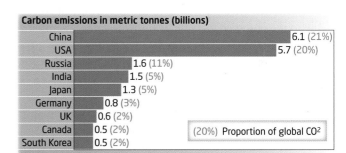

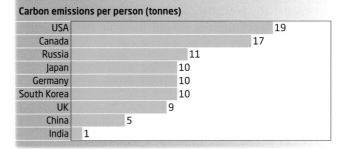

Figure 9 *Top polluting countries in absolute and relative terms.*

Year	Event
1827	French scientist compares the warming of the atmosphere to a greenhouse.
1979	The first World Climate Conference states the possibility of global warming.
1987	The warmest year on record to date.
1995	The warmest year on record to date.
1997	Kyoto Protocol agrees cuts in greenhouse gas emissions but not all countries sign up.
1998	The warmest year on record in the warmest decade.
2005	The second warmest year on record. Kyoto Protocol comes into force. Stern Report on climate change published.
2006	The Intergovernmental Panel on Climate Change (IPCC) confirms the reality of global warming and that human emissions are at least partly responsible.

Table 2 *Global warming factfile.*

Discussion point

What is your school doing to reduce its carbon footprint?

Activities

1 Describe the sources of three greenhouse gases.
2 Write a bullet-point summary of Figure 7 (page 147).
3 a Describe the data presented in Figure 8 (page 149).
   b How significant are the changes indicated?
4 What do you understand by the term 'positive feedback' in terms of the atmosphere?
5 Refer to Figure 9 (page 151). Describe and explain the positions of countries in both graphs.

Global climatic change: environmental consequences

The IPCC is the international body established to assess scientific, technical and socio-economic information on climate change. In 2007 the IPPC concluded:

'Most of the observed increase in global average temperatures since the mid-20th century is very likely due to the observed increase in anthropogenic greenhouse gas concentrations…The observed widespread warming of the atmosphere and ocean, together with ice mass loss, support the conclusion that it is extremely unlikely that global climate change of the past 50 years can be explained without external forcing, and very likely that it is not due to known natural causes alone.'

There are many potential consequences of global climate change. However, there is still much debate about exactly what could happen.

➔ Global temperature variations and heatwaves

In general, higher latitudes and continental regions will experience temperature increases significantly greater than the global average. There will be a rising probability of **heatwaves** with more extreme heat days and fewer very cold days. The Stern Review (2006) quotes the summer of 2003 as Europe's hottest for 500 years and concludes that by 2050, under a relatively high emissions scenario, the temperatures experienced during the heatwave of 2003 could be an average summer. The rise in heatwave frequency will be felt most severely in cities with temperatures amplified by the heat island effect.

➔ Rising sea levels

Sea levels will respond more slowly than temperatures to changing greenhouse gas concentrations. Sea levels are currently rising at around 3 mm per year and the rise has been accelerating. Rising sea levels are due to a combination of **thermal expansion** and the melting of ice sheets and glaciers. Thermal expansion is the increase in water volume due to temperature increase alone. A global average sea-level rise of 0.4 metres from this cause has been predicted by the end of this century.

➔ Increasing acidity in oceans

As carbon dioxide levels rise in the atmosphere, more of the gas is dissolved in surface waters creating carbonic acid. Since the start of the Industrial Revolution the acidity activity of the oceans has increased by 30%. This is having a significant impact on coral reefs and shellfish. As carbon

Increasing acidity in oceans is having an impact on coral reefs, such as the Great Barrier Reef.

dioxide dissolves in water, it produces acidic hydrogen ions which attack the carbonate ions that are the building blocks of the calcium shells and skeletons used by corals and shellfish. In 2009 a leading scientist stated that the Arctic Ocean is becoming acidic so quickly that it will reach corrosive levels within 10 years. This forecast suggests that 10% of the ocean will be corrosively acidic by 2018, rising to 50% in 2050. By 2100 the entire Arctic Ocean will be inhospitable to shellfish. Ocean acidity is particularly advanced in the polar regions because gas is more soluble in cold water than warm water.

⊙ Melting of ice caps and glaciers

Satellite photographs show ice melting at its fastest rate ever. The area of sea ice in the Arctic Ocean has decreased by 15% since 1960, while the thickness of the ice has fallen by 40%. Sea temperature has risen by 3°C in the Arctic in recent decades. A report in the Science section of the *Guardian* in March 2007 claimed that the Arctic Ocean may lose all its ice by 2040. This would disrupt global weather patterns. For example, it would bring intense winter storms and heavier rainfall to western Europe. Table 3 gives examples of recently observed environmental changes in the Arctic linked to higher temperatures.

The warm water of the Gulf Stream, which originates in the Gulf of Mexico, and its continuation the North Atlantic Drift has a major influence on the climates of the east coast of North America and western Europe (Figure 10). Climatologists are concerned that melting Arctic ice could disrupt these warm ocean currents resulting

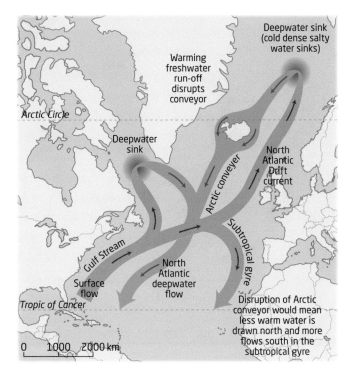

Figure 10 *The Gulf Stream.*

in temperatures in western Europe falling by at least 5°C. Winters in the UK, and in other neighbouring countries such as Italy and Greece, would be much colder than they are now. It is too early to say that this will happen, but scientists are monitoring the situation carefully.

The Antarctic continent (Figure 11, page 154) comprises two main regions separated by the Transantarctic

Theme	Location	Observed changes	Climate link
Sea ice	Circum-Arctic	Reduction in areal extent and thickness	Warmer air
Glacier	Circum-Arctic	Reduction in areal extent and mass	Warmer air
Permafrost	Alaska	Thawing	Warmer air, changes in snow cover
Ice sheet	Greenland	Overall reduction in mass and recession at margins	Warmer air
River	Siberia (Lena, Ob and Yenisei)	Increase in base flow, especially in winter	Reduced permafrost generating more groundwater flow
Treeline	Alaska	Advancing poleward	Warmer air, warmer soil
Birds	Alaska	Changed range	Longer growing season
Caribou	Northern Canada, Alaska	Improved calf survival but reduced health	Warmer air, more insects

Table 3 *Environmental changes in the Arctic.*

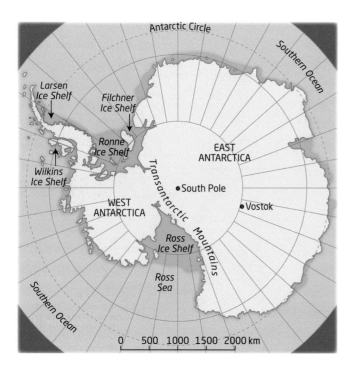

Figure 11 *Map of Antarctica.*

Melting ice on the Qinghai-Tibet plateau.

Geographical skills

Look at an atlas to find the Qinghai-Tibet plateau. Name some of the main glaciers on the plateau and the major rivers that flow out from the region. To where do these rivers flow?

Mountains. Both regions are covered in ice which is on average 2000 metres thick. East Antarctica is a mountainous plateau as big as Europe. Its huge ice sheet appears on the whole to be stable. However, there is much greater concern over the West Antarctic Ice Sheet (WAIS). It is inherently less stable because much of the ice base is under water. Temperatures in western Antarctica have increased sharply in recent years, melting ice shelves and changing plant and animal life on the Antarctic Peninsula.

In 2007, the sea ice around Antarctica had melted back to a record low. At the same time, the movement of glaciers towards the sea had speeded up. A satellite survey between 1996 and 2006 found that the net loss of ice rose by 75%. In 2002 instabilities in the Larsen Ice Shelf led to the collapse of a huge section of the shelf (over 3200 km² and 200 metres thick) from the Antarctic Peninsula. The Larsen A ice shelf, 1600 km² in area, broke off in 1995. In 1998 the 1100 km² Wilkins ice shelf broke away. There are now questions about the long-term stability of Antarctica's two biggest ice shelves, the Ross ice shelf and the Filchner ice shelf.

Measurements of the Greenland ice sheet have shown a slight inland growth, but significant melting and an accumulation of ice flows near the coast. Antarctica and Greenland are the world's two major ice masses. Total melting of these ice masses (which is not predicted at present) could raise global sea levels by 70 metres.

Research published by Chinese scientists in 2006 shows that glaciers in the Qinghai-Tibet plateau are melting faster than anyone previously thought. Warming has speeded up the shrinkage of more than 80% of the 46 377 glaciers in this major plateau region. This could eventually result in water shortages in China and large parts of South Asia. The increasing rate of melting from the plateau has led to a rise in water runoff from the plateau which has increased soil erosion and desertification. The United Nations has warned that Tibet's glaciers could disappear within 100 years.

Ice melting could cause sea levels to rise by a further 5 metres (on top of thermal expansion). Hundreds of millions of people live in coastal areas within this range.

● Thawing peat bogs

An area of permafrost spanning a million square kilometres has started to melt for the first time since it formed 11 000 years ago at the end of the last ice age. The area, which covers the entire sub-Arctic region of western Siberia, is the world's largest frozen peat bog and scientists fear that as it thaws, it will release billions of tonnes of methane, a greenhouse gas 20 times more potent than carbon dioxide, into the atmosphere.

El Niño

This phenomenon is a change in the pattern of wind and ocean currents in the Pacific Ocean. This causes short-term changes in weather for countries bordering the Pacific such as flooding in Peru and drought in Australia. El Niño events tend to occur every two to seven years. There is concern that rising temperatures could increase their frequency or intensity.

Growth of the tropical belt

A study published in 2007 warned that the Earth's tropical belt was expanding north and south. A further 8.5 million square miles of the Earth are experiencing a tropical climate compared with that in 1980. The poleward movement of subtropical dry belts could affect agriculture and water supplies over large areas of the Mediterranean, the south-western USA, northern Mexico, southern Australia, southern Africa and parts of Latin America. The extension of the tropical belt will put more people at risk from tropical diseases.

Changing patterns of rainfall

The amount and distribution of rainfall in many parts of the world could change considerably. Generally, regions that get plenty of rainfall are likely to receive even more, and regions with low rainfall are likely to get less. The latter will include the poor arid and semi-arid countries of Africa. In 2009, the heaviest rain in 53 years battered Dhaka, the capital of Bangladesh – a total of 33.3 cm of rain fell in 12 hours.

Declining crop yields

Higher temperatures have already had an impact on global yields of wheat, corn and barley. A recent study revealed that crop yields fall between 3% and 5% for every 0.5°C increase in average temperature. Food shortages could begin conflicts between different countries.

Impact on wildlife

Many species of wildlife may be wiped out because they will not have a chance to adapt to rapid changes in their environments. The loss of Arctic ice will have a huge effect on polar bears and other species that live and hunt among the ice floes.

Giant climate change banner, Brussels, 2009.

Activities

1 Explain thermal expansion.
2 With reference to Table 3 (page 153), discuss the changes related to global warming that have occurred in the Arctic region. What do you think may happen in the future?
3 With the help of Figure 10 (page 153), explain what could happen if melting Arctic ice disrupts the warm waters of the Gulf Stream and North Atlantic Drift.
4 What is happening to the Antarctic and Greenland ice sheets?
5 How might climate change affect:
   a growth of the tropical belt
   b crop yields
   c wildlife?

Global climatic change: solutions

Human response to climate change must take two forms:

- acting to reduce the causes of greenhouse gas emissions
- preparing for the consequences of significant climatic change.

For both sets of actions it will be vitally important to manage the problem in a sustainable manner. If this does not happen, other major problems may be created in the process. In 2007 the Intergovernmental Panel on Climate Change (IPCC) warned that the world had until 2020 to avoid the most dangerous effects of climate change.

Table 4 summarises the views of the IPCC with regard to measures to combat climate change. The technology is already available to lower emissions in some areas. Examples are nuclear power, renewable energy generation and measures promoting energy efficiency. However, there are two significant problems:

- It will need a very large investment to put some measures into widespread global use.
- Some measures are already considered to be unsustainable. For example, there is growing controversy about the increasing use of biofuels. This source of energy takes valuable land away from food production and uses a considerable amount of energy in the production process. Nuclear power is, as ever, a controversial issue.

Sector	Currently available	Available by 2030
Energy supply	Improved supply and distribution efficiency; switching from coal to gas; nuclear power; renewable energy	Carbon capture and storage for fossil fuel generating facilities; advanced nuclear and renewable energy
Transport	Higher fuel efficiency; hybrid vehicles; cleaner diesel vehicles; biofuels; shifts to rail, public transport and bicycles	Higher-efficiency biofuels; higher-efficiency aircraft; more powerful and reliable electric/hybrid vehicle batteries
Industry	Heat and power recovery; recycling and substitution of materials; control of emissions	Technological changes in the manufacture of cement, ammonia, iron and aluminium
Agriculture	Management of land to increase carbon stored in soil; dedicated energy crops to replace fossil fuel use	Improvement of crop yields; reductions in emissions from some agricultural practices
Forests	Increase in forested area; use of forestry products for bioenergy to reduce fossil fuel use	Tree species improvement to increase biomass productivity and therefore carbon capture

Table 4 *Technologies and practices to combat climate change.*

Global climate action day: Vienna, October, 2009.

For example, in the UK, improvement to the sewer network and drainage systems will be needed to cope with more severe storm events. Many homes will have to be made more flood resilient. An example of this is using stone, concrete or tiled floors so that if a house is flooded it can be hosed down and dried out more easily than a house with carpets. It costs about £40,000 to make an average house flood-resilient. In flood-prone areas in Japan, properties are being built on raised ground with sports fields and parkland used to hold floodwater. In Germany, marshland has been used to construct 'wells' to hold floodwater.

More money is being directed into research to combat global warming. For example, agricultural scientists are trying to develop crops that can better withstand heat and drought.

Government legislation

In 2007 the British government stated its intention to become the first country in the world to set legally binding targets to reduce carbon dioxide emissions. The aim is to cut the UK's carbon dioxide emissions by 60% by 2050. A new system of five-year 'carbon budgets' will be introduced to set limits on total emissions. The limits will be set 15 years in advance. This will allow businesses and public organisations to plan ahead.

Many environmentalists want higher 'green taxes'. However, this is difficult at a time of great concern over the global economy. In the transition to a **low-carbon economy** many proposals have been put forward which include:

- a ten-year programme to convert all taxis to electric or hybrid power
- putting a halt on the expansion of airports
- huge investment in public transport
- free electric coaches operating on motorways in their own lanes.

Many countries are looking at the concept of **community energy**. This is generally where small-scale electricity generation units are incorporated into new building developments. Examples are wind turbines and solar panels built in schools, shopping centres and business parks. Of course, such energy installations can also be added to existing developments. Energy is lost in transmission if the source of supply is a long way away. Energy produced locally is much more efficient.

An example of community energy: small wind turbine on the science block of a school.

 Discussion point

Do you think that the world can reduce emissions before catastrophic climate changes occur? Give reasons for your opinion.

 **Activities**

1 Discuss the technologies and practices that can be used to combat climate change.
2 Why is it important to move towards a low-carbon economy?
3 What are the advantages of developing community energy on a larger scale?

Key terms

Climate change long-term sustained change in the average global climate.

Natural greenhouse effect the property of the Earth's atmosphere by which long wavelength heat rays from the Earth's surface are trapped or reflected back by the atmosphere.

Enhanced greenhouse effect this results from human activities which increase the concentration of naturally occurring greenhouse gases and leads to global warming and climate change.

Global warming the increase in the average temperature of the Earth's near-surface air in the 20th and early 21st centuries and its projected continuation.

Tipping point the point at which the damage caused to global systems by climate change becomes irreversible.

Insolation the heat energy from the sun consisting of the visible spectrum together with ultraviolet and infrared rays.

Energy balance the balance between incoming solar radiation and outgoing terrestrial radiation.

Solar constant the amount of solar energy received per unit area, per unit time on a surface at right-angles to the sun's beam at the edge of the Earth's atmosphere.

Sensible heat the heat energy that causes a change in temperature of a substance but does not contribute to a change in state.

Conduction the transfer of heat by contact.

Convection the transfer of heat by the movement of a gas or a liquid.

Latent heat the quantity of heat absorbed or released by a substance undergoing a change of state, such as water vapour condensing into water droplets.

Evaporation the change in state from a liquid into a vapour.

Condensation the change in state from a gas to a liquid.

Ground heat the warming of the subsurface of the Earth.

Albedo the proportion of solar radiation that is reflected by a particular body or surface.

External forcings processes both outside and within the atmosphere that can force changes in climate.

Solar forcing radiative forcing caused by changes in incoming solar radiation.

Global dimming a worldwide decline of the intensity of the sunlight reaching the Earth's surface, caused by particulate air pollution and natural events, for example volcanic ash.

Global brightening an increasing amount of sunlight reaching the Earth's surface caused by an intensification of solar radiation.

Ice sheet a thick layer of ice covering extensive regions of the world, notably Antarctica and Greenland.

Troposphere the lowest layer of the atmosphere

Tropospheric ozone human produced ozone, a result of air pollution

Positive feedback when an increase of one phenomenon results in an increase in another.

Heatwave a prolonged period of excessively hot weather.

Thermal expansion as sea and ocean temperatures increase, the water molecules near the surface move further apart, so the water volume increases and the sea level rises.

Low-carbon economy where significant measures have been taken to reduce carbon emissions in all sectors of the economy.

Community energy energy produced close to the point of consumption.

Review

Examination-style questions

1 Refer to Figure 12 which shows the link between greenhouse gases and climate change.

a Define greenhouse gases.

b Describe two consequences of climate change shown on the diagram.

c Explain how feedbacks operate in the climate change system.

2 Refer to Figure 13.

a Name the main greenhouse gases.

b Describe how three of the sources shown in Figure 13 contribute to greenhouse gas emissions.

c Explain how these three sources could reduce their greenhouse gas emissions in the future.

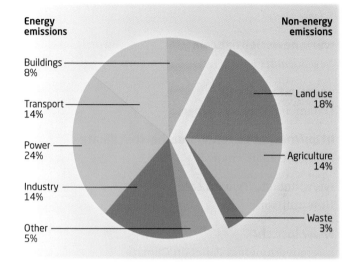

Figure 13 *Greenhouse gas emissions by source.*

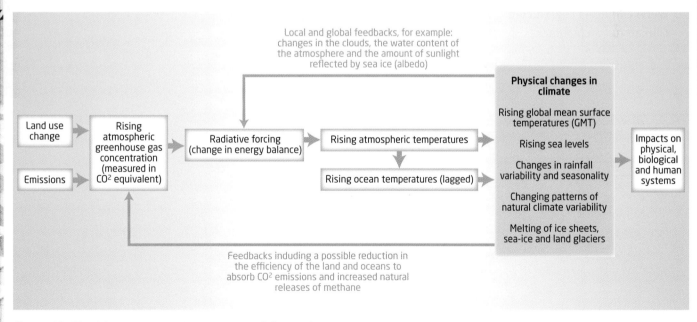

Figure 12 *The link between greenhouse gases and climate change.*

Websites

www.sciencedaily.com
Science Daily

www.newscientist.com
New Scientist

www.oxfam.org.uk
Oxfam and climate change

http://news.bbc.co.uk/weather/hi/climate
BBC on climate change

www.howstuffworks.com
Howstuffworks

www.ipcc.ch/
Intergovernmental Panel on Climate
Change (IPCC)

www.skeptic.com
SKEPTIC (Promoting Science and Critical
Thinking)

www.climateresearch.com
Climateresearch.com

10 Soil and change

KEY QUESTIONS

- What are the causes of soil degradation?
- What are the environmental and socio-economic consequences of soil degradation?
- What management strategies can be used to combat soil degradation?

Lower than average rainfalls can make soils more vulnerable to degradation.

The extent of soil degradation

Soil plays a vital role in the functioning of the planet. It supports agriculture, wildlife and the built environment. It also filters water, stores carbon and preserves records of the ecological and cultural past. Soil scientists have asked for more targeted research and strict guidelines to stop what they say is the massive degradation of land and soil around the world, which is contributing to climate change and food insecurity.

Soil degradation is a global process. It involves both the physical loss (erosion) and the reduction in quality of topsoil associated with nutrient decline and contamination. It has a significant impact on agriculture and also has implications for the urban environment, pollution and flooding. The loss of the upper soil horizons containing organic matter and nutrients and the thinning of **soil profiles** reduces crop yields on degraded soils. Soil degradation can cancel out gains from improved crop yields. The statistics on soil degradation make worrying reading:

- Globally it is estimated that 2 billion hectares of soil resources have been degraded. This is equivalent to about 15% of the Earth's land area. Such a scale of soil degradation has resulted in the loss of 15% of world agricultural supply in the last 50 years.

- For three centuries ending in 2000, topsoil had been lost at the rate of 300 million tonnes a year. Between 1950 and 2000 topsoil was lost at the much higher rate of 760 million tonnes a year.

- During the past 40 years nearly one-third of the world's cropland has been abandoned because of soil erosion and degradation.

- In Sub-Saharan Africa, nearly one million square miles of cropland has shown a 'consistent significant decline' according to a March 2008 report by a consortium of agricultural institutions. Some scientists consider this to be a 'slow-motion disaster'.

- In the UK, 2.2 million tonnes of topsoil is eroded annually and over 17% of arable land shows signs of erosion.

- It takes natural processes about 500 years to replace 25 mm of topsoil lost to erosion. The minimum soil depth for agricultural production is 150 mm. Thus, from this perspective, productive fertile soil can be considered a non-renewable, endangered ecosystem.

A recent study has highlighted the severity of human-induced soil change (Figure 1, page 162), stating that soils around the world are being transformed by human activities in ways that we poorly understand. The loss of the ability of degraded soils to store carbon is given particular attention. Over the last 50 years or so global soils have lost about a hundred billion tonnes of carbon to the atmosphere in the form of carbon dioxide, due to the depletion of soil structure. The idea that the extent of human impacts on the environment could represent a new geological age was first put forward in 2002 by Nobel Prize-winning chemist Paul Crutzen.

Human activities triggering 'Global Soil Change'

Earth's climate and biodiversity aren't the only things being dramatically affected by humans – the world's soils are also shifting beneath our feet, a new report says.

'Global soil change' due to human activities is a major component of what some experts say should be recognised as a new period of geologic time: the Anthropocene, or human-made age.

This new era will be defined by the pervasiveness of human environmental impacts, including changes to Earth's soils and surface geology, proponents of the theory say.

'Unquestionably we are entering the Anthropocene,' said Daniel Richter of Duke University, who authored the new study of Earth's changing soils.

In the December 2007 issue of the journal *Soil Science*, Richter warns that Earth's soils already show a reduced capacity to support biodiversity and agricultural production.

As the amount of depleted and damaged soils increases, global cycles of water, carbon, nitrogen, and other materials are also being affected.

Richter's report supports an independent proposal in the current issue of the journal *GSA Today* that calls for official recognition of the Anthropocene epoch.

In that paper, Jan Zalaseiwicz of the University of Leicester in England and colleagues argue that the fossil and geologic record of our time will leave distinct signatures that will be apparent far into the future.

To future geologists, Zalaseiwicz said, 'the Anthropocene will appear about as suddenly as [the transition] triggered by the meteorite impact at the end of the Cretaceous 65.5 million years ago, when the dinosaurs became extinct'.

Figure 1 *Human activities triggering global soil change.*

The Global Assessment of Human-induced Soil Degradation (GLASOD) is the only global survey of soil degradation to have been undertaken. Figure 2 is a generalised map of the findings of this survey. It shows that substantial parts of all continents have been affected by various types of soil degradation. The GLASOD calculation is that damage has occurred on 15% of the world's total land area – 13% light and moderate with 2% severe and very severe.

Geographical skills

Describe the distribution of soil degradation types shown in Figure 2. Refer to all elements of the key and make reference to all continental areas.

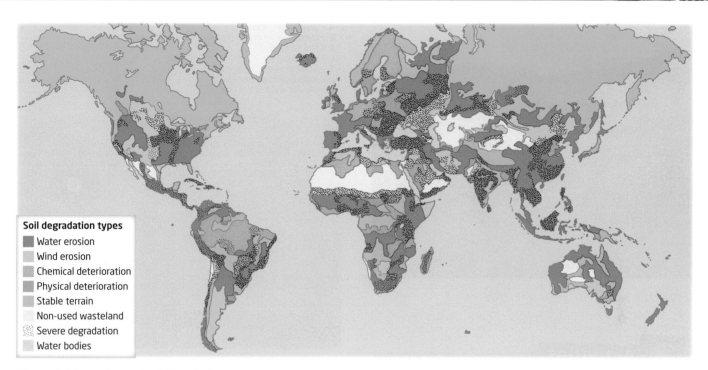

Figure 2 *Human-induced soil degradation.*

The International Forum of Soils, Society and Global Change in September 2007 referred to 'the massive degradation of land and soil around the world which is contributing to climate change and threatening food security'. The Forum noted that:

- At least a quarter of the excess carbon dioxide in the atmosphere has come from changes in land use, such as deforestation, in the last century.

- Without the cover of vegetation, land becomes more reflective. It also loses fertility and the capacity to support vegetation and agricultural crops.

- The Intergovernmental Panel on Climate Change should develop a special report on the link between land degradation and climate change. By addressing soils and protecting the land cover and vegetation we can obtain high value in terms of mitigating climate change.

- A better understanding of the capacity for carbon sequestration in soil is needed.

- Degradation of soil and land in already marginally productive land is a significant issue for many developing countries, particularly in northern Africa, the Sahara region and parts of Asia, including China. Many of these regions have fragile ecosystems where any human interventions can lead to serious degradation.

Research idea

For the country in which you live, find out where the problem of soil degradation is most severe. What is the extent of the problem?

Developed and developing world contrasts

In temperate areas much soil degradation is a result of market forces and the attitudes adopted by commercial farmers and governments. In contrast, in the tropics much degradation results from high population pressure, land shortages and lack of awareness. The greater climate extremes and poorer soil structures in tropical areas give greater potential for degradation in such areas compared with temperate latitudes. This difference has been a significant factor in development or the lack of it.

Gully erosion and remedial measures in southern Italy.

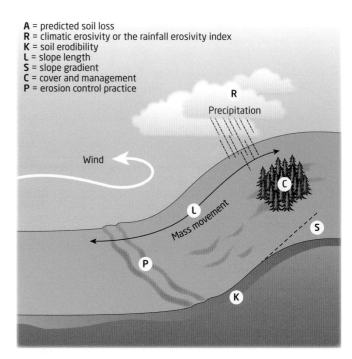

A = predicted soil loss
R = climatic erosivity or the rainfall erosivity index
K = soil erodibility
L = slope length
S = slope gradient
C = cover and management
P = erosion control practice

Figure 3 *The universal soil loss equation.*

Activities

1 Define soil degradation.
2 What is the evidence in the photo above that soil degradation has occurred?
3 Write a 60-word summary of Figure 1 (page 162).
4 Briefly state the different reasons for soil degradation in the developed and developing worlds.

The causes of soil degradation

The **universal soil loss equation** A = R K LS C P is an attempt to predict the degree of erosion that will occur in an area on the basis of certain factors which increase susceptibility to erosion. Figure 3 and Table 1 illustrate the equation. The universal soil loss equation predicts the long-term average annual rate of erosion on a field slope based on rainfall pattern, soil type, topography, crop system and management practices. It only predicts the amount of soil loss that results from sheet or rill erosion on a single slope and does not account for additional soil losses that might occur from gully, wind or tillage erosion. Although it has limitations, it is a useful model to consider when beginning to investigate this globally important topic.

The main cause of soil degradation is the removal of the natural vegetation cover, leaving the surface exposed to the elements. Figure 4 shows the human causes of degradation, with deforestation and overgrazing as the two main problems. The resulting loss of vegetation cover is a leading cause of wind and water erosion. **Deforestation** occurs for a number of reasons, including the clearing of land for agricultural use, for timber, and for other activities such as mining. Such activities tend to happen quickly whereas the loss of vegetation for fuelwood – a massive problem in many developing countries – is generally a more gradual process. Deforestation means that rain is no longer intercepted by vegetation, with rainsplash loosening the topsoil and leaving it vulnerable to removal by overland flow.

Overgrazing is the grazing of natural pastures at stocking intensities above the livestock carrying capacity. Population pressure in many areas and poor agricultural practices have resulted in serious overgrazing. This is a major problem in many parts of the world, particularly in marginal ecosystems. The process occurs in this way:

● trampling by animals (and humans) damages plant leaves

● some leaves die away, reducing the ability of plants to photosynthesise

● now there are fewer leaves to intercept rainfall and the ground is more exposed

● plant species sensitive to trampling quickly disappear

● soil begins to erode when bare patches appear and trampling will compact the soil and damage its structure

Factor	Description
Ecological conditions	
Erosivity of soil R	Rainfall totals, intensity and seasonal distribution. Maximum erosivity occurs when the rainfall occurs as high-intensity storms. If such rain is received when the land has just been ploughed or full crop cover is not yet established, erosion will be greater than when falling on a full canopy. Minimal erosion occurs when rains are gentle, and fall onto frozen soil or land with natural vegetation or a full crop cover.
Erodibility K	The susceptibility of a soil to erosion. Depends upon infiltration capacity and the structural stability of soil. Soils with high infiltration capacity and high structural stability that allow the soil to resist the impact of rainsplash, have lowest erodibility values.
Length-slope factor LS	Slope length and steepness influence the movement and speed of water down the slope, and thus its ability to transport particles. The greater the slope, the greater the erosivity; the longer the slope, the more water is received on the surface.
Land use type	
Crop management C	Most control can be exerted over the cover and management of the soil. This factor relates to the type of crop and cultivation practices. Established grass and forest provide the best protection against erosion. Of agricultural crops, those with the greatest foliage and thus greatest ground cover are optimal. Fallow land or crops that expose the soil for long periods after planting or harvesting offer little protection.
Soil conservation P	Soil conservation measures, such as contour ploughing, bunding (a wall or barrier designed to prevent leaks) and use of strips and terraces, can reduce erosion and slow runoff water.

Table 1 *Factors relating to the universal soil loss equation.*

- loose surface soil particles are the first to be carried away, either by wind or water
- the loss of soil structure means that less water can infiltrate to the lower soil horizons; the growth rate of plants is reduced and it is more difficult for damaged plants to recover.

Agricultural mismanagement is also a major problem due to a combination of a lack of knowledge and the pursuit of short-term gain against consideration of longer-term damage. Such activities include shifting cultivation without adequate fallow periods, absence of soil conservation measures, cultivation of fragile or marginal lands, unbalanced fertiliser use, and the use of poor irrigation techniques. On a global scale industrialisation/urbanisation accounts for only 1%, but on a smaller scale its impact can be much more significant. Table 2 (page 166) provides more detail on human activities and their impact on soil erosion.

 **Discussion point**

Why do you think overgrazing continues to be a problem in many areas when the local population understand what is happening?

Overgrazing and agricultural mismanagement affect more than 12 million km² worldwide. Approximately 20% of the world's pasture and rangelands have been damaged and the situation is most severe in Africa and Asia. Huge areas of forest are cleared for logging, fuelwood, farming or other human uses.

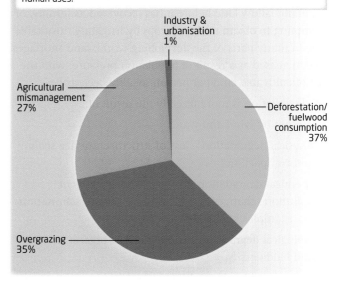

Figure 4 *Causes of land degradation.*

Action	Effect
Removal of woodland or ploughing of established pasture	The vegetation cover is removed, roots binding the soil die and the soil is exposed to wind and water. Particularly susceptible to erosion if on slopes.
Cultivation	Exposure of bare soil surface before planting and after harvesting. Cultivation on slopes can generate large amounts of runoff and create rills and gullies.
Grazing	Overgrazing can severely reduce the vegetation cover and leave the surface vulnerable to erosion. Grouping of animals can lead to trampling and creation of bare patches. Dry regions are particularly susceptible to wind erosion.
Roads or tracks	They collect water due to reduced infiltration which can cause rills and gullies to form.
Mining	Exposure of the bare soil. Degradation from chemical dumping.

Table 2 *Human activities and their impact on soil erosion.*

The role of demographic factors in land degradation cannot be ignored, particularly when high population growth pushes cultivation onto marginal lands. Examples are settlers cultivating soils which are too shallow or too steep, ploughing fallow land before it has recovered its fertility, or attempting to obtain multiple crops by irrigating unsuitable soils. In many parts of the developing world, land shortages have increased as a result of population pressure, with the area of cultivable land per person steadily decreasing.

Soil degradation is more directly the result of:

- erosion by wind and water
- physical degradation – loss of structure, surface sealing and compaction
- chemical degradation through various forms of pollution (changes in pH, acidification and salinisation are examples of chemical degradation)
- biological degradation through loss of organic matter and biodiversity
- climate and land use change which may accelerate the above factors.

Water and wind erosion

These two agents of erosion account for approximately 80% of the world's degraded landscapes. The impact of water erosion is influenced by a number of factors, which are explained in Figure 5. There are many types of water erosion including surface, gully, rill and tunnel erosion. In the UK erosion by water is more widespread than wind erosion. The rate of soil erosion by water in the UK is estimated at 0.1–0.3 tonnes per hectare per year. Forty-four per cent of arable land in the UK is at risk of water erosion. In contrast, in desert regions wind erosion dominates, although water erosion can have devastating short-term impacts.

Physical degradation

The signs of physical degradation are soil crusting, sealing and compaction which can be caused by several factors, like compaction through heavy machines or animals. These problems occur in all continents, under nearly all climates and soil physical conditions. Soil crusting and compaction tend to increase runoff, decrease the infiltration of water into the soil, prevent or inhibit plant growth and leave the surface bare and subject to other forms of degradation. Severe crusting of the soil surface because of the breakdown of soil aggregates can inhibit water entry into the soil and prevent seedling emergence.

Chemical degradation

Chemical deterioration involves loss of nutrients or organic matter, salinisation, acidification, soil pollution, and fertility decline. The removal of nutrients reduces the capacity of soils to support plant growth and crop production and causes acidification. **Acidification** results from a change in the chemical composition of soil. The acidity (or alkalinity) of a soil is measured on the pH scale. Most soils in the UK are slightly acidic. However, in upland areas in the UK acidity increases as the heavier rainfall leaches out elements such as calcium faster than they can be replaced by weathering. In areas where there is a balance between rainfall and evapotranspiration, soils are often neutral, as in the Prairies of North America. In areas with water deficiency, soils are more likely to be alkaline.

Acid rain can have a significant impact on some soils in particular. Some soils are naturally acidic, but this can be considerably increased by acid rain or dry deposition of acid gases and particles. The combustion of fossil fuels is the main source of acidity in the atmosphere.

WATER EROSION

Rainfall intensity and runoff: the impact of raindrops on the soil surface can break down soil aggregates and disperse the aggregate material. Lighter aggregate materials, such as very fine sand, silt, clay and organic matter, can be easily removed by raindrop splash and runoff water; greater raindrop energy or runoff amounts might be required to move the larger sand and gravel particles. Runoff can occur whenever there is excess water on a slope that cannot be absorbed into the soil or trapped on the surface. The amount of runoff can be increased if infiltration is reduced due to soil compaction, crusting or freezing. Runoff from agricultural land may be greatest during spring months when the soils are usually saturated, snow is melting and vegetative cover is minimal. Gully and rill erosion are the dominant forms of water erosion. They provide flow paths for subsequent flows, and the gullies or rills are in turn eroded further. This process leads to the self-organised formation of networks of erosional channels.

Soil erodibility: an estimate of the ability of soils to resist erosion, based on the physical characteristics of each soil. Generally, soils with faster infiltration rates, higher levels of organic matter and improved soil structure have a greater resistance to erosion. Sand, sandy loam and loam-textured soils tend to be less erodible than silt, very fine sand, and certain clay-textured soils.

Slope gradient and length: naturally, the steeper the slope of a field, the greater the amount of soil loss from erosion by water. Soil erosion by water also increases as the slope length increases due to the greater accumulation of runoff.

Vegetation: plant and residue cover protects the soil from raindrop impact and splash, tends to slow down the movement of surface runoff and allows excess surface water to infiltrate.

WIND EROSION

Erodibility of soil: very fine particles can be suspended by the wind and then transported great distances. Fine and medium-sized particles can be lifted and deposited, while coarse particles can be blown along the surface (commonly known as the saltation effect).

Soil surface roughness: soil surfaces that are not rough or ridged offer little resistance to the wind. Excess tillage can contribute to soil structure breakdown and increased erosion.

Climate: the speed and duration of the wind have a direct relationship to the extent of soil erosion. Soil moisture levels can be very low at the surface during periods of drought, thus releasing the particles for transport by wind.

Unsheltered distance: the lack of windbreaks (trees, shrubs, residue etc.) allows the wind to put soil particles into motion for greater distances, thus increasing abrasion and soil erosion. Knolls are usually exposed and suffer the most.

Vegetative cover: the lack of permanent vegetation cover in certain locations has resulted in extensive erosion by wind. Loose, dry, bare soil is the most susceptible. The most effective vegetative cover for protection should include an adequate network of living windbreaks combined with good tillage, residue management, and crop selection.

Figure 5 *The factors influencing the erosion of soil by water and wind.*

In arid and semi-arid areas problems due to accumulation of salts can arise, which impedes the entry of water in plant roots. **Salinisation** is the concentration of abnormally high levels of salts in soils due to evaporation. It frequently occurs in association with irrigation and leads to the death of plants and loss of soil structure. Salt-affected soils are common in arid areas, coastal zones and in marine-derived sediments, where capillary action brings salts to the upper part of the soil.

Soil toxicity can be brought about in a number of ways, but typical examples are from municipal or industrial wastes, oil spills, the excessive use of fertiliser, herbicides and insecticides, or the release of radioactive materials and acidification by airborne pollutants.

Frequent causes of contamination are farmyard waste and sewage sludge which may contain high levels of heavy metals. Individual serious pollution events such as the Chernobyl nuclear power plant accident in 1986 can contaminate a large area for a very long period of time. In other areas soils have been contaminated by radioactive isotopes from nuclear weapons testing.

Biological degradation

Many key soil functions are underpinned by biodiversity and organic matter. Organic matter enters soils mainly from plant remains and organic manure additions. The loss of organic matter degrades the soil and in particular its ability to produce reasonable crop yields. Loss of organic matter also reduces the stability of soil aggregates which under the impact of rainfall may then break up. This may result in the formation of soil crusts which reduce infiltration of water into the soil. This increases the likelihood of runoff and water erosion happening. Loss of soil structure can also occur because of compaction from agricultural machinery and cultivation in wet weather.

In the UK, about 18% of the organic matter present in arable topsoils in 1980 had been lost by 1995. A prominent factor was the ploughing of grasslands for arable use. Some soil scientists in the UK consider that the amount of organic matter in some soils may be so depleted that crop production may not be sustainable in the long-term.

Climate and land use change

Changes to how land and soil are managed may be more important than changes in the soil due to climate modification. For example, in the UK wetter winters may lead to increased muddy flooding unless land use changes are made. Muddy flooding occurs when bare soil is left exposed at the wettest time of the year. In the South Downs in the UK, changes in land management practices occurred in response to floods in the early 1990s. This included the reversion of some winter cereal fields to permanent grassland under the EU's set-aside scheme. No muddy floods have occurred locally since these measures were adopted.

Drier summers may result in wind erosion becoming more of a problem as soils dry out. This may cause problems with air quality and visibility, and have possible adverse health implications.

In low-lying coastal areas land degradation from seawater inundation is a potential concern. River deltas and low-lying islands are particularly at risk. Salinity can reach levels where farming becomes impossible.

Good-quality pastoral farmland – the Cotswold Hills, UK.

The impact of artificial fertilisers and pesticides

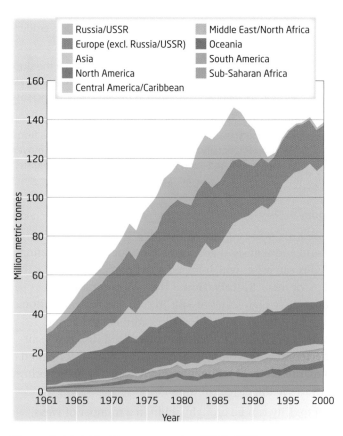

Figure 6 *World fertiliser consumption, 1961–2001.*

Figure 6 shows the considerable global increase in the use of fertiliser by world region. Research has shown that the heavy and sustained use of artificial fertiliser can result in serious soil degradation. In Figure 7, soil profile

Dry landscape in north-east Brazil.

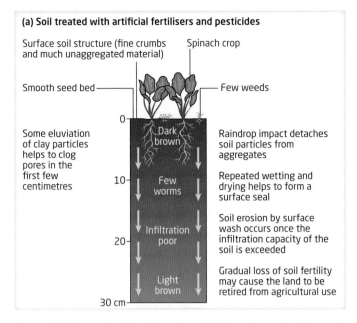

(a) Soil treated with artificial fertilisers and pesticides

Surface soil structure (fine crumbs and much unaggregated material)

Spinach crop

Smooth seed bed

Few weeds

Some eluviation of clay particles helps to clog pores in the first few centimetres

Dark brown

Raindrop impact detaches soil particles from aggregates

Few worms

Repeated wetting and drying helps to form a surface seal

Infiltration poor

Soil erosion by surface wash occurs once the infiltration capacity of the soil is exceeded

Light brown

Gradual loss of soil fertility may cause the land to be retired from agricultural use

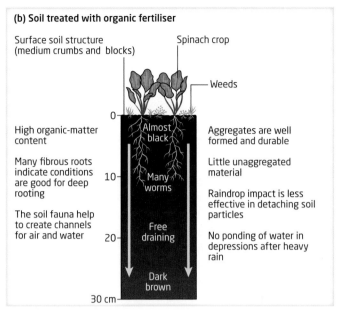

(b) Soil treated with organic fertiliser

Surface soil structure (medium crumbs and blocks)

Spinach crop

Weeds

High organic-matter content

Almost black

Aggregates are well formed and durable

Many fibrous roots indicate conditions are good for deep rooting

Many worms

Little unaggregated material

Raindrop impact is less effective in detaching soil particles

The soil fauna help to create channels for air and water

Free draining

No ponding of water in depressions after heavy rain

Dark brown

Figure 7 *Two soil profiles: (a) with artificial fertilisers (b) with organic fertiliser.*

(a) illustrates the problems that can result. In contrast, soil profile (b) shows a much healthier soil treated with organic fertiliser.

In the artificially fertilised soil the ability of the soil to infiltrate water has been compromised by the breakdown of **soil aggregates** to fine particles which have sealed the surface. Pore spaces have been filled up by the fine soil material from the broken crumbs. This can result in ponding in surface depressions followed by soil erosion.

Local soil degradation

Figure 8 illustrates how a combination of causes and processes can operate in an area to result in soil degradation. The diagram shows a range of different economic activities which affect the soil. Can you think of other economic activities that you could reasonably expect to find in such an area? What impact would these activities have on the soil? Notice how the diagram shows an increase in the area characterised by sealing as the urban area expands at the expense of farmland.

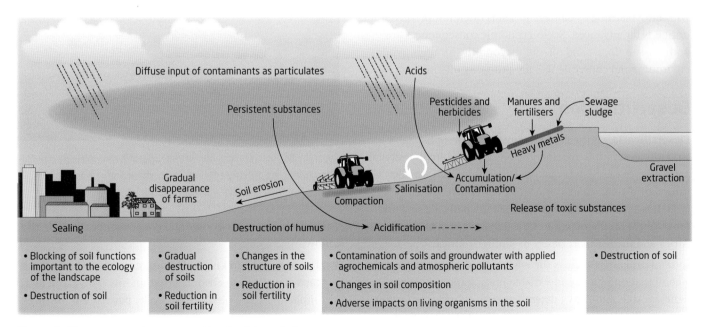

Figure 8 *The causes and processes of local soil degradation.*

Urban soils can be degraded by pollution, removal or burial. Soil quality can be contaminated by building waste and the whole range of pollutants that are particularly concentrated in urban areas. The role of soils in urban areas has only received limited attention to date.

Activities

1 **a** Explain the universal soil loss equation.
   b Briefly suggest the merits and limitations of this model.
2 **a** Define (i) deforestation (ii) overgrazing.
   b Describe the causes of land degradation shown in Figure 4 (page 165).
3 With reference to Figure 5 (page 167), describe and explain the factors that control the rate and magnitude of water erosion and wind erosion.
4 Comment on the changes in world fertiliser consumption illustrated in Figure 6 (page 168).
5 Describe and explain the differences between the two soil profiles shown in Figure 7 (page 169).
6 Briefly explain the causes and processes of land degradation shown in Figure 8 (page 169).

Environmental and socio-economic consequences

The environmental and socio-economic consequences of soil degradation are considerable. Such consequences can occur with little warning as damage to soil is often not perceived until it is far advanced. Socio-economic consequences are both on-site (local) and off-site (beyond the locality), while environmental consequences are primarily off-site.

Desertification

Desertification is the gradual transformation of habitable land into desert. It is arguably the most serious environmental consequence of soil degradation. Desertification is usually caused by climate change and/or by destructive use of the land. It is a considerable problem in many parts of the world, for example on the margins of the Sahara Desert in North Africa and the Kalahari Desert in southern Africa.

In semi-arid areas such as the edge of the Kalahari Desert, a combination of low and variable precipitation, nutrient-deficient soils and heavy dependence on subsistence farming makes soil degradation a significant threat. The problem has been exacerbated in recent decades by political changes which have disrupted traditional communal land ownership patterns, social networks and agricultural practices.

In this fragile ecosystem, soil disturbance and removal of vegetation cover through grazing or preparing the ground for planting increases the probability of wind and water erosion. Finer and organic-rich particles are more readily removed, reducing soil nutrient levels and damaging soil structure.

Other degradation processes contributing to desertification in this region are salinisation and acidification. Bush encroachment is also a problem in some areas. This occurs where the heavy grazing of grasslands leads to them becoming overgrown by woody shrubs.

The United Nations estimates that up to 75% of agricultural areas in dryland Africa are degraded. In South Africa the National Botanical Institute notes that soil degradation exists mainly in the former black communal homelands established by the apartheid policies of the former white South African government.

Dust storms, which can seriously damage crops, may also be a problem in such areas. Dust storms occur naturally wherever dry soils and strong winds combine, but human activity can increase their severity significantly. These human activities are removal of vegetation, overgrazing, overcultivation and surface disturbance by vehicles. All these practices can add to the severity of the problem. In the Sahel the increase in dust-storm frequency has been shown to coincide with periods of severe drought.

Darkhan, Mongolia during one of the regular dust storms that are contributing to soil degradation. The number and strength of dust storms has increased here in recent years.

Other important environmental consequences include the following:

- The reduction in **soil buffering capacity:** this is the capacity of soil to absorb contaminants. This has a direct impact on the global carbon cycle, particularly through the decrease in soil organic matter and the release of carbon dioxide to the atmosphere.

- Impact on water bodies: soil degradation can have a significant impact on receiving water courses (rivers, wetlands and lakes). Soil, along with its nutrients and contaminants, may be delivered in large quantities to water environments, having a huge detrimental influence. Eutrophication has become a significant problem in many rivers and lakes, as has the contamination of groundwater. Eroded soil can block water courses and drains, affect fisheries and increase the risk of flooding. It can also silt up reservoirs and harbours, reducing their lifetime and adding to the maintenance costs of these structures. A study published in July 2006 stated that the costs of treating water contaminated with agricultural pollutants in the UK amounted to £203 million a year.

- Loss of biological diversity: soil degradation may lead to the disappearance of the climax vegetation and the decrease in animal habitat resulting in a biodiversity loss and animal extinction. Soil deposition can harm wildlife habitat by covering nesting areas and wildlife food sources.

- Mudflows and floods: soil degradation reduces the infiltration capacity of soils, resulting in greater surface runoff. On steeper slopes in particular this can result in mudflows which can cause serious damage and in extreme cases, loss of life. Higher levels of surface runoff also increase the potential for flooding.

Soil degradation: a threat to food security?

The increasing world population and the rapidly changing diets of hundreds of millions of people as they become more affluent is placing more and more pressure on land resources. Some soil and agricultural experts say that a decline in long-term soil productivity is already seriously limiting food production in the developing world.

Various studies have concluded that soil quality on three-quarters of the world's agricultural land has been relatively stable since the middle of the 20th century. However, on the remaining quarter, degradation is widespread and its pace has increased over the last half-century. Productivity has fallen significantly on about 16% of agricultural land in developing countries. Almost 75% of Central America's farmland has been seriously degraded, as has 20% of Africa's and 11% of Asia's. There are several consequences for the areas affected:

- a reduced food supply, which can have a devastating effect in areas where food security is already a problem

- lower farming income and economic growth – a reduction in farm income can adversely affect all other aspects of the rural economy, and such a reverse multiplier effect can be very difficult to turn around

- higher food prices, which can put some staple foods beyond the reach of many people

- increased child malnutrition – children and the elderly usually bear the brunt of food shortages and higher food prices

- rural to urban migration, which often results in the transfer of population pressure from rural to urban areas.

The poorest people in regions affected by soil degradation suffer most as they are particularly dependent on:

- agriculture

- annual crops which generally degrade soils more than perennial crops

- common property lands which usually have higher levels of degradation than privately managed land.

The poorest people also lack the capacity to make land-improving investments. This would seem to be a vicious circle. The relationship between poverty and soil quality has attracted closer investigation in recent years.

On a global scale, degradation poses a modest rather than a severe threat to world food supply over the next decade or so. This is because of the global capacity for supply substitution and the dominance of the less degraded temperate regions in world food production and trade. However, greater impact may be felt in terms of higher food prices and malnutrition. Countries that depend on agriculture as their dominant economic sector are likely to suffer the most.

Activities

1 **a** Define desertification.
   b What are the reasons for desertification?
2 **a** What are dust storms?
   b Describe the photograph on page 170.
3 What is the effect of soil degradation on water bodies?
4 To what extent is soil degradation a threat to food security?

Case study

Australia: soil degradation and carbon farming

Large parts of Australia have been in the grip of drought for much of the last decade. Rainfall has decreased significantly in the Murray-Darling basin which produces more than a fifth of Australia's food. One scientific prediction is that the Murray-Darling basin will receive 41% less rainfall on average annually by 2030 due to climate change.

Low rainfall has combined with a range of farming techniques to degrade soils over a considerable area. Soils in Australia now contain only half the carbon they did prior to European settlement. Centuries of ploughing, burning stubble and removing crop waste has gradually lowered the carbon content of the soil. This has weakened soil structure and left it unable to hold as much water as before.

Some Australian soil scientists are proposing **carbon farming** as a strategy to combat this trend. This involves using the plants grown on a farm to 'harvest' carbon from the atmosphere and return it to the soil. The process works this way:

- plant leaves absorb carbon dioxide which makes its way to the expanding root system
- the roots release chemicals containing carbon molecules into the soil, which attract fungi
- fungi grow on the root system, assimilating the carbon
- as the roots decay and break down, the carbon becomes incorporated into the soil.

The benefits of this process are two-fold. First, it improves **soil structure,** retaining more nutrients and being able to hold more water, allowing the soil to cope better with temperature extremes. Second, it could become a valuable form of carbon sequestration. Alex McBratney, Professor of Soil Science at the University of Sidney, estimates that if the carbon content of a quarter of the world's soils was increased by 1% it would remove 300 gigatonnes of carbon dioxide from the atmosphere. This could be achieved by changing agricultural practices. Such practices include planned grazing and growing **perennial crops.**

Planned grazing involves moving cattle from paddock to paddock on a careful rotational basis to avoid overgrazing. This ensures a higher root volume compared with overgrazed land, allowing greater carbon sequestration. The idea is that when a plant is grazed it needs adequate time to recover. If this does not happen the plant will be weakened for the next season.

The answer to many of the world's current agricultural problems may lie in the development of perennial crops. Today's annual crops die off once harvested and new seeds have to be planted before the cycle of production can begin again. The soil is most vulnerable to erosion in the period between harvesting and the next planting. Perennial crops would protect the soil from erosion and also offer other advantages. Plant biologists hope to breed plants that closely resemble domestic crops but retain their perennial habit. Classical crossing methods have been proved to work in the search for perennial crop plants but the process is slow. Some plant breeders aim to speed up the process by using genetic engineering. The objective is to find the genes that are linked to domestication and then insert these into wild plants.

Perennial crops offer advantages beyond helping to protect soils from erosion. They tend to retain more nutrients than annual crops and so require less fertiliser.

Some farmers argue that they should be paid for sequestering carbon while others are concerned that in the future they may be charged for the greenhouse gases they produce. The agricultural sector accounts for 16% of Australia's greenhouse gas emissions.

Management strategies

A range of management strategies can be employed to reduce soil degradation. Many of the strategies used can be subdivided into (a) mechanical methods and (b) cropping techniques. Mechanical methods focus on preventing or slowing the movement of rainwater downslope and reducing the impact of wind on the soil.

Afforestation (planting trees on areas which has not been a forest) or **reforestation** have been widely used comprehensively over sizeable areas or as part of a wider package of strategies. The selection of the areas to be forested is of crucial importance, with steeper slopes being the natural starting point, but also taking other factors into account, such as the predominant wind direction. Contour ploughing is a tried and trusted technique which prevents or diminishes the downslope movement of water and soil. Such ploughing ensures that the ridges and furrows are at right-angles to the slope. Where slopes are too steep for contour ploughing, then terracing may be practised. Here the steep slope is converted into a series of flat steps with raised outer edges (bunds). The monsoon regions of South-east Asia exhibit widespread terracing.

The planting of trees in shelterbelts and the use of hedgerows can do much to dissipate the impact of strong winds, reducing the wind's ability to disturb topsoil and erode particles.

Various cropping techniques can be employed to reduce soil degradation. These include:

- converting land from arable to pastoral uses – the planting of grass helps to bind soil particles together, reducing the action of wind and rain

- including grasses in crop rotations

- leaving unploughed grass strips between ploughed fields

- keeping a crop cover on the soil for as long as possible, thus minimising the 'bare soil' period

- encouraging biological diversity by planting several different types of plants together

- increasing the organic content of the soil by applying animal manure, compost or sewage sludge – this enables soil to hold more water, preventing aerial erosion and stabilising soil structure

- selecting and using farm machinery carefully, in particular avoiding where possible the use of heavy machinery on wet soils to prevent damage to the soil structure and using low ground pressure set-ups on machinery when possible

- leaving the stubble and root structure in place after harvesting

- using reduced or shallow cultivation to maintain or increase near-surface organic matter

- shepherding livestock and moving forage areas to avoid overgrazing.

Managing salt-affected soils

Periodic soil testing and treatment, combined with proper management procedures, can improve the conditions in salt-affected soils that contribute to poor plant growth. There are three ways to manage saline soils. First, salts can be moved below the root zone by applying more water than the plant needs. This method is called the leaching requirement method. The second method, where soil moisture conditions dictate, combines the leaching requirement method with artificial drainage. Finally, salts can be shifted away from the root zone to locations in the soil, other than below the root zone, where they are not harmful. This third method is

called managed accumulation. Sometimes, selecting salt-tolerant crops may be needed in addition to managing soils.

Saline soil in the south of France.

The rise of no-till farming

The traditional practice of turning the soil before planting a new crop is a leading cause of soil degradation. An alternative is no-till farming which minimises soil disruption. Here, farmers leave crop residue on the fields after harvest, where it acts as a mulch to protect the soil and provide nutrients. To sow seeds, farmers use seeders that penetrate through the residue to the undisturbed soil below. This important sustainable approach to farming is spreading, but so far it has been mainly confined to major farming nations because of the high equipment costs involved in changing from traditional practices.

The top five countries with the largest areas of no-till are the USA, Brazil, Argentina, Canada and Australia. Approximately 85% of no-till farmland is located in North and South America. The advantages of no-till farming are that it reduces soil erosion, conserves water, improves soil health, cuts fuel and labour costs, reduces sediment and fertiliser pollution in lakes and streams, and the process sequesters carbon. The obstacles to overcome are that new machinery required is costly, there is heavier reliance on herbicides, more nitrogen fertiliser may initially be required, there may be a greater prevalence of weeds and other pests, and yields may be reduced.

Figure 9 (page 175) compares no-till farming with conventional tillage and conservation tillage. The latter is a half-way stage between no-till and conventional tillage. In the USA about 41% of all planted cropland was farmed using conservation tillage or no-till systems in 2004, compared with 26% in 1990.

Case study

Sustainable farming in Sub-Saharan Africa

Sub-Saharan Africa has suffered more from soil degradation than any other world region, with the arid and semi-arid zones being particularly affected. Here depletion of nutrients and soil organic matter and erosion are the main forms of soil degradation. The main causes are overgrazing and cultivation practices that are not adapted to local environments. However, **sustainable agriculture** is being successfully practised in some areas. Examples include the following:

- In the north-west of Burkina Faso, Aly Ouedraogo from the village of Gourcy has reclaimed many hectares of barren land over a 15-year period, turning a hard-pan gravel surface into fields that are able to produce dense stands of sorghum. The techniques employed were stone lines reinforced by seeding of perennial grasses and fruit trees, while areas between the stone lines have been dug with planting pits. The pits trap runoff, drifting soil, dried leaves and other matter which termites break down. At harvest time, Aly leaves at least 20 cm of stubble to slow wind speeds and provide further material on which termites can feed. A compost and manure pit on the edge of his field provides a handful of fertiliser for each pit. A careful watch is kept for straying livestock. These techniques have been successfully copied in many other communities.

- In the highlands of northern Shewa, Ethiopia, farmers have traditionally used drainage ditches across their fields as a means of protecting land from being washed away when rains are heavy, and to reduce surface runoff. This contrasts markedly with the huge terracing programmes carried out in the Ethiopian Highlands, supported by government and donor agencies in the 1980s. However, having played no role in planning and designing these programmes, local farmers felt no sense of ownership or interest in the terrace structures, which now lie abandoned.

- The Dogon people of eastern Mali use a range of soil and water conservation techniques to produce high yields in a very difficult environment. Every square centimetre of soil is used. The crops are carefully selected to make the most of each site. Drier fields grow the fine-grained grassy cereal fonio; damp spots grow rice; patches near water are for irrigated vegetables. On bare, baking rock ledges, crevices only 20 cm wide, as long as they have a little soil are planted with millet

and beans. Narrow hollows among huge boulders are planted with millet, thatching grass and gourds. When weeding takes place, the waste is raked into mounds 15–20 cm high in between the stalks, creating a trellis of mounds and hollows which slows runoff, allowing it to filter slowly without eroding the soil. The mounds, rich in humus from decaying weeds, are used to plant next year's seed. Along the downhill edge of fields, rocks are piled in long lines level with the contour.

In 2008 a $180 million 5-year project to improve Sub-Saharan Africa's depleted soils was launched in Nairobi. The Alliance for Green Revolution in Africa's Soil Health Programme aims to work with 4.1 million farmers to regenerate 6.3 million hectares of land. The programme will give particular attention to the role of women in promoting sustainable farming. The idea is to adapt farming techniques to local conditions to avoid repeating the mistakes of the past. Soil depletion on long-established farmland has 'pushed' farmers to clear forests and savannas in the search for new arable land, placing new pressures on fragile ecosystems.

Oasis in the Sahel, Africa.

The food situation in many parts of Africa is critical. The continent has been affected by famine and drought on a regular basis. However, the difficulties of the physical environment alone are far from fully responsible for the food problem. Human conflict and the host of pathologies that trail in its wake have dogged the continent in the latter part of the 20th century. Sustainability therefore is not just about an approach to natural resource exploitation. This cannot happen unless peaceful human interaction is sustained first.

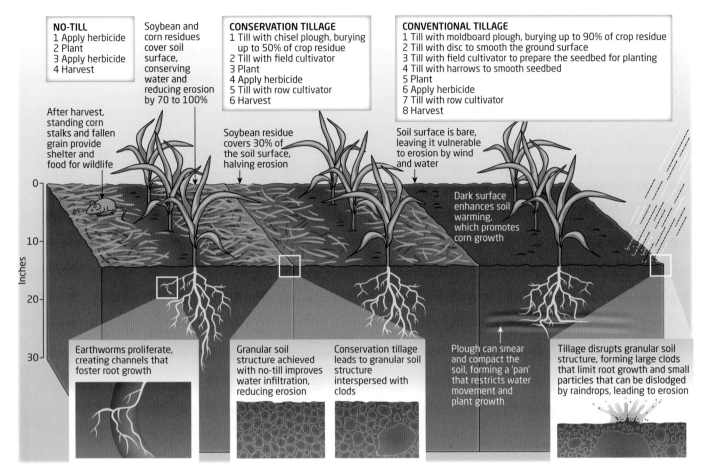

NO-TILL
1 Apply herbicide
2 Plant
3 Apply herbicide
4 Harvest

Soybean and corn residues cover soil surface, conserving water and reducing erosion by 70 to 100%

CONSERVATION TILLAGE
1 Till with chisel plough, burying up to 50% of crop residue
2 Till with field cultivator
3 Plant
4 Apply herbicide
5 Till with row cultivator
6 Harvest

CONVENTIONAL TILLAGE
1 Till with moldboard plough, burying up to 90% of crop residue
2 Till with disc to smooth the ground surface
3 Till with field cultivator to prepare the seedbed for planting
4 Till with harrows to smooth seedbed
5 Plant
6 Apply herbicide
7 Till with row cultivator
8 Harvest

After harvest, standing corn stalks and fallen grain provide shelter and food for wildlife

Soybean residue covers 30% of the soil surface, halving erosion

Soil surface is bare, leaving it vulnerable to erosion by wind and water

Dark surface enhances soil warming, which promotes corn growth

Earthworms proliferate, creating channels that foster root growth

Granular soil structure achieved with no-till improves water infiltration, reducing erosion

Conservation tillage leads to granular soil structure interspersed with clods

Plough can smear and compact the soil, forming a 'pan' that restricts water movement and plant growth

Tillage disrupts granular soil structure, forming large clods that limit root growth and small particles that can be dislodged by raindrops, leading to erosion

Figure 9 *A comparison of no-till, conservation tillage and conventional tillage.*

Activities

1 What is (a) afforestation (b) reforestation (c) contour ploughing?
2 Discuss the cropping techniques that can be used to reduce soil degradation.
3 Describe and explain the expansion of carbon farming in Australia (page 172).
4 Examine two types of sustainable farming adopted in Sub-Saharan Africa.
5 **a** What is no-till farming?
   b Compare the three types of farming system shown in Figure 9 (above).
   c Why is there so little no-till farming in developing countries at present?

Theory of Knowledge

Climate change is such an important issue that it is of interest to academics from a wide variety of disciplines. When this happens it is easier for a person to possibly overrate the importance of their own specialist area of knowledge in relation to areas of knowledge that they know less about. This 'knowledge imbalance' can also make it difficult for important relationships to be recognised at an early stage. For example, soil scientists feel that the relationship between land cover and vegetation and climate change has not been given enough recognition at the international level and thus not enough attention, in terms of real investment, has been given to soil degradation. Are you inclined to agree with them?

Key terms

Soil degradation the physical loss (erosion) and the reduction in quality of topsoil associated with nutrient decline and contamination.

Soil profile the vertical variations that occur in the characteristics of a soil from the surface to the underlying rock.

Universal soil loss equation a mathematical model used to describe soil erosion processes.

Deforestation the process of destroying a forest and replacing it with something else, especially by an agricultural system.

Overgrazing the grazing of natural pastures at stocking intensities above the livestock carrying capacity.

Acidification the change in the chemical composition of soil, which may trigger the circulation of toxic metals.

Salinisation the condition in which the salt content of soil accumulates over time to above normal levels; occurs in some parts of the world where water containing high salt concentration evaporates from fields irrigated with standing water.

Soil aggregates soil particles that are closely bound together are called peds or aggregates.

Desertification the gradual transformation of habitable land into desert.

Dust storms a severe windstorm that sweeps clouds of dust across an extensive area, especially in an arid region.

Soil buffering capacity the capacity of soil to absorb contaminants.

Carbon farming involves using the plants grown on a farm to 'harvest' carbon from the atmosphere and return it to the soil.

Soil structure the shape and arrangement of aggregates gives soils a characteristic structure, e.g. blocky, platy, crumb or prismatic.

Perennial crops crops that do not die off once harvested (annual crops), existing for years before reseeding may be required.

Afforestation planting seeds or trees to make a forest on land has not been a forest recently, or which has never been a forest.

Reforestation re-establishing a forest after its removal.

Sustainable agriculture agricultural systems emphasising biological relationships and natural processes, which maintain soil fertility thus allowing current levels of farm production to continue indefinitely.

Websites

www.fao.org/landandwater
UN Food and Agriculture Organisation, Land and Water Development Division

www.scidev.net
Science and Development Network

www.infonet-biovision.org
infonet-biovision

www.geographical.co.uk
Geographical magazine

www.unccd.int
UN Convention to Combat Desertification (UNCCD)

www.earthwire.org
EarthWire/

Review

Examination-style questions

1 Refer to Figure 10.

a Define (i) overgrazing (ii) deforestation.

b Describe how the principal causes of soil degradation vary by world region.

c Discuss the reasons for these variations in the causes of soil degradation.

2 Refer to Figure 11.

a Suggest what is meant by the soil loss ratio.

b Describe the relationship shown by Figure 11.

c With reference to examples, explain the reasons for this relationship.

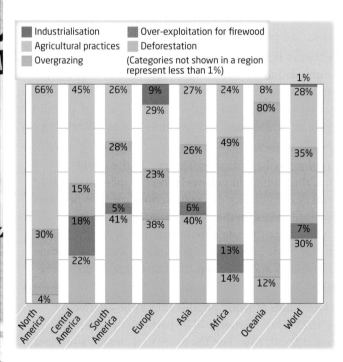

Figure 10 *The principal causes of soil degradation.*

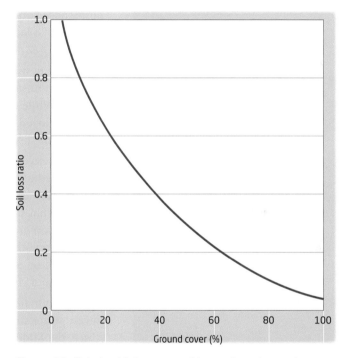

Figure 11 *Relationship between soil loss ratio and ground cover.*

11 Water and change

The global water crisis

Water collection/distribution in Central Asia.

The longest a person can survive without water is about ten days. All life and virtually every human activity needs water. It is the world's most essential resource and a pivotal element in poverty reduction. But for about 80 countries, with 40% of the world's population, lack of water is a constant threat. And the situation is getting worse, with demand for water doubling every 20 years. In those parts of the world where there is enough water, it is being wasted, mismanaged and polluted on a grand scale. In the poorest nations it is not just a question of a lack of water; the paltry supplies available are often polluted.

Securing access to clean water is a vital aspect of development. The lack of clean, safe drinking water is estimated to kill almost 4500 children per day. Out of the 2.2 million unsafe drinking water deaths in 2004, 90% were children under the age of 5. While deaths associated with dirty water have been virtually eliminated from developed countries, in developing countries most deaths still result from water-borne disease.

Water scarcity has been presented as the 'sleeping tiger' of the world's environmental problems, threatening to put world food supplies in jeopardy, limit economic and social development, and create serious conflicts between countries that share drainage basins. In the 20th century, global water consumption grew sixfold – twice the rate of population growth. Much of this increased consumption was made possible by significant investment in water infrastructure, particularly dams and reservoirs, affecting nearly 60% of the world's major river basins.

The UN estimates that two-thirds of world population will be affected by 'severe water stress' by 2025. The situation will be particularly severe in Africa, the Middle East and South Asia. The UN notes that already a number of the world's great rivers such as the Colorado in the USA are running dry, and that **groundwater** is also being drained faster than it can be replenished. Many major **aquifers** have been seriously depleted which will present serious consequences in the future.

The Middle East and North Africa face the most serious problems. Since 1972 the Middle East has withdrawn more water from its rivers and aquifers each year than is being replenished. Yemen and Jordan are withdrawing 30% more from groundwater resources annually than is being naturally replenished. Israel's annual demand exceeds its renewable supply by 15%. In Africa, 206 million people live in **water-stressed** or **water-scarce areas**.

The Pilot Analysis of Global Ecosystems (PAGE), undertaken by the World Resources Institute, calculated water availability and demand by river basin. This analysis estimated that at present 2.3 billion people live in water-stressed areas

with 1.7 billion resident in water-scarce areas. The PAGE analysis forecasts that these figures will rise to 3.5 billion and 2.4 billion people respectively by 2025.

The Water Project, a leading non-government organisation (NGO), has recently stated the following with regard to water:

- at any one time, half of the world's hospital beds are occupied by patients suffering from water-borne diseases
- over one-third of the world's population has no access to sanitation facilities
- in developing countries, about 80% of illnesses are linked to poor water and sanitation conditions
- one out of every four deaths under the age of five worldwide is due to a water-related disease
- in developing countries, it is common for water collectors, usually women and girls, to have to walk several kilometres every day to fetch water; once filled, pots and jerry-cans can weigh as much as 20 kg.

Millennium Development Goal (MDG) target 10 states: 'Halve, by 2015, the proportion of people without sustainable access to safe water and basic sanitation.' A World Health Organization (WHO) report in 2004 estimated that to meet the target, an additional 260 000 people per day up to 2015 should gain access to improved water sources and an extra 370 000 people per day should gain access to improved sanitation. This is a rate of improvement that may prove much too difficult to achieve in a number of countries given the current resources available. In an effort to add impetus to global water advancement the UN proclaimed the period 2005–15 as the International Decade for Action, 'Water for Life'.

The link between poverty and water resources is very clear, with those living on less than $1.25 a day roughly equal to the number without access to safe drinking water. Access to safe water is vital in the prevention of diarrhoeal diseases which result in 1.5 million deaths a year, mostly among children under five. Improving access to safe water can be among the most cost-effective means of reducing illness and mortality. The UN World Water Development Report stated:

'The real tragedy is the effect it has on the everyday lives of poor people, who are blighted by the burden of water-related disease, living in degraded and often dangerous environments, struggling to get an education for their children and to earn a living, and to get enough to eat. The brutal truth is that the really poor suffer a combination of most, and sometimes all, of the problems in the water sector.'

The narrow irrigation zone along the banks of the river Nile, Egypt.

Discussion point

How far do you think you could walk carrying water weighing 20 kg?

Theory of Knowledge

Expanding access to water and sanitation is an ethical and moral imperative rooted in the cultural and religious traditions of many communities around the world. The UN sees the right to water as 'indispensable for leading a life in human dignity'. How important is the right to water compared with other human rights, such as education or freedom?

Water utilisation at the regional scale

Every year, 100 000 cubic kilometres of precipitation falls onto the Earth's land surface. This would be more than adequate for the global population's needs, but much of it cannot be captured and the rest is very unevenly distributed. For example:

- over 60% of the world's population live in areas receiving only 25% of global annual precipitation
- the arid regions of the world cover 40% of the world's land area, but receive only 2% of global precipitation

● the Congo river and its tributaries account for 30% of Africa's annual runoff in an area containing 10% of Africa's population.

Figure 1 shows what happens to the precipitation reaching land surfaces. **'Green' water** is that part of total precipitation that is absorbed by soil and plants, then released back into the air. As such it is unavailable for human use. However, green water scarcity is the classic cause of famine. Green water accounts for 61.1% of total precipitation. The remaining precipitation, known as **'blue' water**, collects in rivers, lakes, wetlands and groundwater. It is available for human use before it evaporates or reaches the ocean. As Figure 1 shows, only 1.5% of total precipitation is directly used by people.

Total world blue water withdrawals are estimated at 3390 km³, with 74% for agriculture, mostly irrigation (Figure 2). About 20% of this total comes from groundwater. Although agriculture is the dominant water user, industrial and domestic uses are growing at faster rates. Demand for industrial use has expanded particularly rapidly.

The amount of water used by a population depends not only on water availability but also on levels of urbanisation and economic development. As global urbanisation continues, the demand for **potable water** in cities and towns will rise rapidly. In many cases demand will outstrip supply.

In terms of agriculture, more than 80% of crop **evapotranspiration** comes directly from rainfall, with the remainder from irrigation water diverted from rivers and groundwater. However, this varies considerably by region. In the Middle East and North Africa, where rainfall is low and unreliable, more than 60% of crop evapotranspiration originates from irrigation.

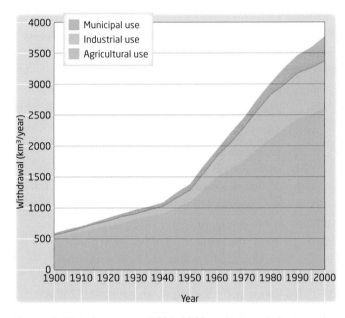

Figure 2 *Global water use 1900–2000: agriculture, industry and domestic.*

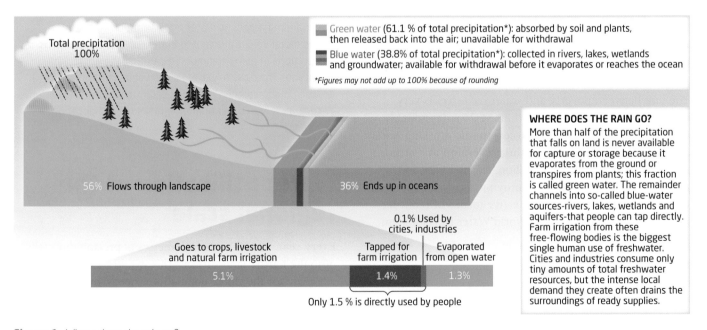

Figure 1 *Where does the rain go?*

3 Patterns in environmental quality and sustainability

Figure 3 contrasts water use in developed and developing countries. In the latter, agriculture accounts for over 80% of total water use, with industry using more of the remainder than domestic allocation. In the developed world agriculture accounts for slightly more than 40% of total water use. This is lower than the amount allocated to industry. As in the developing world, domestic use is in third place.

As developing countries industrialise and urban-industrial complexes expand, the demand for water grows rapidly in the industrial and domestic sectors. As a result the competition with agriculture for water has intensified in many countries and regions. This is a scenario that has already played itself out in many developed countries where more and more difficult decisions are having to be made about how to allocate water.

Large variations in water allocation can also exist within countries. For example, irrigation accounts for over 80% of water demand in the west of the USA, but only about 6% in the east.

Figure 4 shows the divide by world region between rainfed water for crop use and irrigation water. The figures in the circles refer to the total amount of rainfed water used. Here the highest totals are for East Asia, South Asia, and Sub-Saharan Africa. The highest proportion of irrigation

Geographical skills

Draw up a table to show how global water use changed for municipal, industrial and agricultural uses for the following years: 1900, 1940, 1980 and 2000.

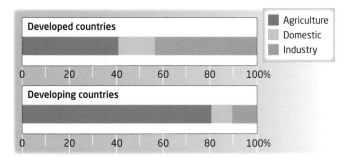

Figure 3 *Water used for agriculture, industry and domestic purposes in the developed and developing worlds.*

water use is in the Middle East, North Africa and South Asia. Irrigated farming accounts for 70% of global annual water consumption. This rises to over 90% in some countries such as India.

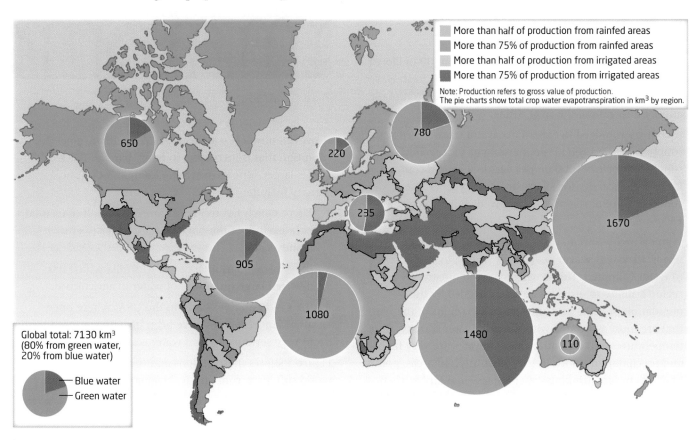

Figure 4 *Rainfed and irrigation water for crop use.*

Activities

1 Write a brief explanation of the information presented in Figure 1 (page 180).
2 Describe and explain the different ways in which water is used in (a) high-income countries and (b) developing countries.
3 Examine the regional variations in rainfed and irrigation agriculture shown in Figure 4 (page 181).

The environmental and human factors affecting water scarcity

The world's population is increasing by about 80 million a year. This converts to an increased demand for fresh water of around 64 billion m³ per year, which equates to the total annual flow rate of the river Rhine.

A country is judged to experience water stress when water supply is below 1700 m³ per person per year. When water supply falls below 1000 m³ per person a year, a country faces water scarcity for all or part of the year. These concepts were developed by the Swedish hydrologist Malin Falkenmark.

Water scarcity is to do with the availability of potable water. **Physical water scarcity** is when physical access to water is limited. This is when demand outstrips a region's ability to provide the water needed by the population. It is the arid and semi-arid regions of the world that are most associated with physical water scarcity. Here temperatures and evapotranspiration rates are very high and precipitation is low. In the worst-affected areas, points of access to safe drinking water are few and far between.

However, annual precipitation figures fail to tell the whole story. Much of the freshwater supply comes in the form of seasonal rainfall, as exemplified by the monsoon rains of Asia. India gets 90% of its annual rainfall during the summer monsoon season from June to September. Also, national figures can mask significant regional differences. Analysis of the supply and demand situation by river basin can reveal the true extent of such variations. For example, the USA has a relatively high average water-sufficiency figure of 8838 m³ per person a year. However, the Colorado river basin has a much lower figure of 2000 m³ per person a year, while the Rio Grande river basin is lower still at 621 m³ per person a year.

The dried-up bed of the Rio Oja, northern Spain.

However, physical water scarcity is a human-made condition that is increasing in many parts of the world. This is largely due to overuse. Examples of physical water scarcity include:

- Egypt which has to import more than half of its food because it does not have enough water to grow it domestically
- the Murray-Darling basin in Australia which has diverted large quantities of water to agriculture
- the Colorado river basin in the USA, where once-abundant resources have been heavily overused leading to very serious physical water scarcity downstream.

Figure 5 shows these regions and the other parts of the world suffering from physical water scarcity.

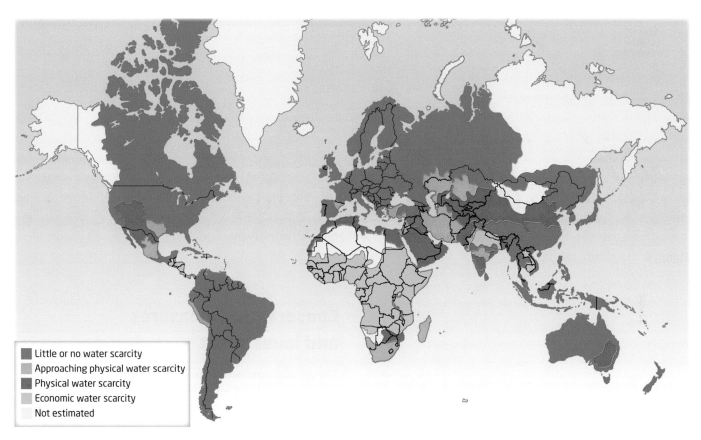

Figure 5 *Physical water scarcity and economic water scarcity worldwide.*

Legend:
- Little or no water scarcity
- Approaching physical water scarcity
- Physical water scarcity
- Economic water scarcity
- Not estimated

Economic water scarcity exists when a population does not have the necessary monetary means to utilise an adequate source of water. The unequal distribution of resources is central to economic water scarcity where the crux of the problem is lack of investment. This occurs for a number of reasons, including political and ethnic conflict. Figure 5 shows that much of Sub-Saharan Africa is affected by this type of water scarcity.

Scientists expect water scarcity to become more severe largely because:

- the world's population continues to increase significantly
- increasing affluence is inflating per capita demand for water
- demands for biofuel production are increasing, and biofuel crops are heavy users of water
- climate change is increasing aridity and reducing supply in many regions
- many water sources are threatened by various forms of pollution.

The Stockholm International Water Institute has estimated that each person on the Earth needs a minimum of 1000 m³ of water per year for drinking, hygiene and growing food for sustenance. Whether this water is available depends largely on where people live on the planet, as water supply is extremely inequitable. For example, major rivers such as the Yangtze, Ganges and Nile are severely overused and the levels of underground aquifers beneath major cities such as Beijing and New Delhi are falling.

In many parts of the world the allocation of water is largely down to the ability to pay. A recent article in *Scientific American* entitled 'Facing the freshwater crisis' quotes an old saying from the American West: 'Water usually runs downhill, but it always runs uphill to money'. Thus poorer people and non-human consumers of water – the fauna and flora of nearby ecosystems – usually lose out when water is scarce.

Figure 6 (page 184) illustrates the huge extent of the global water gap using selected groups of developed and developing countries. The daily usage figures for the USA and Australia are particularly high. Many of the developing countries illustrated have water use figures below the water poverty threshold. Water scarcity is playing a significant role in putting the brake on economic development in a number of countries.

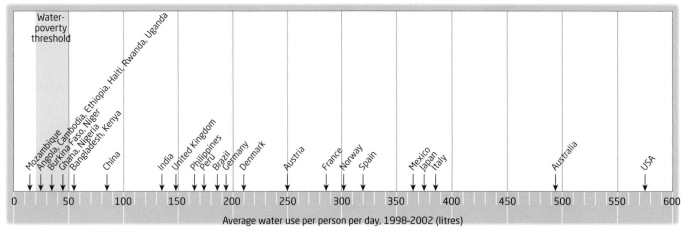

Figure 6 *The global water gap.*

Public drinking water point: Vienna.

Conservation measures and investment

The general opinion in the global water industry is that in the past the cost of water in the developed world has been too low to encourage users to save water. Higher prices would make individuals and organisations, both public and private, think more carefully about how much water they use. Higher prices would:

- encourage the systematic reuse of used or **'grey' water**
- spur investment in recycling and reclamation systems
- lead to greater investment in the reduction of water losses.

However, many consumers still see water as a 'free' or very low-cost resource and campaign groups are concerned that higher prices would have an unfair impact on people on low incomes. Water pricing for both domestic and commercial users is a sensitive issue. It has also become much more of a political issue as more and more countries have privatised their water resources.

Conserving irrigation water would have more impact than any other measure. Most irrigation is extremely inefficient, wasting half or more of the water used. A 10% increase in irrigation efficiency would free up more water than is evaporated by all other users. The most modern drip irrigation systems are up to 95% efficient (Table 1), but require significant investment.

Although some industries have significantly reduced their use of water per unit of production, most water analysts believe that much more can be done. For example, production of 1 kg of aluminium can require up to 1500 litres of water. Other industries such as paper production are also very water-intensive. Some countries such as Japan and Germany have made considerable improvements in industrial water use. For example, Japanese industry recycles more than 75% of processed water.

	Efficiency
Surface - used in over 80% of irrigated fields worldwide	
Furrow traditional method; cheap to install; labour-intensive; high water losses; susceptible to erosion and salinisation	20-60%
Basin cheap to install and run; needs a lot of water; susceptible to salinisation and waterlogging	50-75%
Aerial (using sprinklers) - used in 10-15% of irrigation worldwide	
Costly to install and run; low-pressure sprinklers preferable	60-80%
Subsurface ('drip') - used in 1% of irrigation worldwide	
High capital costs; sophisticated monitoring; very efficient	75-95%

Table 1 *Main types of irrigation.*

Irrigation canal, Egypt.

As water scarcity becomes more of a problem, the investment required to tackle this global challenge will rise. Table 2 shows the estimated investment needed by world region for the period 2005–30. There are very large contrasts between the different regions of the world. Delivering water to the points where it is required is a costly business in terms of both constructing and maintaining infrastructure. Overall, the sums of money illustrated in Table 2 are huge and funding may need to be diverted from other sectors of national government funding. However, investment in water as a proportion of GDP has fallen by half in most countries since the late 1990s.

Urban sanitation services are very heavy users of water. Demand could be reduced considerably by adopting dry, or low-water use, systems such as dry composting toilets with urine separation systems. A number of pilot projects are in operation such as the Gebers Housing Project in Stockholm.

	Trillions of dollars
Asia/Oceania	9.0
South/Latin America	5.0
Europe	4.5
USA/Canada	3.6
Africa	0.2
Middle East	0.3

Table 2 *Water investment needs by area, 2005–30.*

Maintenance of the water infrastructure is crucial to prevent deterioration, leaks and outright breaches. At the same time, growing populations and those becoming more affluent need new, efficient water-delivery systems. To help conserve freshwater supplies, developed nations and some less developed ones will have to spend trillions of dollars on maintaining and creating efficient infrastructures during the next quarter of a century.

Depleted aquifers

Aquifers provide approximately half of the world's drinking water, 40% of the water used by industry and up to 30% of irrigation water. Falling water tables can bring severe ecological, economic and social consequences. However, detailed knowledge of the state of many major aquifers is very limited. Nevertheless, there is no doubt that the **water table** in many aquifers has fallen significantly. For example, the Ogallala aquifer in the American Midwest has fallen by more than 35 metres in

50 years. In China, the overexploitation of aquifers has been a major factor in the decline in rice production from 140 million tonnes in 1997 to 127 million tonnes in 2005.

Apart from falling water tables due to water withdrawals exceeding natural replenishment:

- in some areas, for example around the Mediterranean, sea water has begun to seep into depleted aquifers, making the water unusable for most purposes
- in other areas sewage is beginning to contaminate some aquifers.

Where aquifers cross international borders, more detailed knowledge of their potential and problems will be required for neighbouring countries to reach agreement about allocating withdrawals of water. An atlas of underground water sources published by UNESCO identifies 273 trans-border aquifers, some crossing as many as four nations. Some of the world's largest untapped aquifers are in North Africa, which could have significant future development potential. Egypt, Libya, Sudan and Chad share the Nubian sandstone aquifer which contains 10 000-year-old 'fossil water'. The four countries have formed a joint organisation to manage the aquifer.

Virtual water

The importance of the concept of **virtual water** is becoming increasingly recognised. Virtual water is the amount of water that is used to produce food or any other product and is thus essentially embedded in the item. One kilogram of wheat takes around 1000 litres of water to produce, so the import of this amount of wheat into a dry country saves this amount of water compared with the dry country producing the wheat itself. According to *Scientific American* (August 2008, page 34):

> 'The virtual water concept and expanded trade have also led to the resolution of many international disputes caused by water scarcity. Imports of virtual water in products by Jordan have reduced the chance of water-based conflict with its neighbour Israel, for example.'

The size of global trade in virtual water is more than 800 billion m³ of water a year. This is equivalent to the flow of ten river Niles. Greater liberalisation of trade in agricultural products would further increase virtual water flows. Table 3 shows the virtual water content of a number of selected products. The virtual water content of a hamburger, for example, is very high relative to its average cost to the consumer.

Product	Virtual water content (litres)
1 glass of beer (250 ml)	75
1 glass of milk (200 ml)	200
1 cup of coffee (125 ml)	140
1 cup of tea (250 ml)	35
1 slice of bread (30 g)	40
1 slice of bread (30 g) with cheese (10 g)	90
1 potato (100 g)	25
1 apple (100 g)	70
1 cotton T-shirt (250 g)	2000
1 sheet of A4 paper (80 g/m²)	10
1 glass of wine (125 ml)	120
1 glass of apple juice (200 ml)	190
1 glass of orange juice (200 ml)	170
1 bag of potato crisps (200 g)	185
1 egg (40 g)	135
1 hamburger (150 g)	2400
1 tomato (70 g)	13
1 orange (100 g)	50
1 pair of shoes (bovine leather)	8000
1 microchip (2 g)	32

Table 3 *Examples of global average virtual water content.*

Grape production in the Rioja region of Spain. Much irrigation water is used for the production of Spanish wine, a large proportion of which is exported.

Discussion point

Do you think that governments should place environmental taxes on products that contain a lot of virtual water to make both producers and consumers think more carefully about these products?

Water footprints

The **water footprint** of a country is the volume of water needed for the production of the goods and services consumed by the population of that country. This can be thought of as being in two parts:

- the internal water footprint is the volume of water used from domestic water resources
- the external water footprint is the volume of water used in other countries to produce goods and services imported and used by the population of the country.

The idea is that because the water footprint includes imports it is a truer reflection of overall water use by a country. For the period 1997–2001, the global average water footprint was 1240 m³/capita/year (cap/yr). The figure for the USA was 2480 m³/cap/yr while China had an average footprint of 700 m³/cap/yr. The major factors determining the water footprint of a country are:

- volume of consumption: largely related to per capita income
- consumption patterns: for example high or low meat consumption
- climate: precipitation and temperature conditions
- agricultural practices: water use efficiency.

The water footprint has been developed following the use and general acceptance of the ecological footprint concept. The water footprint is closely linked to the concept of virtual water. Figure 7 shows national water footprint per capita. If you are surprised by the position of some countries, look again at the

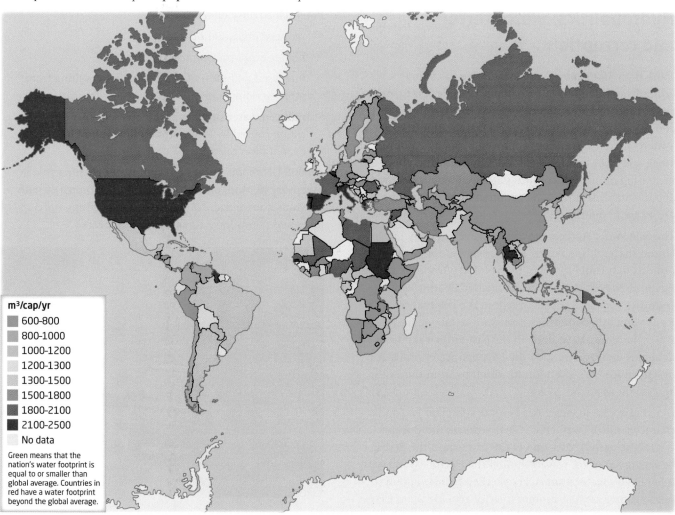

m³/cap/yr

- 600–800
- 800–1000
- 1000–1200
- 1200–1300
- 1300–1500
- 1500–1800
- 1800–2100
- 2100–2500
- No data

Green means that the nation's water footprint is equal to or smaller than global average. Countries in red have a water footprint beyond the global average.

Figure 7 *National water footprint per capita.*

four bullet points to help your understanding. Figure 8 shows the contribution of major countries to the global water footprint. India, China and the USA account for 34% of the global total, but because of its much lower population, per capita usage is much higher in the USA.

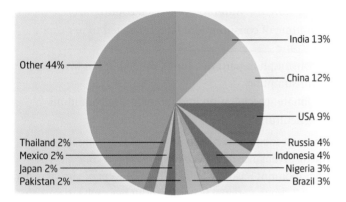

Figure 8 *Contribution of major consumers to the global water footprint.*

Hydropolitics, water terror and corruption

More than 300 major river basins as well as many groundwater aquifers cross national boundaries. However, as yet there are no enforceable laws that govern the allocation and use of international waters. The UN Watercourses Convention, approved by many countries in 1997, still lacks enough signatories to come into effect. An increasing number of countries are becoming concerned about water insecurity. The countries along the river Nile are a case in point.

The Nile Water Agreement of 1929 gave Egypt by far the largest share of Nile water. This agreement forbids any projects that could threaten the volume of water reaching Egypt. However, this has been criticised by upstream countries such as Kenya as a relic of the colonial era. Kenya and other countries now want to take more Nile water than they have done in the past as their domestic demands increase. In 2004 the Egyptian water minister described Kenya's intention to withdraw from the 1929 agreement as an 'act of war'.

Denying access to water has become a familiar characteristic of conflict in recent years. In the Bosnian war of the early 1990s, one of the first acts of the Serbs, besieging Sarajevo, was to shut off the electricity and with it Sarajevo's water pumps. People then had no option but to gather at wells around the city, making them easy targets for Serb snipers and their mortar shells. At about

the same time water terror was also a potent weapon in the Somalian civil war. People retreating from the fighting filled wells with rocks and dismantled all water infrastructure. These two conflicts could be previews of 'water wars' that some environmentalists warn will eventually engulf the world. For example, in the Middle East, King Hussein of Jordan has said that only a dispute over water could break the peace his country has established with Israel.

Corruption at various levels has an impact on the efficient development of water resources. The Fifth World Water Forum held in Istanbul in 2009 heard that some 30% of water-related budgets are being siphoned off by corrupt deals, including falsifying meter readings, nepotism and favouritism in the award of contracts.

Climate change

Many countries, particularly in the developing world, are concerned about the effects climate change may have on the quantity and quality of drinking-water resources. Potential adverse effects include:

- reduced precipitation
- higher evapotranspiration
- increased pollution of water supplies resulting from more flooding
- reduced water supplies and increased costs due to silting caused by lower stream flows and higher evaporation rates.

A 2008 UN report quotes a recent water resources inventory in Mongolia which found that compared with previous knowledge, 22% of rivers and springs and 32% of lakes and ponds have dried up or disappeared.

Reduced stream flow in southern Mongolia.

Case study

Mali: WaterAid in action

Mali, in West Africa, is one of the world's poorest nations. The natural environment is harsh and deteriorating. Rainfall levels, which are already low, are falling further and desertification is spreading. Currently 65% of the country is desert or semi-desert. Eleven million people still lack access to safe water. WaterAid has been active in the country since 2001. Its main concern is that the fully privatised water industry frequently fails to provide services to the poorest urban and rural areas. It is running a pilot scheme in the slums surrounding Mali's capital Bamako, providing clean water and sanitation services to the poorest people. Its objective is to demonstrate to both the government and other donors that projects in slums can be successful, both socially and economically.

WaterAid has financed the construction of the area's water network. It is training local people to manage and maintain the system, and to raise the money needed to keep it operational. Encouraging the community to invest in its own infrastructure is an important part of the philosophy of the project. According to Idrissa Doucoure, WaterAid's West Africa Regional Manager: 'We are now putting our energy into education programmes and empowering the communities to continue their own development into the future. This will allow WaterAid to move on and help others.' Already significant improvements in the general health of the community have occurred. The general view is that it takes a generation for health and sanitation to be properly embedded into people's day-to-day life.

The role of government

The government of a country has a critical role in the delivery of safe drinking water to a population. Responsibilities for water supply may cut across a number of different departments. Here, good cross-departmental cooperation is vital if the benefits of investment are to be maximised. Prior to the 1980s water resources were frequently managed by public utilities under government control. However, in many countries the process of privatisation has seen water resources sold off to private companies answerable to shareholders rather than to the general public. Governments maintain an element of control through 'watchdog' organisations, but they do not have the power they had previously in terms of this vital resource. Water resources in many countries are owned by large transnational companies.

Many pressure groups are concerned about the concept of 'water for capital', citing examples of people in poorer countries being forced to pay for clean water that was once accessible in their own villages.

External development assistance

Individual countries, multilateral organisations, NGOs and private foundations all provide assistance to the drinking-water and sanitation sectors of developing countries. Such aid is provided in various ways and can account for the majority of spending on drinking-water and sanitation in some countries. For some developing countries this figure rises to nearly 90%. For example, the NGO WaterAid is currently working in 30 different countries in Africa, Asia and the Pacific region.

In 2006, the grant and loan aid commitments of bilateral and multilateral external support agencies to the drinking-water and sanitation sectors totalled US$6.4 billion. The total for the period 2002–06 was US$18.3 billion.

Activities

1. Define the terms (a) water stress and (b) water scarcity.
2. Explain the difference between physical water scarcity and economic water scarcity.
3. Present a bullet-point summary of the information presented in Figure 5 (page 183).
4. Comment on the global water gap illustrated in Figure 6 (page 184).
5. What are the main reasons for the considerable difference in water investment needs shown in Table 2 (page 185)?
6. Explain why knowledge of water in aquifers is much more limited than knowledge of surface water.
7. Write brief explanations of the concepts of (a) virtual water and (b) water footprints.
8. Examine the variations in water footprint per capita shown in Figure 7 (page 187).
9. Describe the contribution of major consumers to the global water footprint in Figure 8 (page 188).

Case study

Vadodara City, India

Vadodara is the largest city in the state of Gujarat. A high rate of population increase has led to considerable shortfalls in the potable water supply and in the sanitation system. This has had an impact on water-borne disease in particular, although there are very large variations within the urban area (Figure 9).

There is a very strong relationship between the prevalence rates of gastroenteritis and infective hepatitis and socio-economic grouping. For example, Fatepura, Gajrawadi and Panigate, the wards with the highest rates for both diseases, all have large slum populations.

Disease rates are also high in Shiyabaug and the City where population densities are very high alongside environmental degradation, inadequate water supply and poor sewerage infrastructure. Elsewhere both population density and slum populations are lower.

A recent article entitled 'Development, Environment and Urban Health in India' (*Geography* 2007, pages 158–9) concluded that 'The poorer sections of society can either not afford to take care of their physical and other needs or are unaware of the need to do so, the result being unclean living areas.'

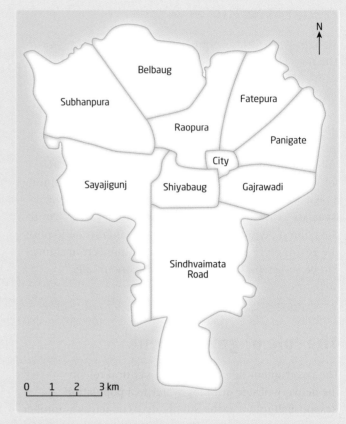

Figure 9 *Vadodara City: distribution of water-borne diseases.*

Ward number	Name of ward	Prevalence rate per 10 000 population	
		Gastroenteritis	**Infective hepatitis**
1	City	16.79	15.95
2	Fatepura	18.22	20.22
3	Gajrawadi	24.42	25.90
4	Sindhvaimata Road	2.99	9.47
5	Shiyabaug	8.31	10.49
6	Sayajigunj	0.47	1.00
7	Belbaug	1.14	4.01
8	Raopura	8.64	13.44
9	Panigate	17.84	14.63
10	Subhanpura	0.45	3.25
	Total	**8.19**	**10.99**

Discussion point

Suggest how you could realistically reduce your use of virtual water.

The factors affecting access to safe drinking water

Less than 50%
50-75%
76-90%
91-100%
No or insufficient data

Figure 10 *Improved drinking-water coverage, 2006.*

Water tower in a reservoir: Lake Vyrnwy, Wales.

Figure 10 shows improved drinking-water coverage in 2006 according to the United Nation's *Global Annual Assessment of Sanitation and Drinking-Water 2008 Report*. From 1990 to 2006, approximately 1.56 billion people gained access to improved drinking-water sources. Currently 87%

of the world uses drinking water from improved sources compared with 77% in 1990. Although the world is on track to meet the Millennium Development Goal drinking-water supply target by 2015 in general, many countries in Sub-Saharan Africa and in Oceania are currently projected to miss MDG country targets.

Access to safe drinking water is influenced by both physical and human factors. Physical factors include:

- amount of precipitation
- seasonal distribution of precipitation
- physical ability of the surface area to store water
- rate of evapotranspiration
- density of surface access points to water
- ease of access to groundwater supplies if they exist.

Human factors include:

- the wealth of a nation or region in terms of its ability to construct and maintain water infrastructure
- the distribution of population between urban and rural areas: in most developing countries people in

Case study

Ethiopia

After Nigeria, Ethiopia is the most populous country in Africa. It is one of the least urbanised countries in the world, with 84% of people living in rural areas. Only 42% of Ethiopians have access to improved water sources, and access in rural areas is about half this figure.

Although the country receives reasonably high annual precipitation, there is an absence of infrastructure for capturing and storing water. This makes the large rural population particularly vulnerable to droughts that periodically affect the region. The rising population has also resulted in smaller, fragmented farms, a situation further contributing to food insecurity when water becomes scarce.

Table 4 shows Ethiopia and the other countries with the least access to an improved water source. These countries are among the world's fastest-growing populations.

	Population with improved drinking water source (%)	Population (millions)	
	2006	**mid-2008**	**mid-2025**
Afghanistan	22	32.7	50.3
Somalia	29	9.0	14.3
Papua New Guinea	40	6.5	8.6
Ethiopia	42	79.1	110.5
Mozambique	42	20.4	27.5
Niger	42	14.7	26.3
Equatorial Guinea	43	0.6	0.9
DR Congo	46	66.5	109.7
Fiji	47	0.9	0.9
Madagascar	47	18.9	28.0
Nigeria	47	148.1	205.4

Table 4 *The countries with the least access to an improved water source.*

urban areas are more likely to have access to safe drinking water than their rural counterparts due to the concentration of investment in urban areas

- socio-economic differences in urban areas: affluent urban districts invariably have better access to safe water than poor districts
- the degree of contamination of urban water supplies by industry and lack of sanitation
- the degree of contamination of rural water supplies by animal use, fertilisers, pesticides, herbicides and lack of human sanitation
- civil war and international conflict.

The quantity versus quality debate

Since the mid-1980s it has become generally accepted that the quantity of water and the convenience of availability can be more important than improvements in quality (beyond a certain level). The rationale behind this view relates to the ways in which different infectious diseases are linked to water:

- Faecal-oral diseases are caused by micro-organisms present in the faeces of infected people. Most of them cause diarrhoea and kill over a million children a year. These diseases, including cholera and typhoid, are not only transmitted by water, but can also be passed on by contaminated food, fingers, utensils and even dirty clothes. Transmission of these diseases can be reduced by having more water available in the home to improve cleanliness.
- Water-washed skin and eye diseases, for example trachoma, are most common in arid regions. These diseases have little to do with water quality but the best preventative measure is greater water availability for personal hygiene.
- Water-based diseases such as schistosomiasis (bilharzia) are caused by parasitic worms which enter the body when people wade or swim in infected water.

The avoidance of such areas for example by having piped water washing areas, or purification of these areas, is the answer here. However, in many impoverished regions neither of these solutions might be an option.

- Water-related insect vector diseases such as malaria and elephantiasis are spread by insects that breed in water. For example, one type breeds in the water storage tanks on large buildings in Indian cities and transmits malaria.

Thus the main public health benefit from improved water supplies (quality or quantity) is the reduction in faecal-oral diseases. It has been estimated that of the deaths in East Africa that can be prevented by water supplies, 90% are in this category. Developing world water engineers, with limited funds, are therefore faced with deciding whether the faecal-oral infections are mainly water-borne, due to poor water quality, or mainly transmitted by food, fingers and other such water-washed routes related to the lack of water. Should money be spent on improving the quality of the existing supply, or go on increasing that supply at the same quality?

The economic benefits of improving access to safe water

The World Health Organization estimates that each dollar invested in achieving MDG 7 would give an economic return of between US$ 3 and US$ 34, depending on the region. The benefits would include:

- avoiding health-related costs of US$ 7.3 billion per year
- adult working days gained to the value of US$ 750 million
- significant time savings through the relocation of water access points closer to user communities
- girls and women in particular having better educational and productive opportunities with time saved fetching water
- the availability of water used to start or expand small enterprises which will increase household disposable income
- demand for agricultural products likely to increase and the potential for tourism to expand
- improved life expectancy at all ages.

Water pollution

Each year about 450 km³ of wastewater are discharged into rivers, streams and lakes around the world.

While rivers in more affluent countries have become steadily cleaner in recent decades, the reverse has been true in much of the developing world. It has been estimated that 90% of sewage in developing countries is discharged into rivers, lakes and seas without any treatment. The UN estimates that almost half the population in many developing world cities do not have access to safe drinking water. For example, the Yamuna river which flows through Delhi has 200 million litres of sewage draining into it each day. For many people the only alternative to using this water for drinking and cooking is to turn to water vendors who sell tap water at greatly inflated prices.

Although most people in developing countries think that their water supplies are clean and healthy, there is growing concern in some quarters about traces of potentially dangerous medicines that may be contaminating tap water and putting unborn babies at risk, according to a report published in the UK in September 2008. One newspaper headline read 'Is our water being poisoned with a cocktail of drugs?' Scientists are worried that powerful and toxic anti-cancer drugs are passing unhindered through sewage works and making their way back into the water supply. The greatest concern is about 'cytotoxic' or cell-killing cancer drugs which are taken by about 250 000 people in the UK. Easily dissolved in water, they remain highly toxic when leaving the body and are hard to destroy in water treatment plants.

Desalination: the answer to water shortages?

Desalination plants are in widespread use in the Middle East where other forms of water supply are extremely scarce. Most of these plants distill water by boiling, generally using waste gases produced by oil wells. Without the availability of waste energy the process would be extremely expensive. This is the main reason why desalination plants are few and far between outside of the Middle East.

However, another method of desalination does exist. Originally developed in California in the mid-1960s for industrial use, the 'reverse osmosis' technique is now being applied to drinking water. Recent advances have substantially reduced the cost of reverse-osmosis systems. Large-scale systems using this new technology have been built in Singapore and Florida.

The sea water will still have to undergo conventional filter treatment to rid it of impurities such as microbes pumped into the sea from sewage plants. It is likely therefore that even when the technology has been refined, desalinated water will always be more expensive than obtaining water from conventional sources. However, desalination does have other advantages:

- it does not affect the water level in rivers
- it could mean that controversial plans for new reservoirs could be shelved.

However, desalination plants are expensive and do not offer a viable solution to the poorest countries unless costs can be drastically reduced.

Activities

1 Look at Figure 10 (page 191).
   a Describe the global variations in improved drinking water coverage.
   b What are the main reasons for such significant differences?
2 How are different infectious diseases linked to water?
3 Discuss the economic benefits of improving access to safe water.
4 To what extent is desalination the answer to water shortages?

Key terms

Groundwater water found below the surface which is not combined chemically with any minerals present.

Aquifer a permeable rock that will hold water and permit its passage.

Water-stressed area place where water supply is below 1700 cubic metres per person per year.

Water-scarce area place where water supply falls below 1000 cubic metres per person a year.

'Green' water that part of total precipitation that is absorbed by soil and plants, then released back into the air.

'Blue' water precipitation that collects in rivers, lakes, wetlands and as groundwater. It is available for human use before it evaporates or reaches the ocean.

Potable water water that is free from impurities, pollution and bacteria, and is thus safe to drink.

Evapotranspiration the combined processes of evaporation, sublimation and transpiration of the water from the Earth's surface into the atmosphere.

Physical water scarcity when physical access to water is limited.

Economic water scarcity when a population does not have the necessary monetary means to utilise an adequate source of water.

'Grey' water water that has already been used for one purpose, but can possibly be reused for another purpose.

Water table the top of the water-saturated part of a permeable rock. During periods of very high rainfall the water table may extend into the soil and possibly reach the surface of the ground.

Virtual water the amount of water that is used to produce food or any other item and is thus essentially 'embedded' in the item.

Water footprint a person's water footprint is the volume of fresh water the individual uses directly and in the production of the goods and services that person consumes.

Desalination the conversion of salt water into fresh water by the extraction of dissolved solids.

Websites

www.worldwaterday.net
World Water Day

www.worldwatercouncil.org
World Water Council

www.worldbank.org
The World Bank

www.unwater.org
UN Water

www.waterfootprint.org
Water Footprint

www.unesco.org/water
UNESCO Water

www.thewaterproject.org
The Water Project

www.scientificamerican.com
Scientific American

Review

Examination-style questions

1 Refer to Figure 11.

a Briefly explain the concept of the water footprint.

b Why do water withdrawals by the four uses shown in the diagram vary between world regions?

c Explain the 'trade' and 'total consumption water footprint' sections of the diagram.

2 Refer to Figure 12.

a Why is access to safe drinking water such an important element of development?

b Why does access to safe drinking water vary so much between urban and rural areas in some parts of the world?

c Explain the major differences between world regions shown in Figure 12.

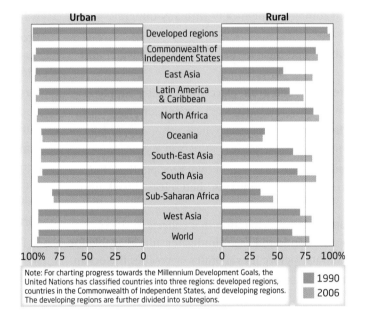

Figure 12 *Access to safe drinking water.*

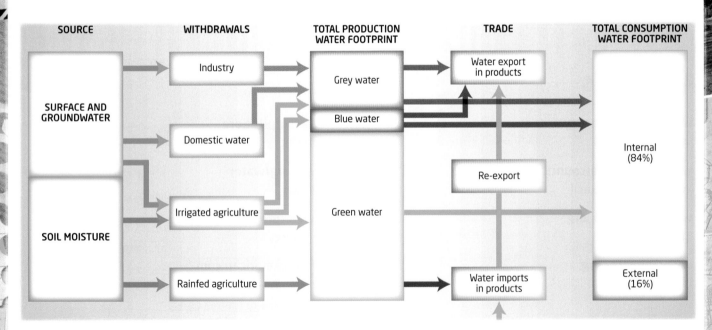

Figure 11 *Components of the water footprint.*

12 Biodiversity and change

The concept of biodiversity

Giant water lilies in an Amazon tributary.

Biodiversity means biological diversity. It is the diversity of animal and plant life, wild and cultivated, in a particular habitat or in the world as a whole. Biodiversity can be viewed at a number of scales:

- Species diversity – the variety of *species* present in a given area. The term 'species richness' is often used in this context.
- Genetic diversity – refers to the variation of genes within species. Variation in genetic make-up more easily allows populations to adapt to changing environments.
- Ecosystem diversity – **ecosystem** diversity encompasses the broad differences between ecosystem types, and the diversity of habitats and ecological processes occurring within each ecosystem type. It is harder to define ecosystem diversity than species or genetic diversity because the 'boundaries' of communities (associations of species) and ecosystems are more fluid.

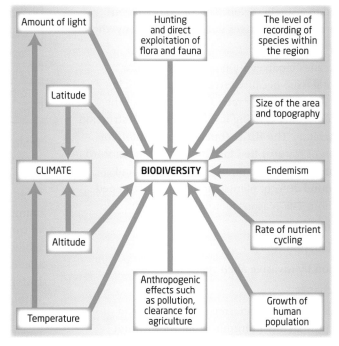

Figure 1 *Factors influencing the level of biodiversity.*

Globally, an estimated 1.7 million species have been identified so far. Estimates for the total number of species in existence vary from 5 million to nearly 100 million. Figure 1 illustrates the factors influencing biodiversity. The most important factor is climate, which can be regarded as a limiting factor as it determines the limits within which an animal or plant can exist. Species richness is concentrated in equatorial regions and tends to decline towards the poles. Also, diversity generally decreases with increasing altitude. For marine ecosystems, species richness tends to be concentrated on continental shelves, though deep-sea communities are also significant.

At low latitudes the climate is warmer and usually more humid compared to high latitudes. Such conditions are ideal for the fast breakdown of dead **biotic** and **abiotic** material resulting in rapid nutrient cycling. In contrast, in those parts of the world where the climate is too cold or too dry, the levels of biodiversity are low. In such regions there are not enough food sources to support large populations. Plants form the basis of land-based food chains and grow best in warm, moist conditions.

Figure 1 shows that human populations can have a major influence on biodiversity. Human population growth has an impact on biodiversity because humans are in competition with other species for resources and space. As human populations increase, this competition becomes more intense. In so many parts of the world the varied natural environment has been largely cleared to make way for monoculture systems of food production. The term **endemism** in Figure 1 refers to a state in which species are restricted to a single region. This often occurs on islands where a species thrives but is not found anywhere else in the world.

In recent decades biodiversity has become a major environmental issue because environments are being degraded at an accelerating rate. In many parts of the world much diversity is being lost through the destruction of natural habitats. The IUCN (International Union for Conservation of Nature) Red List 2004 stated that a third of amphibians, 23% of mammals, 12% of birds and probably around 20% of plants and fish are threatened with extinction. The reasons identified included:

- habitat loss
- overexploitation
- destruction by invasive alien species
- climate change.

Some species, sometimes referred to as 'living dead' species, are now so low in number that they cannot maintain a viable population.

Scientific reports have estimated current species loss at about 1000 times the 'background' rate experienced before the Industrial Revolution. The most alarming predictions are that as many as half of all current species could be lost

in the next century. This is when scientists talk about what the threshold of sustainable biodiversity loss might be. Is it, for example, 50% of all existing species? Beyond this threshold would be catastrophic decline.

Country	Total number
Brazil	59851
Colombia	54649
China	34687
Indonesia	32680
Mexico	28836
South Africa	25052
Venezuela	23429
Ecuador	22065
USA	21474
India	21020
Peru	20081
Bolivia	19561
Australia	17974
Malaysia	17171
Costa Rica	13630
Thailand	13340
Papua New Guinea	13115
Congo, Dem. Rep.	13107
Russia	12468
Vietnam	12034

Table 1 *Number of amphibian, bird, mammal, reptile and vascular plant species, by country.*

Table 1 shows the biodiversity levels for the top twenty countries in the world. Many, but not all, contain areas of tropical rainforest. Brazil and Colombia have levels of biodiversity considerably beyond the other countries in the league table. Scientists have identified **biodiversity hotspots** which are areas of particularly high biodiversity within countries. Many species are endemic to these regions. It has been estimated that 25 land-based hotspots covering just 1.4% of the Earth's surface accommodate:

- 25% of all birds
- 54% of amphibians
- 30% of mammals
- 44% of plants.

Geographical skills

On an outline map of the world:
a   Label the 20 countries shown in Table 1.
b   Use a cartographic technique of your own choice to illustrate the differences in biodiversity between these countries.
c   Make a list of the countries that have areas of tropical rainforest.
d   Explain the presence in the table of countries that do not have tropical rainforest.

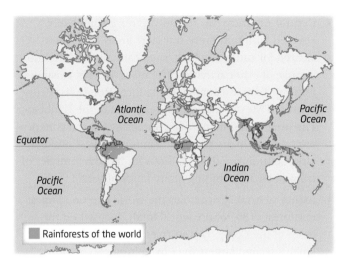

Figure 2 *The tropical rainforests.*

Activities

1   Define the terms (a) biodiversity (b) ecosystem (c) biotic (d) abiotic.
2   Explain the term endemism.
3   Briefly discuss the three scales at which biodiversity can be viewed.
4   Produce a 100-word summary to explain Figure 1 (page 197).
5   What is a biodiversity hotspot?
6   Discuss the geographical locations of the countries shown in Table 1.

- South America: the Amazon is by far the world's largest tropical rainforest. It covers the basin of the river Amazon, the second longest river in the world. The Amazon contains the greatest variety of plants and animals on Earth. This unique region contains a fifth of all the world's plants and birds and about a tenth of all mammal species. Over half of this forest lies in Brazil, which holds about one-third of the world's remaining tropical rainforests. About 13% of the rainforest is in Peru with smaller areas in Colombia, Venezuela, Ecuador, Bolivia, Guyana, Suriname and French Guiana.

The importance of biodiversity in tropical rainforests

The greatest fears have been expressed about the loss of species in **tropical rainforests** (Figure 2), one of the world's great **biomes**. Tropical rainforests, also known as humid tropical forests, have the most productive and diverse ecosystem found on land. These rainforests contain over 50% of the world's species. The Amazon in South America is by far the world's largest area of rainforest. Rainforests once covered almost 15% of the Earth's land surface, but this has declined to only 6% today due to widespread clearance for a range of human activities.

Figure 2 shows the locations of the world's rainforests which straddle the equator and are found between the Tropics of Cancer and Capricorn.

Condensation occurring in giant cumulus clouds over the Amazon rainforest. Such clouds produce very high annual rainfall.

- Central America: this region was once completely covered with rainforest, but large areas have been cleared for cattle ranching, sugarcane plantations and a range of other activities. The main areas of existing rainforest are in Panama, Costa Rica, Honduras, Belize, southern Mexico and on some islands in the Caribbean. The jungles and mangrove swamps of Central America are home to many plants and animals found nowhere else. Central America is famous for its large number of tropical birds, including many kinds of parrot.

- Africa: Central Africa holds the world's second largest rainforest (18% of the world total), focused on the basin of the Congo (Zaire) river. The Congo is the Earth's second largest river by volume. Six nations share the Congo basin. These are: Cameroon, the Central African Republic, the Republic of Congo, the Democratic Republic of Congo, Equatorial Guinea and Gabon. The Congo basin contains 70% of the plant cover in Africa. To the south-east, the large island of Madagascar was once intensively forested, but now much of it has been cut down.

- South and South-east Asia: the rainforests of Asia stretch from India and Myanmar in the west to Malaysia and Indonesia in the east. Most tropical rainforest in Asia is found in Indonesia, the Malay peninsula (Malaysia, Thailand, Myanmar), and Laos and Cambodia. Bangladesh has the largest area of mangrove forests in the world.

- Australasia: Papua New Guinea and the north-eastern coastal zone of Australia have significant areas of rainforest. Nearly 85% of the main island of Papua New Guinea is covered with rainforest. In Australia, tropical rainforest is confined to a narrow 500 km long zone along the North Queensland coast. In total the rainforest covers only 0.1% of Australia's land area. Undergrowth in Australia's tropical forests is dense and lush. The forests lie in the path of wet winds blowing in from the Pacific.

Discussion point

How important are the non-use values identified in Table 2? Does their importance vary from person to person? If so, what are the reasons for different perceptions?

Biodiversity in tropical rainforests and in other biomes is of great importance for a number of reasons. These can be placed in various classes of importance. Table 2 shows

The Amazon and its immediate floodplain near Manaus.

Direct use value (*goods*)	Indirect use value (*services*)	Non-use values	
Food, medicines, building materials, fibre, fuel	Atmospheric and climate regulation, pollination, nutrient recycling	Potential (or option) value	Future value either as a good or a service
	Cultural, spiritual and aesthetic	Existence value	Value of knowing something exists
		Bequest value	Value of knowing that something will be there for future generations

Table 2 *Categorising values.*

one classification that can be used in different biomes. This classification distinguishes between direct use value, indirect use value and non-use values. Of course, values of biodiversity also exist wholly outside the human context, as in the case of the inherent value of species.

Perhaps a more familiar classification is to examine biodiversity in terms of its ecological, economic and cultural importance. In general the same factors are covered in both methods of classification; the difference is in the way of looking at the phenomenon.

Ecological value

All living creatures are supported by the interactions among organisms and ecosystems. Biodiversity loss makes ecosystems less stable and more vulnerable to extreme events. It also weakens their natural cycles. The tropical rainforests play an immense role in all the world's major natural cycles – energy cycle, water cycle, carbon and oxygen cycle and the nitrogen cycle. The Amazon rainforest has been described as the 'lungs of the planet' because it provides the essential environmental service of continuously recycling carbon dioxide into oxygen. More than 20% of the world's oxygen is produced in the Amazon rainforest. While in temperate forests often just half a dozen tree species or fewer make up 90% of the trees, a tropical rainforest may have more than 480 tree species in a single hectare. The forests help to maintain a humid environment. Half of all rainfall in the Amazon basin is produced locally from the forest-atmosphere cycle.

Economic value

A biologically diverse natural environment provides the human population with the necessities of life and forms the basis for the economy. Everything we use and trade comes from the natural world. At least 1650 known tropical forest plants have the potential to be grown as vegetable crops, which could reduce our reliance on the few crops grown today. Just 30 crops supply about 90% of the calories in the global human diet. Since the world depends on so few plant species for food, humankind is vulnerable to environmental changes and crop diseases. Rainforest flora has also been the source of many important drugs. An estimated 25% of Western pharmaceuticals are derived from rainforest ingredients, yet less than 1% of rainforest plants have been tested for their medicinal properties. The US National Cancer Institute has identified 3000 plants that are active against cancer cells, and 70% of these plants are found in the rainforest. Twenty-five per

cent of the active ingredients in today's cancer-fighting drugs come from organisms found only in the rainforest.

Cultural value

Most people feel connected to nature in varying degrees. Some feel a strong spiritual bond that may be rooted in our common biological ancestry. Human cultures around the world profoundly reflect our instinctive attachment to the natural world. Thus cultural diversity is inextricably linked to Earth's biodiversity. Thousands of cultural groups around the world each have distinct traditions and knowledge for relating to the natural world. For example, in rainforests indigenous peoples who have lived in these environments for thousands of years usually place very different values on the rainforest environment from those outside groups or relative newcomers to this biome. However, many more people from other environments now visit or want to visit areas of rainforest because they have become aware of their intrinsic characteristics.

Activities

1 Define the terms (a) tropical rainforest and (b) biomes.
2 Describe the global distribution of tropical rainforests.
3 a Look at the photo on page 199. Describe the type of cloud that is characteristic of tropical rainforests.
   b What can happen to such clouds when large areas of rainforest disappear?
4 Examine the ecological importance of tropical rainforests.
5 What is the economic value of tropical rainforests? Why would it be difficult to arrive at a precise figure for this economic value?
6 What do you understand by the term 'cultural value'? Explain the cultural value of biodiversity.

Theory of Knowledge

The cultural value of the environment, of which biodiversity is a major part, has been the subject of prose, poerty, painting, theatre, sculpture and other forms of communication; it has been discussed for thousands of years by writers from many different disciplines. What has taught you, personally, most about this?

Changes in the Amazon rainforest

Ecosystem characteristics

The Amazon is the world's largest rainforest and the major ecosystem in Brazil in terms of both geographical area and biodiversity. Its land area represents 40% of Brazil's territory. One thousand eight hundred species of birds and 250 varieties of mammals are sheltered by an infinite assortment of trees and plants. It is one of the few places on Earth where new species of plants and animals remain to be discovered. It is estimated that the Amazon rainforest is directly responsible for the production of 20% of the world's replenishable supply of oxygen. The Amazon holds carbon stocks of around 120 billion tonnes. Figure 3 shows some of the main characteristics of the Amazon rainforest with its distinctive layering.

It is a huge low-lying region consisting of a series of regular tabular formations that descend gradually to the Amazon river (Figure 4). Only 3% of the area consists of alluvial deposits of recent Quaternary origin, the tabular formations being mainly sands and clays of Tertiary age. The basin is flanked by the Guiana Plateau to the north and the Central Plateau to the south. The basin has an annual rainfall of approximately 2000 mm and annual average temperatures of 22–26°C (Figure 5).

Essential to the rainforest ecosystem is the Amazon **river system.** The Amazon river has more than one thousand tributaries. Of the twenty largest rivers in the world, ten are in the 5.9 million km² Amazon basin. Seventeen of the Amazon's tributaries flow for more than 1600 km. The Amazon is second only to the Nile in length. However, the Amazon is the world's largest river in volume (Figure 4). Dropping less than 3 cm per kilometre after emerging from

Vegetation growing in shallow water along the banks of an Amazon tributary.

Figure 3 *Characteristics of the Amazon rainforest.*

3 Patterns in environmental quality and sustainability

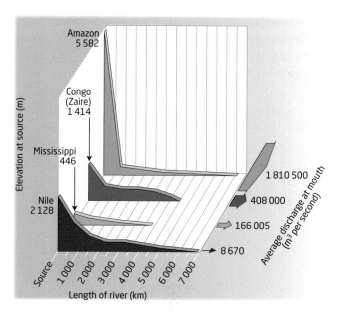

Figure 4 *Comparing the Amazon with other major world rivers.*

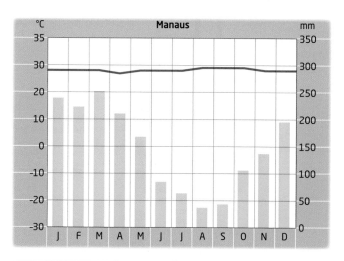

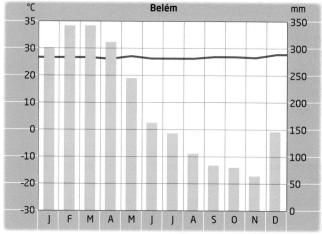

Figure 5 *Climate graphs for Manaus and Belém.*

the Andes, the Amazon drains one-sixth of the planet's runoff into the Atlantic Ocean. Aquatic plant life on the Amazon is plentiful. The best known are the *Victoria amazonica* water lilies (see photo on page 197), whose leaves sometimes grow to 2 metres in diameter.

In general most of the Amazon basin is under high rainforest on acid soils known as **latosols** or tropical red soils (Figure 6). These are old and deep soils with a browny-red colour and crumbly texture. Such ferralitic

The meeting of the waters of major tributaries in the Amazon. Note the different colours of the waters due to the considerable difference in the amount of sediment carried.

(iron-rich) soils form under conditions of constant high temperatures and moisture surplus, so decomposition and leaching are dominant processes. Decomposition of the leaf litter is rapid because of the high temperatures. Unlike most other rainforest areas, the soils of the Amazon are low in nutrients even when a tree cover exists. The forest receives its nutrients from a network of fine roots close to the soil surface which is mixed with organic material. The root system picks up nutrients directly from the decomposed litter, and nutrients do not get deep into the soil in significant quantity. This organic material is absolutely vital to the ecosystem.

As the parent rock disintegrates rapidly, tropical red soils may become deep if they are found on level surfaces. With only a moderate gradient they are easily eroded, particularly when the vegetation is cleared away.

Most of the rainforest grows on dry land and is known as 'terra firma' rainforest. This contrasts with the lower

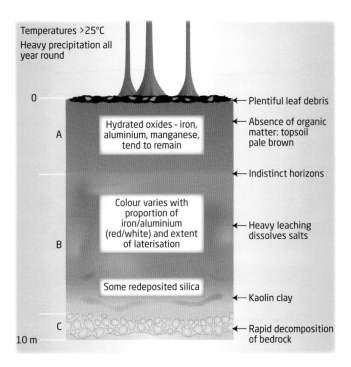

Temperatures >25°C
Heavy precipitation all year round

0

A

Hydrated oxides - iron, aluminium, manganese, tend to remain

B

Colour varies with proportion of iron/aluminium (red/white) and extent of laterisation

Some redeposited silica

C

10 m

← Plentiful leaf debris

← Absence of organic matter: topsoil pale brown

← Indistinct horizons

← Heavy leaching dissolves salts

← Kaolin clay

← Rapid decomposition of bedrock

Figure 6 *Soil profile of rainforest soil.*

igapo forest which grows near the rivers on land that is flooded for at least part of the year. Most trees in the terra firma forest grow to between 25 and 30 metres, although emergents may be 60 metres high (Figure 3). The forest is an essential component of the region's water cycle: it has been estimated that about half of the Amazon's rainfall comes from transpiration.

Early exploitation of the Amazon

The indigenous inhabitants, such as the Yanomami Indians, lived off the forest for thousands of years without creating any significant environmental stress. Throughout colonial times the fringes of the forest were exploited in a limited way for cattle ranching and sugar plantations, but the majority of the region remained untouched apart from an isolated economic cycle based on spices in the north of the Amazon. This was directed in the 17th century by Jesuit missionaries who worked among the settled tribal peoples along the rivers. The Jesuits encouraged the cultivation of various crops such as pepper and indigo, for export to Europe. However, in the 18th century, the missionaries were ejected from Brazil as from many other parts of South America.

The Amazon was the last region of the country to be drawn into the national economy. This integration was based on the exploitation of natural rubber leaves in the

late 19th century. Belem and Manaus emerged as the main centres of the rubber trade. In 1900 nearly a third of Brazil's export trade by value was accounted for by rubber passing through these two ports.

Because of the region's sparse population the rapidly rising labour requirement was met by a considerable migration stream from the north-east. However, the rubber boom ended rapidly in the early years of the 20th century with the development of plantation rubber cultivation in South-east Asia. From then until the 1960s the Amazon was largely ignored in terms of economic development.

House of a farmer in the Amazon, with no connection to services.

Recent development

In recent decades significant areas of rainforest have been cleared. The main reasons have been to:
- provide newly settled smallholders with land and crops
- create huge cattle ranches and soybean farms
- build roads
- exploit mineral deposits
- use wood for fuel
- use wood for furniture manufacture and for pulp and paper
- provide land for urban and industrial uses.

The impact of agriculture

Population growth has focused on the main urban areas of Belém, Manaus, Santarém, Pôrto Velho and Rio Branco. Outside of these settlements the areas of heaviest growth have been along the Belém-Brazilia highway and in Rondônia. The latter has become one of the most devastated parts of the rainforest. Migrants arriving along the BR 364 highway were attracted by the apparent fertility of the soil but the fact is that less than 20% of the state is suitable for agriculture. The catalyst for growth was the paving of the highway in 1984.

Clearing forest for cattle pasture is the main reason for deforestation (Figure 7). Between 2000 and 2005 cattle ranching accounted for 80% of deforestation in the Amazon. In the early 1970s the government decided that significant areas of the Amazon should be cut down to be planted with grass for pasture. A number of foreign transnational companies attracted by the idea set up huge ranches. The most suitable breed for cattle in the region, the Nelore from India, required much more grazing land per head in the Amazon than in more fertile environments. In addition, in many areas the quality of pasture declined considerably after a relatively short period.

In recent years the improved infrastructure along with the eradication of foot-and-mouth disease has led to the emergence of more intensive cattle operations with much higher stocking levels. This has been an important factor in Brazil's rise to become the world's largest exporter of beef.

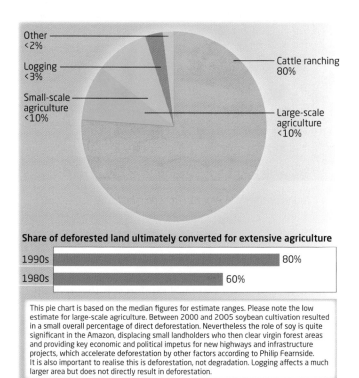

Share of deforested land ultimately converted for extensive agriculture

1990s	80%
1980s	60%

This pie chart is based on the median figures for estimate ranges. Please note the low estimate for large-scale agriculture. Between 2000 and 2005 soybean cultivation resulted in a small overall percentage of direct deforestation. Nevertheless the role of soy is quite significant in the Amazon, displacing small landholders who then clear virgin forest areas and providing key economic and political impetus for new highways and infrastructure projects, which accelerate deforestation by other factors according to Philip Fearnside. It is also important to realise this is deforestation, not degradation. Logging affects a much larger area but does not directly result in deforestation.

Figure 7 *Causes of deforestation in the Brazilian Amazon, 2000–05.*

The impact of logging

Amazonia is the world's last great reserve of tropical timber. For a long time much of the forest was protected by its inaccessibility. However, since the Belém-Brasilia highway was built in 1965, timber companies have flocked to the state of Pará in particular. The frontier town of Paragominas has one of the highest concentrations of sawmills in the world. The typical sequence of environmental destruction is as follows:

- an area of forest is searched for suitable trees to be cut
- the entangled nature of the forest means that when the selected trees crash down they bring many others with them
- more damage is caused when the retrieval team moves in with bulldozers to haul out the selected trees
- although a few trees will repopulate the bulldozer trails, nothing grows where the tyre tracks ran; trees still fall along the trails, brought down by winds channelled along the newly created corridors
- the area is now susceptible to fire for the first time; normally the closed canopy prevents the moist leaf litter on the forest floor from drying enough to allow any chance sparks to spread; but once the canopy has been broken open, fire becomes a very real hazard; throughout Pará fires have wiped out vast areas of logged forest.

However, with careful management the impact of logging can be much reduced. Vine-cutting means that 30% fewer trees may be damaged when felling takes place. Careful route planning can reduce by a quarter the area affected by bulldozers. Smaller gaps in the canopy and less fuel left behind on the forest floor considerably cut the risk of fire.

Manatee at the INPA Amazon Research Institute in Manaus.

Mining: an unstoppable force?

Considerable profits have already been made from mining and the mining industry sees much more to come. Figure 8 shows the location of the largest mining projects in the Amazon. The largest and most ambitious scheme is the Carajas Project. It has been described as a 'Pandora's box' with 18 million tonnes of iron ore reserves, 150 tonnes of gold, as well as significant deposits of silver, manganese, copper, molybdenum, nickel, casserite and bauxite. The iron ore deposits are the world's largest.

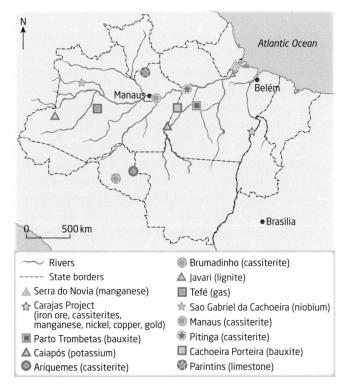

Figure 8 *Mining projects in the Amazon.*

The immense mineral wealth has attracted development on a huge scale. Apart from the advanced opencast mining operation, a completely new network of power generation, transport and processing plants has been constructed, with a rail line to the coast connecting with new port facilities and aluminium factories.

Environmental concern over huge open-pit mining has caused intense debate:

- a large section of rainforest, the home of several thousand Indians, has been transformed into an enormous industrial park

- against the wishes of the local community the railway line to the coast was built through the Gavioes Indian Reserve

- hundreds of Indians died as a result of 'imported' diseases

- in the Xikrin Indian Reserve, independent miners invaded and polluted local rivers with mercury, used to separate out gold after panning

- deforestation has led to the inevitable consequences experienced elsewhere in the Amazon

- air pollution has increased significantly as the scale of economic activity has expanded.

The development of the mine and its associated activities have significantly changed the population structure of the region. The European-origin population of the Carajas region was negligible before 1980, but has risen considerably since then.

Exotic fauna at the INPA Amazon Research Institute in Manaus.

Limited protection

Around 42% of Brazil's tropical rainforest is theoretically protected by many different conservation units under varying sets of rules. Although monitored by satellite there are not enough police and officials on the ground to apprehend bandit loggers. Corruption among officials and violence towards them is also a problem.

Activities

1   With reference to Figure 3 (page 202), describe the characteristics of the Amazon rainforest.
2   With the help of Figure 4 (page 203), describe and explain the climate of the Amazon rainforest.
3   How important is the Amazon river system to the rainforest environment?
4   How does early exploitation of the rainforest compare with its present economic use?
5   What have been the environmental concerns of the Carajas project?

Consequences

The impact of deforestation and the loss of biodiversity in terms of both Brazil and the planet as a whole, have been well documented, focusing on the major problems of:

- depletion of the region's genetic bank
- increased levels of carbon dioxide
- reduced levels of oxygen
- decreased precipitation due to a reduced vegetation cover
- reduced interception capacity leading to greater likelihood of flooding
- the ultimate alteration of the Amazon's discharge regime and sediment transport pattern
- severe soil exhaustion and erosion
- the adverse impact on the indigenous population.

The consequences of reduced biodiversity in the Amazon and other rainforests not only affect the rainforests themselves, but also the planet as a whole because of the vital importance of this biome. Loss of biodiversity makes ecosystems less stable and more vulnerable. Many of the species in rainforest areas are endemic and not found elsewhere. The heavier the burden of human activity on the environment, the greater the pressure on ecological services, increasing the risk of ecosystem collapse. Scientists cannot accurately predict the tipping point at which an ecosystem decline may suddenly speed up or cause a failure that reverberates across other ecosystems.

Deforestation is a significant contributor to global climate change as it is one of the major causes of the enhanced greenhouse effect. Tropical deforestation is responsible for approximately 20% of world greenhouse gas emissions. The rainforests act as huge **carbon sinks**. Trees and other plants remove carbon, in the form of carbon dioxide, from the atmosphere during the process of photosynthesis and release oxygen back into the atmosphere during normal respiration. The decay and burning of wood releases much of this stored carbon back to the atmosphere. Deforestation may cause carbon stores held in soil to be released.

A study carried out by the Brazilian National Institute for Research in Amazonia stated that hydro-electricity dams with reservoirs in tropical forests can sometimes contribute more to global warming than fossil fuel power plants. Emissions of carbon dioxide and methane from rotting vegetation in reservoir waters pose a considerable problem. The study calculated that emissions from the Balbina reservoir had 26 times more impact on global warming than emissions from coal-fired plants generating the same amount of electricity. While the gases released from such reservoirs will slowly reduce as the vegetation decays, this will take a long time.

Trees pump water from the soil and release it into the atmosphere as part of the cycle that provides the planet with fresh water. Tropical rainforest trees play the most vital role on Earth in this process. A serious reduction in rainforest makes climate change more likely. The clearing of forests invariably leaves an impoverished soil which is easily washed away by the heavy rains. This makes it almost impossible for the original forest species to **recolonise** the area.

The 2009 Red List of Threatened Species from the International Union for the Conservation of Nature (IUCN) shows that '17 291 species out of the 47 677 assessed species are threatened with extinction'. Many of these species are in tropical rainforests. Writing at *ecoworldy.com* (2 April 2009), Bryan Nelson states that 'The current rate of extinction is 100 to 1000 times higher than the average, or background rate, making our current period the sixth major mass extinction in the planet's history.' The current rate of biodiversity loss is clearly a crisis situation. Many unknown species are likely to be lost and their benefits will be left undiscovered. Professor Jonathan Baillie, director of conservation programmes at the Zoological Society of London is quoted as saying, 'In our lifetime, we have gone from having to worry about a relatively small number of highly threatened species to the collapse of entire ecosystems.'

World food supply is maintained by cultivating a relatively narrow range of crops. Most food is provided by 15–20 plant species such as maize, wheat and rice. Such a narrow range of important crops makes food supply vulnerable to new diseases. Keeping a significant pool of 'wild' relatives of food plants is a vital insurance policy. Biodiversity loss threatens this position.

The World Wildlife Fund (WWF) has stressed that biodiversity underpins the health of the planet, stating that reduced biodiversity means that millions of people face a future where food supplies are more vulnerable to pests and disease and where water is irregular or in short supply. Reduced biodiversity will result in fewer new medicines, greater vulnerability to natural disasters and more severe effects from global warming.

The displacement of indigenous communities and their traditional way of life is also a factor to be considered. Indigenous peoples often have only very limited political representation and little power against the interests of big business. The loss of indigenous communities has an impact both on the people living in them, and in a wider context because of the knowledge they have of the plants and animals around them and of the environmental balance within their localities. Such knowledge is likely to become more and more important in the future. The threat to cultural diversity should also not be underestimated. The UN Environment Programme has stressed the close links between biodiversity and cultural diversity.

Chinese medical centre in London. Chinese medicines use a wide range of natural ingredients from rainforests and elsewhere.

Key terms

Biodiversity the diversity of plant and animal life in a particular habitat or in the world as a whole.

Ecosystem a dynamic complex of plant, animal and micro-organism communities and their non-living environment interacting as a functional unit.

Biotic the living components of an ecosystem such as plants.

Abiotic the non-living components of an ecosystem such as water and soil.

Endemism a state in which species are restricted to a single region.

Biodiversity hotspot area with a particularly high level of biodiversity.

Tropical rainforest a rainforest found near the equator, typically characterised by high temperature and rainfall, poor soil, and a high diversity of plant and animal species.

Biome a naturally occurring organic community of plants and animals.

River system all of the streams and channels draining a river basin comprising a main river and its tributaries.

Latosol a major soil type of the humid and high temperature tropics with a shallow A horizon but a thick B horizon comprising clay, sand, and sesquioxides of iron and aluminium which, respectively, endow it with a red or yellow colour. Much of the silica has been leached from latosols, and they tend to be of low fertility.

Igapo forest that part of the rainforest which grows near the rivers on land that is flooded for at least part of the year.

Carbon sink an environmental reservoir that absorbs and stores more carbon than it releases, thereby offsetting greenhouse gas emissions.

Recolonise The re-establishment of organisms into habitats that they previously occupied.

Websites

www.iucn.org
International Union for Conservation of Nature (IUCN)

www.inpa.gov.br
Instituto Nacional de Pesquisas da Amazonia (INPA)

www.news.mongabay.com
Mongabay.com – 50 Simple Things Kids Can Do to Save the Earth

www.rain-tree.com
Raintree

www.sciencedaily.com
Science Daily

www.davidsuzuki.org
David Suzuki Foundation

www.globalchange.umich.edu
University of Michigan's Global Change Curriculum

Review

Examination-style questions

1 Refer to Figure 9.

a Define biodiversity.

b Briefly discuss three of the threats to biodiversity shown in Figure 9.

c For a region of rainforest you have studied, examine the causes of reduced biodiversity.

2 Refer to Figure 10.

a Describe the locations of the most biodiverse countries.

b Examine the reasons for high levels of biodiversity in these countries.

c Discuss the consequences of reduced biodiversity in tropical rainforests.

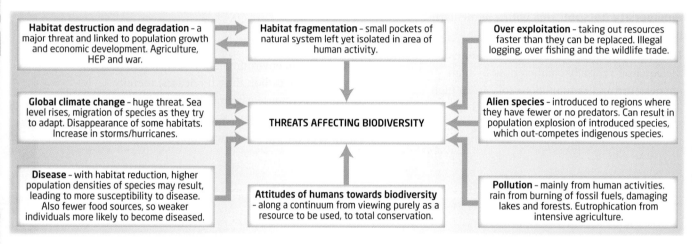

Habitat destruction and degradation – a major threat and linked to population growth and economic development. Agriculture, HEP and war.

Habitat fragmentation – small pockets of natural system left yet isolated in area of human activity.

Over exploitation – taking out resources faster than they can be replaced. Illegal logging, over fishing and the wildlife trade.

Global climate change – huge threat. Sea level rises, migration of species as they try to adapt. Disappearance of some habitats. Increase in storms/hurricanes.

THREATS AFFECTING BIODIVERSITY

Alien species – introduced to regions where they have fewer or no predators. Can result in population explosion of introduced species, which out-competes indigenous species.

Disease – with habitat reduction, higher population densities of species may result, leading to more susceptibility to disease. Also fewer food sources, so weaker individuals more likely to become diseased.

Attitudes of humans towards biodiversity – along a continuum from viewing purely as a resource to be used, to total conservation.

Pollution – mainly from human activities. rain from burning of fossil fuels, damaging lakes and forests. Eutrophication from intensive agriculture.

Figure 9 *Threats affecting biodiversity.*

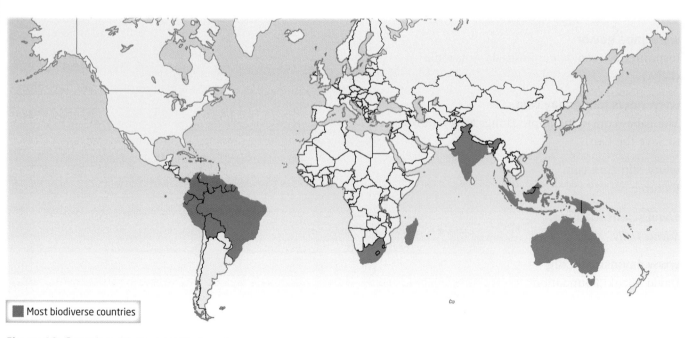

■ Most biodiverse countries

Figure 10 *Countries with the most biodiversity.*

13 Sustainability and the environment

KEY QUESTIONS

- What is environmental sustainability?
- How effective are management strategies in achieving environmental sustainability?

Entrance to National Park in Andalucia, Spain. The graffiti refers to the number of foreigners buying up houses in the nearby village of Frigiliana.

The United Nations has defined **environmental sustainability** as:

'… meeting the needs of the present without compromising the ability of future generations to meet their needs. This encompasses keeping population densities below the carrying capacity of a region, facilitating the renewal of renewable resources, conserving and establishing priorities for the use of non-renewable resources, and keeping environmental impact below the level required to allow affected systems to recover and continue to evolve.'

The concept of sustainability can be applied in various ways:

- To the full range of scales, from the individual to the Earth as a whole. Increasingly governments are reminding individuals and households about their carbon footprint and how these can be reduced. In the UK adults have been asked to think about driving five miles less a week and to reuse plastic bags. At the largest scale, sustainability focuses on the total carrying capacity of the planet.

- To different geographical environments such as rainforests, temperate grasslands and urban areas. Satellite photography has been a major advance in our ability to see what is happening over large land areas. It has allowed short-term changes to be recognised quickly.

- To individual economic activities such as tourism, agriculture and forestry. Each sector has its own impact on the environment which can be modified by careful management. The move towards sustainable tourism is considered below.

Figure 1a (page 212), from the *Living Planet Report 2008*, shows what is likely to happen under the **business-as-usual** scenario. Here, only very limited efforts are made in terms of environmental sustainability and the problem gets steadily worse. Human populations in the most marginal areas will be affected first, but gradually environmental problems will encompass more and more regions and their populations.

In contrast, Figure 1b shows what could happen with environmental sustainability at the forefront of policymaking. The graph shows ecological debt being gradually reduced until once again the planet has a biocapacity reserve and it is living within its means. Environmental sustainability requires political will by governments on both a national and an international basis, and action by all sectors of society. It demands limits on the actions of individuals and organisations whose behaviour damages the environment for personal and organisational gain.

Sustainability need not require a reduction in the quality of life, but it does require a change in attitudes and values toward less consumptive lifestyles. These changes must embrace global interdependence, environmental stewardship, social responsibility, and economic viability. Environmental sustainability in a country or region is difficult to achieve without economic and social sustainability because of the strong interconnectedness between these three vital spheres of life. Economic sustainability involves maintaining income and employment. Social sustainability means maintaining social capital including that devoted to health, education, housing and the rule of law.

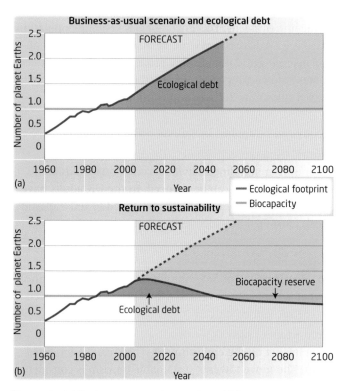

Figure 1 *(a) Business-as-usual scenario and (b) return to sustainability, 1960–2100.*

Charging an electrical car, London.

Sustainable cities

As an increasing proportion of the world's population is living in urban areas and the environmental problems of cities have become more and more obvious, the need for policies to make cities more sustainable has become clear. Cities tend to be large consumers of goods and services, taking resources from their surrounding regions in particular to maintain the living standards of their populations. However, the ecological impact of large cities extends way beyond their local catchment areas due to their demand for a wide range of global goods and services.

Although most cities are far from sustainable in an absolute sense, there are signs of progress in both the developed and developing worlds. In the UK there can be no doubt at all that London's environment is much cleaner than it was 60 years ago. The Clean Air Act, passed in 1956, was a major milestone in improving air quality. The Act was passed in response to London's 'Great Smog' of 1952 in which thousands of people died from respiratory problems. It introduced a number of measures to reduce air pollution, especially by establishing 'smoke control areas' in which only smokeless fuels could be burnt. Similar measures have been passed in many other countries over the past half century. Many subsequent environmental laws passed in the UK have resulted in further improvements in London's environment. For example, water quality measures to improve London's rivers have seen a revival in aquatic life along the Thames in particular.

Although pollution from industry and domestic uses is now minimal compared with 50 years ago, emissions from motor vehicles have risen rapidly to become the major environmental problem in London and many other cities. Recent measures, including the Congestion Charge and the Low Emissions Zone, are helping to tackle this problem. These were controversial measures when they were introduced, but have gradually gained public acceptance. The London Plan, first published in 2004 and revised on a few occasions since then, stresses the importance of environmental sustainability. The latest version (2009) wants London to be 'a city that becomes a world leader in improving the environment'. The Plan stresses measures to move to a low-carbon economy based on new **green technology**, with plans for a new low-carbon bus, electric cars, bike-hire schemes, public transport improvements, better insulated homes, brownfield as opposed to greenfield development, and the planting of more trees.

London's Low Emissions Zone.

The World Resources Institute declared Lanzhou in China the world's most polluted city in 1998. It is a major industrial centre, burning large quantities of coal every day. The city is surrounded by hills, which hinders the dispersal of pollution. The city has addressed its environmental problems by:

- attempting to close some heavy industries
- relocating some industries from inner-city to edge-of-city locations
- restricting emissions based on air quality warnings with yellow and red level alerts to reduce factory pollution
- investing in the supply of natural gas and cleaner coal
- restricting traffic
- planting trees on surrounding hillsides to reduce dust storms.

Lanzhou has a long way to go to match environmental quality in the world's cleanest cities, but it has clearly

Research idea

For the city in which you live or the one nearest to you, find out what has been done to improve environmental sustainability. How successful do you think these policies have been?

turned the corner. People do not like living in poor environments and invariably react in a positive sense once a problem becomes serious enough.

Towards sustainable tourism?

'It is increasingly apparent that tourism is falling victim, but also contributing, to climate change and the reduction of biodiversity. The path ahead is therefore marked by a different type of growth: more moderate, more solid and more responsible.'

Francesco Frangialli, Secretary-General of the United Nations World Tourism Organisation (UNWTO)

As the level of global tourism increases rapidly it is becoming more and more important for the industry to be responsibly planned, managed and monitored. Tourism operates in a world of finite resources where its impact is becoming of increasing concern to a growing number of people. At present, only 5% of the world's population have ever travelled by plane. However, this is undoubtedly going to increase substantially.

Following the 1992 Earth Summit in Rio de Janeiro, the World Travel and Tourism Council (WTTC) and the Earth Council drew up an environmental checklist for tourist development which included waste minimisation, reuse and recycling, energy efficiency, and water management. The WTTC has since established a more detailed programme called 'Green Globe', designed to act as an environmental blueprint for its members.

The Egyptian Red Sea resort of Hurgada. Tourism is a major water user in a dry country.

However, Leo Hickman in his book *The Final Call* claims that the industry is still in a poor state with regard to environmental sustainability. He states:

> 'The net result of a widespread lack of government recognition is that tourism is currently one of the most unregulated industries in the world, largely controlled by a relatively small number of Western corporations such as hotel groups and tour operators. Are they really the best guardians of this evidently important but supremely fragile global industry?'

Environmental groups are keen to make travellers aware of their **destination footprint.** They are urging people to:

- 'fly less and stay longer'
- carbon-offset their flights
- consider 'slow travel'.

In 'slow travel', tourists consider the impact of their activities both for individual holidays and in the longer term too. For example, they may decide that every second holiday will be in their own country (not using air transport). It could also involve using locally run guesthouses and small hotels as opposed to hotels run by international chains. This enables more money to remain in local communities. Virtually every aspect of the industry now recognises that tourism must become more sustainable. **Ecotourism** is at the leading edge of this movement. Ecotourism has helped to bring needed income to some of the poorest countries. It has provided local people with a new, alternative way of making a living. As such it has reduced human pressure on ecologically sensitive areas.

Sustainable tourism model for the Irish uplands.

Discussion point

How does the average person have an adverse impact on the environment when they go on holiday?

National Parks and other protected areas

The world's first National Park was Yellowstone in the western USA. Yellowstone was designated in 1872 when members of a scientific expedition brought back photographs and persuaded the federal government to preserve this part of the west in its unspoilt natural condition. This was a major departure from the attitudes of the time when nature was seen as something to be conquered and exploited for economic gain.

Buffalo in Yellowstone National Park, USA.

The concept of National Parks spread around the world and most countries now have National Parks and other protected areas such as National Forests and Areas of Outstanding Natural Beauty within their borders. Wilderness Areas with the greatest restrictions on access have the highest form of protection. Over time, more parts of the world have benefited from various degrees of protection. Without the designation of National Parks and other protected areas the world's flora, fauna and other resources would be in a much worse state today.

However, some protected areas are under severe pressure. The Maasai Mara National Reserve in Kenya is losing animal species at a considerable rate, according to a recent scientific study. This is due to increased human settlement in and around the reserve. The study, which was funded by the World Wildlife Fund (WWF), monitored hoofed species in the Maasai Mara on a monthly basis for 15 years. According to this study, six species including giraffes, impala, warthogs, topis and water-bucks have declined significantly at an alarming rate in the reserve. The study says that losses were as high as 95% for giraffes, 80% for warthogs, 76% for hartebeest and 67% for impala.

Only about 12% of the world's land area is covered by national protection schemes. In four of the largest countries with high biodiversity – Brazil, China, India and Russia – the levels are 7%, 8%, 5% and 8% respectively.

While the main concerns about environmental sustainability relate to areas beyond National Parks and other protected areas, the latter are a continuous reminder of the importance of the natural environment and what can be done when there is sufficient political will to act. Much of our knowledge about the environment has been gained from protected areas over a significant period of time.

Mule deer in Yellowstone National Park, USA.

The Environmental Sustainability Index

The Environmental Sustainability Index (ESI) benchmarks the ability of nations to protect the environment over the next several decades. The ESI integrates 76 data sets – tracking natural resource endowments, past and present pollution levels, environmental management efforts, and

Theory of Knowledge

Nineteenth-century American writers such as Henry David Thoreau and Ralph Waldo Emerson did much to raise environmental awareness in the USA. Writers and artists in other countries have also done much to raise appreciation of the natural world. How important do you think such contributions are compared with the impact of scientific evidence?

the capacity of a society to improve its environmental performance – into 21 indicators of environmental sustainability. These indicators allow comparison across a range of issues that are grouped into five broad categories:

- environmental systems
- reducing environmental stresses
- reducing human vulnerability to environmental stresses
- societal and institutional capacity to respond to environmental challenges
- global stewardship.

The higher the ESI score the better the situation with regard to environmental sustainability. Virtually no country scores very high or very low on all 21 indicators. The ESI does not include a number of important measures because of a lack of comprehensive data at present. This includes quality of waste management, wetlands destruction, and exposure to heavy metals.

The ESI is compiled by environmental scholars from Yale and Columbia Universities in the USA. Table 1 (page 216) shows selected countries from the most recent ranking, while Figure 2 illustrates the global situation by quintile (that is where population data or statistics can be divided into five equal groups, according to the distribution of the values of a particular variable). According to the ESI method, the most sustainable countries are mainly affluent, sparsely populated nations with significant natural resources. The lowest-ranking countries are North Korea, Iraq, Taiwan, Turkmenistan and Uzbekistan. All these countries face numerous environmental issues, natural and human-induced, and have a poor environmental policy record.

The ESI shows that wealth contributes to the potential for good environmental stewardship, although it does not guarantee it as a number of affluent nations occupy low-ranking positions on the list. The relationship between economic development and environmental sustainability is complex, with countries facing environmental challenges at every level of development. The report highlights the need for improved data to underpin better environmental policymaking in the future. The ESI provides a useful tool for tracking environmental performance, identifying the progress of countries on an issue-by-issue basis. It promotes a quantitative and systematic approach to environmental policymaking. The report stresses that environmental sustainability issues have to be tackled at a range of scales from local to global.

Geographical skill

Study Figure 2.
a Explain the grouping of countries by quintile.
b What are the merits of this techniques?
c Suggest why quintiles were used rather than octiles or deciles.

ESI rank	Country	ESI score
1	Finland	75.1
2	Norway	73.4
3	Uruguay	71.8
4	Sweden	71.7
5	Iceland	70.8
6	Canada	64.4
7	Switzerland	63.7
8	Guyana	62.9
8	Argentina	62.7
10	Austria	62.7
11	Brazil	62.2
12	Gabon	61.7
30	Japan	57.3
33	Russia	56.1
45	USA	52.9
65	UK	50.2
101	India	45.2
133	China	38.6
146	North Korea	29.2

Table 1 *The 2005 Environmental Sustainability Index for selected countries.*

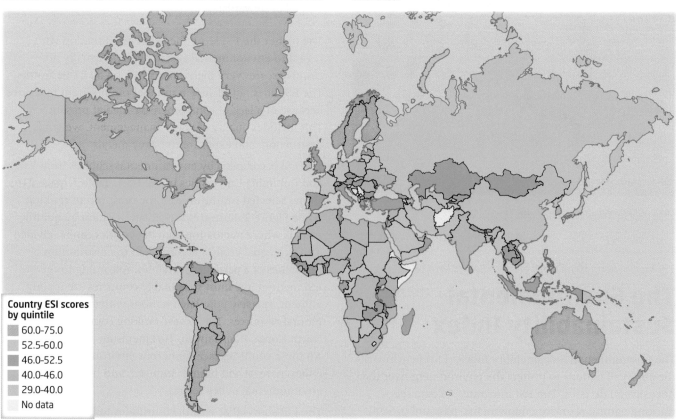

Country ESI scores by quintile
- 60.0–75.0
- 52.5–60.0
- 46.0–52.5
- 40.0–46.0
- 29.0–40.0
- No data

Figure 2 *Environmental Sustainability Index, 2005.*

3 Patterns in environmental quality and sustainability

Development and environmental sustainability

It has become the norm in most countries to consider the environmental impact of a development scheme before planning permission is granted. In some countries **environmental impact assessment** is a rigorous process truly linked to sustainable development, but in still too many instances environmentalists claim that this is a cosmetic process where the profit motive dominates thinking. However, action by environmental groups and changing public attitudes have placed increasing pressure on politicians worldwide.

Figure 3 illustrates what should happen in assessing the sustainability of development schemes. Four key strands are highlighted:

- Eco-friendly: there has been increasing recognition that long-term development has to be environmentally sustainable. The ability to design sustainable development schemes has improved considerably in recent years as more data has become available from earlier schemes whose merits and limitations have been studied. Environmental science has come a long way in recent decades.

- Public participation: too often in the past this has been a question of going through the motions and then ignoring public opinion if their views were contrary to the desires of business people and politicians. Environmentalists advocate bottom-up strategies which frequently involve the use of intermediate technology. If people feel that their opinion matters they are more likely to actively participate in sustainable projects.

- Social justice and equity: development that is just and fair means that poor people become stakeholders in development schemes. Direct involvement with a reasonable share of the benefits available gives a strong incentive to ensure that the development is sustainable. Local people want income improvement to be long term and to be available to their children and grandchildren. The concept of **pro-poor strategies** has expanded considerably in recent decades, gaining recognition for its many successes. The development of microcredit and social business are examples of such strategies.

- Futurity: trans-generational responsibility is central to the concept of environmental sustainability. The development of new technologies to conserve resources has attracted increasing investment in recent years.

In some countries the 'green industrial sector' is now a significant part of the economy, employing an increasing number of people.

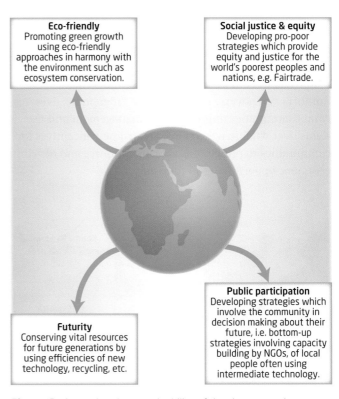

Eco-friendly
Promoting green growth using eco-friendly approaches in harmony with the environment such as ecosystem conservation.

Social justice & equity
Developing pro-poor strategies which provide equity and justice for the world's poorest peoples and nations, e.g. Fairtrade.

Futurity
Conserving vital resources for future generations by using efficiencies of new technology, recycling, etc.

Public participation
Developing strategies which involve the community in decision making about their future, i.e. bottom-up strategies involving capacity building by NGOs, of local people often using intermediate technology.

Figure 3 *Assessing the sustainability of development schemes.*

Activities

1 What is environmental sustainability?
2 Suggest how this concept could be applied to an individual person.
3 Describe the scenarios shown in Figure 1a and 1b (page 212).
4 What is the Environmental Sustainability Index?
5 Discuss the differences in ESI shown in Figure 2 and Table 1.
6 What has been the role of National Parks and other protected areas in environmental sustainability?
7 Present an analysis of Figure 3.

Case study

Management strategy: Namibia's community conservancies

Namibia in south-west Africa is a sparsely populated country with a generally dry climate. Approximately half its 2.1 million people live below the international poverty line of $1.25 a day. Environmental sustainability is a significant issue in its marginal landscapes, with the government attempting to tackle this issue and reduce poverty at the same time.

Namibia's Communal Conservancy Programme is regarded as a successful model of community-based natural resource management with an improving record for wildlife numbers and poverty reduction. The Programme gives rural communities unprecedented management and use rights over wildlife which have created new incentives for communities to protect this valuable resource and develop economic opportunities in tourism.

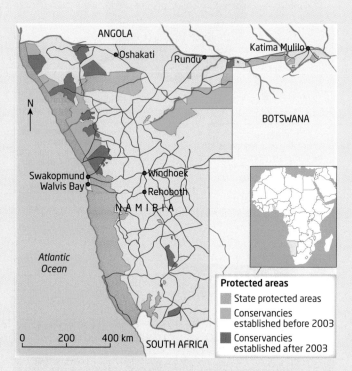

Figure 4 *Namibia's community conservancies.*

The conservancy programme began in 1996. By 2007 it had expanded to 50 registered conservancies which now cover nearly 11.9 million hectares (Figure 4).

This encompasses over 14% of the area of the country, benefiting more than 230 000 rural dwellers. Many more communities are in the process of formally establishing conservancies. **Communal conservancies** are legally recognised common property resource management organisations in Namibia's communal lands. The use rights given to conservancies include the rights to hunt, capture, cull and sell 'huntable game'. However, the government determines the overall culling rate and establishes quotas for protecting game used for trophy hunting.

An obvious sign of success is the significant increase in the numbers of wildlife in the conservancies after decades of decline. In the north-west conservancies, elephant numbers more than doubled between 1982 and 2000, and populations of oryx, springbok and mountain zebra rose tenfold. This improvement results from a decline in illegal hunting and poaching due to the economic value that conservancy communities now place on healthy wildlife populations.

The conservancies benefit from a number of 'new' economic activities including:

- contracts with tourism companies
- selling hunting concessions
- managing campsites
- selling wildlife to game ranchers
- selling crafts.

These activities are in addition to traditional farming practices which were usually at the subsistence level. The diversification of economic activity made possible by the conservancy programme has increased employment opportunities where few existed beforehand and also raised incomes.

The significant participation of conservancy populations has been central to the design of the programme. Conservancies are built around communities' willingness to work collectively. Often, they form when neighbouring villages and tribal authorities agree to trace a boundary around their shared borders and manage the wildlife within this area. The conservancy programme has inbuilt flexibility which allows communities to choose diverse strategies for wildlife management and distributing benefits.

Support from and cooperation between a number of different institutions has been important to the development of the programme (Table 2). Such institutions bring substantial experience and skills in helping conservancies to develop. Running skills-training programmes has been an important aspect of such support. For example, communal conservancies are able to call on the experience of various NGOs for help and advice. This enables good practice in one area to be applied in other areas. The Namibian Community-based Tourism Association has been instrumental in helping communities negotiate levies and income-sharing agreements with tourism companies.

Figure 5 (page 220) shows the rapid expansion of the total land area under management of conservancies from 1998 to 2005. From less than 20 000 km² in 1998, the total land area went beyond 100 000 km² in 2005. The rate of increase was particularly impressive between 2002 and 2005. The population living in conservancy areas also rose rapidly in the same period and now exceeds 200 000 (Figure 6, page 220). This is about one-tenth of the country's population.

Organisation	Support activities
Legal Assistance Centre	Supplies legal advice and advocacy on issues related to community-based natural resource management (CBNRM).
Namibia Community-based Tourism Association	Serves as an umbrella organisation and support provider for community-based tourism initiatives.
Namibia Non-Governmental Organisation Forum	Represents a broad range of NGOs and community-based organisations.
Namibia Nature Foundation Rössing Foundation	Provides assistance through grants, financial administration, technical support, fundraising, and monitoring and evaluation.
Multi-disciplinary Research Centre	Provides training and materials for CBNRM partners.
Namibia Development Trust	Centre of the University of Namibia provides research-related support.
Centre for Research Information	Provides assistance to established and emerging conservancies in southern Namibia.
Action in Africa – Southern Africa Development and Consulting	Provides research, developmental assistance and market linkages for natural plant products.
!NARA	Conducts capacity training in participatory democratic management for conservancy communities and institutions supporting communities.
Desert Research Foundation of Namibia	Researches arid land management, conducts participatory learning projects with communities about sustainable management, and engages policymakers to improve regulatory framework for sustainable development.
Rural People's Institute for Social Empowerment	Provides assistance to established and emerging conservancies in southern Kunene and Erongo regions.
Integrated Rural Development and Nature Conservation	A field-based organisation working to support conservancy development in Kunene and Caprivi regions.
Nyae Nyae Development Foundation	Supports San communities in the Otjozondjupa region in the Nyae Nyae Conservancy.
Ministry of Environment and Tourism	MET is not a formal member, but attends meetings and participates in NACSO working groups. Provides a broad spectrum of support in terms of policy, wildlife monitoring and management, and publicity.

Table 2 *Namibian Association of CBNRM support organisations.*

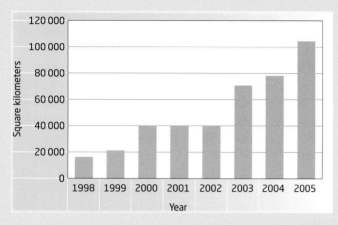

Figure 5 *Communal conservancies: total land under management, 1998–2005.*

Although rural poverty remains significant in Namibia, the conservancy programme has resulted in substantial progress, with income rising year on year. Figure 7 shows the development of conservancy income between 1994 and 2005, while Table 3 shows the detailed breakdown of conservancy-related income in 2006. In 2006, conservancy income reached nearly Namibian dollars (N$)19 million. Income from small businesses associated with the conservancies but not directly owned by them brought in another N$ 8 million.

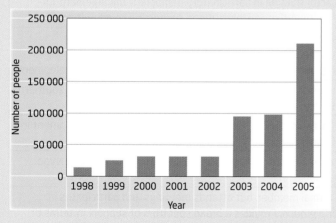

Figure 6 *Communal conservancies: population living in conservancy areas, 1998–2005.*

An important aspect of development has been the involvement of women in the employment benefits. Such jobs have included being game guards and natural resource monitors, as well as serving tourists in campgrounds and lodges.

Rising income from conservancies has made possible increasing investment in social development projects. Expenditure on such projects more than doubled between 2003 and 2005. This has made conservancies an increasingly important element in rural development.

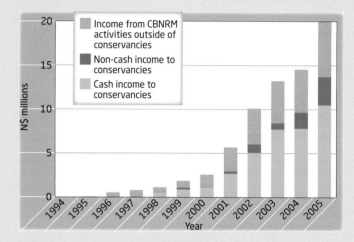

Figure 7 *Income from conservancies and other community-based natural resource management in Namibia, 1994–2005.*

Source of income	Value (N$)	% of total conservancy income
Miscellaneous	34 788	0.1
Premium hunting	43 600	0.2
Veld products	39 000	0.1
Thatching grass	2 450 481	9.1
Shoot and sell hunting	504 883	1.9
Interest earned	161 807	0.6
Craft sales	474 343	1.8
Campsites and CBTEs*	3 746 481	14.0
Trophy meat distribution	870 219	3.2
Game donation	860 950	3.2
Use of own game	739 629	2.8
Trophy hunting	6 113 923	22.8
Joint venture tourism	10 794 668	40.2
Total	**26 834 772**	**100.0**
* community-based tourism enterprises		

Table 3 *Conservancy-related income, 2006.*

Scaling-up resource management

Following the perceived success of community conservancies, the Namibian government has extended the concept to community forests (Figure 8). Establishing

Based in large part on the success of CBNRM in the conservancies, the Namibian government enacted legislation in 2001 allowing the formation of community forests - areas within the country's communal lands for which a community has obtained management rights over forest resources such as timber, firewood, wild fruits, thatch grass, honey, and even some wildlife. The establishment of the community forest programme shows how the scaling-up process can reach across natural resource systems, affecting natural resource policy at the broadest level. Although the community forest programme and the conservancy programme are now administered separately by different ministries, some groups have expressed interest in merging the programmes to allow a more integrated approach to managing natural resources at the community level.

Establishing a community forest is similar to the process of forming a conservancy. Communities must:

- submit a formal application to the government
- elect a forest management committee from the community
- develop a constitution
- select, map, and demark a community forest area
- submit a forest management plan describing how the community will harvest forest resources sustainably and manage other activities such as grazing and farming within the forest area
- specify use rights and bylaws necessary to act on their management plan
- craft a plan to ensure the equitable distribution of revenues to all community members
- obtain permission from the area's traditional authority.

As of April 2008, a total of 45 community forests had been formed (although only 13 were officially gazetted), encompassing 2.2 million ha and benefiting some 150 000 Namibians. In the north-eastern region alone, 16 registered forests have generated more than N$ 300 000 (US$ 38 000) since 2005.

a community forest is similar to the process of forming a conservancy. This is a good example of the **scaling-up process** from one natural resource system to another. Based on the Forest Act of 2001, the project helps local communities to establish their own community forests, and to manage and utilise them in a sustainable manner. Because many rural Namibians are poor, it is important that they have a greater say in how forest resources are managed, and share the benefits of properly managed forest resources.

Forest fires and uncontrolled cutting have been two of the main problems facing forest-protection efforts in Namibia for some time. About four million hectares of forest and veld are burnt annually, mostly as a result of fires started deliberately to improve grazing and to clear hunting grounds.

The advent of community forests has led to improved forest resource management. It has also improved the livelihoods of local people based on the empowerment of local communities with forest use rights. Villagers in community forests derive an income by marketing forestry products such as timber and firewood, poles, wild fruits, devil's claw, thatching grass, tourism, honey from bee-keeping, wildlife, woven baskets and other crafts.

Activities

1. Look at Figure 4 (page 218). Describe the geographical location of (a) state-protected areas, (b) conservancies established before 2003 and (c) conservancies established after 2003.
2. How have employment opportunities expanded under the conservancy programme?
3. Comment on the importance of the Namibian Association of CBNRM organisations to the success of the communal conservancy programme.
4. Describe the development of the communal conservancy programme shown in Figures 5 and 6.
5. Analyse the data presented in Figure 7.
6. Comment on the distribution of conservancy-related income shown in Table 3.
7. Describe and explain the extension of the conservancy concept to forests in Namibia.
8. Can you think of any other environments in Namibia where the conservancy concept could be applied?

Figure 8 *Extending the conservancy concept: community forests in Namibia.*

Key terms

Environmental sustainability meeting the needs of the present without compromising the ability of future generations to meet their needs.

Business-as-usual the scenario for future patterns of production and consumption which assumes that there will be no major changes in attitudes and priorities.

Green technology new technologies that aim to conserve the natural environment and resources.

Destination footprint the environmental impact caused by an individual tourist on holiday in a particular destination.

Ecotourism a specialised form of tourism where people experience relatively untouched natural environments such as coral reefs, tropical forests and remote mountain areas, and ensure that their presence does no further damage to these environments.

Environmental impact assessment a document required by law detailing all the impacts on the environment of a project above a certain size.

Pro-poor strategies development schemes that focus on the reduction of poverty and the narrowing of the income gap between poor people and the population as a whole. Environmental sustainability has become central to such approaches in recent years.

Communal conservancies legally recognised common property resource management organisations in Namibia's communal lands.

Scaling-up process expanding effective programmes to reach larger numbers of people in a broader geographical area.

Websites

www.sedac.ciesin.columbia.edu
Socioeconomic data and applications centre

www.cfnen.org.na
Community Forestry in North-Eastern Namibia

www.met.gov.na
Ministry of Environment and Tourism, Namibia

www.rightsandresources.org
Rights and Resources Initiative

www.uneca.org
UN Economic Commission for Africa (UNECA)

www.responsibletravel.com
Responsibletravel.com

www.tourismconcern.org.uk
Tourism Concern

Review

Examination-style questions

1 Refer to Figure 9.

a Define environmental sustainability.

b Describe and explain the relationships shown in the diagram.

c Discuss a range of measures that could be undertaken to improve the environmental sustainability of large cities.

2 Refer to Figure 10.

a Why are national actions so important in environmental sustainability?

b Discuss the actions that can have short-term effects in the movement to environmental sustainability.

c Why do some actions require a longer timespan before they can improve environmental sustainability?

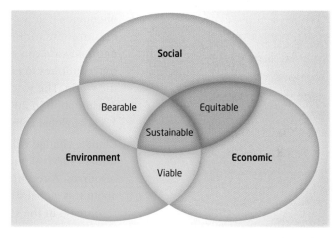

Figure 9 *Social, economic and environmental sustainability.*

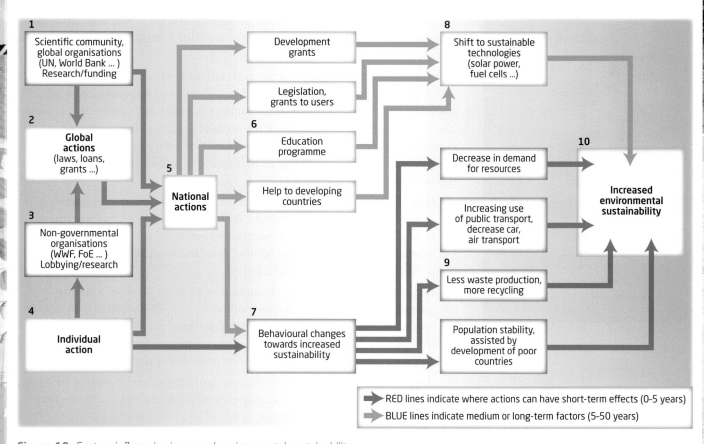

Figure 10 *Factors influencing increased environmental sustainability.*

14 Patterns of resource consumption

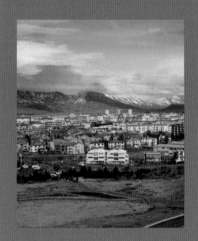

Reykjavik, Iceland. Built-up land is part of the ecological footprint.

The enormous growth of the global economy in recent decades has had a phenomenal impact on the planet's resources and natural environment. Many resources are running out and waste sinks are becoming full. The remaining natural world can no longer support the existing global economy, much less one that continues to expand. The main responsibility lies with the rich countries of the world. The world's richest 20% accounted for 76.6% of the world's private consumption in 2005, while the world's poorest 20% were responsible for only 1.5% of global consumption.

Climate change will have an impact on a number of essential resources for human survival, increasing the competition between countries for such resources. A recent article in the British newspaper *The Times* (9 March 09) about this global situation was entitled 'World heading for a war of the resources'. In the same month an article appeared in *The Guardian newspaper* (20 March 09) entitled 'Deadly crop fungus brings famine threat to developing world'. It reported that leading crop scientists had issued a warning that a deadly airborne fungus could devastate wheat harvests in poor countries and lead to famines and civil unrest over significant regions of central Asia and Africa. A further article in *The Times* (14 May 09) was entitled 'Russia warns of war within decade over hunt for oil and gas'.

Concerns about the relationship between humankind and the biological capacity of the planet cross many different academic disciplines. For example, within economics the field of ecological economics has expanded rapidly. This branch of the subject argues that the scale of the economy must be kept within sustainable limits. Scholars from various disciplines have devised a number of indicators to measure the environmental impact of humanity on the natural environment. These measures include the following:

- Index of Sustainable Economic Welfare: an economic indicator intended to replace Gross Domestic Product. Rather than simply adding together all expenditures like the Gross Domestic Product does, consumer expenditure is balanced by such factors as income distribution and cost associated with pollution and other unsustainable costs.

- Genuine Progress Indicator: an attempt to measure whether a country's growth, increased production of goods and expanding services have actually resulted in the improvement of the well-being of the people in the country. GPI advocates the claim that it can more reliably measure economic progress, as it distinguishes between worthwhile growth and uneconomic growth.

- Happy Planet Index: combines environmental impact with human well-being to measure the environmental efficiency with which, country by country, people live long and happy lives.

- Living Planet Index: tracks populations of 1313 vertebrate species – fish, amphibians, reptiles, birds, mammals – from all around the world.
- Ecological footprint: a measure of human demand on the Earth's ecosystems.

A common strand linking all of these relatively new indicators is that humanity must switch its focus from quantitative growth to qualitative development, and set strict limits on the rate of global resource consumption. Ecological economists argue that in such a 'steady-state' economy, the value of goods produced can still increase, for example through technological innovation or better distribution.

Ecological footprint

The **ecological footprint** has arguably become the world's foremost measure of humanity's demands on the natural environment. It was conceived in 1990 by M. Wackernagel and W. Rees at the University of British Columbia. The concept of ecological footprints has been used to measure natural resource consumption, how it varies from country to country, and how it has changed over time. The ecological footprint (Figure 1) for a country has been defined as 'the sum of all the cropland, grazing land, forest and fishing grounds required to produce the food, fibre and timber it consumes, to absorb the wastes emitted when it uses energy, and to provide space for its infrastructure' (*Living Planet Report 2008*). Thus the ecological footprint, calculated for each country and the world as a whole, has six components (Figure 1):

- built-up land
- fishing ground
- forest
- grazing land
- cropland
- carbon footprint.

In previous years an additional component reflecting the electricity generated by nuclear power plants was included in ecological footprint accounts. This component is no longer used because the risks and demands of nuclear power are not easily expressed in terms of **biocapacity.**

The ecological footprint is measured in **global hectares.** A global hectare is a hectare with world-average ability to produce resources and absorb wastes. In 2005 the global ecological footprint was 17.5 billion global hectares (gha) or 2.7 gha per person. This can be viewed as the

demand side of the equation. On the supply side, the total productive area, or biocapacity, of the planet was 13.6 billion gha, or 2.1 gha per person. With demand greater than supply, the Earth is living beyond its environmental means.

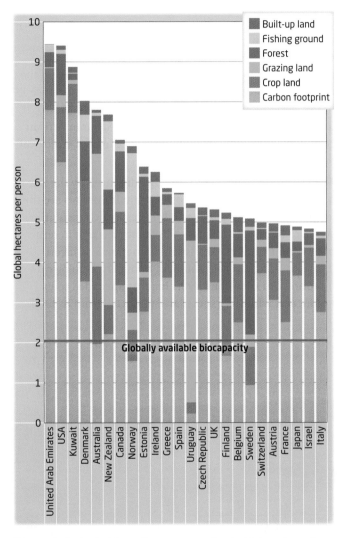

Figure 1 *Ecological footprint per person for the highest footprint countries.*

Figure 1 shows the ecological footprint of countries with the highest per capita figures and how the footprint of each country is made up. The United Arab Emirates, the USA, Kuwait and Denmark have the highest ecological footprints per person in the world. All four countries have figures above 8 global hectares per person. Nations at different income levels show considerable disparities in the extent of their ecological footprint. The lowest per capita figures were attributed to Bangladesh, Congo, Haiti, Afghanistan and Malawi. All these countries have an ecological footprint of about 0.5 gha per person. Footprint and biocapacity figures for individual countries are calculated annually by Global Footprint Network.

In many of the countries illustrated in Figure 1, the **carbon footprint** is the dominant element of the six components that comprise the ecological footprint, but in others, like Australia, Uruguay and Sweden, other aspects of the ecological footprint are more important. In Uruguay, the demand on grazing land is by far the dominant component of the ecological footprint. In Sweden, the demand on its forests is the country's major impact on the natural environment. In general the relative importance of the carbon footprint declines as the total ecological footprint of countries falls. In many Sub-Saharan African countries the contribution of carbon to the total ecological footprint is extremely low indeed.

The ecological footprint is strongly influenced by the size of a country's population. The other main influences are the level of demand for goods and services in a country (the standard of living), and how this demand is met in terms of environmental impact. International trade is taken into account in the calculation of a country's ecological footprint. For each country its imports are added to its production while its exports are subtracted from its total.

Forested landscape, the Azores, Atlantic Ocean. Depletion of forest resources is part of the ecological footprint.

The expansion of world trade has been an important factor in the growth of humanity's total ecological footprint. In 1961, the first year for which full datasets are available, global trade accounted for 8% of the world's ecological footprint. By 2005, this had risen to more than 40%. In the latter year the footprint of imports in high-income countries was as much as 61% of their total consumption footprint. In middle-income countries it was 30% and

in low-income countries 13%. The USA had the largest export footprint in the world in 2005, followed by Germany and China. The USA also had the largest import footprint, with China second and Germany third.

The ecological footprint includes only those aspects of resource consumption and waste production for which the Earth has regenerative capacity, and where data exist that allow this demand to be expressed in terms of productive area. For example, toxic releases do not figure in ecological footprint accounts. Ecological footprint calculations provide snapshots of past resource demand and availability. They do not:

- attempt to predict the future
- indicate the intensity with which a biologically productive area is being used
- evaluate the social and economic dimensions of sustainability.

Assessing human pressure on the planet is a vital starting point. The ecological footprint can be calculated at the full range of scales, from the individual to the total global

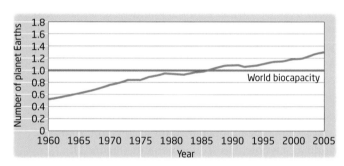

Figure 2 *Global ecological footprint, 1961–2005.*

population. Knowing the extent of human pressure on the natural environment helps us to manage ecological assets more wisely on both an individual and a collective basis. It is an important tool in the advancement of sustainable development.

Figure 2 shows how humanity's ecological footprint increased from 1961 to 2005. According to the *Living Planet Report 2008*, the global ecological footprint now exceeds the planet's regenerative capacity by about 30%. This global excess is increasing and as a result ecosystems are being run down and waste is accumulating in the air, land and water. The resulting deforestation, water shortages, declining biodiversity and climate change are putting the future development of all countries at risk.

Human demand on the Earth has more than doubled over the past 45 years due to a combination of population growth and rising living standards which has involved greater individual consumption. In 1961, most countries in the world had more than enough biocapacity to meet their own demand. But by the mid-1980s humankind's ecological footprint had reached the Earth's biocapacity. Since then humanity has been in ecological **overshoot** with annual demand on resources each year exceeding the Earth's regenerative capacity. The WWF calculates that it now takes the Earth one year and four months to regenerate what the global population uses in a year. This is a very significant threat to both the well-being of the human population and the planet as a whole.

Figure 3 divides the world into eco-debt and eco-credit countries. The former are living beyond their ecological means while the latter still have 'spare' biocapacity. The eco-debt nations are only able to meet their needs by importing resources from other countries and by using the atmosphere as a dumping ground. The WWF estimates that if present trends continue – the so-called 'business-as-

usual' approach – the global population will require two planets to satisfy the demand for goods and services by the early 2030s. However, there are many effective ways to change this situation. For example, the *Living Planet Report* argues that:

- technology transfer and support for local innovation can help emerging economies maximise their well-being while leap-frogging resource-intensive phases of industrialisation
- cities can be designed to support good lifestyles while at the same time minimising demand on both local and global ecosystems
- moving to clean energy generation and efficiency based on current technologies could allow the world to meet the projected 2050 demand for energy services with large reductions in associated carbon emissions
- empowerment of women through education and access to voluntary family planning can slow or even reverse population growth.

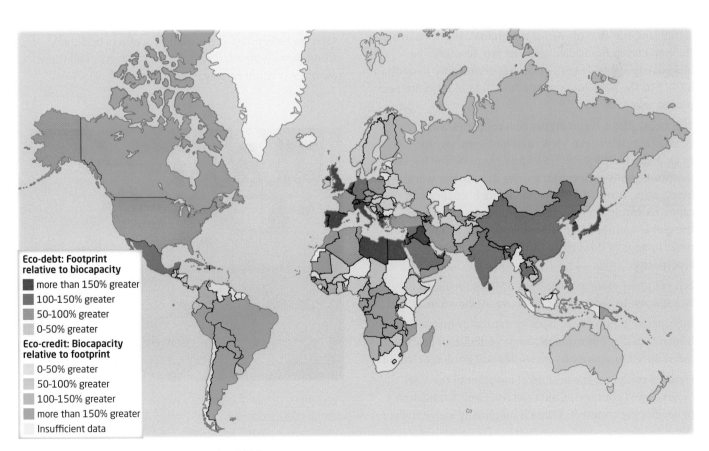

Figure 3 *Eco-debt and eco-credit countries, 2005.*

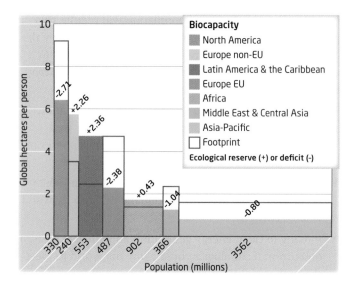

Figure 4 *Biocapacity and ecological footprint by region.*

	Country	% share
1	USA	11.2
2	Brazil	10.1
3	Russia	8.7
4	China	8.5
5	Canada	4.8
6	India	3.4
7	Argentina	2.4
8	Australia	2.3
9	Indonesia	2.3
10	Congo Dem. Rep.	1.8

Table 1 *Countries with the largest share of the world's biocapacity.*

Figure 4 shows biocapacity and ecological footprint by world region. The width of each bar is proportional to each region's population. The graph shows that three regions still have an ecological reserve. These are Europe non-EU, Latin America and the Caribbean, and Africa. The reserves in the two former regions are significant, but that for Africa is marginal. In Africa, where the population has tripled over the last 40 years, the biocapacity available per person has declined by more than 67%. For the planet as a whole the fall in biocapacity per person was 49%.

The *Living Planet Report* argues that countries with ecological reserves can view their biological wealth as an asset. In 2005, the USA and China had the largest footprints, with each country using 21% of the world's biocapacity. However, China had a much smaller per capita footprint than the USA although its impact on the global natural environment is growing at a faster pace. India is in third place using 7% of the planet's total biocapacity.

Ten countries alone contain over 55% of the Earth's biocapacity. In order of size these are as shown in Table 1.

Biocapacity is influenced both by natural events and human activity. For example, some agricultural practices can reduce biocapacity by increasing soil erosion or salinity.

Figure 5 compares the ecological footprint of the USA (a developed country), China (an NIC) and Bangladesh (a developing country). China is marginally above the per

capita globally available biocapacity whereas the USA's ecological footprint is about four and a half times this level. In comparison, the footprint for Bangladesh is extremely low indeed. Table 2 shows actual figures for a number of individual resources. Per capita oil consumption is a good indicator of contrasts in economic development.

Oil consumption in the USA is almost 14 times higher than in China. In turn, per capita oil consumption in China is almost 9 times that of Bangladesh. The contrast in meat, water and electricity consumption is also considerable, although, as with oil, consumption in China of all these resources is rising rapidly.

Fish being sold from the back of a van, Lemnos, Greece – fish are a major food resource here.

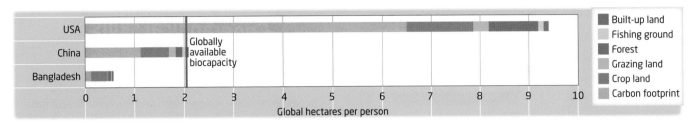

Figure 5 *Ecological footprints of the USA, China and Bangladesh.*

	Oil consumption per capita 2005*	Meat consumption 2002*	Average water use 2006*	Electricity consumption per capita 2006*
USA	68.838	124.8	576	12187
China	4.943	52.4	86	2140
Bangladesh	0.565	3.1	46	120
	* barrels/day/1000 people	* kg/person	* per person per day (litres)	* (kWh/year)

Table 2 *Individual resource use for USA, China and Bangladesh.*

Figure 6 is a simplified model showing the contrast in (a) the level of resource use and (b) the rate of change in resource use, between developing countries, NICs and developed countries. Figure 6 can be compared with the rates of change in consumption of four commodities between 1990 and 2005 (Figure 7, page 230).

Bangladesh is one of the most densely populated countries in the world. Although the rate of population growth has fallen, it was still estimated at 1.6% a year in 2006. This compares with 0.5% in China and 0.6% in the USA. Almost half of its population live on less than one dollar a day. The majority of people are employed in agriculture but there is simply not enough work in this sector to go around. The government is trying to attract foreign investment into the manufacturing and energy sectors and has achieved some degree of success. A large pool of low-cost labour is certainly an attraction to foreign TNCs, particularly when labour costs in other Asian countries are rising. If Bangladesh can transform itself into one of the next generation of newly industrialised countries, its demand for a wide range of resources will increase rapidly and, along with this, its ecological footprint!

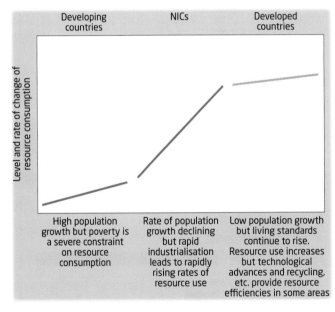

Figure 6 *Model of the relationship between resource use and the level of economic development.*

a) Meat, 1990–2005

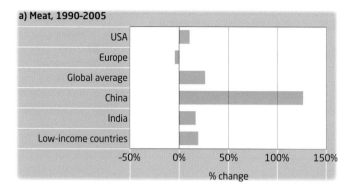

b) Fish, 1990–2005

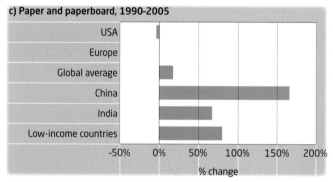

c) Paper and paperboard, 1990–2005

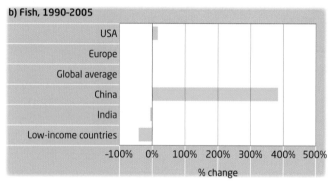

d) Gas and diesel, 1990–2005

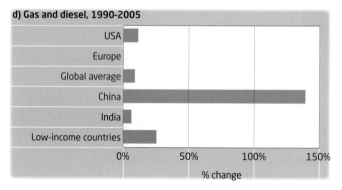

Figure 7 *Trends in consumption of selected commodities, 1990–2005.*

Geographical skills

Look at Figure 6 which is a model of the relationship between resource consumption and the level of economic development.

Now study Figure 7 which shows real data for a number of countries and world regions. To what extent does the real data follow the trends indicated in the model?

Activities

1   Define:
    a ecological footprint
    b global hectares.
2   Describe and suggest reasons for the variations by country shown in Figure 1 (page 225).
3   Draw up a table to illustrate the trend shown in Figure 2 (page 226).
4   **a** Describe the geographical patterns shown in Figure 3 (page 227).
    b What are the main reasons for these patterns?
5   Write a bullet-point summary to describe the data presented in Figure 4 (page 228).
6   Describe the differences in the ecological footprint per person in the USA, China and Bangladesh (Figure 5, page 229).

Research idea

Visit www.footprint.wwf.org.uk to calculate your own ecological footprint. What do you think you could reasonably do to reduce this figure? How does your ecological footprint differ from that of other people in your class?

Opposing views on the relationship between population and resources

Resources can be classed as either natural or human. Natural resources are naturally occurring substances such as oil, forests and fish which are considered to have value by human populations. They can be used directly or they can be processed to make other products.

For natural resources the traditional distinction is between renewable and non-renewable or stock resources. Many renewable resources naturally regenerate within a human defined timespan to provide new supplies of these resources. Such resources, like soil and forests, are often connected in ecological systems. However, if renewable resources are used up at a level greater than their natural rate of replacement, the standing stock of such a resource will decline and may eventually become exhausted. Examples are the destruction of rainforest and the overfishing of marine species in high demand. Sustainable development policies are required to redress the balance between supply and demand for these renewable resources.

The distinction between non-renewable and renewable is not absolutely clearcut for all resources. In some cases it is useful to think in terms of the extent of renewability. This applies to resources such as forests and fish where renewal depends on the rate at which they are used and the resource management techniques employed.

Solar power – a flow resource. Solar power is used for road lighting in southern Italy.

Flow renewable resources are renewable resources that do not need regeneration. Such resources are in constant supply. These include renewable energy sources such as solar, wind and tidal power. Such resources have been utilised to only a limited extent so far due to problems regarding technology and cost. However, the use of flow resources will undoubtedly increase significantly in the future as fossil fuel deposits become further depleted and environmental concerns about nuclear power remain.

In contrast, non-renewable resources such as coal and oil take millions of years to form. Thus in human terms these resources are fixed in the supply available. **Resource depletion** can occur relatively quickly and eventually become exhausted with no viable further production possible. In the EU, many coalfields where large quantities of coal were mined in the 19th and early 20th centuries no longer produce any coal at all.

Historical views on the population/ resources relationship

The relationship between population and resources has concerned those with an understanding of the subject for thousands of years. However, the assumptions made by earlier writers were based on very limited evidence as few statistical records existed more than two centuries ago. These are just some of the views that have been expressed through time:

- Confucius, the ancient Chinese philosopher, said that excessive population growth reduced output per worker, depressed the level of living and produced strife. He discussed the concept of optimum numbers, arguing that an ideal proportion between land and numbers existed and any major deviation from this created poverty. When imbalance occurred he believed the government should move people from overpopulated to underpopulated areas.

- Plato and Aristotle also considered the question of optimum size: on this depended man's potential being fully developed and his 'highest good' realised.

- Medieval writers generally favoured a high birth rate because of the constant threat of sudden depopulation as a result of wars, famine and epidemics.

- The Mercantilist schools of political economy during the 17th and 18th centuries emphasised the economic, political and military advantages of a large and growing population.

- Thomas Malthus, who was concerned that population was rising too rapidly, wrote his first essay in 1798 entitled 'An essay on the principle of population as it affects the future improvement of society'.

- In the 19th century Karl Marx made the most powerful attack of any on the work of Malthus, stating 'an abstract law of population exists for plants and animals only'. Socialist and Marxist writers believed that any population problems would be solved through the re-organisation of society.

- In the 20th century demographic debate has been based on the availability of increasingly sophisticated data in terms of both depth and breadth of coverage. Concern about the 'population explosion' developed in the 1960s.

The ideas of Thomas Malthus

The Revd Malthus (1766–1834) produced his *Essay on the principle of population* in 1798. He said that the crux of the population problem was 'the existence of a tendency in mankind to increase, if unchecked, beyond the possibility of an adequate supply of food in a limited territory'. Malthus thought that an increased food supply was achieved mainly by bringing more land into arable production. He maintained that while the supply of food could, at best, only be increased by a constant amount in arithmetical progression (1 – 2 – 3 – 4 – 5 – 6), the human population tends to increase in geometrical progression (1 – 2 – 4 – 8 – 16 – 32), multiplying itself by a constant amount each time. In time, population would outstrip food supply until a catastrophe occurred in the form of famine, disease or war. The latter would occur as human groups fought over increasingly scarce resources. These limiting factors maintained a balance between population and resources in the long term. In a later paper Malthus placed significant emphasis on 'moral restraint' as an important factor in controlling population.

Clearly Malthus was influenced by events in and before the 18th century, and could not have foreseen the great advances that were to unfold in the following two centuries which have allowed population to grow at unprecedented rates alongside a huge rise in the exploitation and use of resources. There have been many advances in agriculture since the time of Malthus which have contributed to huge increases in agricultural production. These advances include the development of artificial fertilisers and pesticides, new irrigation techniques, high-yielding varieties of crops, cross-breeding of cattle, greenhouse farming and the reclamation of land from the sea.

However, nearly all of the world's productive land is already exploited. Most of the unexploited land is either too steep, too wet, too dry or too cold for agriculture. In Asia, nearly 80% of potential arable land is now under cultivation.

Theory of Knowledge

When you are reading about the opinions of a particular writer it is always important to consider the position from which they are writing, because this is likely to have a significant influence on their views. What differences between the social positions and life histories of Malthus and Marx could account for opposing views?

Farmers graze goats in desert areas when production land is scarce.

Optimum population

The idea of **optimum population** has been mainly understood in an economic sense (Figure 8). At first, an increasing population allows for a fuller exploitation of a country's resource base, causing living standards to rise. However, beyond a certain level rising numbers place increasing pressure on resources, and living standards begin to decline. The highest average living standard marks the optimum population, or more accurately the **economic optimum**. Before that population is reached, the country or region can be said to be **underpopulated**. As the population rises beyond the optimum, the country or region can be said to be **overpopulated**.

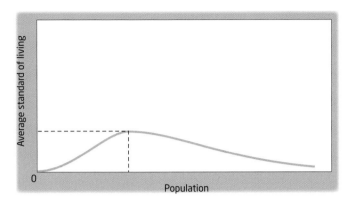

Figure 8 *The optimum population.*

There is no historical example of a stationary population having achieved appreciable economic progress, although this may not be so in the future. It is not coincidental that in the past periods of rapid population growth have paralleled eras of technological advance that have increased the carrying capacity of countries and regions. Thus we are led from the idea of optimum population as a static concept to the dynamic concept of **optimum rhythm of growth** (Figure 9) whereby population growth responds to substantial technological advances. For example, Abbé Raynal (*Révolution de l'Amérique*, 1781) said of the United States: 'If ten million men ever manage to support themselves in these provinces it will be a great deal'. Yet today the population of the USA is over 300 million and hardly anyone would consider the country to be overpopulated.

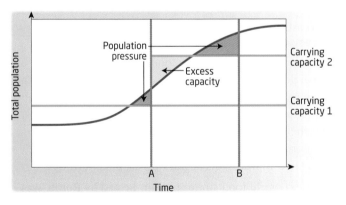

Figure 9 *Optimum rhythm of growth.*

The most obvious examples of **population pressure** are in the developing world but the question here is – are these cases of absolute overpopulation or the results of underdevelopment that can be rectified by adopting remedial strategies over time?

There are two opposing views of the effects of population growth:

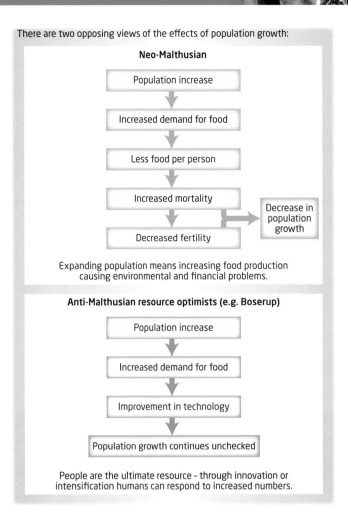

Figure 10 *The opposing views of the neo-Malthusians and the anti-Malthusians.*

Figure 10 summarises the opposing views of the **neo-Malthusians** and the resource optimists such as Esther Boserup (1910–99). Neo-Malthusians argue that an expanding population will lead to unsustainable pressure on food and other resources. In recent years neo-Malthusians have highlighted:

- the steady global decline in the area of farmland per person
- the steep rise in the cost of many food products in recent years
- the growing scarcity of fish in many parts of the world
- the already apparent impact of climate change on agriculture in some world regions
- the switchover of large areas of land from food production to the production of biofuels, helping to create a food crisis in order to reduce the energy crisis

- the continuing increase in the world's population
- the global increase in the level of meat consumption as incomes rise in newly industrialised countries in particular.

The **anti-Malthusians** or resource optimists believe that human ingenuity will continue to conquer resource problems, pointing to many examples in human history where, through innovation or intensification, humans have responded to increased numbers. Resource optimists highlight a number of continuing advances which include:

- the development of new resources
- the replacement of less efficient with more efficient resources
- the rapid development of green technology with increasing research and development in this growing economic sector
- important advances in agricultural research
- stabilising levels of consumption in some developed countries.

Canada's Central Experimental Farm, an important centre of agricultural research.

Activities

1 Explain the following:
   a underpopulation
   b overpopulation
   c optimum population.
2 Study Figure 9 (page 233).
   a Suggest why the population initially started to increase.
   b What could account for the increases in carrying capacity at Times A and B?
   c Why can Figure 9 (page 233) be described as a dynamic model while Figure 8 (page 233) is a static model?
4 With the aid of Figure 10 (page 233), explain the opposing views of the neo-Malthusians and the resource optimists.

Discussion point

What is your view on the relationship between population and resources?

World food summits

Forecasts of famine tend to appear every few decades or so. In 1974 a world food summit held in Rome met against a background of rapidly rising food prices and a high rate of global population growth. The major concern was that the surge in population would overwhelm humankind's ability to produce food in the early 21st century. The possibility that the predictions of Thomas Malthus were going to come true was very real in the opinion of some experts. These neo-Malthusians began to issue dire warnings.

The next world food summit, again hosted by Rome, was held in 1996. It too met against a background of rising prices and falling stocks. But new concerns, unknown in 1974, had appeared. Global warming threatened to reduce the productivity of substantial areas of land and many scientists were worried about the long-term consequences of genetic engineering. The errors of past strategies had also become all too apparent in many parts of the world.

Across Asia vast areas of irrigated land had become waterlogged and rendered almost totally unproductive. In many regions the intensive use of chemical fertilisers was taking a heavy toll in terms of both runoff into rivers and lakes and the re-emergence of crop diseases – such as the

Sugarcane in Brazil. Cropland is a major element in the ecological footprint.

virulent fungus responsible for the Irish potato famine in the mid-19th century – plants having developed resistance to traditional farm chemicals.

Lester Brown, president of the environmental organisation the Worldwatch Institute and seen by some as the world's leading modern Malthusian, argued that the world was entering an era of food scarcity. He contended that growing demand for grain, from China in particular, could soon overwhelm the capacity of all the world's grain-producing countries. However, the modern anti-Malthusians counselled against panicking over very short-term fluctuations, pointing in particular to the way in which food production grew significantly faster than population in the second half of the 20th century.

New concerns about food supply arose in 2007 as the prices of most basic foodstuffs increased rapidly, leaving many more people in poor countries unable to afford the most basic diet. In early 2009 the chief scientific adviser to the UK government argued that increasing population, declining energy sources and food shortages will combine to create the 'perfect storm' by 2030 (Figure 11). Similar concerns were echoed at the 2009 world food summit.

'Perfect storm' of energy, food and water crises

By Richard Alleyne
Science Correspondent

GROWING populations, falling energy sources and food shortages will create the 'perfect storm' by 2030, said the government's chief scientific adviser.

Professor John Beddington predicted that the demand for resources would create a crisis with dire consequences. Demand for food and energy would jump 50% by 2030 and for fresh water by 30%, as the global population topped 8.3 billion.

Climate change would exacerbate matters in unpredictable ways.

'It's a perfect storm,' Prof Beddington told the fourth annual Sustainable Development UK conference in Westminster yesterday.

'There's not going to be a complete collapse but things will start getting really worrying if we don't tackle these problems.

'My main concern is what will happen internationally. There will be food and water shortages.

'We're relatively fortunate in the UK. There may not be shortages here, but we can expect prices of food and energy to rise.'

He said the world needed more disease-resistant and pest-resistant plants and better harvesting procedures.

Prof Beddington said the 'storm' would create war, unrest and mass migration. Growing populations and success in alleviating poverty in the Third World would create huge demand for food and water in the next two decades, with climate change depleting resources.

He said food reserves were at a 50-year low but the world would require 50% more energy, food and water by 2030.

Prof Beddington said climate change would mean northern Europe would become new key centres for food production and other areas would need to use more advanced pesticides.

The United Nations Environment Programme predicts widespread water shortages across Africa, Europe and Asia by 2025.

Figure 11 *From* The Daily Telegraph, *20 March 2009.*

Three agricultural worlds

In terms of agricultural production the nations of the world can be placed into three groups:

- The haves – Europe, North America, Australia and New Zealand – have sufficient cropland to meet most of their food needs and efficient farm production systems enabling the production of more food from the same amount of land.

- The rich have-nots – this is a mixed grouping of countries which includes land-short Japan and Singapore, along with rapidly developing countries such as Indonesia and China, Chile, Peru, Saudi Arabia and the other Gulf States. These countries are unable to grow enough food for their populations but can afford to purchase imports to make up the deficit.

- The poor have-nots – consisting of the majority of the developing world. These countries, with over three billion people, are unable to produce enough food for their populations and cannot afford the imports to make up the deficit.

The Green Revolution: a re-assessment

The package of agricultural improvements generally known as the **Green Revolution** was seen as the answer to the food problem in many parts of the developing world. India was one of the first countries to benefit when a high-yielding variety seed programme (HVP) commenced in 1966–67. In terms of production it was a turning point for Indian agriculture, which had virtually reached stagnation. The HVP introduced new hybrid high-yielding varieties (HYVs) of five cereals: wheat, rice, maize, sorghum and millet. All were drought-resistant with the exception of rice, were very responsive to the application of fertilisers, and had a shorter growing season than the traditional varieties they replaced. Although the benefits of the Green Revolution are clear, serious criticisms have also been made. The two sides of the story can be summarised as follows:

Advantages

- Yields are twice to four times greater than traditional varieties.

- The shorter growing season has allowed the introduction of an extra crop in some areas.

- Farming incomes have increased, allowing the purchase of machinery, better seeds, fertilisers and pesticides.

- The diet of rural communities is now more varied.

- Local infrastructure has been upgraded to accommodate a stronger market approach.

- Employment has been created in industries supplying farms with inputs.

- Higher returns have justified a significant increase in irrigation.

Disadvantages

- High inputs of fertiliser and pesticide are required to optimise production. This is costly in both economic and environmental terms. In some areas rural indebtedness has risen sharply.

- HYVs require more weed control and are often more susceptible to pests and disease.

- Middle and higher-income farmers have often benefited much more than the majority on low incomes, thus widening the income gap in rural communities. Increased rural to urban migration has often been the result.

- Mechanisation has increased rural unemployment.

- Some HYVs have an inferior taste.

- The problem of salinisation has increased, along with the expansion of the irrigated area.

The Green Revolution: the latest concern

In recent years a much greater concern has arisen about Green Revolution agriculture. In the early 1990s nutritionists noticed that even in countries where average food intake had risen, incapacitating diseases associated with mineral and vitamin deficiencies remained commonplace and in some instances had actually increased. A 1992 UN report directly linked some of these deficiencies to the increased consumption of Green Revolution crops. The problem is that the HYVs introduced during the Green Revolution are usually low in minerals and vitamins. Because the new crops have displaced the local fruits, vegetables and legumes that traditionally supplied important vitamins and minerals, the diet of many people in the developing world is now extremely low in zinc, iron, vitamin A and other micronutrients.

This is threatening to lock parts of the developing world into an endless cycle of ill-health, low productivity and underdevelopment. In some developing countries the majority of the population suffer this hidden starvation. People who are continually starved of micronutrients never fulfil their physical or intellectual potential.

The World Bank has estimated that deficiencies of iron, iodine and vitamin A are responsible for reducing the GDP of the developing world by as much as 5%. According to a 1996 report by the International Food Policy Research Institute, the only real solution is an international effort to breed new crop strains for the developing world that are both high-yielding and rich in vitamins and minerals.

In December 2007 the price of wheat broke through the $10 a bushel level, sparking protests in Pakistan and other countries as rising wheat prices were passed on to consumers. As Figure 12 shows the price of wheat on the global market has risen considerably in recent years.

---

29 JULY 2007

Wheat: Growing Concerns about Global Supplies

Some people worry about peak oil. I worry more about peak grain. The fact is that world per capita cereal production has already passed its peak, which was back in the mid-eighties, not least because of collapsing production in the former Soviet Union and Sub-Saharan Africa. Simultaneously, however, rising incomes in Asia are causing a surge in worldwide food demand. Already the symptoms of the coming food shortage are detectable. The International Monetary Fund recorded a 23% rise in world food prices during the last 18 months. For a long time we have deluded ourselves that 'illimitable improvement' was attainable. As the world approaches a new era of dearth, expect misery – and its old companion vice – to make a mighty Malthusian comeback.

Niall Ferguson *The Sunday Telegraph*

Figure 12 *Wheat: growing concerns about global supplies.*

There can be little doubt that the days of easy grain surpluses are a thing of the past. For example, India, the second largest consumer of wheat, became a large net importer in 2006 after a six-year period as a net exporter. In 2007 India tried to buy 50% more of the grain than suppliers were offering. At about the same time Russia was considering curbs on wheat exports to prevent domestic prices of this cereal rising too rapidly. In addition, Australia, the third biggest exporter of wheat, warned that its output might be 18% less than a previous government estimate, due to a second year of drought.

A late-season drought in the Ukraine had a considerable impact on production. In Morocco the crop was down 76%. Argentina temporarily halted wheat exports to assess damage caused by cold weather.

Demand for grain and other crops is rising because:

- global population continues to increase significantly and will reach 7 billion by 2010

- living standards are improving in many countries, especially in highly populated China and India – higher incomes result in the increasing demand for meat; however, it takes 7 kg of grain to produce 1 kg of beef – consumers in NICs are following the lifestyles developed in richer countries

- In some areas agricultural resources are being diverted from food production to biofuel manufacture because of concerns about energy security – this is reducing food production significantly in some areas.

The main problems with the supply of grain is that:

- most good-quality farmland is already being used

- about a third of this farmland and has been significantly degraded by intensive farming in the last half-century – the worst predictions are that 30% of all agricultural land could be unusable by 2025

- the world's deserts expanded by 160 million hectares between 1970 and 2000

- the global land area used for the cultivation of wheat and barley has been falling for 25 years

- ocean freight transportation rates reached record highs in 2007

- drought and other adverse environmental factors are significantly reducing yields in key producing countries – more and more countries are becoming concerned about the impact of climate variability on food production

In terms of global ending stocks to use ratio, the recent estimate for 2007/08 is 17%, a 30-year low (Figure 13).

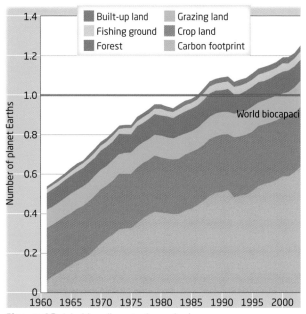

Figure 13 *World ending stocks and price.*

This compares with 36% between 1998 and 2001. A global stock of 25% is considered to be a 'safe' level – anything below causes concern.

Steep price increases are not confined to wheat. Corn prices doubled in 2006/07, with the price of soybeans 50% higher. Agricultural economists are concerned as historically prices have tended to move in long cycles driven by extended periods of mismatched supply and demand. The main impact of rising food prices is of course on the low-income populations of developing countries.

Activities

1 Write a brief bullet-point summary of Figure 11 (page 235).
2 To what extent is it realistic to recognise 'three agricultural worlds'?
3 Discuss the advantages and disadvantages of the Green Revolution.
4 Explain why there is growing concern about global stocks of wheat.
5 Analyse the trends shown in Figure 12 (page 237).

Key terms

Ecological footprint a sustainability indicator, which expresses the relationship between population and the natural environment. It sums the use of natural resources by a country's population.

Biocapacity the capacity of an area or ecosystem to generate an ongoing supply of resources and to absorb its wastes.

Global hectare one global hectare (gha) is equivalent to one hectare of biologically productive space with world average productivity.

Carbon footprint 'the total set of GHG (greenhouse gas) emissions caused directly and indirectly by an individual, organisation, event or product' (UK Carbon Trust 2008).

Overshoot occurs when humanity's demand on nature exceeds the biosphere's supply, or regenerative capacity.

Resources any aspect of the environment that can be used to meet human needs.

Flow renewable resources are resources that do not need regeneration, such as solar power.

Resource depletion the consumption of non-renewable, finite resources which will eventually lead to their exhaustion.

Optimum population the one that achieves a given aim in the most satisfactory way.

Economic optimum the level of population which, through the production of goods and services, provides the highest average standard of living.

Underpopulated when there are too few people in an area to use the resources available efficiently.

Overpopulated when there are too many people in an area relative to the resources and the level of technology available.

Optimum rhythm of growth the level of population growth that best utilises the resources and technology available. Improvements in the resource situation or/and technology are paralleled by more rapid population growth.

Population pressure when population per unit area exceeds the carrying capacity.

Neo-Malthusians also Malthusians; the pessimistic lobby who fear that population growth will outstrip resources leading to the consequences predicted by Thomas Malthus.

Anti-Malthusians also known as resource optimists; the optimists who argue that either population growth will slow well before the limits of resources are reached or that the ingenuity of humankind will solve resource problems when they arise.

Green Revolution the introduction of high-yielding seeds and modern agricultural techniques to developing countries.

Websites

www.earthtrends.wri.org
Earth Trends (World Resource Institute)

www.footprint.wwf.org.uk
WWF footprint calculator

www.prb.org
Population Reference Bureau

www.statistics.gov.uk
UK National Statistics

www.fao.org/WorldFoodSummit
FAO World Food Summit

www.oxfam.org
Oxfam

www.reliefweb.int
Relief Web

www.newscientist.com
New Scientist

www.greeneconomics.ca
Green Economics, the Pembina Institute, Canada

www.wwf.org.uk
WWF

www.bestfootforward.com
Best Foot Forward

Review

Examination-style questions

1 Refer to Figure 14.

a Define ecological footprint.

b Describe the changes in the ecological footprint by component between 1961 and 2005.

c Discuss the reasons for these changes.

2 Refer to Figure 15.

a Describe the relationship shown on the graph.

b Why are today's neo-Malthusians concerned about the relationship between population size and resource consumption?

c Explain the views of the anti-Malthusians.

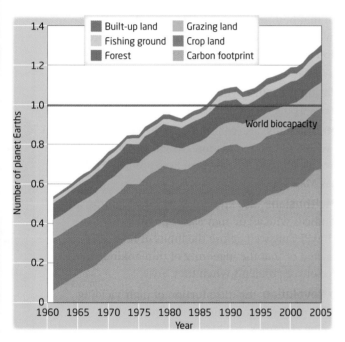

Figure 14 *Ecological footprint by component, 1960–2005.*

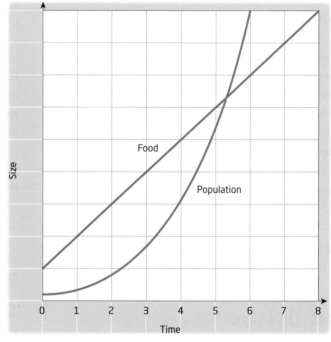

Figure 15 *The relationship between population and food supply.*

15 Changing patterns of energy consumption

KEY QUESTIONS

- What are the global trends and patterns in the production and consumption of oil?
- What are the geopolitical and environmental impacts of the changing patterns and trends in oil?

Oil production in Dorset, UK – the largest inland oilfield in the country.

The distribution of energy resources

The fossil fuels dominate the global energy situation. Their relative contributions are (2008):

- oil 34.8%
- coal 29.3%
- natural gas 24.1%.

In contrast, hydro-electricity accounted for 6.4% and nuclear energy 5.5% of global energy; other renewable energy sources, such as wind power and solar power, provide only a tiny percentage, but their growth is very rapid – see Chapter 16. The main data source used in this chapter is the BP Statistical Review of World Energy. It includes commercially traded fuels only. It excludes fuels such as wood, peat and animal waste which, although important in many countries, are unreliably documented in terms of production and consumption statistics.

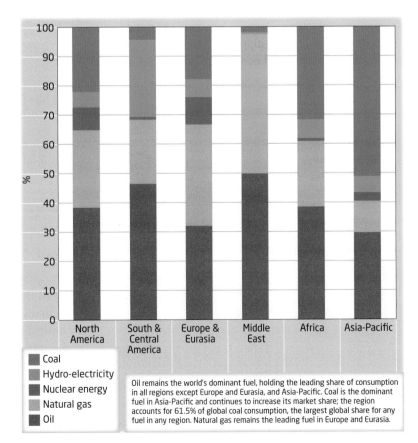

Legend:
- Coal
- Hydro-electricity
- Nuclear energy
- Natural gas
- Oil

Oil remains the world's dominant fuel, holding the leading share of consumption in all regions except Europe and Eurasia, and Asia-Pacific. Coal is the dominant fuel in Asia-Pacific and continues to increase its market share; the region accounts for 61.5% of global coal consumption, the largest global share for any fuel in any region. Natural gas remains the leading fuel in Europe and Eurasia.

Figure 1 *The regional pattern of energy consumption, 2008.*

Figure 1 shows the regional pattern of energy consumption for 2008. Consumption by type of fuel varies widely by world region:

- Oil: nowhere is the contribution of oil less than 30% and it is the main source of energy in four of the six regions shown in Figure 1 (page 241). In the Middle East it accounts for approximately 50% of consumption.

- Coal: only in the Asia-Pacific region is coal the main source of energy. In contrast it accounts for only 4% in South and Central America and 1.5% in the Middle East.

- Natural gas: natural gas is the main source of energy in Europe and Eurasia and it is a close second to oil in the Middle East. Its lowest share of the energy mix is 11% in Asia-Pacific.

- Hydro-electricity: the relative importance of hydroelectricity is greatest in South and Central America (26.3%). Elsewhere its contribution varies from 6.2% in Africa to less than 1% in the Middle East.

- Nuclear energy: nuclear energy is not presently available in the Middle East and it makes the smallest contribution of the five energy sources in Asia-Pacific, Africa, and South and Central America. It is most important in Europe and Eurasia, and North America.

Figure 2 shows how global consumption of the five major traditional sources of energy changed between 1983 and 2008. In 2008 the global consumption of primary energy was 11 294.9 million tonnes oil equivalent, an increase of 1.4% over the previous year.

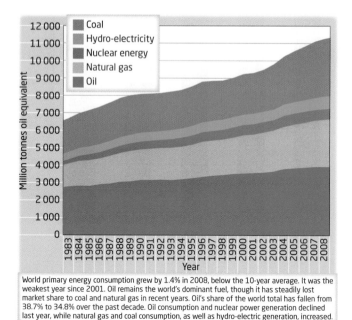

World primary energy consumption grew by 1.4% in 2008, below the 10-year average. It was the weakest year since 2001. Oil remains the world's dominant fuel, though it has steadily lost market share to coal and natural gas in recent years. Oil's share of the world total has fallen from 38.7% to 34.8% over the past decade. Oil consumption and nuclear power generation declined last year, while natural gas and coal consumption, as well as hydro-electric generation, increased.

Figure 2 *Global consumption of major energy sources, 1983–2008.*

Oil: global patterns and trends in production and consumption

The data quoted below is taken from the *BP Statistical Review of World Energy 2009*. Not everyone agrees with this data, as we will find out later in this chapter. Figure 3 shows the change in daily oil consumption by world region from 1983 to 2008. From less than 60 million barrels a day globally in the early 1980s, demand rose steeply to 84.5 million barrels a day in 2008. The largest increase has been in the Asia-Pacific region which now accounts for 30.1% of consumption. This region now uses more oil than North America which accounts for 27.45% of the world total. In contrast, Africa consumed only 3.4% of global oil, behind South and Central America with 6.9%.

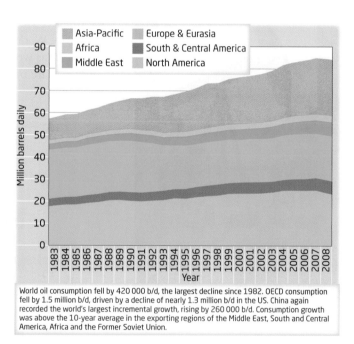

World oil consumption fell by 420 000 b/d, the largest decline since 1982. OECD consumption fell by 1.5 million b/d, driven by a decline of nearly 1.3 million b/d in the US. China again recorded the world's largest incremental growth, rising by 260 000 b/d. Consumption growth was above the 10-year average in the exporting regions of the Middle East, South and Central America, Africa and the Former Soviet Union.

Figure 3 *Oil consumption by world region, 1983–2008.*

The pattern of regional production is markedly different from that of consumption. In 2008, the Middle East accounted for 31.9% of production, followed by Europe and Eurasia (21.7%), North America (15.8%), and Africa (12.4%). Within the Middle East, Saudi Arabia dominates production, alone accounting for 13.1% of the world total. Russia accounts for over half the total production of Europe and Eurasia.

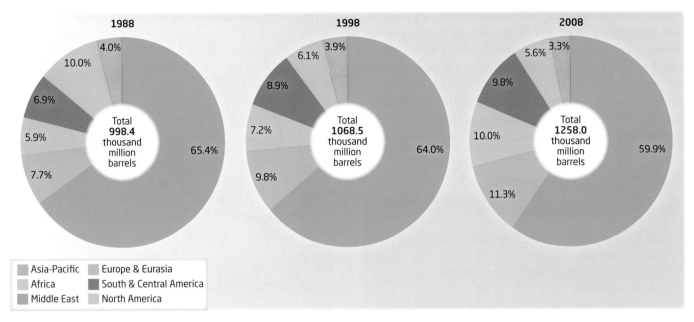

| 1988 | 1998 | 2008 |

1988
4.0%
10.0%
6.9%
5.9%
7.7%
Total
998.4
thousand
million
barrels
65.4%

1998
3.9%
6.1%
8.9%
7.2%
9.8%
Total
1068.5
thousand
million
barrels
64.0%

2008
3.3%
5.6%
9.8%
10.0%
11.3%
Total
1258.0
thousand
million
barrels
59.9%

Asia-Pacific   Europe & Eurasia
Africa   South & Central America
Middle East   North America

Figure 4 *Distribution of proven oil reserves, 1988, 1998 and 2008.*

Figure 4 illustrates the spatial distribution of **proved oil reserves**. In the period 1988–2008, proved reserves rose considerably but much more so in the latter part of the period than in the earlier part. However, the problem is that demand is increasing at a faster rate than proved reserves. In 2008, the Middle East accounted for almost 60% of global proved reserves. The main countries contributing to the latter figure are: Saudi Arabia 21%;

Iran 10.9%; Iraq 9.1%; Kuwait 8.1% and the United Arab Emirates 7.8%. Europe and Eurasia held the second largest proved reserves, with 11.3% of the world total. Russia accounted for over half of the latter figure.

Table 1 shows the **reserves-to-production (R/P) ratio** for the world in 2008. While the R/P ratio is almost 79 years in the Middle East, it is only 14.8 years in North America and 14.5 years in Asia-Pacific.

Aircraft being refuelled at Gatwick airport. Aviation fuel is a major product of the oil industry.

Region	Reserves/production ratio (years)
North America	14.8
South and Central America	50.3
Europe and Eurasia	22.1
Middle East	78.6
Africa	33.4
Asia-Pacific	14.5
World	42.0

Table 1 *Oil reserves-to-production ratio at end of 2008.*

The US government's Energy Information Agency predicts that the demand for oil will rise by 54% in the first quarter of the 21st century. This amounts to an extra 44 million barrels of oil each day by 2025. Much of this extra demand will come from Asia. All estimates indicate that the Persian Gulf's share of the oil trade will rise steadily over the next two decades and along with it the risk of terrorist attack and embargo by the key producing countries.

Research idea

Look at the latest BP Statistical Review of World Energy: www.bp.com/statisticalreview. Use the energy charting tool to create custom charts for your own analysis of the global energy situation.

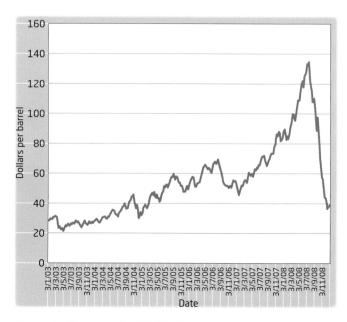

Figure 5 *The price of oil, 2003–08.*

Recent price changes

The price of oil has increased sharply over the last decade or so. It rose from $10 a barrel in 1998 to more than $130 a barrel in 2008 (Figure 5), before falling back sharply in the global recession of 2008–09. As the world moves out of recession the price is beginning to rise again.

The price of oil affects the cost of almost all other products and activities. The previous three global economic recessions were all strongly linked to a substantial increase in oil prices. However, up to early 2007 the global economy had managed to ride out the rise in the price of oil but some economists doubted that this could continue. Previous sharp and significant increases in the price of oil have mainly been the result of **supply shocks**: the **Organization of the Petroleum Exporting Countries (OPEC)** oil embargo in 1973–74, the Iranian revolution in 1979, Iraq's invasion of Kuwait in 1990. The recent high price situation was due mainly to rising demand. This means that prices are more likely to remain high although the level may fall back to a certain extent when economic conditions deteriorate.

There were a number of reasons for the rapid rise in the price of oil in the mid-2000s:

- The significant increase in the demand for oil was the largest for almost 30 years. Very high growth in demand in China, India, the USA and some other economies has had a marked impact on the rest of the world. Many emerging economies, such as India and China, subsidise oil which encourages consumption.

- There has been insufficient investment in exploration and development over the last two decades. The low oil prices for most of this period did not provide enough incentive for investment.

- Problems in the Middle East centred on Iraq. Exports of oil from Iraq are well below potential because of terrorist attacks and the slow pace of reconstruction after the War.

- Major buyers, particularly governments, stock up on oil to guard against disruptions to supply.

- Hurricanes have had a significant impact, particularly on US oil production in the Gulf of Mexico.

- Refining capacity in the USA was limited due to inadequate investment in recent decades. US refineries are ageing and thus require more maintenance which in turn reduces capacity.

- There was a lack of spare oil production capacity. In the past Saudi Arabia has maintained a significant amount of spare capacity (wells it was not pumping oil from) to prevent global supply problems when supplies were interrupted in other producing countries. This spare capacity has declined to a 20-year low.

Marine petrol station on the Amazon river near Manaus, Brazil.

Million tonnes oil equivalent		
Country	1997 consumption	2007 consumption
Developed countries		
USA	2204.8	2361.4
Japan	506.6	517.5
Germany	337.8	311.0
UK	220.4	215.9
NICs		
South Korea	179.6	234.0
Malaysia	37.8	57.4
China	961.4	1863.4
India	260.6	404.4
Developing countries		
Bangladesh	10.6	20.3
Pakistan	41.2	58.3
Peru	10.9	13.8
Algeria	26.5	34.7

Table 2 *Primary energy consumption, 1997–2007.*

Trends in developed countries

The USA consumes almost one-quarter of global oil output but has only 2.5% of its proven reserves. Although petrol prices have risen significantly in the USA in recent years, they remain less than half the price in the UK. Of the 20 million barrels a day consumed in the USA, 25% is used for transportation. However, the oil efficiency of US vehicles is at a 20-year low, a result of complacency in the period of low energy prices. The USA's high dependence on oil leaves it vulnerable to supply shocks and also pushes prices higher for the rest of the world. The only realistic way to limit the demand for oil in the USA is to increase the tax on petrol substantially. However, it is unlikely that any American President would take such a big political risk.

De-industrialisation and increasing energy efficiency in developed countries in general has resulted in a relatively modest increase in demand compared with that in NICs (Table 2). In fact, Germany and the UK actually show a decrease. This is partly due to higher efficiency rates, but also to the fact that the data only includes the five traditional sources of energy and this excludes renewable energy such as wind power. The other developed countries in Table 2 are the USA and Japan.

Trends in NICs

It is the NICs that are increasing their energy demand by the fastest rate. China alone has accounted for one-third of the growth in global oil demand since 2000. China passed Japan as the world's second largest user of oil in 2004. Its average daily consumption of 6.63 million barrels is about twice its domestic production. Because of this situation its oil imports doubled between 1999 and 2004. However, oil consumption per person is still only one-fifteenth of that in the USA. As this gap narrows it will have a considerable impact on global demand. The demand for oil in China is expected to increase by 5–7% a year. If this occurs, China will take over from the USA as the world's largest consumer of oil by 2025. Rising demand is concentrated on the large industrial cities which are located mainly in the eastern coastal zone.

China is by far the largest consumer of coal and the gap between China and the rest of the world will increase steadily in the future. China is expected to need 3242 million tonnes of coal a year by 2025. It is likely that China will build several hundred new coal-fired power stations to satisfy its demand for energy. This will have a huge impact on greenhouse gas emissions. Industry accounts for 71% of total energy demand, which is very high indeed. China accounts for half of world cement production and a third of world steel production. Other NICs such as India, Malaysia and South Korea (Table 2) are also recording high increases in energy demand.

Trends in developing countries

Most developing countries struggle to fund their energy requirements. In Table 2 data is presented for Bangladesh, Pakistan, Peru and Algeria. As you might expect there is considerable variation in the rate of growth. Energy demand is influenced by a number of factors, two of which are the rate of economic development and the rate of population growth.

There is a strong positive correlation between GNP per capita and energy use. In poor countries it is the high-income and middle-income groups that generally have enough money to purchase sufficient energy and they also tend to live in locations where electricity is available. Around the world 2 billion people lack access to household electricity. It has been estimated that connecting these people to electricity services would add only 1% extra to emissions of greenhouse gases. In the poorest countries of the world, traditional biomass often accounts for 90% or more of total energy consumption.

When will global peak oil production occur?

There has been growing concern about when global oil production will peak and how fast it will decline thereafter. For example, in the USA oil production peaked in 1970. There are concerns that there are not enough large-scale projects underway to offset declining production in well-established oil production areas. The rate of major new oilfield discoveries has fallen sharply in recent years.

It takes six years on average from first discovery for a very large-scale project to start producing oil. The International Energy Agency expects **peak oil production** somewhere between 2013 and 2037, with a fall by 3% a year after the peak. The US Geological Survey predicts that the peak is 50 years or more away.

In a report published by OPEC in 2009, this major energy organisation stated that 'the global reserve/resource base can easily meet forecast demand growth for decades to come'. OPEC highlights improved recovery techniques in existing oilfields, the number of new discoveries and the increasing use of non-conventional oil resources. The organisation argues that technological advance continues to blur the distinction between conventional and non-conventional oil.

However, in total contrast, the Association for the Study of Peak Oil and Gas (ASPO) predicts that the peak of global oil production would come as early as 2011 (Figure 6), stating 'Fifty years ago the world was consuming 4 billion barrels of oil per year and the average discovery was around 30 billion. Today we consume 30 billion barrels per year and the discovery rate is now approaching 4 billion barrels of crude oil per year'. If ASPO is correct and the oil peak is imminent, it will not allow time to shift energy use to alternative sources.

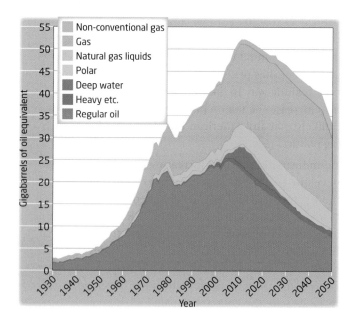

Figure 6 *Peak oil production, 1930–2050.*

About Peak Oil
Understanding Peak Oil

By Colin J. Campbell

The peak of oil discovery was passed in the 1960s, and the world started using more than was found in new fields in 1981. The gap between discovery and production has widened since. Many countries, including some important producers, have already passed their peak, suggesting that the world peak of production is now imminent. Were valid data available in the public domain, it would be a simple matter to determine both the date of peak and the rate of subsequent decline, but as it is, we find a maze of conflicting information, ambiguous definitions and lax reporting procedures. In short, the oil companies tended to report cautiously, being subject to strict Stock Exchange rules, whereas certain OPEC countries exaggerated during the 1980s when they were competing for quotas based on reported reserves. Despite the uncertainties of detail, it is now evident that the world faces the dawn of the Second Half of the Age of Oil, when this critical commodity, which plays such a fundamental part in the modern economy, heads into decline due to natural depletion. A debate rages over the precise date of peak, but rather misses the point, when what matters – and matters greatly – is the vision of the long, remorseless decline that comes into sight on the other side of it. The transition to decline threatens to be a time of great international tension. Petroleum Man will be virtually extinct this century, and Homo sapiens faces a major challenge in adapting to his loss. Peak Oil is by all means an important subject.

Figure 7 *Understanding peak oil.*

ASPO has been criticised because it has changed its prediction of the year when peak oil will occur a number of times. ASPO argues that this is understandable as new data becomes available. It also points out that hard information is often jealously guarded, making the true nature of the supply/demand balance difficult to judge. As Figure 7 illustrates, it is not pinpointing peak oil to an exact year that is important, but realising that this situation is imminent, and developing sustainable policies to cope with it.

OPEC

OPEC is an intergovernmental organisation comprising 12 oil-producing nations. Recently Indonesia decided to leave the organisation. This was because the country had become a net importer of oil. OPEC was founded in 1960 after a US law imposed quotas on Venezuelan and Persian Gulf oil imports in favour of the Canadian and Mexican oil industry. OPEC's stated objective is 'to coordinate and unify the petroleum policies of member countries and ensure the stabilisation of oil markets in order to secure an efficient, economic and regular supply of petroleum to consumers, a steady income to producers and a fair return on capital to those investing in the petroleum industry'. Figure 8 (page 248) shows OPEC's share of world crude oil reserves in 2008. Over the years, OPEC's decisions have had a substantial influence of oil prices.

OPEC has been heavily criticised at times for the allegedly political nature of some of its decisions. This has generally happened when the oil-rich Arab nations have wanted to put pressure on the USA and other Western countries with regard to the Israel-Palestinian issue. At an OPEC meeting in November 2007, Venezuela's President Hugo Chavez urged the organisation to take a 'stronger political and geopolitical role'. He argued that OPEC should ensure that:

- the price of oil remained high at between $80 and $100 a barrel
- a method should be found to compensate the world's poorest countries for the high price
- affluent countries should pay a high price in order to combat climate change.

At the same conference, Iran urged OPEC to take a tougher line with consumer countries.

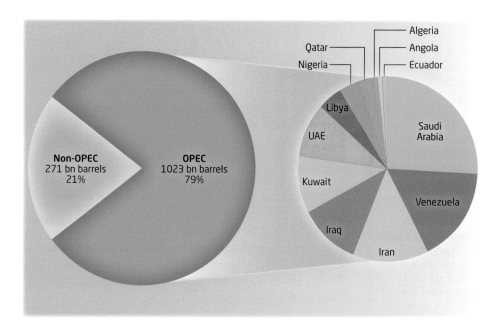

OPEC proven crude oil reserves, end 2008 (billion barrels/%)		
Saudi Arabia	264	25.8%
Venezuela	172	16.8%
Iran	138	13.4%
Iraq	115	11.2%
Kuwait	102	9.9%
UAE	98	9.6%
Libya	44	4.3%
Nigeria	37	3.6%
Qatar	25	2.5%
Algeria	12	1.2%
Angola	10	0.9%
Ecuador	7	0.6%

Figure 8 *OPEC share of world crude oil reserves, 2008.*

The headquarters of OPEC in Vienna.

Activities

1 Explain why the locations of global oil production and consumption vary so widely.
2 Define the 'reserves/production ratio'. Describe how this varies around the world.
3 **a** Why is the prediction of peak oil production so important?
  b Suggest why the predictions of when peak oil production will occur vary so widely.
4 Discuss the importance of OPEC in the global energy situation.

The geopolitical impact of changes in patterns and trends in oil

Energy security depends on resource availability, domestic and foreign, and security of supply. It can be affected by **geopolitics**, and is a key issue for many economies. Because there is little excess capacity to ease pressure on energy resources, energy insecurity is rising, particularly for non-renewable resources. The key energy issues for individual countries are the three S's: Sustainability,

Security and Strategy. Look at the World Energy Council's website (www.worldenergy.org) for more information on these issues.

Following the 1973 Arab–Israeli war, the Arab nations reduced the supply of oil to the USA and Western Europe in an effort to lessen their support for Israel. This led to a serious energy shortage which became known as the **energy crisis**. Other less serious shortages of supply have occurred since then which have pushed energy prices up and reminded us that we cannot take energy for granted. Figure 9 is a preview of what could happen in the USA during a major energy crisis.

Energy Crisis America: A Preview

✳ As the energy crisis deepens, people will make fewer trips, plan trips better, drive less and carpool. High mileage cars will be in demand and the SUV market will die. With less and slower driving due to high petrol prices the number of accidents will go down. Park and Ride schemes will become more prevalent and the government will encourage energy savings with tax breaks.

✳ Businesses will turn off advertising lights and more people will wash their clothes in cold water. In poor areas there will be more deaths from heat in the summer and more deaths from cold in the winter due to energy costs. Fuel riots may occur.

✳ The energy crisis will increase illegal immigration from Mexico where there is increasing unemployment. This will add to social tensions. Chronic heating oil shortages may cause a greater migration to the Sun Belt. The middle class may shrink with more people sinking into poverty. There will be more homelessness. Eventually energy efficiency measures unthinkable today will become the law of the land. Extreme right wing politicians will call for military control of all Middle East oil for the good of the world.

Figure 9 *The energy crisis.*

The USA, gravely concerned about the political leverage associated with imported oil, began in 1977 the construction of a **Strategic Petroleum Reserve**. The oil was to be stored in a string of salt domes and abandoned salt mines in southern Louisiana and Texas which could be easily linked up to pipelines and shipping routes. The initial aim was to store one billion barrels of oil which could be used in the event of supply discontinuation.

When Hurricane Katrina disrupted supplies of Gulf Coast petroleum in 2005 the US government said it would consider lending oil from the Strategic Petroleum Reserve, the country's emergency stockpile, to refiners that requested it. The loaned oil would be returned to the SPR when supplies got back to normal levels. The SPR currently holds 700 million barrels.

Oil storage tanks, Parry Sound, Canada.

Figure 10 shows the major trade movements for oil in 2007. The map clearly shows that the Middle East is the major global focal point of oil exports. The long-running tensions that exist in the Middle East have at times caused serious concerns about the vulnerability of oilfields, pipelines and oil tanker routes. The destruction of oil wells and pipelines during the Iraq War showed all too clearly how energy supplies can be disrupted. Middle East oil exports are vital for the functioning of the global economy.

 Geographical skills

Figure 10 is quite a complex map showing oil links between producers and consumers. Data is provided for each link. With the help of an atlas, identify the most important links and make a note of the figures provided.

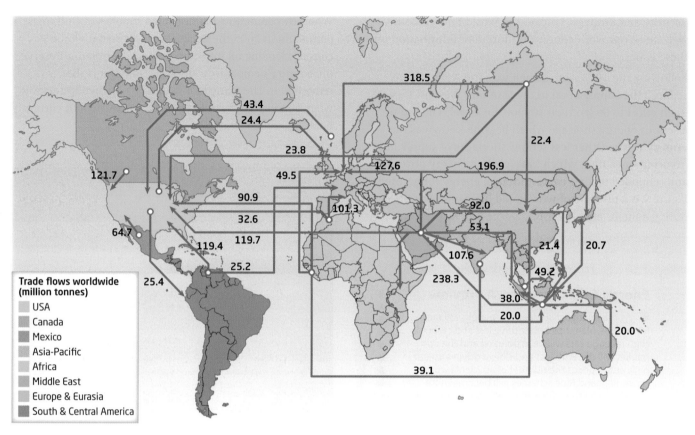

Figure 10 *Major trade movements for oil, 2007.*

Most Middle East oil exports go by tanker through the Strait of Hormuz, a relatively narrow body of water between the Persian Gulf and the Gulf of Oman. The strait at its narrowest is 55 km wide. Roughly 30% of the world's oil supply passes through the strait, making it one of the world's strategically important chokepoints. Iran has at times indicated that it could block this vital shipping route in the event of serious political tension. This could cause huge supply problems for many importing countries.

Concerns about other key **energy pathways** have arisen from time to time. These include the following:

- Nigeria: At times local rebel groups have attacked the oil installations in the Niger delta either out of frustration at the paucity of benefits accruing to the region or in an attempt to gain payouts. In 2006, an armed rebel group known as the Movement for the Emancipation of the Niger Delta (MEND) intensified attacks on oil platforms and pumping stations. A rising tide of violence has affected the country's financial

stability and its ability to supply crude oil to the outside world. There is ongoing concern about the political situation in Nigeria and the impact this might have on global oil supplies. In 2007 Nigeria was the 12th largest oil producer in the world and the largest in Africa.

- Venezuela: The left-wing government of Hugo Chavez was hostile to the American government of George Bush. The USA has voiced concern about its reliance on oil supplies from Venezuela. In February 2008 Venezuela's state oil company said it had stopped selling crude oil to Exxon Mobil. This was in response to the American oil company's move to use the courts to seize billions of dollars of Venezuela's assets. The dispute is over the nationalisation of energy TNC assets in the country. Venezuela has threatened to cut off oil supplies to the USA. Venezuela is the USA's fourth largest oil supplier and the USA is the number one buyer of Venezuelan oil.

(continued on page 253)

Case study

Russia: An energy giant flexes its muscles

Tensions can exist between energy producers and consumers. This can cause economic problems in terms of supply disruptions and rising costs. It can also result in political problems if sellers and buyers of energy seriously disagree. This has happened between energy-rich Russia and some of its customer countries. Russia has flexed its energy muscles a number of times in recent years.

Russia is one of the world's major producers and exporters of oil and gas. World Bank statistics show that oil and gas account for over 20% of Russia's GDP. The production of these fossil fuels is vital to the country's economic success. The high energy prices of recent years have been of massive benefit to the Russian economy. And there is no shortage of demand for Russian oil and gas. To the west lies energy-hungry Europe. To the south and east are the rapidly expanding economies of India and China, along with the developed economies of South Korea and Japan. European countries in particular have become increasingly reliant on energy supplies from their giant neighbour.

Country	% of world total
Saudi Arabia	13.1
Russia	12.4
USA	7.8
Iran	5.3
China	4.8

Table 3 *Major oil producing countries, 2008.*

Russian oil production has increased considerably over the last decade to put it alongside Saudi Arabia in the global league table (Table 3). Russia vies with the USA as the world's number one gas producer.

Russian gas is piped to a large number of countries via an extensive pipeline network. The pipeline networks for both oil and gas are owned by the state. Gas supplies by Gazprom (a state company with a monopoly on Russian gas exports) account for approx 23% of gas consumption in the EU. Countries of central, eastern and southern Europe remain heavily dependent on imports from Russia. Some, such as the Baltic states, are 100% reliant. The largest buyer of Russian gas in absolute terms is Germany, followed by Ukraine and Italy. At present Russia does not export gas to east Asian countries or to the USA. The most important route for Russian gas exports are the pipelines crossing the Ukraine. They account for over 80% of all Russian gas sent beyond the CIS.

Russia has had a number of disputes with neighbouring countries over its exports of oil and gas. The following are some of the most recent:

- The 2006 'gas war' between Russia and the Ukraine was thought to be largely the result of Russia's displeasure with Ukraine due to the latter's political shift towards the West after the 'Orange Revolution' in 2004. Russia increased the price of gas to the Ukraine considerably to put political pressure on the country (as well as increasing its revenue).

- In January 2007 Belarus cut off a transit pipeline carrying Russian oil. The closure of the 4000 km Druzhba pipeline halted the movement of Russian oil supplies to a number of countries. The pipeline carries more than 1.2 million barrels a day of oil, providing almost a quarter of Germany's needs and 96% of Poland's imports as well as supplies to Hungary, Ukraine, the Czech Republic and Slovakia. This action was the latest round in the dispute between the two countries over the steep increases in the prices of Russian oil and gas: on 31 December 2006 Gazprom raised gas prices for Belarus from US \$47 per 1000 cubic metres to US \$100. To counter the rising cost of Russian energy, Belarus announced it would charge an import duty of $45 a tonne on Russian oil shipped across its territory to western Europe. When Belarus halted pumping, Russia accused Belarus of illegally siphoning off oil from the pipeline. Russia then closed the pipeline on its side of the border. Fortunately, a negotiated settlement was reached which allowed the pipeline to flow again.

- In late 2006 / early 2007 Azerbaijan was also in dispute with Russia. The former had suspended oil exports to Russia following a pricing dispute with Gazprom.

Such disputes have again raised EU fears about its increasing reliance on energy supplies from Russia. Critics argue that Russia has a habit of manipulating gas and oil supplies for political purposes. The German Chancellor Angela Merkel said that the dispute illustrated that Europe's energy sources needed to be more diverse. Thus the EU is looking to:

- build interconnecting pipelines and power lines, such as electricity hook-ups between Germany, Poland and Lithuania and between France and Spain
- diversify supply – an important example is the Nabucco pipeline which will connect Europe with gasfields in the Middle East, Caucasus and Central Asia via the Balkans and Turkey
- build more terminals for the import of liquefied natural gas.

Serious doubts have been expressed about the management and efficiency of the energy industry in Russia. In May 2006, the head of the International Energy Agency (IEA) voiced concerns that Gazprom may not have enough gas to supply Europe over the next decade. An IEA study concluded that Gazprom was not re-investing enough to ensure continued adequate supplies in the future. Gazprom relies on a very limited number of large gasfields and has so far failed to invest in developing new resources in the Arctic. Already Gazprom makes up the difference between its exports to Europe and its falling output from western Siberia by increasing imports from Central Asia.

Russia has also taken a very tough line with foreign investors in the energy sector, making life difficult in a number of different ways. There is some concern that the country risks scaring off vital foreign investment as well as potential oil and gas customers. It is not just foreign investment that is needed to keep Russia's oil and gas sector on track; it is also the expertise of foreign firms. According to the *Economist* (16 December 2006, page 13):

'In the early part of the decade new production from the former Soviet Union accounted for most of the growth in the world's supply of oil and gas. But when Mr Putin began his campaign to take control of Russia's resources, that growth stalled, just as China's demand for energy was taking off. The present high prices for oil and gas are the result. With exploration prospects drying up in most of the Western world, and with the countries of the Organisation of the Petroleum Exporting Countries unwilling to open the taps, Russia is one of the few countries that could produce more oil – if only Mr Putin changed his thuggish ways.'

According to the *Financial Times (13 November 2006):*

'Nato advisers have warned the military alliance that it needs to guard against any attempt by Russia to set up an "OPEC for gas" that would strengthen Moscow's leverage over Europe.'

The study warned that Russia could seek to construct a gas cartel including the countries of Central Asia, Algeria, Qatar, Libya and perhaps Iran.

Case study

The Niger delta: Oil pollution

The Niger delta covers an area of 70 000 km², making up 7.5% of Nigeria's land area. It contains over 75% of Africa's remaining mangrove. A report published in 2006 estimated that up to 1.5 million tonnes of oil have been spilt in the delta over the past 50 years. The report, compiled by WWF, says that the delta is one of the five most polluted spots on Earth. Pollution is destroying the livelihoods of many of the 20 million people who live in the delta. The pollution damages crops and fishing grounds and is a major contributor to the upsurge in violence in the region. People here are dissatisfied with bearing the considerable costs of the oil industry but seeing very little in terms of the benefits. The report accused the oil companies of not using the advanced technologies that are evident in other world regions, to combat pollution. However, Shell claims that 95% of oil discharges in the last five years have been caused by sabotage.

The flaring (burning) of unwanted natural gas found with the oil is a major regional and global environmental problem. The gas found here is not useful because there is no gas pipeline infrastructure to take it to consumer markets. It is estimated that 70 million m³ are flared off each day. This is equivalent to 40% of Africa's natural gas consumption. Gas flaring in the Niger delta is the world's single largest source of greenhouse gas emissions.

One of the world's largest wetlands and Africa's largest remaining mangrove forest. has suffered an environmental disaster:

- Oil spills, acid rain from gas flares and the stripping away of mangroves for pipeline routes have killed off fish.
- Between 1986 and 2003, more than 20 000 hectares of mangroves disappeared from the coast, mainly due to land clearing and canal dredging for oil and gas exploration.
- The oilfields contain large amounts of natural gas. This is generally burnt off as flares rather than being stored or re-injected into the ground. Hundreds of flares have burned continuously for decades. This causes acid rain and releases greenhouse gases.
- The government has recognised 6817 oil spills in the region since the beginning of oil production. Critics say the number is much higher.
- Construction and increased ship traffic has changed local wave patterns causing shore erosion and the migration of fish into deeper water.
- Various types of construction have taken place without adequate environmental impact studies.

The federal environmental protection agency has only existed since 1988 and **environmental impact assessments** were not compulsory until 1992.

- China: Chinese politicians have expressed concern about the country's energy security situation. Four-fifths of China's oil imports pass through the Straits of Malacca, the busiest shipping lane in the world. China is looking to bypass the Straits of Malacca to a certain extent through the construction of new pipeline systems through neighbouring countries such as Pakistan and Myanmar.

The rapid expansion of air travel in China has been a major source of increasing energy demand.

Case study

Oil sands in Canada and Venezuela

Huge **oil sand**, or tar sand, deposits in Alberta, Canada and Venezuela could be critical over the next 50 years as the world's production of conventional oil falls. Such synthetic oil, which can also be made from coal and natural gas, could provide a vital bridge to an era of new technologies.

The estimates of economically recoverable oil sand reserves in Canada vary considerably. *Oil & Gas Journal* estimates are close to 180 billion barrels while the BP Statistical Review of World Energy puts the figure at about 17 billion barrels, based on oil sands under active development. And the Canadian oil sands don't even turn up on the International Energy Agency's industry lists of the ten countries with the largest proven oil reserves. Even the higher industry estimate is only about a six-year world supply, as the world now consumes close to 30 billion barrels of oil a year.

At present about 33 000 employees work the Alberta oil sands. Tar sands production reached 1 million barrels a day in 2005 and is projected to increase fivefold by 2030 – still about half of Saudi Arabia's current output and less than 5% of world production in 2030.

However, there are serious environmental concerns about the development of tar sands:

- it takes two tonnes of mined sand to produce one barrel of synthetic crude, leaving lots of waste sand
- it takes about three times as much energy to produce a barrel of Alberta oil-sands crude as it does a conventional barrel of oil; thus oil sands are large creators of greenhouse gas emissions.

Venezuela's heavy-oil production has not kept pace with that of Canada, but is now about 500 000 barrels of synthetic crude a day, with plans to expand production to 1 million barrels a day by 2010 in the Orinoco tar belt.

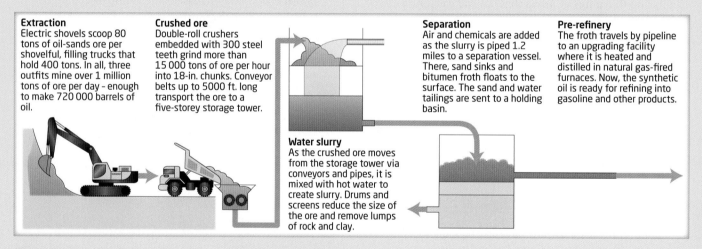

Extraction
Electric shovels scoop 80 tons of oil-sands ore per shovelful, filling trucks that hold 400 tons. In all, three outfits mine over 1 million tons of ore per day – enough to make 720 000 barrels of oil.

Crushed ore
Double-roll crushers embedded with 300 steel teeth grind more than 15 000 tons of ore per hour into 18-in. chunks. Conveyor belts up to 5000 ft. long transport the ore to a five-storey storage tower.

Water slurry
As the crushed ore moves from the storage tower via conveyors and pipes, it is mixed with hot water to create slurry. Drums and screens reduce the size of the ore and remove lumps of rock and clay.

Separation
Air and chemicals are added as the slurry is piped 1.2 miles to a separation vessel. There, sand sinks and bitumen froth floats to the surface. The sand and water tailings are sent to a holding basin.

Pre-refinery
The froth travels by pipeline to an upgrading facility where it is heated and distilled in natural gas-fired furnaces. Now, the synthetic oil is ready for refining into gasoline and other products.

Figure 11 *Squeezing oil from sand.*

National companies

A relatively new group of national (state) energy companies has become increasingly powerful and a big challenge to the influence of the so-called oil 'majors'. National companies such as Russia's Gazprom, Saudi's Aramco and Venezuela's PdVSA control about 80% of the world's oil reserves and 50% of the gas reserves. A number of these state energy companies have been formed fairly recently as part of a process that has become known as **resource nationalisation**. This has resulted in the wholesale or partial exclusion of the major energy TNCs from a number of important producing areas. Where the major energy TNCs operate in countries with active national energy companies, the former have been under pressure to accept harsher economic terms. Resource nationalisation has resulted in a significant shift of power within the energy industry.

The environmental impact of changes in patterns and trends in oil

Pathways crossing difficult environments

As energy companies have had to search further afield for new sources of oil, new energy pathways have had to be constructed. Some major oil and gas pipelines cross some of the world's most inhospitable terrain. The trans-Alaskan pipeline crosses three mountain ranges and several large rivers. Much of the pipeline is above ground to avoid the permafrost problem. Here, the ground is permanently frozen down to about 300 metres, apart from the top metre which melts during the summer. Building foundations and the uprights which hold the pipeline above ground, have to extend well below the melting zone (called the active layer). The oil takes about six days to make the 1270 km journey. Engineers fly over the pipeline every day by

helicopter to check for leaks and other problems. Problems such as subsidence have closed the pipeline for short periods.

Increasing energy insecurity has stimulated exploration of technically difficult and environmentally sensitive areas. Such exploration and development is economically feasible when energy prices are high, but becomes less so when prices fall.

Research idea

Look at the Oil Sands Story website www. oilsandsdiscovery.com to find out more about this potentially huge energy resource.

Activities

1. What do you understand by the terms (a) geopolitics and (b) energy crisis?
2. What are energy pathways and why are they so important?
3. Discuss Russia's role in geopolitics.
4. Why does the USA have a strategic petroleum reserve?
5. What is resource nationalisation and why has it occurred in some countries?
6. The Niger delta has been described as an 'environmental disaster area'. Briefly discuss this assertion.
7. Outline the advantages and disadvantages of exploiting oil sands deposits.
8. Why are energy companies increasingly searching for oil in difficult environments such as the Arctic and the Falkland Islands?

Case study

The Arctic Circle

As global warming causes the polar ice to recede, potentially oil-rich seabeds are being uncovered beneath the Arctic Circle. This region has long been thought to hold substantial reserves. Some estimates say up to 25% of the world's undiscovered oil and natural gas may be located here.

The big issue is who can lay claim to what parts of the ocean. In June 2007, Russian scientists claimed they found evidence of 70 billion barrels of oil and natural gas reserves on the Lomonosov Ridge, a huge rock formation that extends through the North Pole from Siberia to Greenland.

Russia has claimed nearly half the Arctic – a territory of half a million square miles – and granted a monopoly to its own companies to exploit it. Denmark has objected, saying it, too, has rights to the ridge. Other interested countries too, such as the USA, Canada and Norway, have failed to recognise the legitimacy of the Russian claim.

The US Geological Survey has calculated that a billion-barrel field would cost about $37 per barrel to extract, plus at least another $3 in exploration costs. By comparison, it costs about $2 per barrel to pump oil from the ground in Saudi Arabia, and $5 to $7 per barrel in Venezuela. Environmental groups want UN protection for Arctic wildlife and ecosystems. Oil spills would be a major concern in this fragile environment.

South Atlantic: the Falkland Islands

The Falkland Islands is one of the latest energy frontier regions. Test wells have shown promising results and full-scale drilling began in 2010. This is a hostile physical environment where huge floating oil rigs will be used. Such rigs cost about $500 000 a day to hire. The remoteness of the Falkland Islands adds to the logistical problems associated with drilling there. The British Geological Survey has estimated there is a one in five chance of finding commercially viable oil in the basin north of the Falklands, falling to a one in ten chance in the basin to the south. Other major issues are:

- the prospect of interference from Argentina which has a territorial claim to the Falkland Islands
- protecting the pristine ecosystem of these islands.

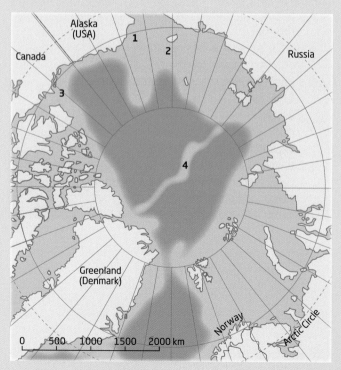

Figure 12 *The Arctic oil rush.*

1 USA Continental Shelf
If the USA ratified the Law of the Sea treaty, it could claim territory here roughly half the size of Alaska.

2 Chukchi Sea
Shell has plans to explore here. But since Russia is claiming nearly half the Arctic Ocean, it may run into trouble.

3 Beaufort Sea
A 260 km^2 area in this body of water is said to be rich in oil and gas, but it's in dispute - so no one has bid on a drilling lease offered by both Canada and the USA.

4 Lomonosov Ridge
This giant undersea landmass extends from Russia to Greenland - and the two countries are fighting over it. In June, 2007 Russia said its scientists found evidence of a 70-billion-barrel deposit and claimed rights to the whole ridge.

The Arctic National Wildlife Refuge (ANWR) is under threat from energy development. So far the environmental lobby has managed to hold the line under intense oil company pressure. However, as the USA becomes more and more concerned about its energy situation the ANWR will undoubtedly come under the threat of development again.

Key terms

Proved oil reserves quantities of oil that geological and engineering information indicates with reasonable certainty can be recovered in the future from known reservoirs under existing economic and operating conditions.

Reserves-to-production (R/P) ratio the reserves remaining at the end of any year are divided by the production in that year. The result is the length of time that those remaining reserves would last if production were to continue at that level.

Supply shock a significant interruption to supply due to an environmental, economic or political event.

Organization of the Petroleum Exporting Countries (OPEC) the current members are: Algeria, Angola, Ecuador, Iran, Iraq, Kuwait, Libya, Nigeria, Qatar, Saudi Arabia, United Arab Emirates and Venezuela.

Peak oil production the year in which the world or an individual oil-producing country reaches its highest level of production, with production declining thereafter.

Geopolitics political relations among nations, particularly relating to claims and disputes pertaining to borders, territories and resources.

Energy crisis a serious shortage of energy which interrupts domestic supplies and has an impact on all sectors of the economy.

Strategic Petroleum Reserve the USA's reserve supply of oil, which should last for about three months in the event of severe interruptions to imported oil.

Energy pathways supply routes between energy producers and consumers which may be pipelines, shipping routes or electricity cables.

Environmental impact assessment a document required by law detailing all the impacts on the environment of an energy or other project above a certain size.

Oil sands also known as tar sands or extra heavy oil: naturally occurring mixtures of sand or clay and water which form an extremely dense and viscous form of petroleum called bitumen.

Resource nationalisation when a country decides to place part (or all) of one or a number of natural resources (e.g. oil and gas) under state ownership.

Websites

www.peakoil.net
The Association for the Study of
Peak Oil and Gas (ASPO)

www.bp.com/statisticalreview
BP Statistical Review of World Energy

www.oilsandsdiscovery.com
Oil Sands Story

www.opec.org
Organization of the Petroleum Exporting
Countries (OPEC)

www.world-petroleum.org
World Petroleum Council

Review

Examination-style questions

1 Refer to Figure 13.

a Describe China's changing consumption of oil.

b Suggest reasons for such a significant change in consumption.

c What impact do you think such changes have had on the global oil situation?

2 Refer to Figure 14.

a Describe the differences in the cost of developing different types of oil resources.

b What are the reasons for such considerable variations in cost?

c Explain why the environmental impact of developing some types of oil resource is greater than for others.

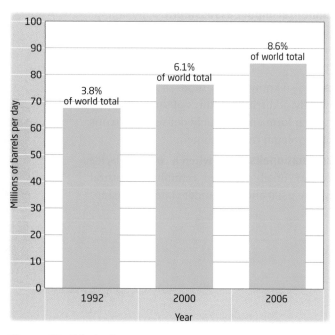

Figure 13 *China's oil consumption.*

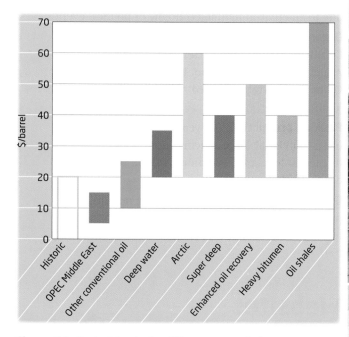

Figure 14 *Cost of developing different types of oil resource.*

16 The changing importance of other energy sources

Wind farm in northern Spain.

Traditional sources of energy

Between 1998 and 2008 global oil production increased 11%. Over the same period this compares with the following changes in the other four traditional sources of traded energy:

- a rise of 35% in natural gas production
- a 49% increase in coal production
- a 13% increase in nuclear energy
- a 22% rise in hydro-electricity.

A number of renewable energy sources showed more spectacular percentage gains, but from a much lower base.

Natural gas

Global production of natural gas increased from 2273 billion cubic metres in 1998 to 3066 billion cubic metres in 2008 (Table 1). All eight world regions showed an increase in production. However, the largest producing world regions, Europe/Eurasia and North America, recorded the lowest percentage increases between 1998 and 2008. The highest relative changes were in the Middle East and Africa.

On an individual country basis, natural gas production is dominated by Russia and the USA, accounting for 19.6% and 19.35% of the global total respectively. There is a very substantial gap between these two natural gas giants and the next largest producers, which are Canada (5.7%), Iran (3.8%) and Norway (3.2%).

Theory of Knowledge

Alternatives to fossil fuel in electricity generation all have associated costs. For example, nuclear power stations are:

- expensive in the short-term (massive resources are expended in building them)
- attractive in the medium-term (zero carbon emissions)
- possibly very expensive in the long-term (safe storage of radioactive waste).

How should we weigh up the costs and benefits of alternative power sources across these differnet time scales? How much 'debt' are we entitled to impose on future generations?

Region	1998	2008	% change
North America	750.5	812.3	8.2
South & Central America	88.8	158.9	78.9
Europe & Eurasia	895.8	1087.3	21.3
Middle East	185.0	381.1	106.0
Africa	107.2	214.8	100.2
Asia-Pacific	245.7	411.2	67.3
Total world	2273.0	3065.6	34.8

Table 1 *Natural gas production by world region 1998–2008.*

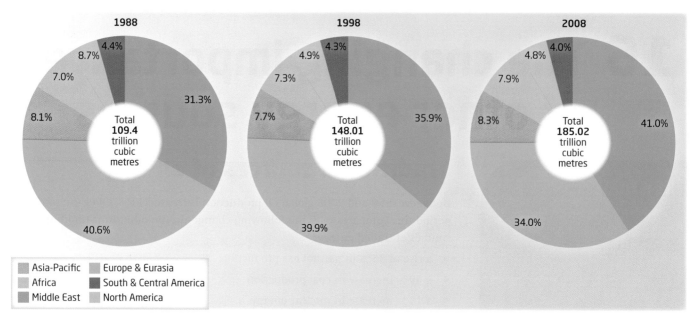

Figure 1 *Distribution of proved reserves of natural gas, 1988, 1998 and 2008.*

There is a much stronger correlation between consumption and production of natural gas than for oil, due mainly to the different ways these two energy products are transported. Global consumption of natural gas in 2008 was led by Europe and Eurasia (37.8%), North America (27.6%) and Asia-Pacific (16.0%).

During the period 1988–2008, proved reserves of natural gas increased substantially (Figure 1). The global share of proved reserves in the Middle East rose considerably, while the share held in Europe and Eurasia declined significantly. On an individual country basis the largest reserves in 2008 were in

Russia (23.4%), Iran (16%) and Qatar (13.8%). In 2008 the global reserves-to-production ratio stood at 60.4 years.

Coal

Figure 2 shows the production and consumption of coal by world region for 1998 and 2008. Coal production is dominated by the Asia-Pacific region, accounting for 61.1% of the global total in 2008. Much of this coal is produced in China which alone mines 42.5% of the world total. The next largest producing countries were the USA (18.0%), Australia (6.6%), India (5.8%) and Russia (4.6%). As for natural gas, there is a strong relationship between the production and consumption of coal by world region. Consumption is led by Asia-Pacific (61.5%), North America (18.4%) and Europe and Eurasia (15.8%). China alone consumed 42.6% of world coal in 2008.

Natural gas is a major source of energy for cooking in many countries.

Region	Share of total (%)	R/P ratio (years)
North America	29.8	216
South & Central America	0.1	n/a
Europe & Eurasia	33.0	218
Middle East & Africa	4.0	131
Asia-Pacific	31.4	64
Total world	100.0	122

Table 2 *Proved coal reserves at end 2008.*

Table 2 shows proved reserves of coal at the end of 2008. There is a fairly even spread between three regions: Europe/Eurasia, Asia-Pacific and North America. However, in terms of the reserves-to-production ratio then the figure for Asia-Pacific at 64 years is significantly below that for other world regions. Coal reserves can become exhausted within a relatively short time period. In the 19th and early 20th centuries, countries such as Germany, the UK and France were significant producers. Today there are very

few operational coal mines in these three countries. The photo below shows a mine in the Massif Central region of France which was closed in the early 1990s. It is now a museum to the coal industry in the region.

Closed coal mine in the Massif Central, France – now a museum.

Extending the 'life' of fossil fuels

There are a number of technologies that can improve the use and prolong the life of fossil fuels. These include **coal gasification**, **clean coal technologies** and the extraction of **unconventional natural gas**. Such techniques may be very important in buying time for more renewable energy to come on-line.

Coal is the most polluting source of energy. Environmental legislation in a number of countries has required coal-burning power plants to reduce pollutants such as nitrogen oxides and sulphur dioxide by installing building-size scrubbers and catalytic units. However, at present, all the carbon dioxide produced is still released into the atmosphere. This amounts to nearly two billion tonnes each year from US coal power plants alone.

Coal gasification is the technology that could transform the situation. At present electricity from coal gasification is more expensive than that from traditional power plants but if tougher pollution laws are passed in the future this situation could change significantly.

The coal industry in a number of areas may be on the point of a limited comeback with the development of clean coal technologies. This new technology has developed forms of coal that burn with greater efficiency and capture coal's pollutants before they are emitted into the atmosphere. The latest 'supercritical' coal-fired power

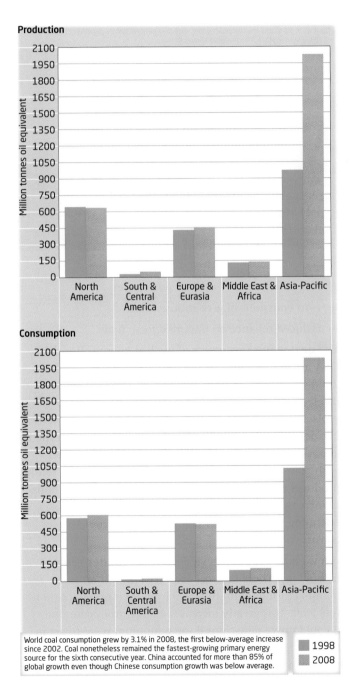

Figure 2 *Coal production and consumption.*

stations, operating at higher pressures and temperatures than their predecessors, can operate at efficiency levels 20% above those of coal-fired power stations constructed in the 1960s. Existing power stations can be upgraded to use clean coal technology.

Conventional natural gas, which is generally found within a few thousand metres or so below the surface, has accounted for most of the global supply to date. However, in recent years 'unconventional' deposits have begun to contribute more to supply. The main categories of unconventional natural gas are:

- deep gas
- tight gas
- gas-containing shales
- coalbed methane
- geopressurised zones
- Arctic and sub-sea hydrates.

Unconventional deposits are clearly more costly to extract but as energy prices rise and technology advances, more and more of these deposits are attracting the interest of governments and energy companies.

Nuclear power: a global renaissance?

No other source of energy creates such heated discussion as nuclear power. The main concerns about nuclear power are:

- power plant accidents, which could release radiation into air, land and sea
- radioactive waste storage/disposal
- rogue state or terrorist use of nuclear fuel for weapons
- high construction costs
- the possible increase in certain types of cancer near nuclear plants.

With 103 operating reactors the USA leads the world in the use of nuclear electricity. This amounts to 31% of the world's total, producing 20% of the USA's electricity. At one time the rise of nuclear power looked unstoppable. However, a serious incident at the Three Mile Island nuclear power plant in Pennsylvania in 1979 and the much more serious Chernobyl disaster in the Ukraine in 1986 brought any growth in the industry to a virtual halt. No new nuclear power plants have been ordered in the USA since then, although public opinion has become more favourable in recent years as (a) Three Mile Island and Chernobyl recede into the past and (b) worries about polluting fossil fuels increase.

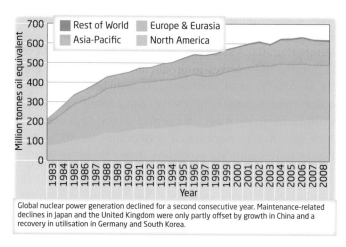

Global nuclear power generation declined for a second consecutive year. Maintenance-related declines in Japan and the United Kingdom were only partly offset by growth in China and a recovery in utilisation in Germany and South Korea.

Figure 3 *Nuclear energy consumption by world region.*

Geographical skills

With reference to Figure 3, describe and explain the changes in nuclear energy consumption. Make particular note of any changes in trend for each of the world regions shown in the graph.

The big advantages of nuclear power are:

- zero emissions of greenhouse gases
- reduced reliance on imported fossil fuels.

The next major consumers of nuclear energy after the USA are France and Japan with 16.1% and 9.2% of the 2008 world total respectively. France obtains 78% of its electricity from nuclear power and is thinking about replacing its older plants with new ones. But it has yet to decide on this course. Other countries, deeply concerned about their ability to satisfy demand, are going ahead with plans for new nuclear power plants. China currently produces 6600 MW of power from nine reactors. It aims to increase this to 40 000 MW. India already has 15 operating nuclear power plants with eight more under construction.

A few countries have developed **fast-breeder reactor** technology. These reactors are very efficient at manufacturing plutonium fuel from their original uranium fuel load. This greatly increases energy production but it could prove disastrous if the plutonium were to get in the wrong hands, as plutonium is the key ingredient for nuclear weapons.

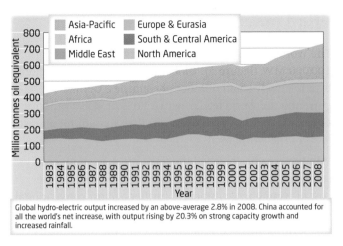

Global hydro-electric output increased by an above-average 2.8% in 2008. China accounted for all the world's net increase, with output rising by 20.3% on strong capacity growth and increased rainfall.

Figure 4 *Hydro-electricity consumption by world region, 1983–2008.*

Research idea

What are the government's current views on nuclear energy in the country in which you live?

Activities

1 Compare the changes in production of the five traditional forms of energy between 1998 and 2008.
2 Using Table 1 (page 259), describe how the global production of natural gas changed between 1998 and 2008.
3 Draw up a table to present the information illustrated in Figure 1 (page 260).
4 Discuss recent changes in the production and consumption of coal.

Renewable energy

Hydro-electricity (HEP) dominates renewable energy production. The newer sources of renewable energy which make the largest contribution to global energy supply are wind power and biofuels.

Hydro-electric power

Of the five traditional major sources of energy, HEP is the only one that is renewable. It is by far the most important source of renewable energy. The 'big four' HEP nations of China, Canada, Brazil and the USA account for almost 50% of the global total. However, most of the best HEP locations are already in use so the scope for more large-scale development is limited. In many countries, though, there is scope for small-scale HEP plants to supply local communities.

Figure 4 shows the pattern of consumption by world region from 1983. In 2008 the countries with the largest share of the world total were: China (18.5%), Canada (11.7%), Brazil (11.5%) and the USA (7.9%).

Inside the Itaipù hydro-electric power plant, Brazil.

Although HEP is generally seen as a clean form of energy it is not without its problems, which include:

- large dams and power plants can have a huge negative visual impact on the environment
- the obstruction of the river for aquatic life
- deterioration in water quality
- large areas of land may need to be flooded to form the reservoir behind the dam
- submerging large forests without prior clearance can release significant quantities of methane, a greenhouse gas.

Wind power

The worldwide capacity of wind energy is approaching 100 000 MW (Figure 5). Global wind energy is dominated by a relatively small number of countries. Germany is currently the world leader with 23.6% of global capacity. Germany, the USA and Spain together account for almost 58% of the world total.

Wind energy has reached the 'take-off' stage both as a source of energy and a manufacturing industry. As the cost of wind energy improves further against conventional energy sources, more and more countries will expand into this sector. However, projections regarding the industry still vary considerably because of the number of different factors that will have an impact on its future.

Costs of generating electricity from wind today are only about 10% of what they were 20 years ago, due mainly to advances in turbine technology. Thus, at well chosen locations wind power can now compete with conventional sources of energy. Wind energy operators argue that costs should fall further due to (a) further technological advances and (b) increasing economies of scale. One large turbine manufacturer has stated that it expects turbine costs to be reduced by 3.5% a year for the foreseeable future.

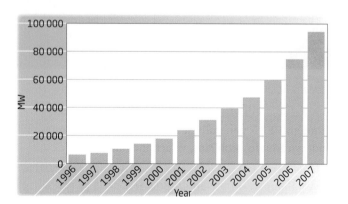

Figure 5 *Wind energy – global cumulative installed capacity, 1996–2007.*

Apart from establishing new wind energy sites, **repowering** is also beginning to play an important role. This means replacing first-generation wind turbines with modern multi-megawatt turbines which give a much better performance. The advantages are:

- more wind power from the same area of land
- fewer wind turbines
- higher efficiency, lower costs

- enhanced appearance as modern turbines rotate at a lower speed and are usually more visually pleasing due to enhanced design
- better grid integration as modern turbines use a connection method similar to conventional power plants.

As wind turbines have been erected in more areas of more countries, the opposition to this form of renewable energy has increased:

- people are concerned that huge turbines located nearby could blight their homes and have a significant impact on property values
- there are concerns about the hum of turbines disturbing both people and wildlife
- skylines in scenically beautiful areas might be spoiled forever
- turbines can kill birds – migratory flocks tend to follow strong winds but wind companies argue that they avoid building on migratory routes
- suitable areas for wind farms are often near the coast where land is expensive
- turbines can affect TV reception nearby
- the cost of investing in wind energy is high when compared with the alternatives.

The recent rapid increase in demand for turbines has resulted in a shortage of supply. New projects now have to make orders for turbines in large blocks up to several years in advance in order to ensure firm delivery dates from manufacturers. Likewise the investment from manufacturers is having to rise significantly to keep pace with such buoyant demand.

Wind farm, Palm springs, California.

Case study

China: The Three Gorges Dam

The Three Gorges Dam across the Yangtze river in China is the world's largest electricity generating plant of any kind. The dam is over 2 km long and 100 metres high. The lake impounded behind it is over 600 km long. All of the originally planned components were completed in late 2008. Currently there are 32 main generators with a capacity of 700 MW each. Six additional generators in the underground power plant are being installed and should become fully operational in 2011. At full strength the generating capacity of the dam will be a massive 22 500 MW.

One objective of such a large capacity is to reduce China's dependence on coal. The dam supplies Shanghai and Chongqing in particular with electricity. This is a multipurpose scheme that also increases the river's navigation capacity and reduces the potential for floods downstream. The dam has raised water levels by 90 metres upstream, transforming the rapids in the gorge into a lake, allowing shipping to function in this stretch of the river. The dam will protect an estimated 10 million people from flooding.

However, there was considerable opposition to the dam because:

- more than a million people had to be moved to make way for the dam and the lake
- much of the resettlement has been onto land above 800 metres above sea level which is colder and has less fertile soils
- the area is seismically active and landslides are frequent
- there are concerns that silting will quickly reduce the efficiency of the project
- significant archaeological treasures were drowned
- the dam interferes with aquatic life
- the total cost is estimated at $70 billion – many people argue that this money could have been better spent.

Examples of new developments in wind energy:

- In 2008 a Dutch company installed the world's first floating wind turbine off the southern coast of Italy in water 110 metres deep. The technology is known as the 'submerged deepwater platform system'.
- The Swedish company Nordic has recently brought a two-bladed turbine onto the market.

Biofuels

Biofuels are fossil fuel substitutes that can be made from a range of agri-crop materials including oilseeds, wheat, corn and sugar. They can be blended with petrol and diesel. In recent years, increasing amounts of cropland have been used to produce biofuels. Initially, environmental groups such as Friends of the Earth and Greenpeace were very much in favour of biofuels, but as the damaging environmental consequences have become clear, such environmental organisations were the first to demand a rethink of this energy strategy.

The main methods of producing biofuels are:

- Farmers grow crops high in sugar (sugarcane, sugar beet, sweet sorghum) or starch (corn/maize). Then yeast fermentation is used to produce ethanol.
- Plants containing high amounts of vegetable oil, such as oilpalm, soybean and jatropha, are grown. The oils are then heated to reduce their viscosity and they can be burned directly in a diesel engine, or chemically processed to produce fuels such as biodiesel.
- Wood can be converted into biofuels such as woodgas, methanol or ethanol fuel.
- Cellulosic ethanol can be produced from non-edible plant parts, but costs are not economical at present. This method is seen as the potential second generation of biofuels.

Ethanol is the most common biofuel produced globally, particularly in Brazil and the USA. It accounts for over 90% of total biofuel production. Ethanol can be used in petrol engines when mixed with gasoline. Most existing petrol engines can run on blends of up to 15% ethanol. Global production of ethanol has risen rapidly in recent decades. For example, in the USA the amount of maize turned into ethanol increased from 15 million tonnes in 2000 to 85 million tonnes in 2007. This amounts to about one-third of US maize production. The USA and Brazil are by far the largest producers of ethanol. Together these two countries produce 87.9% of the world total. However, production in the European Union and China is growing significantly.

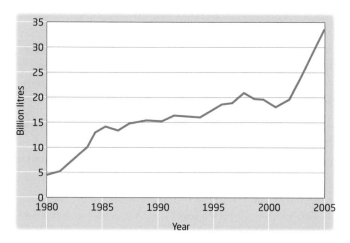

Figure 6 *World ethanol production, 1980–2005.*

In contrast to the USA, Brazil uses sugarcane to produce ethanol. More than half of Brazil's sugarcane crop is now used for this purpose. Sugarcane-based ethanol can be produced in Brazil at about half the cost of maize-based ethanol in the USA. This difference is due to:

- climatic factors
- land availability
- the greater efficiency of sugar in converting the sun's energy into ethanol.

The USA has set a target of increasing the use of biofuels to 35 billion gallons by 2017. This is about five times the current level. The objective is to replace approximately 15% of imported oil with domestically produced ethanol. Subsidies are an important element in encouraging biofuel production. In 2006, US tax credits for maize-based ethanol production amounted to around $2.5 billion. This sum is expected to increase with rising production.

Global biodiesel production and capacity have risen significantly in recent years. Biodiesel is the most common biofuel produced in Europe, with the continent accounting for over 63% of global production. Germany and France are the leading producers within Europe. Biodiesel can be used in any diesel engine when mixed with mineral diesel, usually up to a limit of 15% biodiesel. Rapeseed oil is the major source of Europe's biodiesel. After the EU, the USA is the second most important producer of biodiesel. In the latter, soybean oil is the main source for production.

Increasing investment is taking place in research and development of the so-called 'second generation' biodiesel projects including algae and cellulosic diesel. Other important trends in the industry are a transition to larger plants and consolidation among smaller producers.

The optimism of only a few years ago about the green credentials of biofuels has largely faded as one organisation after another has voiced a variety of concerns. It now seems likely it will take the technological advances of the second generation of biofuels to satisfy at least some critics about the sustainability of this form of energy. The key areas to be addressed are (a) the growing of food crops rather than non-food crops and (b) the need to ensure that there is a clear net environmental benefit in the production and use of biofuels. Not all biofuels are the same. Investment should be concentrated on the most sustainable ones.

Geothermal electricity

Geothermal energy is the natural heat found in the Earth's crust in the form of steam, hot water and hot rock. Rainwater may percolate several kilometres in permeable rocks where it is heated due to the Earth's **geothermal gradient**. This is the rate at which temperature rises as depth below the surface increases. The average rise in temperature is about 30°C per km, but the gradient can reach 80°C near plate boundaries.

This source of energy can be used to produce electricity, or its hot water can be used directly for industry, agriculture, bathing and cleansing. For example, in Iceland, hot springs supply water at 86°C to 95% of the buildings in and around Reykjavik. At present virtually all the geothermal power plants in the world operate on steam resources, and have an extremely low environmental impact.

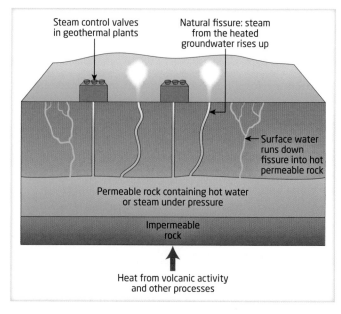

Figure 7 *Using geothermal power.*

Geothermal power plant in Iceland.

First begun in Larderello, Italy in 1904, electricity generation using geothermal energy is now taking place in 24 countries, five of which use it to produce 15% or more of their total electricity. In the first half of 2008, total world installed geothermal power capacity passed 10 000 MW. This is enough electricity to meet the needs of 60 million people. In 2010, capacity could increase to 13 500 MW across 46 countries, which would be equivalent to 27 coal-fired power plants. The USA is the world leader in geothermal electricity with plants in Alaska, California, Hawaii, Nevada and Utah. Total production accounts for 0.37% of the electricity used in the USA. Other leading geothermal electricity using countries are the Philippines, Italy, Mexico, Indonesia, Japan, New Zealand and Iceland.

The Geysers in California, USA, is the largest complex of geothermal power plants in the world. Fifteen geothermal power plants here have a net generating capacity of about 725 MW of electricity – enough to power 725 000 homes, or a city the size of San Francisco. The Geysers accounts for about a quarter of the green power produced in California.

Solar power

From a relatively small base the installed capacity of solar electricity is growing rapidly. Experts say that solar power has huge potential for technological improvement which could make it a major source of global electricity in years to come. According to some estimates, over $30 billion was invested in the solar sector in 2007. A recent study has predicted that the global solar market could grow to a $100 billion industry by 2013, reaching 23 GW installed capacity from 4.9 GW in 2008. Spain, Germany, Japan and the USA currently lead the global market for solar power.

Solar electricity is currently produced in two ways:

- **Photovoltaic systems** – these are solar panels that convert sunlight directly into electricity. Germany has the largest installed PV capacity which rose from 100 MW in 2000 to 4150 MW at the end of 2007. Much of this increase is due to the revised 'feed-in tariff system' which is part of the Renewable Energy Sources Act. This has made solar power a more attractive proposition for electric utilities. Spain has moved into third place in PV capacity after introducing a similar feed-in tariff structure in 2004. Rapid growth in other countries such as France, Italy, South Korea and the USA has been due to various incentive packages and local market conditions.

- Concentrating solar power (CSP) systems use mirrors or lenses and tracking systems to focus a large area of sunlight into a small beam. This concentrated light is then used as a heat source for a conventional thermal power plant. The most developed CSP systems are the solar trough, parabolic dish and solar power tower. Each method varies in the way it tracks the sun and focuses light. In each system a fluid is heated by the concentrated sunlight, and is then used for power generation or energy storage.

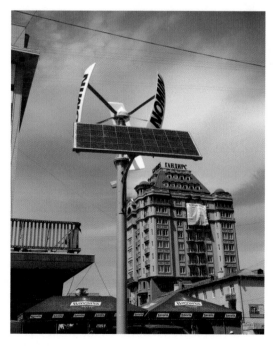

Solar panels and mini wind turbines powering street lights.

Another idea being considered is to build solar towers. Here a large greenhouse area would be constructed with a very tall tower in the middle. The hot air in the greenhouse would rise rapidly up the tower, driving turbines along the way.

Traditional solar panels comprise arrays of photovoltaic cells made from silicon. These cells absorb photons in light and transfer their energy to electrons, which form an electrical circuit. However, standard solar panels are:

- costly to install
- have to be tilted and carefully positioned so as not to shade nearby panels.

A number of companies are now using a new technique to manufacture solar panels. This involves using different materials and building them in very thin layers or films, almost like printing on paper, to produce the photovoltaic effect. The cost of production is reduced because (a) the layers or films use less material and (b) they can be deposited on bases such as plastic, glass or metal.

World	7841.00
Germany	3862.00
Japan	1919.00
USA	830.50
Spain	655.00
Italy	120.20
Australia	82.50
South Korea	77.60
France	75.20
Netherlands	53.30

Table 3 *Installed photovoltaic capacity (Mw).*

Tidal power

Although currently in its infancy, a study by the Electric Power Research Institute estimated that as much as 10% of US electricity could eventually be supplied by tidal energy. This potential could be equalled in the UK and surpassed in Canada.

Tidal power plants act like underwater windmills, transforming sea currents into electrical current. Tidal power is more predictable than solar or wind and the infrastructure is less obtrusive, but start-up costs are high. The 240 MW Rance facility in north-western France is the only utility-scale tidal power system in the world. However, the greatest potential is at Canada's Bay of Fundy in Nova Scotia. A pilot plant was opened at Annapolis Royal in 1984, which at peak output can generate 20 MW. More ambitious projects at other sites along the Bay of Fundy are under consideration, but there are environmental concerns. The main concerns are potential effects on fish populations, levels of sedimentation building up behind facilities, and the possible impact on tides along the coast.

Activities

1. Suggest reasons for the variations and trends in the consumption of hydro-electricity by world region.
2. Discuss recent changes in the installed capacity of wind energy.
3. **a** What are biofuels?
   b Why has biofuel production expanded so rapidly?
   c Examine the advantages and disadvantages of biofuels.
4. **a** What is geothermal energy?
   b Explain the geographical locations of the main producing countries.
5. Explain the difference between photovoltaic and concentrated solar power systems.

Research idea

For the country in which you live, find out which forms of renewable energy are used and how much they contribute to total energy production.

Fuelwood in developing countries

Fuelwood and charcoal are collectively called fuelwood, and account for just over half of global wood production. In developing countries about 2.5 billion people rely on fuelwood, charcoal and animal dung for cooking. Fuelwood provides much of the energy needs for Sub-Saharan Africa. It is also the most important use of wood in Asia. Table 4 shows the number of people living without electricity in the world.

Although at least one study claims that the global demand for fuelwood peaked in the mid-1990s, there can be no doubt that there are severe shortages in many countries. This is a major factor in limiting development.

In developing countries the concept of the 'energy ladder' is important. Here, a transition from fuelwood and animal dung to 'higher-level' sources of energy occurs as part of the process of economic development. Income, regional electrification and household size are the main factors having an impact on the demand for fuelwood. Thus forest depletion is initially heavy near urban areas but slows down as cities become wealthier and change to other forms of energy. It is the more isolated rural areas that are most likely to lack connection to an electricity grid. It is in such areas that the reliance on fuelwood is greatest. Wood is likely to remain the main source of fuel for the global poor in the foreseeable future.

Case study

The USA: a Solar Grand Plan

In an article in *Scientific American* (January 2005), three leading experts in solar electricity presented a 'Solar Grand Plan' for the USA. Their overall objective is to end US dependence on foreign oil, and slash greenhouse gas emissions by 2050. Under the plan, solar power could provide 69% of US electricity and 35% of its total energy (including transportation) by 2050. They argue that this solar energy could be provided at prices equivalent to today's rates for conventional energy.

The essential element of the plan is the large-scale development of photovoltaic farms covering a total area of around 80 000 km². The National Renewable Energy Laboratory in Golden, Colorado has shown that more than enough land is available in the south-west without requiring the use of environmentally sensitive areas, populated areas or difficult terrain. Figure 8 shows the variations in average daily total radiation across the USA.

The main disadvantage of solar power is that it generates no power at night, and little when skies are cloudy. Thus excess electricity must be produced during sunny hours and stored for use during the hours of darkness. The plan advocated the use of new state-of-the-art compressed-air energy storage.

The authors of the plan estimate that US carbon dioxide emissions in 2050 would reduce to 62% below 2005 levels due to (a) significantly lower emissions from power plants and (b) the displacement of gasoline vehicles by plug-in hybrids fuelled by a new solar power grid. To fund the Solar Grand Plan, the US government would need to invest more than $400 billion over the next 40 years. However, there would be huge savings on eliminating imported oil and there would be a very substantial cut in the US trade deficit.

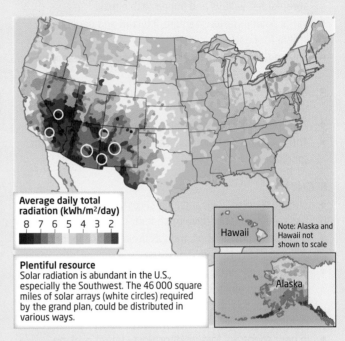

Figure 8 *Average daily total solar radiation across the USA.*

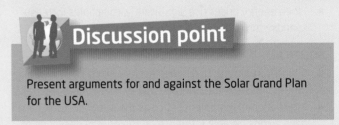

Discussion point

Present arguments for and against the Solar Grand Plan for the USA.

Region	Number (people)
South Asia	706 million
Sub-Saharan Africa	547 million
East Asia	224 million
Other regions	101 million

Table 4 *Number of people living without electricity, 2004.*

The collection of fuelwood does not cause deforestation on the same scale as the clearance of land for agriculture, but it can seriously deplete wooded areas. The use of fuelwood is the main cause of indoor air pollution in developing countries. Indoor air pollution is responsible for 1.5 million deaths in developing countries every year. More than half of these deaths are of children below the age of five.

The reasons for variations in energy supply

As you might expect, global variations in energy supply occur for a number of reasons. These can be broadly subdivided into physical, economic and political factors. Figure 9 (page 270) shows examples for each of these groupings.

Technological change has had a major impact. For example, offshore oilrigs can now drill in much deeper water than 30 years ago. Public perception has become increasingly important. People have never been more aware of environmental and other issues surrounding the development of energy resources (for example the Gulf of Mexico oil diaster in 2010).

PHYSICAL

- Deposits of fossil fuels are only found in a limited number of locations.
- Large-scale HEP development requires high precipitation, steep-sided valleys and impermeable rock.
- Large power stations require flat land and geologically stable foundations.
- Solar power needs a large number of days a year with strong sunlight.
- Wind power needs high average wind speeds throughout the year.
- Tidal power stations require a very large tidal range.
- The availability of biomass varies widely due to climatic conditions.

ECONOMIC

- The most accessible, and lowest cost, deposits of fossil fuels are invariably developed first.
- Onshore deposits of oil and gas are usually cheaper to develop than offshore deposits.
- Potential HEP sites close to major transport routes and existing electricity transmission corridors are more economical to build than those in very inaccessible locations.
- In poor countries foreign direct investment is often essential for the development of energy resources.
- When energy prices rise significantly, companies increase spending on exploration and development.

POLITICAL

- Countries wanting to develop nuclear electricity require permission from the International Atomic Energy Agency.
- International agreements such as the Kyoto Protocol can have a considerable influence on the energy decisions of individual countries.
- Potential HEP schemes on 'international rivers' may require the agreement of other countries that share the river.
- Governments may insist on energy companies producing a certain proportion of their energy from renewable sources.
- Legislation regarding emissions from power stations will favour the use, for example, of low-sulphur coal, as opposed to coal with a high sulphur content.

Figure 9 *Reasons for global variations in energy supply.*

Variable energy patterns over time

The use of energy in all countries has changed over time for a number of reasons:

- Technological development: for example (a) nuclear electricity has only been available since 1954, (b) oil

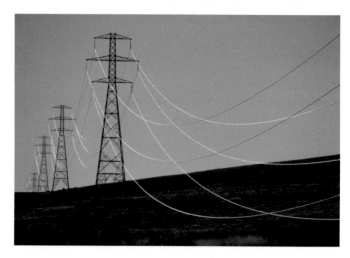

Electricity transmission corridor.

and gas can now be extracted from much deeper waters than in the past, (c) renewable energy technology is advancing steadily.

- Increasing national wealth: As average incomes increase, living standards improve which involves the increasing use of energy and the use of a greater variety of energy sources.

- Changes in demand: at one time all of Britain's trains were powered by coal and most people also used coal for heating in their homes. Before natural gas was discovered in the North Sea, Britain's gas was produced from coal (coal gas).

- Changes in price: the relative prices of the different types of energy can influence demand. Electricity production in the UK has been switching from coal to gas over the past 20 years mainly because power stations are cheaper to run on natural gas.

- Environmental factors/public opinion: public opinion can influence decisions made by governments. People today are much better informed about the environmental impact of energy sources.

Activities

1. **a** What is fuelwood?
   b Why is fuelwood so important in many developing countries?
2. Discuss the main reasons for variations in energy supply.
3. Give three reasons for changes in a country's energy sources.

Key terms

Coal gasification a process that converts solid coal into a gas that can be used for power generation.

Clean coal technology power plant processes that both increase the efficiency of coal-burning and significantly reduce emissions.

Unconventional natural gas natural gas that is more difficult to access and therefore more expensive to extract than 'conventional' reserves.

Fast-breeder reactor a nuclear reactor in which the chain reaction is maintained mainly by fast neutrons. It is capable of producing more fissionable material than it consumes.

Repowering replacing first-generation wind turbines with modern multi-megawatt turbines which give a much better performance.

Biofuels fossil fuel substitutes that can be made from a range of agri-crop materials including oilseeds, wheat, corn and sugar.

Geothermal energy the natural heat found in the Earth's crust in the form of steam, hot water and hot rock.

Geothermal gradient the rate at which temperature rises as depth below the surface increases.

Photovoltaic systems solar panels that convert sunlight directly into electricity.

Websites

www.earthpolicy.org
Earth Policy Institute

www.bp.com/statisticalreview
BP Statistical Review of World Energy

www.savetheplanetnews.com
Save the Planet

Review

Examination-style questions

1 Refer to Figure 10.

a Define the reserves-to-production ratio.

b Describe and suggest reasons for the variations shown on the graph.

c Examine the implications of such differences in the reserves-to-production ratio.

2 Refer to Figure 11.

a Define renewable energy.

b Explain why renewable energy contributes only a relatively small fraction to total global energy production.

c Discuss the recent development of one source of renewable energy.

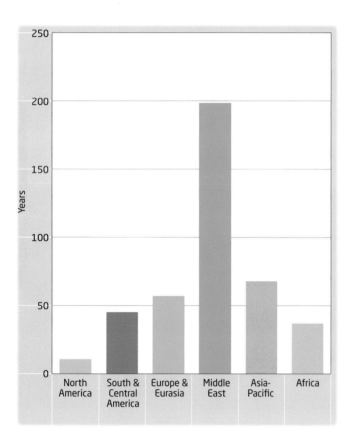

Figure 10 *Natural gas – reserves-to-production ratio.*

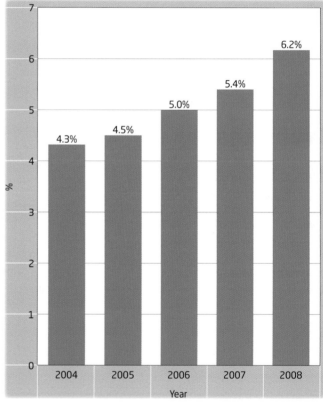

Figure 11 *Renewable energy as a percentage of global capacity.*

17 Conservation strategies

KEY QUESTIONS

- How can resource consumption be reduced by conservation, waste reduction, recycling and substitution?
- What strategies can be used to reduce the consumption of one resource?

Aluminium cans awaiting collection for recycling, Italy.

Conservation of resources

The **conservation of resources** is the management of the human use of natural resources to provide the maximum benefit to current generations while maintaining capacity to meet the needs of future generations. Conservation includes both the protection and rational use of natural resources. Conservation and the use of natural resources are social processes since they rely on people's behaviour, values and decisions. Both the demand for, and supply of, resources need to be planned and managed to achieve a sustainable system. In addition, there is growing pressure from individual governments and international organisations for a greater degree of equity in the use of the world's resources. They argue that there is a need for environmental policies and laws that contribute to more equitable sharing of the costs and benefits of conservation.

Non-renewable resources, such as fossil fuels, are replaced over geological timescales, so the available stock of many of these resources may eventually be used up completely. Conservation involves actions to use these resources most efficiently, thus extending their life as long as possible. For example, by **recycling** aluminium, the same piece of material is reused in a series of products, reducing the amount of aluminum ore that must be freshly mined. Similarly, energy-efficient products help to conserve fossil fuels since the same energy services, such as lighting or transportation, can be attained with smaller amounts of fuel.

Conservation also involves the **reuse** of resources. Plastic bags are an obvious example, but there are many others. These include returning wire hangers to dry-cleaners, donating clothes and other items you no longer want to charities rather than dumping them, and repairing household items where possible rather than buying anew. In the recent recession, many shoe-repairers increased their trade as people looked to extend the life of their shoes rather than have the expense of buying new ones.

In many developing countries there has long been a culture of reuse and recycling because people could not afford to buy new replacements. It is a common sight to see waste collectors roaming streets in search of reusable items. The reuse of rubber tyres is an example.

Renewable resources, in contrast, can be seriously depleted if they are subjected to excessive harvest or otherwise degraded. No substitutes may be available for food products such as fish or agricultural crops. When the demise of biological resources causes the complete extinction of a species or the loss of a particular habitat, there can be no substitute for that diversity of life.

Theory of Knowledge

Energy conservation is a sensitive topic. Individuals are being encouraged to make small savings, such as not leaving electrical equipment on stand-by. At the same time major international events, which admittedly give pleasure to many, go ahead unchallenged. Examples of spectacularly resourced and energy hungry events are motor racing (the Formula One Grand Prix Championship) and the Olympic Games – not just the cost of venues, competitors and equipment, but also the movement of spectators, etc. What would be your choice of major event to be discontinued, in order to save energy? Why?

Various strategies can be used in the attempt to conserve resources. The agreement of quotas is an increasingly frequent resource management technique, illustrated by the case study of the European Union's (EU) Common Fisheries Policy below. **Quotas** involve agreement between countries to take only a predetermined amount of a resource. Quotas may change on an annual or longer time period basis. Much further along the line is **rationing**. This is very much a last resort management strategy when demand is massively out of proportion to supply. For example, individuals might only be allowed a very small amount of fuel and food per week. Some senior citizens will remember that this happened during the Second World War.

Green waste recycling in the UK.

At various times the use of **subsidies** has been criticised by environmentalists. It has been argued that reducing or abandoning some subsidies would aid conservation. In the late 1990s a report entitled 'Perverse Subsidies', published by the International Institute for Sustainable Development, highlighted the huge amounts of money that taxpayers worldwide pay out to subsidise industry, energy, transport, farming, water and fishing. But taxpayers then have to spend almost as much again to help repair the damaging effects subsidies can have on the environment and the economy. The report concluded that 'by removing perverse subsidies we find that economies become more efficient and productive, at the same time as being more conserving of our natural resources'.

Discussion point

To what extent should the world's richer countries lead the way in the conservation of resources?

Waste reduction and recycling

Recycling involves the concentration of used or waste materials, their reprocessing, and their subsequent use in place of new materials. If organised efficiently, recycling can reduce demand considerably on fresh deposits of a resource. Recycling also involves the recovery of waste. New technology makes it possible to recover mineral content from the waste of earlier mining operations. However, the proportion of a material recycled is strongly related to the cost in proportion to the price of the original raw material, although governments are doing more and more to weaken this relationship.

The literature on sustainable consumption highlights recycling, but some attention is also given to promoting slow(er) consumption through focusing on product lifespan, design for reuse, and reuse through various second-hand markets. A number of studies have focused on participation rates in recycling. Such studies have highlighted **recycling deserts** alongside areas of high participation.

Supermarkets have made significant efforts in recent years to reduce the number of plastic bags used. Some now charge for bags while others just encourage reuse of bags. Supermarkets like Tesco in the UK claim to have drastically reduced the number of new plastic bags used by customers each year. However, environmental groups are putting pressure on supermarkets to do more, claiming that many products have far too much packaging and that the supermarkets themselves are high users of energy.

Recycling depot in the UK.

Case study

The EU's Common Fisheries Policy

Many of the world's fishing grounds are in crisis because of **overfishing**. In the worst-affected areas it is feared that fish stocks may not recover for a long time, if at all. The EU's Common Fisheries Policy (CFP) is a significant example of resource management although perceptions vary widely as to its effectiveness.

The **tragedy of the commons** is a term used to explain what has happened in many fishing grounds, including European waters. Because the seas and oceans have historically been viewed as common areas, open to everyone, the capacity of fishing vessels operating in many areas has exceeded the amount of fish available. The result has been resource depletion (Figure 1). To try to solve this problem, countries have extended their territorial waters to 200 miles (320 km) from their shores and instigated a variety of management techniques within these waters. Outside of these limits nations have sought to come to agreements, with varying degrees of success.

The CFP has evolved over a number of stages. Current measures to conserve fish stocks include:

- taking a long-term approach by fixing total allowable catches (TACs) on the basis of fish stocks

Fishing vessels in an Irish port.

- introducing accompanying conservation measures
- setting recovery plans for stocks below the safe biological limits
- managing the introduction of new vessels and the scrapping of old vessels in such a way as to reduce the overall capacity of the EU fleet
- EU aid for the modernisation of vessels finishing at the end of 2004
- measures to neutralise the socio-economic consequences of fleet reduction
- measures to encourage the development of sustainable aquaculture.

Fish stocks need to renew themselves due to losses from both fishing and natural causes. Thus it is important that small fish must be allowed to reach maturity so that they can reproduce. With this in mind the CFP sets the maximum quantity of fish or **total allowable catch** that can be caught each year. This is divided among the member states to give the national quota for each country. The number of small fish caught is limited by:

- minimum mesh sizes
- closure of certain areas to protect fish stocks
- the banning of certain types of fishing
- recording catches and landings in special log books.

Supporters of the CFC argue that it makes a strong contribution to the quest for sustainable fishing. However, environmentalists believe that short-term economic and political concerns override the objective of sustainability.

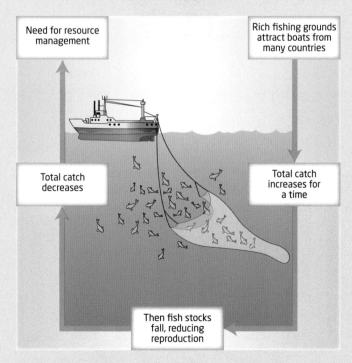

Need for resource management

Rich fishing grounds attract boats from many countries

Total catch decreases

Total catch increases for a time

Then fish stocks fall, reducing reproduction

Figure 1 *The need for resource management in fishing.*

Tesco supermarket, London. Plastic bag use has fallen considerably, but supermarkets are under pressure to do more, such as to reduce packaging.

Recycling not only conserves valuable resources, it is also fundamental in the reduction of **landfill**. Landfill is undesirable for a number of reasons:

- leachate pollution: leachate is solution formed when water percolates through a permeable medium – the leachate may be toxic or carry bacteria when derived from solid waste

- biodegradable waste rotting in landfill creates methane gas which is 21 times more potent than carbon dioxide

- increasingly large areas of land are required for such sites.

In the UK, Landfill Tax was introduced in the Finance Act of 1996. It was established as the UK's first tax with 'an explicit environmental purpose'. Since then the tax has been raised twice to provide a greater incentive to local authorities to reduce the amounts of waste they send to landfill. At the same time advances in waste treatment, such as mechanical biological treatment (MBT), have emerged as a competitive

alternative to landfill. The overall objective is to drive waste streams higher up the waste hierarchy (Figure 2). The starting point is to reduce disposal, much of which occurs in landfill sites. Figure 3 shows how municipal waste management varied in the EU in 2006 for 15 countries. While landfill dominates in countries such as Greece, Portugal and the UK, it is at a very low level in Sweden, Belgium, Denmark and the Netherlands.

The Waste Resources Action Programme (WRAP) is the lead agency in the UK in terms of the waste hierarchy. WRAP was originally set up to focus on recycling, but its

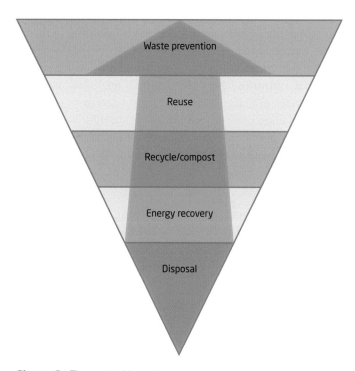

Figure 2 *The waste hierarchy.*

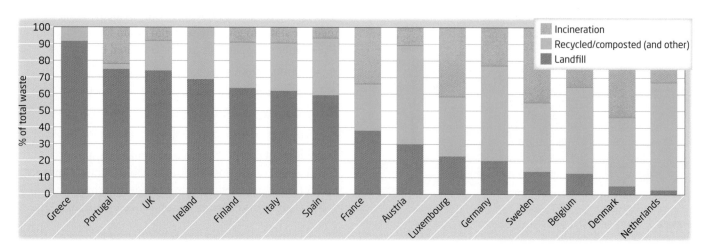

Figure 3 *Municipal waste management in the EU.*

Case study

Beijing

It is not surprising that developed countries generally lead the way in recycling although there are some exceptions. However, changes are beginning to take place elsewhere! In July 2009, the Beijing municipal government launched a strategy for the improved disposal of the 18 410 tonnes of domestic refuse generated by the city every day. These measures include:

- building more environmentally friendly disposal sites
- improving incineration technologies
- enforcing household waste separation and recycling.

The last Saturday of every month has been designated as a 'recyclable resources collecting day'. However, people in China are not yet as 'recycling aware' as populations in richer countries. Much needs to be done in terms of environmental education to improve this situation.

Figure 4 shows the increase in rubbish generated from Chinese cities between 1990 and 2008, and the way in which this rubbish was disposed in the latter year. Beijing will run out of space for landfills in just four years. More than a third of Chinese cities are facing a similar crisis. At present, only 10% of waste is incinerated. However, significantly increasing **incineration** requires substantial investment and there is always considerable opposition from people living close to the sites selected for new incinerators. The main concern is the significant amounts of heavy metals and dioxins released into the atmosphere by incinerators. The city government has promised to

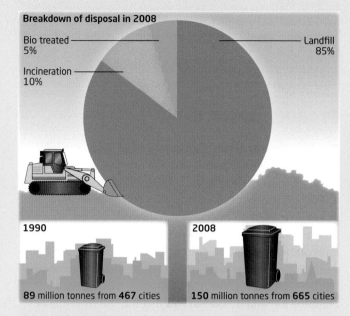

Figure 4 *Rubbish generation and disposal in China.*

improve incineration standards to reach the level required in the EU. China lags far behind the likes of Japan and the USA where 90% and 30% respectively of all refuse is burned.

Bio-treatment, where refuse is turned into fertiliser is another method Beijing is keen to develop. Planned new facilities will see the proportion of incineration, bio-treatment and landfill reach 2:3:5 in 2012 and 4:3:3 in 2015.

role has evolved to encompass the higher rungs of the waste hierarchy also. An important principal here is that 'waste that isn't created does not need to be dealt with'. When the Welsh Assembly was looking for a means to reduce the country's ecological footprint from a current 5.16 gha per person, waste became a prime consideration with an action plan based on the waste hierarchy.

The UK government-funded Envirowise claims that bad waste practices cost UK industry at least £15 billion per year. Commercial waste dominates the total amount of waste the country produces. Approximately 70% of office waste is recyclable, but on average only 7.5% is actually recycled. Envirowise has urged companies to look at their waste hierarchy, beginning with what can be reduced and reused.

Collecting and sorting plastic bottles.

Product stewardship

Product stewardship is an approach to environmental protection in which manufacturers, retailers and consumers are encouraged or required to assume responsibility for reducing a product's impact on the environment. Also called 'extended producer responsibility' it is a growing aspect of recycling. In many cases this is a system of environmental responsibility whereby producers take back a product, recycling it as far as possible, after the customer has finished with it. For manufacturers, this includes planning for, and if necessary paying for, the recycling or disposal of the product at the end of its useful life. This may be achieved in part by redesigning products to use fewer harmful substances, to be more durable, reuseable and recycleable, and to make products from recycled materials.

Many states in the USA require retailers that sell lead acid batteries to accept used batteries for recycling when consumers purchase new batteries. Germany was the first nation to institute a comprehensive product stewardship programme, passing a law in 1991 requiring manufacturers to assume the costs of collecting and recycling used packaging. Schemes for product stewardship for beverage containers operate in a number of countries.

Substitution

Substitution is the use of common and thus less valuable resources in place of rare, more expensive resources. An example is the replacement of copper by aluminium in the manufacture of a variety of products. Historically, when non-renewable resources have been depleted, new technologies have been developed that effectively substitute for the depleted resources. New technologies have often reduced pressure on these resources even before they are fully depleted. For example, fibre optics has been substituted for copper in many electrical applications.

Energy from Waste (EfW) techniques has advanced considerably in recent years. New EfW techniques can treat non-recyclable waste and produce electricity, heat and fuel, thus saving on the use of fossil fuels. Figure 5 describes the four main EfW techniques in use. The modern EfW industry argues that it should not be blamed for the poor environmental performance of older plants, some of which may actually now be closed. The industry also argues that the health concerns of people living close to older plants should not be applied to modern facilities.

A number of companies are working on advanced systems of gasification which will both get rid of rubbish and produce energy. Although standard techniques for gasification have been around for some time, the current

Anaerobic digestion (AD)

It is one of the most talked about technologies following a government backing in the English Waste Strategy 2007. The biological process works whereby feedstock with a high moisture content – such as food waste, animal manure and sewage sludge – is recycled into a biogas, which can be upgraded to pipeline-quality gas and biofertiliser.

Mechanical biological treatment (MBT) and Biological Mechanical Treatment (BMT)

During MBT, materials such as metals, glass and plastics are mechanically removed. The leftover organic fraction can then be sent for aerobic composting or AD (see above).

BMT differs whereby the materials are separated after the biological treatment. Waste is dried to reduce its mass and water content. Materials such as metals and glass are then removed and the remaining residue can be processed into a refuse derived fuel (RDF) or solid recovered fuel (SRF) and used for energy production.

Gasification and pyrolysis

Gasification and pyrolysis are both thermal processes and are identified as advanced conversion technologies (Renewables Obligation). Gasification, sometimes described as partial combustion, occurs when a hydrocarbon-carbon based substance is heated in a restricted amount of air and produces a synthetic gas (syngas); pyrolysis occurs when air is completely excluded and typically produces liquids.

Incineration

Waste-to-energy plants, or incinerators with energy recovery, treat municipal waste (household and similar wastes), which remains after waste prevention, reuse and recycling activities. They can produce both electricity and heat for industrial and household users.

Figure 5 *Energy from Waste (EfW) techniques.*

cost of waste disposal is making more viable the possibility of disposing of household waste using higher-energy methods once reserved only for hazardous materials such as medical waste and asbestos.

Figure 6, which appeared in a recent waste management and recycling article in the British newspaper *The Times*, gives tips to businesses to reduce waste. The wording of the tips recognises that the majority of businesses in the UK today are in the service sector.

Energy efficiency

Meeting future energy needs in developing, emergent and developed economies while avoiding serious environmental degradation will require increased emphasis on radical new approaches which include:

- much greater investment in renewable energy
- conservation
- recycling
- carbon credits
- 'green' taxation.

To be effective in the long term, energy solutions must be sustainable. In his acceptance speech (for the presidency of the USA) in August 2008, Barack Obama stated:

> Now is the time to end this addiction (to oil) and to understand that drilling is a stop-gap measure, not a long-term solution. Not even close. As President, I will tap our natural gas reserves, invest in clean coal technology, and find ways to safely harness nuclear power. I'll help our auto companies re-tool, so that the fuel-efficient cars of the future are built right here in America. And I'll invest $150 billion over the next decade in affordable, renewable sources of energy.

Figure 6 *Ten top tips to reduce waste.*

1. Get advice from a body like Envirowise on how to audit your waste to identify the costs and opportunities.
2. Engage staff and appoint champions to collate waste data.
3. Work with your suppliers to reduce waste like packaging and avoid over-production of material for marketing and publicity.
4. Make it easy – recycling bins should be as close as the nearest waste bin.
5. Make sure your contract cleaners know what you are doing.
6. Set the office printer to default print on both sides, use electronic communication where possible and reuse paper and envelopes whenever you can.
7. Where suitable, give used but non-recyclable work supplies to a local school or voluntary group.
8. Only shred sensitive documents as the process drastically reduces paper quality for recycling.
9. For un-needed furniture and equipment seek out local recycling specialists.
10. It's all in the detail. For example, avoid purchasing disposable catering products. Swap plastic cups for mugs.

Activities

1. Explain the term 'conservation of resources'.
2. Define (a) reuse (b) recycling.
3. Briefly explain the purpose and methods of the EU's Common Fisheries Policy.
4. With reference to Figure 2 (page 276), explain the concept of the waste hierarchy.
5. Describe the information shown in Figure 4 (page 277).
6. What is product stewardship?
7. How can substitution help to conserve important resources?
8. Briefly outline the EfW processes described in Figure 5.
9. Comment on the suggestions for reducing waste identified in Figure 6.

Restaurant in the Azores using geothermal heat for cooking.

Managing energy supply is often about balancing socio-economic and environmental needs. We have all become increasingly aware that this requires detailed planning and management. **Carbon credits** and **carbon trading**

Case study

Germany: satisfying energy demand in a sustainable way

- Germany is one of the world leaders in promoting renewable energy. In 2005 renewable energy accounted for 4.6% of Germany's primary energy supply and 10.2% of its total electricity consumption. Renewable energy is now an important industrial sector in Germany.

- Germany meets 5% of its electricity needs from hydro-electricity. Its installed output of 4600 MW is concentrated mainly in the pre-Alpine region where physical and precipitation characteristics are most favourable.

- By early 2007, Germany had over 18000 wind turbines on line, producing more than 20000 MW. Germany now obtains 5.7% of its electricity from wind, employing over 64000 people in the process. Germany is now looking to build offshore wind farms to accompany its land-based turbines. The German government has legislated to promote wind energy since 1991 with the most important impetus coming from the Renewable Energy Sources Act of 2000 and its amendment in 2004. The central element is a minimum price, guaranteed for more than 20 years, which will be paid for electricity fed into the grid that has been generated from renewable energy sources. Power companies have to take this electricity by law. The renewable energy industry also benefits from favourable tax concessions.

- Germany boasts a $5 billion photovoltaic industry which accounts for 52% of the world's installed solar panels. The world's largest photovoltaic system is Bavaria Solarpark in Muehlhausen, Germany. It generates 10 MW from 57600 photovoltaic panels spread over three sites covering a total of 25 hectares.

- Bioenergy is also a source of interest. Jühnde, near Göttingen, is Germany's first model bioenergy village.

- Only a few regions in Germany have potential for harnessing geothermal power. The exploitation of deep geothermal power is little more than an idea at present but geothermal sources close to the surface have provided hot water and heating to households in a few areas for 30 years.

Discussion point

Suggest why Germany has been ahead of most nations in the pursuit of sustainable energy.

Australia's national strategy on energy efficiency, 2009-20

Figure 7 shows that Australia is a high energy use society and that consumption has been rising steadily. Australia's total energy use increased by 15% over the six years to 2009, according to a report by the Australian Bureau of Statistics.

The report stated that in 2006–07, Australia's total supply of energy products was 21359 petajoules – predominantly from natural gas (44%), black coal, uranium concentrates and refined products (the latter three at 19% each). While investment in renewable energy is rising, renewables such as hydro-electricity, wood biomass, wind and solar currently made up just over 1% of Australia's total energy production.

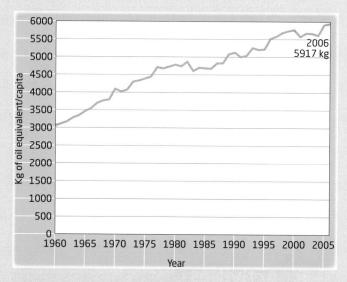

Figure 7 *Energy use in Australia.*

Although there have been large decreases in energy intensity in some industries, such as transport (50%) and construction (74%), energy intensity has increased in others, such as mining. In mining, energy use has doubled over the last 30 years due to a number of factors, including a shift towards more opencast mining.

Australia's production of crude oil fell 21% in the six years to 2009, and its export of oil and refined products dropped 31%. In the same period oil imports grew by 35%.

Sydney's central business district.

In an effort to significantly reduce its consumption of energy, Australia has recently launched a National Strategy on Energy Efficiency for the period 2009–20. Work began in August 2004 on the strategy. There is general agreement at all levels of government that improvements in energy efficiency can:

- improve productivity in the economy
- allow households and businesses to achieve savings on their energy bills
- deliver significant greenhouse gas abatement.

The national government in Australia has proposed the Carbon Pollution Reduction Scheme as the main mechanism for reducing greenhouse gas emissions. This will place a cap, and therefore a price (carbon price), on greenhouse gas emissions.

There are several key elements of the strategy:

➔ Assisting households and businesses in transition to a low-carbon future

This part of the strategy will encompass financial assistance with the installation of roof insulation and solar hot water systems, auditing of the energy efficiency of public housing stock and consideration of implementing cost-efficiency upgrades, encouraging businesses to identify and implement cost-effective energy-efficiency measures, and incentives to improve the energy efficiency of buildings and equipment.

➔ Reducing impediments to the uptake of energy efficiency

Measures will include improving the extent and accessibility of information and advice to households and businesses, broadening the range of appliances covered by minimum energy performance standards, identifying and developing measures to address market barriers to the rapid deployment of energy-efficiency technologies and practices, with a particular focus on land transport. Incentives in the private rental market will be split between landlords and tenants.

➔ Making buildings more energy efficient

The overall objective here is to substantially increase the number of energy-efficient houses and commercial buildings, and to raise the energy efficiency of the existing building stock.

➔ Government working in partnership and leading the way

There is clear recognition that each level of government – national, state, territory and local – has an important role to play in improving energy efficiency. Collaboration between the different levels of government will be essential to achieve all the objectives at a high level. The agreed funding arrangements and a significant ongoing work programme are seen as a landmark example of collaboration between different levels of government.

The Strategy will be evaluated and reviewed in 2015 to determine the level of improvement in energy-efficiency performance in its first five years. The review will evaluate all major aspects of the strategy.

Australia's National Strategy on Energy Efficiency has been generally well received nationally and internationally because:

- it is a collaborative effort by all levels of government
- it is comprehensive in its approach
- progress will be reviewed about halfway through the specified time period
- it will adopt a carrot and stick approach – certain things will be legally binding, but attractive incentives will also be on offer.

The major criticism is that clear targets in terms of reductions in energy usage per capita have not been set, but these may be introduced at a later date.

are an important part of the EU's environmental and energy policies. Under the EU's emissions trading scheme, heavy industrial plants have to buy permits to emit greenhouse gases over the limit they are allowed (carbon credits) by government. However, this could be extended to other organisations such as banks and supermarkets. From 2008 the British government is offering the free provision of visual display electricity meters so that people can see exactly how much energy they are using at any time. Many countries are looking increasingly at the concept of **community energy** (see also chapter 9). Much energy is lost in transmission if the source of supply is a long way away. Energy produced locally is much more efficient. This will invariably involve **microgeneration.**

In March 2006 J.M. Barrosa took the European Commission's first shot at creating an EU energy policy. He argued that the EU can no longer afford 25 different and uncoordinated energy policies. Coordination of energy policies in the EU has the potential to create a more efficient energy market, but it may be difficult to achieve. If the EU is successful in coordinating energy policies, this may well provide a model for other parts of the world to follow. This will be most likely where countries are already linked together in trade blocs such as NAFTA (the USA, Canada and Mexico).

Figure 8 summarises some of the measures governments and individuals can undertake to reduce the demand for energy and thus move towards a more sustainable situation.

Geographical skills

When a number of options are available it is important to be able to prioritise. Study Figure 7 and discuss the three measures in each section which you think are the most important to implement. Make sure you justify your choices.

Activities

1. How can the production of community energy be seen as a conservation measure?
2. What is microgeneration?
3. Define (a) carbon credits (b) carbon trading. How can these concepts help the conservation of energy?
4. In what ways is Germany attempting to be more sustainable in energy production?
5. Present an analysis of Australia's National Strategy on Energy Efficiency.

GOVERNMENT

- Improve public transport to encourage higher levels of usage.
- Set a high level of tax on petrol, aviation fuel etc.
- Ensure that public utility vehicles are energy efficient.
- Set minimum fuel consumption requirements for cars and commercial vehicles.
- Congestion charging to deter non-essential car use in city centres.
- Offer subsidies/grants to households to improve energy efficiency.
- Encourage business to monitor and reduce its energy usage.
- Encourage recycling.
- Promote investment in renewable forms of energy.
- Pass laws to compel manufacturers to produce higher-efficiency electrical products.

INDIVIDUALS

Transport
- Walk rather than drive for short local journeys.
- Use a bicycle for short to moderate distance journeys.
- Buy low fuel consumption/low-emission cars.
- Reduce car usage by planning more multipurpose trips.
- Use public rather than private transport.
- Use car pools.

In the home
- Use low-energy light bulbs.
- Install cavity wall insulation.
- Improve loft insulation.
- Turn boiler and radiator setting down slightly.
- Wash clothes at lower temperatures.
- Purchase high energy efficiency appliances.
- Don't leave electrical appliances on standby.

Figure 8 *Examples of energy conservation measures.*

Key terms

Conservation of resources management of the human use of natural resources to provide the maximum benefit to current generations while maintaining capacity to meet the needs of future generations.

Recycling the concentration of used or waste materials, their reprocessing, and their subsequent use in place of new materials.

Reuse this involves extending the life of a product beyond what was the norm in the past, or putting a product to a new use and extending its life in this way.

Quotas involving agreement between countries to take only a predetermined amount of a resource. Quotas may change on an annual or longer time period basis.

Rationing very much a last resort management strategy when demand is massively out of proportion to supply. For example, individuals might only be allowed a very small amount of fuel and food per week.

Subsidy financial aid supplied by government to an industry for reasons of public welfare, the balance of payments etc.

Recycling deserts areas where rates of recycling are well below the national or regional average.

Overfishing a level of fishing resulting in the depletion of the fish stock.

Tragedy of the commons the idea that common ownership of a resource leads to over-exploitation as some nations will always want to take more than other nations see as their fair share.

Total allowable catch the maximum quantity of fish that can be caught each year.

Landfill a site at which refuse is buried under layers of earth.

Incineration a waste treatment technology that involves the combustion of organic materials and/or substances. Incineration and other high-temperature waste treatment systems are described as 'thermal treatment'.

Product stewardship a system of environmental responsibility whereby producers take back a product, recycling it as far as possible, after the customer has finished with it.

Substitution the use of common and thus less valuable resources in place of rare, more expensive resources. An example is the replacement of copper by aluminium in the manufacture of a variety of products.

Carbon credit a permit that allows an organisation to emit a specified amount of greenhouse gases; also called an emission permit.

Carbon trading a company that does not use up the level of emissions it is entitled to, can sell the remainder of its entitlement to another company that pollutes above its entitlement.

Community energy energy produced close to the point of consumption.

Microgeneration generators producing electricity with an output of less than 50 KW.

Websites

www.oecd.org
Organisation for Economic Co-operation and Development (OECD)

www.worldwatch.org
Worldwatch Institute

www.coag.gov.au
Council of Australian Governments (COAG)

www.recyclenow.com
Recyclenow

www.recycling-guide.org
Recycling Guide

Review

Examination-style questions

1 Refer to Figure 9.

a What do you understand by the term 'municipal waste generation'?

b Suggest reasons for the significant differences between the countries illustrated in Figure 9.

c Discuss the strategies that can be adopted to reduce per capita waste generation.

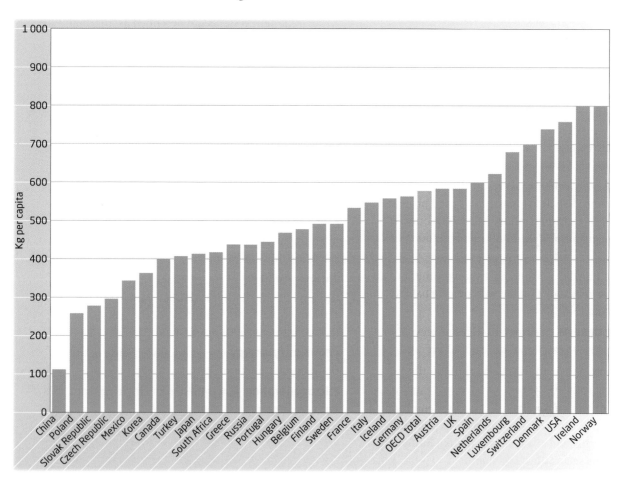

Figure 9 *Municipal waste generation.*

4 Patterns in resource consumption

2 Refer to Figure 10.

a Define recycling.

b Describe and explain the recycling of batteries illustrated in Figure 10.

c Discuss the recycling of other products.

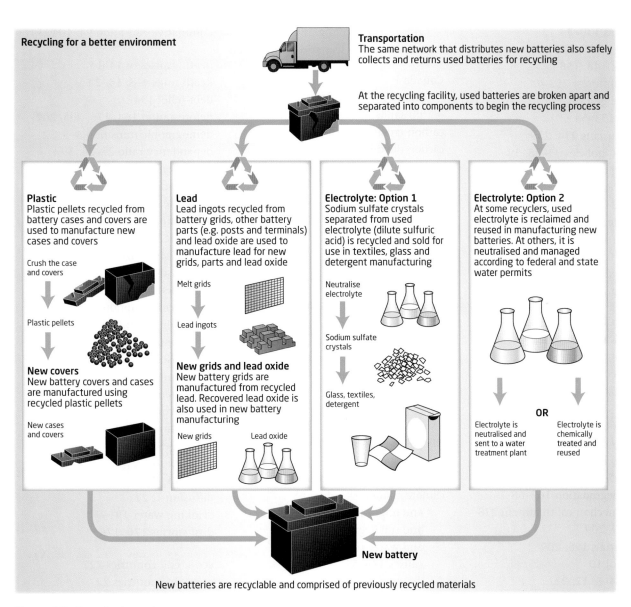

Recycling for a better environment

Transportation
The same network that distributes new batteries also safely collects and returns used batteries for recycling

At the recycling facility, used batteries are broken apart and separated into components to begin the recycling process

Plastic
Plastic pellets recycled from battery cases and covers are used to manufacture new cases and covers

Crush the case and covers

Plastic pellets

New covers
New battery covers and cases are manufactured using recycled plastic pellets

New cases and covers

Lead
Lead ingots recycled from battery grids, other battery parts (e.g. posts and terminals) and lead oxide are used to manufacture lead for new grids, parts and lead oxide

Melt grids

Lead ingots

New grids and lead oxide
New battery grids are manufactured from recycled lead. Recovered lead oxide is also used in new battery manufacturing

New grids   Lead oxide

Electrolyte: Option 1
Sodium sulfate crystals separated from used electrolyte (dilute sulfuric acid) is recycled and sold for use in textiles, glass and detergent manufacturing

Neutralise electrolyte

Sodium sulfate crystals

Glass, textiles, detergent

Electrolyte: Option 2
At some recyclers, used electrolyte is reclaimed and reused in manufacturing new batteries. At others, it is neutralised and managed according to federal and state water permits

OR

Electrolyte is neutralised and sent to a water treatment plant

Electrolyte is chemically treated and reused

New battery

New batteries are recyclable and comprised of previously recycled materials

Figure 10 *Recycling batteries.*

Index